Ruth St. Denis
A Biography of the Divine Dancer

American Studies Series
William H. Goetzmann, Editor

Ruth St. Denis

A Biography
OF THE
Divine Dancer

SUZANNE SHELTON

UNIVERSITY OF TEXAS PRESS, AUSTIN

International Standard Book Number 0-292-77046-4
Library of Congress Catalog Card Number 90-70933

First University of Texas Press Edition, 1990
Published by arrangement with Doubleday, a division of Bantam
Doubleday Dell Publishing Group, Inc., whose edition was titled *Divine
Dancer: A Biography of Ruth St. Denis.*

Requests for permission to reproduce material from this work should be sent to
Permissions, University of Texas Press, Box 7819, Austin, Texas 78713-7819.

♾ The paper used in this publication meets the minimum requirements of
American National Standard for Information Sciences—Permanence of Paper
for Printed Library Materials, ANSI Z39.48-1984.

Designed by Beverley Vawter Gallegos

Some of the information connected with the research of this book appeared in
the January 1979 issue of *Dance* magazine, and in the author's lecture, *Ruth St.
Denis: Dance Popularizer with "High Art" Pretensions,* in the book *American
Popular Entertainment: Program and Papers of the Conference on the History of
American Popular Entertainment,* published by Greenwood Press.

Specified material from *Ruth St. Denis, An Unfinished Life: An Autobiography.*
Copyright 1939 by Harper & Row, Publishers, Inc.; renewed © 1967 by
Ruth St. Denis. Reprinted by permission of the publisher.

"Dance Divine" and "Calling," poems from *Lotus Light* by Ruth St. Denis,
copyright 1932, by Ruth St. Denis. Reprinted by permission of
Houghton Mifflin Company.

For Thea

CONTENTS

LIST OF ILLUSTRATIONS

following page 54

following page 78

Hugo von Hofmannsthal. Courtesy Gernsheim Collection, Humanities Research Center, University of Texas.

Ruth St. Denis in *The Cobras,* 1906, Berlin. Photograph by Emil Schwalb, Berlin. Courtesy Phillip Baribault.

The Yogi, created in Vienna in 1908. Courtesy Phillip Baribault.

The fashionable dancer, home from Europe, 1910. Photograph by White, New York. Courtesy Phillip Baribault.

Ruth St. Denis in "The Flower Arrangement" from *O-Mika,* 1913. Photograph by White, New York. Courtesy Dance Collection, New York Public Library.

Ruth and Brother St. Denis in *O-Mika.* Photograph by White, New York. Courtesy Dance Collection, New York Public Library.

Ted Shawn. Photograph by Arnold Genthe. Courtesy Hoblitzelle Theatre Arts Library, University of Texas.

Ruth with her husband, Ted Shawn. Photograph by Nickolas Muray. Courtesy Phillip Baribault.

Ruth St. Denis, Ted Shawn, and the first Denishawn company, 1915. Courtesy Phillip Baribault.

Ted and Ruth in *The Garden of Kama,* 1915. Photograph by Putnam & Valentine, Los Angeles. Courtesy Dance Collection, New York Public Library.

Ruth St. Denis as Egypta. Photograph by Otto Sarony. Courtesy Phillip Baribault.

Ruth St. Denis as *Kuan Yin,* 1916. Photograph by Ira Hill, New York. Courtesy Dance Collection, New York Public Library.

following page 126

Strutting in *Legend of the Peacock.* Photograph by Sotoff, Evanston, Illinois. Courtesy Phillip Baribault.

Ruth St. Denis at Denishawn Theatre, Westlake Park. Photograph by Putnam & Valentine. Courtesy Phillip Baribault.

Ruth St. Denis in *Dance of the Royal Ballet of Siam,* 1918. Photograph by Lou Goodale Bigelow. Courtesy Phillip Baribault.

Ruth St. Denis and Denishawn Dancers in a nautch dance c. 1918. Photograph by Putnam & Valentine. Courtesy Phillip Baribault.

Ruth St. Denis in an East Indian dance, c. 1924. Photograph by Arthur Kales. Courtesy Phillip Baribault.

St. Denis demonstrating a pose from *Second Arabesque.* Photograph by Youngborg, St. Paul. Courtesy Phillip Baribault.

St. Denis in *A Tagore Poem*. Photograph by Marcus Blechman. Courtesy Phillip Baribault.

Sum Nung Au-Young. Courtesy University Research Library, UCLA.

Ruth St. Denis and her temple dancers at Denishawn House, 1933. Courtesy Dance Collection, New York Public Library.

Ruth St. Denis as the Duchess of Marlborough in the 1944 Paramount film *Kitty*. Courtesy Phillip Baribault.

following page 270

Ruth St. Denis in *Incense* in later years. Courtesy Phillip Baribault.

St. Denis in *White Jade*. Photograph by Marcus Blechman. Courtesy Phillip Baribault.

St. Denis as the Gold Madonna in *Color Study of the Madonna*, c. 1934. Courtesy Phillip Baribault.

Ruth St. Denis in a nautch, 1960's. Courtesy Phillip Baribault.

Ruth St. Denis and Phil Baribault, 1955. Courtesy Phillip Baribault.

Ruth St. Denis and Rhythmic Choir in *Gregorian Chant*. Photograph by Phillip Baribault. Courtesy Phillip Baribault.

Ruth St. Denis' expressive hands. Photograph by Arthur Muray. Courtesy Phillip Baribault.

The "Dance of Touch" from *Radha* revival, 1941. Photograph by Marcus Blechman. Courtesy Phillip Baribault.

"Siddhas of the Upper Air," married fifty years, 1964. Courtesy Phillip Baribault.

ACKNOWLEDGMENTS

BIOGRAPHY, like the life it attempts to reflect, is not a solo act. I am indebted to the many people and institutions that contributed ideas and materials to this book. Foremost among them is my doctoral committee in American Civilization at The University of Texas at Austin: William H. Goetzmann, Robert M. Crunden, William Stott, Stanley Hall, David Hovland, and Selma Jeanne Cohen. Miss Cohen, particularly, offered encouragement and advice and her own example of meticulous dance history scholarship.

I must also thank the curators of the libraries from which much of this material is drawn. Genevieve Oswald of the Dance Collection of the Library and Museum of the Performing Arts, the New York Public Library at Lincoln Center, contributed not only her professional assistance but also her personal interest in this project. Brooke Whiting and Hilda Bohem of the University Research Library, the University of California at Los Angeles, gave freely of their time and expertise. Jane Allen Combs and Edwin Neal of the Hoblitzelle Theatre Arts Collection, Humanities Research Center, The University of Texas at Austin, opened their library shelves and their hearts to this project.

I also received invaluable help from Evelyn S. DeVito of the Packer Collegiate Institute, Julia Mason of the Somerset County (N.J.) Library, Frank Evina of the Library of Congress, Betty Wainio of the Somerville (N.J.) Free Public Library, Bette Barker of the State Library of New Jersey, and Mary Jo Pugh of the Bentley Historical Library, the University of Michigan.

Of particular help with knotty research problems were Clyde Maffin, the Ontario (N.Y.) County Historian, and Ronald Seeliger and Goldie Hester of the Perry-Casteñada Library, The University of Texas at Austin. I must also thank Susan L. Pustejovsky and Douglas Hickman, who translated documents from the German and French.

Among the friends and students of Ruth St. Denis, Jane Sherman

Lehac was my faithful correspondent, critic, supplier of information, and source of moral support. Phillip Baribault gave generously of his reminiscences, his photographs and films. La Meri or Russell Meriwether Hughes and Henrietta Buckmaster helped me to understand the offstage St. Denis. I am also indebted to Clifford Vaughan, Rosemary Glenn, Estelle Dennis, Dwight Godwin, Arthur R. Mathis, Jr., Anna Austin Crane, and others associated with St. Denis and Denishawn.

Thanks for help with photographs to Frank Derbas and Mary Ellen MacNamara.

I must acknowledge a special debt to Christena L. Schlundt, the dance historian whose published chronology and groundwork in the St. Denis materials made my task much easier.

My colleagues in dance history, criticism, and writing, shared materials and offered valuable information: John Mueller, Judith B. Alter, Iris M. Fanger, Selma Odom, Camille Hardy, Carol Spencer Howard, Marcia B. Siegel, and Walter Terry.

My editor at Doubleday, Sally Arteseros, gave this book her full support and the benefit of her critical eye.

Finally, I wish to thank Glenn E. Shelton, who introduced me to writing, and Frank and Irina Pal, who brought me to dance. My family, John and Thea Buckley, deserve my deepest gratitude. With generosity and grace, they lived with this book.

PREFACE

RUTH ST. DENIS is often called the mother of modern dance in America. Unlike her contemporaries Isadora Duncan and Loie Fuller, St. Denis made her career in America, touring as a solo artist until 1914 when she met and married Ted Shawn. Together they founded Denishawn, the dance company and school that trained the core of first-generation modern dancers in America—Martha Graham, Doris Humphrey, and Charles Weidman.

St. Denis herself was not a "modern dancer." She was an "interpretive dancer," dedicated to the belief that behind each physical gesture was an emotional or spiritual motivation. Like that other late Romantic Isadora Duncan, St. Denis read the American Transcendentalists and agreed with Ralph Waldo Emerson that natural facts are signs of spiritual facts, that the artist must penetrate to the spiritual truth beyond physical appearances. She used nature as her model for movements that were inherently expressive, dynamic, and organic. She also studied the techniques of François Delsarte and Émile Jaques-Dalcroze who explored the correspondences between movement and expression, movement and music.

Modern dance was a direct outgrowth of "interpretive dance." If the harsh angularities of Martha Graham's early work seemed foreign to Ruth St. Denis' exotic dance pictures, they both shared a commitment to expressive movement, a fascination with the female psyche, and a basic theatricality. Much of Doris Humphrey's mature work grew out of the music visualizations she created with St. Denis. Charles Weidman's dance cartoons owed more to Ted Shawn's choreography, but he learned theatrical and gestural skills from St. Denis, particularly the deft use of the hands. All of these modern dancers employed technical tools that St. Denis developed—the use of bare feet, a freer use of the torso, subtle modulations of weight, gradations in dynamics, the expressive use of the arms.

St. Denis lived to see her art grow passé, then popular again. Her ideas also went in and out of fashion. She was a mystic of the eclectic variety that seems typically American. In her search for an inner unity and harmony she explored Swedenborgianism, Transcendentalism, Christian Science, Buddhism and Vedanta, and varieties of Christian thought. Her dances were nominally Japanese, Indian, Siamese, Egyptian, Javanese, Chinese, or merely lyrical, but each of them focused on the merger of the individual with the divine.

At the moment of dancing, Ruth St. Denis submerged herself in this divine experience, but offstage her life was an erratic series of exploitative relationships, destructive passions, and unfulfilled dreams. Her personal life reflected a chronic tension between spirituality and sexuality that plagued other charismatic women of her day—Mary Baker Eddy, Aimee Semple McPherson, Madame Blavatsky.

I have tried in this critical biography to travel the road between Ruth St. Denis' inner aspirations and their outer manifestation in dance. I have not attempted to write a history of Denishawn nor a history of early American modern dance. I have merely tried to follow one figure in that history.

Dance Divine

We are free of time and space.
The gestures
Of our right and left hands
In the meetings and partings
Of our rhythms
Are the fulfillment of our completed selves.
In the endless avowal
Of that selfhood which is divine,
We use our translucent bodies
In a new language
To express the glory of our love.

RUTH ST. DENIS

ONE

THE FAMILY

On the evening of January 27, 1893, Ruth Emma Dennis stood inside the Adamsville School, shrewdly surveying the crowd of neighbors and friends gathering for her production of *The Old Homestead,* a popular play celebrating rural virtues and temperance. The play was tailor-made for these New Jersey farmers from the Bridgewater foothills, their hired hands, and workers from the nearby rock quarry. They were plain but pious folk, not nearly as sophisticated as 'Em Dennis herself, who at the age of forty-eight was considered worldly-wise and something of an eccentric. An educated woman with a medical degree, she dispensed folk medicine to her neighbors, along with lectures on women's rights. She refused to wear corsets, bustles, or rats in her hair. She had tasted the heady world of Utopian communities and once lived among artists and intellectuals, but now was reduced to operating a bohemian boardinghouse on the family farm. Undaunted, 'Em Dennis brought the world to the foothills. She entertained prominent authors, lecturers, and actors on the veranda of her Pin Oaks farmhouse, near Somerville, New Jersey, and she founded the Pin Oaks Dramatic Club. Most of her nearest neighbors appeared in its maiden play on that winter evening in 1893.

Among the cast of *The Old Homestead* were Clark Miller, the local iceman; the Van Nostrand boy, whose farm lay just up the road from the Adamsville schoolhouse; and Lizzie Logan, the Bridgewater belle, who appeared in the role of Rickety-Ann. The heart of the play, however, was Emma Dennis' own family, and she cleverly used the talents of her brood. The males took a back seat: her stepson, Tom, Jr., appeared in a minor supporting role, while her seven-year-old son, Brother, who had never received a Christian name, stayed strictly behind the scenes. To her husband, the genial Tom Dennis, Sr., went what should have been the juiciest role, that of Uncle Josh to his wife's Aunt Jerusha, but the critics agreed that even Tom was outshone. "The life of the play," declared the Somerset *Unionist-Gazette,* "was the Whistling Joe of Ruthie Dennis," Emma's lively, resourceful, fourteen-year-old daughter. "For so young a person she displayed really remarkable talent, and she was never at a loss for business from beginning to end."

On the strength of Ruthie's talent and her mother's organization, *The Old Homestead* moved into a grander theatre, Somerset Hall, the following month. Located four miles from the schoolhouse, on the corner of Main and Union Streets in downtown Somerville, Somerset Hall contained a tiny stage tucked up three flights of rickety stairs. On this stage Mrs. Dennis expanded her production to include entr'actes. Again, Ruthie was the star, performing a vivacious dance and a burlesque of "physical culture" exercises. "Her posing is excellent and her dancing very pretty, although not so graceful as it will be after a little more practice," said the preachy local critic who was remarkably prescient.

With a little more practice, Ruthie became a founder of modern dance in America, and the story of her unfolding career begins within the chemistry of the Dennis family. As the reigning star in a family constellation which included willful mother, dreamy father, nameless brother, and stepbrother, Ruthie learned from childhood a role which her life and art came to serve. She was a madonna surrounded by acolytes, a goddess attended by devotees. With all the emotional complexities that role implied, she sustained the aspirations of a family whose interrelationships spawned grief as well as genius.

The hub of the family was Ruth Emma Dennis, an austere woman of extraordinary will. Born Ruth Emma Hull on September 19, 1844 or 1845, she was the youngest child of a poor family raised in Canandaigua, New York. Her hometown lay in western New York's "burned-over district," where religious revivalism flourished in the early nineteenth century, and during Emma's childhood Canandaigua remained the scene of fervent camp meetings. The Hulls were devout Methodists, and they lived among the phrenologists, mesmerists, Fourierists, land reformers, and Swedenborgians who kept the social and intellectual climate of western New York in ferment. In this atmosphere young Emma Hull developed the paradoxical mixture of religious fundamentalism and freethinking that marked her mature years. Her mother, the frail but pious Ann Hull, bore thirteen children, whom she tried to protect from the abuse of their alcoholic father. William Hull, a sometime carpenter, ultimately deserted his family, and the children were sent packing to the Fairhaven, Connecticut, home of a relative, Betsey Hull, just before the Civil War. During this bitter period Emma developed a chronic nervous condition, though as the youngest child in the family, she was petted by her siblings. She was closest to her brother Drew and her sister Mary, who married into money after a career as a schoolteacher. Mary Hull Wright's newfound fortune may have been the financial source for her younger sister's medical education.

By the time she was twenty-five, Emma Hull had become intrigued with the mysteries of human physiology. Motivated by the need to understand her own nervous disorder, she became one of eighteen new female recruits at the University of Michigan Medical School in 1870. Medical education for women was rare in those days, with female students segregated from males, particularly during anatomy classes. Michigan physicians had resisted coeducation until the university regents ordered open enrollment in 1870, and the first women students found themselves the target of hostility and ridicule. In self-defense, some of the new students became strident in their feminism and publicly agitated for full acceptance by the male-dominated medical and university communities. Ann Arbor, during the 1870s, was rife with women's suffrage campaigns and university unrest, and this climate fed Emma Hull's nascent feminism. Through her studies in physiology, anatomy, *materia medica,* and chemistry, Emma also developed an attitude toward health that would influence her own daughter's outlook and career.

A major influence on medical education in the 1870s was the work of Samuel Hahnemann, the founder of homeopathy, who advocated the gradual attenuation of drugs in treating physical ailments. Emma took his arguments a step further in her graduate thesis, written in 1872 and given the Latin title "Vis Medicatrix Naturae." Arguing for natural methods of healing, she outlined the benefits of fresh air, sunshine, sleep and pure draughts of water, as opposed to allopathic remedies. She based her opposition to drugs upon "my own observation and my own experience, which though not extensive has been to my mind very forcible," and presented an intriguing case study which surely was autobiographical. The youngest daughter in an unstable family, she reported, had been plagued for years by intermittent insanity. Drugs were applied to no effect, and only after enforced rest, country walks, and bland diet did the young woman conquer her nervous headaches. "Through many untoward circumstances and hard buffetings against wind and tide she has clung like a drowning man to as plain and simple a method of living as circumstances would allow, and is now accomplishing more than her friends ever believed she would be able to do." Miss Hull's heartfelt argument was enough to win her a medical diploma, the second in the school's history awarded to a female, but a subsequent nervous relapse ended her hopes of a medical career.

After graduation Emma sought a cure from the renowned Dr. James C. Jackson, the abolitionist-physician whose Jackson Sanitarium in Dansville, New York, was a fashionable resort for neurasthenic females. In Dansville women donned short dresses without corsets and followed a regimen of hip baths, rest, and careful diet. Freed from conventional social restrictions, the patients indulged in spirited discussions of dress-reform and women's rights. For a year Emma attended daily baths and listened to Dr. Jackson's lectures on hygienic clothing and social reform.

Women of Emma Hull's day literally bore the weight of social oppression on their shoulders in the form of heavy, voluminous clothing. A typical winter costume might include boots and stockings, cotton drawers, a whalebone corset and muslin corset-cover, several short flannel skirts, a long waterproof skirt topped by a cotton overskirt, an alpaca dress-skirt, a dress laden with flounces and trimming, and a cloak. Each of the skirts was attached to tight bands about the waist which exerted enormous downward pressure on the hips and abdomen. The corset itself squeezed the diaphragm in a vise, obstructed respiration, and as one female physician observed at an autopsy, even displaced the internal organs. This torturous attire became the target of feminists after Amelia Bloomer suggested in the 1850s a new costume, modeled after Turkish trousers, which became the symbol of the dress-reform movement. In London the Rational Dress Society advocated divided skirts and modified corsets, and in Boston the Committee on Dress-Reform opened a shop which sold hoops and suspenders to distribute the weight of clothing and flannel undersuits for warmth. A lecture series on dress-reform, sponsored in 1874 by the National Dress Association, featured speeches by four female physicians, and Emma Hull herself occasionally took to the podium to preach the evils of oppressive dress.

She passed on this legacy to her daughter, who as a child wore clothing that made her the object of ridicule. As an adult, Ruth St. Denis declared, "I am going to live to be 100 years old because I refuse to accept the mandates of fashion. My dances are a protest against tight lacing, tight shoes, tight clothes."

Not only did her mother hear the doctrine of dress-reform at Dr. Jackson's sanitarium, she also learned to dance, from Dr. Jackson himself. Though he was a minister, Dr. Jackson advocated therapeutic social dancing, in defiance of Christian clergy who regarded dancing as a ticket to perdition. In a spirited essay directed toward his detractors, Dr. Jackson defended dancing for two central reasons: first, he felt that social dancing was the only amusement in which the sexes necessarily mingled, thus benefiting women who usually were excluded from male-dominated recreation, if not from "almost all the forms of higher power," he added pointedly. Second, Dr. Jackson felt that dancing promoted "the development and culture of the moral and spiritual nature" by providing "a counterbalancing emotional and physical outlet for persons of highly sensitive spiritual organization." This defense of dancing on social, moral, and physiological grounds may have suggested to Emma Hull the rationale on which her daughter ultimately based her career. Certainly Dr. Jackson's theories of feminism, dress-reform, and the moral function of art became the basis for Emma's own mature beliefs.

Armed with her new theories, Emma left the sanitarium and gradually drifted into an artists' colony near Perth Amboy, New Jersey, where she met her future husband. The Eagleswood colony was the last remnant of the Raritan Bay Colony, which the Marcus Spring family founded in 1853 as an experiment in Christian socialism. The Springs and their followers had been members of the North American Phalanx, a Utopian community in New Jersey, but they left to form a more religious community "where industry, education and social life may in principle and practice be arranged in conformity to the Christian religion." Economically, the new Raritan Bay Union consisted of a joint stock association in which cooperation replaced the evils of competition. This venture in Christian socialism survived only eight years, but during its brief life the Raritan Bay Union attracted such visionaries as Margaret Fuller, Theodore Dwight Weld, Angelina Grimké Weld, and her sister Sarah Grimké, plus assorted abolitionists, socialists, feminists, and Quaker pacifists. Though the Raritan Bay Union dissolved in

1861, its intellectual atmosphere lingered in the Eagleswood Military Academy established by Weld, which in 1871 was converted into a residential hotel for artists and intellectuals. Prominent painters, among them George Inness and William Page, maintained nearby studios and shared with hotel residents the latest art gossip, the mystical theories of Emanuel Swedenborg, and the Single Tax arguments of Henry George. Swedenborg was the patron saint of Eagleswood, and residents eagerly discussed such Swedenborgian doctrines as Correspondence, the notion that the natural world is but a metaphor for the spiritual world. At the center of these lively discussions was Marcus Spring's widow, Rebecca, who lived at the Eagleswood hotel with her sculptor son Edward, another son Herbert, and her daughter Jennie, who was divorced from the playwright Steele MacKaye. In the same hotel Emma Hull set up housekeeping with Thomas Laban Dennis.

A machinist by trade, Tom Dennis probably came to Eagleswood to take advantage of its cooperative machine shop, as well as its intellectual climate. An avid reader and confirmed agnostic, he argued with Eagleswood's Christian believers and swore by the essays of Tom Paine and Robert Ingersoll. He was a clever, charming, handsome roughneck who liked to swig whiskey and play the violin. Dreamy by nature, he spent his spare hours designing inventions—a dynamo, a bicycle, an electric light, a flying machine—most of which never came to fruition.

He was born in Stourbridge, England, on November 11, 1846, and emigrated with his family to Boonton, New Jersey, where his father kept a saloon. His mother, Julia Chapman Dennis, kept house in Boonton and doted on her only child until the family adopted a daughter, Mary, at the onset of the Civil War. By wartime Tom was almost grown, fifteen years old and an apprentice with the Jr. Mile machine shop in Boonton. He loved to tinker with machines but longed even more to enlist in the Union Army, and in September 1864 he lied about his age and joined Captain Peter G. Van Winkle's regiment of New Jersey Cavalry Volunteers. As part of the Army of the Southwest, the regiment camped near New Orleans, where Tom caught a severe cold that led to his honorable discharge at the rank of private in June 1865. He returned home and two years later married Emely Alice Piere, a seventeen-year-old girl from the neighboring town of Mendham who was already pregnant with his first child. After the birth of their son, Tom, Jr., the younger Dennises settled with Tom's parents in Boonton, but something went disastrously wrong with the marriage.

The couple separated in December 1875, about the time Tom met his Eagleswood friend Emma Hull, and on December 4, 1878, Tom divorced Alice Dennis on grounds of her desertion and adultery. He was granted custody of their son, and two days later he married Emma Hull in an unorthodox ceremony in the studio of the painter William Page. Edward Spring was witness to this "marriage by contract" in which the parties simply agreed to be wed, without license or clergy. One month later, on January 20, 1879, their daughter Ruthie was born.

The circumstances of the Dennises' common-law marriage and Ruthie's untimely birth shadowed the family from the start and followed Ruth St. Denis into old age. In her late years she confided to a close friend that she was "born illegitimate," and she deliberately obfuscated her birth date over the years, either out of vanity or shame. When she was past fifty, she wrote in her diary, "I have always the feeling that I am working under the idea of illegitimacy or disorder. That is one reason why I never have the feeling of having accomplished anything—or having anything under my feet." In another veiled allusion to the circumstances of her birth, she blamed her own lifelong insecurity on her mother's "fears when I was conceived," and added that by osmosis, "I seem to have been born a kind of rebel to law and order." Her very birth seemed to place her outside the social norm, and when the family moved to Pin Oaks Farm near Somerville, New Jersey, in late 1884, social pressures grew even more intense.

Neighboring farmers thought the Dennises odd, and at least one Somerville oldtimer today remembers her grandmother's warning that young Ruthie Dennis was to be avoided, as she had a "bad reputation." Rumors of the Dennises' common-law marriage may have followed the family to Somerville, or the gossip may have been generated by Tom's drinking bouts or by 'Em's refusal to wear the conventional corsets and layered petticoats. Perhaps the local gossip was only the natural snobbery of Somerville townfolk toward their backhills neighbors, but whatever its origin, the whispering wounded Ruthie. One ugly incident loomed in her memory. An unmarried servant girl from a nearby farm became pregnant, and the Dennis family took her in. The neighboring farmers began to gossip that Mrs. Dennis planned to administer an abortion, and their righteous wrath boiled into a public confrontation. 'Em Dennis was called to testify. In characteristic fashion 'Em set her neighbors straight and sent them shamefaced back to their farms, but the memory of that trauma fueled young Ruthie's insecurity. She equated sex with shame and ostracism and was further confused when she heard her mother reject her father's advances with a half-humorous "Don't, the neighbors won't think we're married." As an adult, Ruthie still bore these scars. She craved social acceptance and prided herself on respectability. Years after she left the farm, as she traveled on her first tour abroad, she wrote her family that she could not believe that "poor me—running barefoot about Pin Oaks and being snubbed and spat upon by certain 'respectable and God-fearing persons'—would ever get here."

Despite the social ostracism, Pin Oaks was a haven for a six-year-old girl. If the farm lacked the sophisticated gaiety of Somerville's quilting parties and soirées, it was a wonderland for a leggy tomboy. Dressed in blue jeans, her hair cut short like a boy's, Ruthie ran free over twenty acres of land which extended up a sloping hillside covered with maple, oak, and pine groves. She loved to dress her bulldog Tige in baby clothes and monitored spats between the family cat, Pickles, and the rooster, Brigham Young. In winter Ruthie delighted in sleigh rides; in summer she waded in the cool stream that trickled between the farm and the frame schoolhouse which she attended each autumn. At least thirty-five farm children of all ages enrolled each fall in the Adamsville School, where they received marks in attendance, punctuality, deportment, and recitation. Ruthie's weak subject was deportment. Ever the rebel to law and order, she once answered a schoolboy's taunts by bashing his head with a rusty coal shovel. She preferred the freedom of the farm to the discipline of school, and after her lessons each afternoon, she raced up the present-day Steele Gap Road, past the Van Nostrand farm, and up the hill to her beloved Pin Oaks.

The Dennises' home had once been the County Poor House, and though dilapidated, it was roomy enough for a piano and a parlor full of Tom's favorite books on engineering and Emma's well-worn medical texts. Just months after moving into the house, the family made room for a new baby, Brother, and Mrs. Dennis began to worry about finances. Her husband could not keep a steady job. He puttered around the farm, designed grandiose inventions, and built Ruthie a fine swing next to the barn, but most of his energy and spare money went to the Somerville saloons. Many an evening Tom returned to the farm, drunk and dozing, behind Old Dan, the family's horse who followed his head from Somerville, home to Pin Oaks. Sometimes Tom's drunkenness took a vicious turn, and Ruthie remembered family tableaux of "Dad very angry and sullen and Mother frightened, and we children hanging behind her skirts wondering wide-eyed what was going to happen."

Tom blamed his inability to work on an old wartime eye ailment, on his rheumatism, vertigo, and varicose veins, and he petitioned the government for a veteran's pension which was granted only after years of delay. To sustain the family in the meantime, Mrs. Dennis sold produce from the farm's vegetable garden, prescribed herbal medicines for sick neighbors, and converted the family home into a boardinghouse. Borrowing money from a New York friend, Mrs. Nancy Miller, Emma added an upper story to the house and a veranda where the roomers could sit in their rocking chairs. She hoped for an arty clientele and may have envisioned a miniature Eagleswood, but paying residents were hard to come by in the Bridgewater foothills. Only in the summer season did Mrs. Dennis manage to make ends meet, and her name regularly appeared on the county's delinquent tax rolls, adding to the family shame. Arguments between Emma and Tom increased. She complained of insomnia and nervous headaches and badgered Tom about his drinking. He countered with snide comments about her religion, and always, they argued about money.

When family quarrels flared, Ruthie escaped by reading, roaming, or best of all, playacting. She had a flair for drama and loved to make up melodramas for her friends. "Fainting and falling were my specialties in those days," she said, "and I used to pride myself that I did it rather gracefully too." Sometimes her play took a serious turn, inspired by her mother's incessant Bible reading. When nervous headaches threatened, Emma called Ruthie to her side to read the holy verses aloud, and the child came to regard religion as a haven from arguments and ailments. On one occasion, after a New Testament reading, Ruthie fashioned a costume from two bath towels and stood with outstretched arms in the north bedroom, with a "deep feeling awareness of an inner sensation of being the 'boy Jesus.'" Intuitively, through her child's play, she was planting the seeds of her art.

So theatrical was her temperament, so persuasive her personality, that her friends' parents began to disapprove of Ruthie Dennis. Sally Aspell, a childhood companion, remembered "almost breaking my neck trying to emulate her acrobatics off the woodshed," and receiving for her pains a spanking from her parents for following Ruthie home after school. If friends were unavailable, Ruthie clowned for her baby brother or followed her adolescent stepbrother around the farm. Both boys adored her and like complementary bookends, they framed her central position in the family. Of the three children, Ruthie was the undisputed queen, the object of her mother's determined tutelage, the darling of her daddy who liked to summon her with two long whistles. Everywhere, Ruthie found an appreciative audience, especially among the boarders, many of whom had artistic and intellectual pretensions. They applauded her acrobatics from the veranda while discussing the New York theatre season or the finer points of Theosophy versus Christian Science.

Among the Christian Scientists who boarded at the farm were Paul and Pearl Plunkett, children of the flamboyant Mary Plunkett, who cheerfully admitted that her offspring had different fathers. Mrs. Plunkett had been a student of Mary Baker Eddy until she engineered a rival Christian Science faction. While her children stayed behind on the Dennis farm, Mrs. Plunkett directed the International Christian Scientist Association in New York. On visits to Pin Oaks she introduced the Dennises to Christian Science, the new religion founded in 1875 with the publication of Mrs. Eddy's *Science and Health with Key to Scriptures*. The themes of Christian Science might have been a page from Mrs. Dennis' own medical dissertation. Christian Scientists believed in the primacy of mind over matter, in an infinite Spirit that left no room for evil, which they dismissed as an erroneous point of view. Most important to Mrs. Dennis, Christian Scientists advocated spiritual healing and rejected drugs and medical science as unnatural interference with God's revealed will. Mrs. Dennis may have identified with Mrs. Eddy, who also suffered from neurasthenia, and she took up the study of Christian Science. A decade later her own daughter became a convert.

A close friend of Mrs. Plunkett's, John W. Lovell, frequently visited her children at Pin Oaks Farm, and he contributed his own theory of Theosophy to the veranda discussions. A prosperous New York publisher, Lovell was one of the earliest members of the Theosophical Society, founded in New York in the same year as the publication of Mrs. Eddy's *Science and Health*. The Theosophists, like the Christian Scientists, were influenced by the mid-century cults of Spiritualism and Mesmerism, but while Mrs. Eddy drew upon the Holy Bible, the Theosophists borrowed the basic Indian religious doctrines of karma, reincarnation, and a Divine Absolute as rhetorical camouflage for their obsession with the occult. Lovell became a Theosophist in the early

1880s and lent his publishing empire to Theosophist enterprises. One of his publications, *The Idyll of the White Lotus*, became a formative influence on Ruthie Dennis.

Written by Mabel Collins Cook and originally published in London by the Theosophical Society, *The Idyll of the White Lotus* told the story of a young priest in ancient Egypt whose visions of the "Lady of the White Lotus" threatened the religious establishment and cost him his life. As a Theosophical tract, the novel was an elaborate allegory, with the hero representing the human soul surrounded by the five senses and the six emotions of human life. In her later career Ruth St. Denis echoed this dramatic theme and structure in her choreography, but as a child she simply thrilled to the sheer romance of the novel. In her play-acting she became the "Lady of the White Lotus," the white-robed goddess who clasped a lotus blossom to her breast and warned of sensuality which poisoned the flower within each human soul. The book and its heroine "seized upon my imagination," St. Denis said, "and had a tremendous influence on my whole inner life."

The beloved Mr. Lovell also presented Ruthie with a black pony named Jack. Astride her horse, Ruthie streaked about the foothills, feeling "again and again that I was a bird or a cloud or the wind." To tame her spirited daughter, Mrs. Dennis drilled Ruthie in physical culture exercises based on the teachings of François Delsarte, a French professor of declamation. Mrs. Dennis had discovered the Delsarte system during a visit to her sister in New Haven, where she met Aurilla Colcord Poté. Madame Poté maintained a studio in Carnegie Hall in New York City and taught physical culture with particular attention to the alleviation of nervous trouble. Her approach must have appealed to the neurasthenic Mrs. Dennis, who began teaching "Delsarte" to her daughter, who in turn made Delsartism the basis of her dance technique.

In its original form, Delsarte's doctrine was a scientific analysis of body gesture and corresponding emotional and spiritual states. His "Law of Correspondences," like that of Swedenborg, assigned a metaphysical equivalent to each physical fact, for in Delsarte's words, "To each spiritual function responds a function of the body. To each grand function of the body corresponds a physical act." Delsarte divided bodily movement into three great orders: oppositional movement, with body parts moving in opposite directions simultaneously to express force and power; parallel movements, with body parts moving simultaneously in the same direction, denoting physical weakness; and successive movements which pass through the entire body, expressive of emotion.

These ideas first came to America in the 1870s when a Delsarte disciple, Steele MacKaye (the same MacKaye who had married into the Marcus Spring family), imported the system as a training tool for actors. Eventually "Delsarte" became a popular movement. Americans, eager to understand the laws of motion and to rationalize their own fascination with the human body, ignored Delsarte's lofty theories and instead extracted from his system an applied technology. By the 1880s "Delsarte" encompassed every aspect of self-expression from elocution to statue-posing to dress-reform, and a "Delsarte corset" even appeared on the American market. Many a progressive American household had a daughter doggedly memorizing Delsarte's symbolic body zones: the head or the mental zone, the upper torso or emotional zone, the lower torso and limbs which comprised the physical zone. In the Dennis household Emma drilled Ruthie, who practiced "holding onto the old brass bedstead, swinging my legs and being told that my emotions were in the middle of me and that my physical impulses were from the hips down, and then from the shoulders up all was spiritual." Small wonder that her later dances moved chiefly from the waist up!

After Ruthie mastered her Delsarte exercises, Mrs. Dennis allowed her to compose dances to stories which she dictated from her sickbed. Soon Ruthie began to attend Maud Davenport's dancing classes in Somerville. Ruthie arrived for her first lesson, keenly aware that her faded farm clothing looked dowdy beside the organdy and ribbons of the other girls, but her energy and agility made her the school's star. In a recital at the Armory Hall in Somerville, Ruthie joined Miss Bertie Barcalow in a charming Cavalier's Love Dance, and the highlight of the afternoon was Ruthie's solo exhibition of skirt dancing which, the local critic felt, displayed "remarkable talent."

As Ruthie's dancing talent developed, her mother began to see a way out of the family's financial bind. Of all the Dennises, only Ruthie seemed to have potential earning power: Tom, Sr., was hopeless, and Tom, Jr., already had left the farm to make his own way as a machinist. If Ruthie could be put to work as a variety dancer, the family's finances might be assured. As a first step, Mrs. Dennis needed a professional opinion from a teacher of greater stature than Somerville's Maud Davenport, and she wrote to the New York dancing master Karl Marwig, requesting an audition. Not only was Marwig a ballet teacher of note, he also was a chief booking agent for New York showgirls and served as "Master of Dance" for the powerful producer Augustin Daly. Always on the lookout for new talent, Marwig granted Ruthie an interview.

In the spring of 1891 the twelve-year-old farm girl peddled watercress to earn enough money for the New York trip. She never forgot her first audition. Arriving with her mother at the Marwig studio, Ruthie gyrated through an improvised Spanish dance. "All I remember," she later wrote, "was placing a tambourine on the floor and pirouetting in it on my right foot while I took what I considered to be a splendid arabesque and slowly inched myself around until I had completed a circle. I also waved my arms about with a lovely sense of choreographic adventure." With that, Marwig pronounced his verdict: the child had talent, which was all Emma Dennis needed to hear.

Back home at Pin Oaks, Mrs. Dennis began a two-year campaign to launch Ruthie in a theatrical career. Time was short. As Emma wrote her creditor and friend, Mrs. Miller, the Dennises had counted on their one permanent boarder, a Mrs. McDermott, "to bridge the gap until Ruthie's money starts coming in." But Mrs. McDermott suddenly died, and with her went eight dollars a week, creating "a chasm—instead of a bridge" and leaving the Dennis family desperate for funds. Emma borrowed more money and advice from Mrs. Miller, tirelessly wrote theatrical agents and producers, and took Ruthie on job-hunting trips to New York, where they lodged in Mrs. Miller's hotel. On one of those trips, in the winter of 1892, Ruthie experienced what she later called "the real birth of my art life."

The occasion was a Delsarte matinee, presented on behalf of the National Christian League for the Benefit of Social Purity at the Madison Square Theatre. The artist was Genevieve Stebbins, a leading American exponent of the Delsarte system, author of a popular Delsarte text, and principal of the New York School of Expression. As Ruthie and her mother watched from the audience, the curtain rose on *The Dance of Day*. Mrs. Stebbins lay onstage, clad in Grecian robes. "This was the day of the garden set," Ruth St. Denis remembered. "Stebbins was sleeping à la Greek statuary at the back of the stage. She unfolded from sleep—rose—got to noon—began to wilt as the setting sun until she slept in the opposite direction." In this series of simple plastiques, Ruthie saw her tedious Delsarte exercises translated into dance.

Unlike most Delsartists, Mrs. Stebbins transformed a mechanical system of gesture into a dynamic art form. She called her adaptation of the Delsarte theory "statue-posing," but her art was anything but static. Forgotten by dance historians today, she deserves credit as a forerunner of modern dance in America, not only because she became a model for the young Ruth St. Denis, but because she added dynamism to dance. By the late nineteenth century, American theatrical dance had become a static art, a series of poses, a string of isolated, bravura feats. The challenge for early modern dancers was the revitalization of dance, the discovery of a logic of motion. Stebbins was one of the first to discover an energy source, a dynamo for dance, and she found it in the spiral form.

In her 1893 book *Dynamic Breathing and Harmonic Gymnastics,* Stebbins formulated a theory of motor energy based on her eclectic studies in yoga, Swedish gymnastics, Buddhism, oriental dance, and Delsarte. "LIFE," she declared, "is a something which, while we may not know its real nature and genesis, we do know is the basic root principle of all expression." And what, according to Stebbins, was "LIFE"? What motivates man to breathe and feel and move? She decided that just as the sun was the dynamo for physical life, so the mysterious substance called ether was the dynamo for spiritual life. With these twin forces fueling the dancer, he would move in physical and spiritual harmony. Stebbins went a step further and identified the form that such harmonious movement would assume: "There is no such thing as a straight line in the nascent life of nature," she reasoned, so "the spiral motion is the type of life." She observed the slowly shifting weight of an oriental dancer which, "coupled with the natural balance of head, arm, and torso, produces the spiral line from every point of view." This spiral form, a three-dimensional movement which contained the seeds of its own evolution, was Stebbins' breakthrough. Long before the thirteen-year-old girl in her audience created her own dynamic, organic, and spiritually motivated dance, Stebbins took a step toward modern dance movement.

Stebbins' Delsarte drills are a catalogue of movements we now perceive as "modern": oppositional swings of the arms and legs, foot flexion, spirals, lateral bending of the trunk, subtle shifts of weight, backfalls to the floor. She built her system of exercises on breath-rhythms and emphasized "the diaphragm, the great centre muscle, the roof of the stomach and the floor of the lungs. In its rise and fall, contraction and relaxation, it carries with it all muscles attached, and all the vital functions of life are toned and invigorated by its energetic action." She combined her breath-propelled exercises into exotic routines: an Eastern Temple Drill, a Spanish Drill (the Carmen), a Roman Drill (the Amazon). Her Serpentine Arm Drill became the basis for Ruth St. Denis' arm undulations, and Stebbins' Athenian Drill, based on studies of the famed "Victory of Samothrace" sculpture, could have inspired Isadora Duncan's Greek style. One can envision a Martha Graham gesture in Stebbins' "Angular Arm Twist" Drill—"With arms hanging at sides, clench hands and turn elbows well in"—or the art of Doris Humphrey in Stebbins' "leg pendulum swings." One of the most familiar poses from St. Denis' *Radha* is the simple, first gesture from Stebbins' Eastern Temple Drill: "Place the backs of the hands on the forehead, fingers touching, while standing erect on both feet." The importance of Stebbins' method as a basis for modern technique was its energizing of neglected areas of the body—the torso, arms, sides, and head—and its creative placement of the body in space, use of varying levels from lying to kneeling to standing, and its built-in dynamic based on breath motivation. Stebbins, or in broader terms "Delsarte," was the source of St. Denis' dance technique and, by inheritance, that of her successors.

Certainly on that winter afternoon in 1892, Ruthie etched in her memory the themes, if not the form, of Stebbins' dances. The closing pantomime on the program was *The Myth of Isis,* a three-part Egyptian dance which "chronicled the cycle of life, beginning with Chaos or the Birth of Nature, continuing through Life and Death, and finally resurrection and Immortality." The same themes and cyclic form, on a grander scale, reappeared a decade later in the rudiments of Ruth St. Denis' first dance composition, *Egypta.* In an echo of Stebbins, two scenes in that work were titled "Dance of Day" and "The Mystery of Isis." Yet, more than a source of dance ideas, Stebbins was a role model for Ruthie Dennis, the first spiritually, artistically, and socially acceptable dancer the young girl had ever seen. "Through Mrs. Stebbins I glimpsed for the first time the individual possibilities of expression and dignity and truth of the human body," she said, and Stebbins' blend of "spirituality and spectacle" became the blueprint for her own career.

A few months before the Stebbins performance, another production with an Egyptian theme whetted Ruthie's appetite for a stage career. In the summer of 1892, the friendly John Lovell took the Plunkett children and Ruthie to the Eldorado resort on the Jersey Palisades, where they saw *Egypt Through Centuries.* This outdoor extravaganza chronicled "110 centuries of Egyptian culture" in a succession of colorful tableaux. Ruthie watched in fascination as the first act began with the gods Osiris and Isis demanding the sacrifice of a virgin in the River Nile. The chosen victim dramatically ascended a sacred altar which loomed above the stage. From its heights the virgin "indicated the four points of the Universe," then flung herself into the Nile. In the next moment, hundreds of young dancers filled the stage for the Grand Ballet of the Virgins. Five hundred limbs followed the movements of prima ballerina Elena Salmoirachi in a synchronized echo. A flower ballet followed, then a burst of fireworks, and Ruthie tucked away in her memory the Egyptian themes, the virginal persona, the grandeur and spectacle which later shaped her own art.

Dazzled by these glimpses of theatrical magic, Ruthie returned to the farm more determined than ever to pursue a stage career. The normal adolescence of a Jersey farm girl was not to be hers. She did attend Somerville High School, but the budding sexual awareness of her classmates, their giggles and whispers, "made me shrink and turn a little cold." Her first boyfriend, Clark Miller, was a fatherly figure, a stable and thoughtful young man who, to Ruthie's relief, "was never demonstrative." Mrs. Dennis had warned her daughter of the perils of traffic with the opposite sex. "Very simply mother called it by an old-fashioned term, 'playing with fire,'" Ruthie remembered. "How often in those years when she was with me night and day, struggling to keep the little family together, and a roof over our heads, did she note my mischievous eyes and hear the taunting challenge of my voice, when boys or men that caught my fancy drew near to me. Many times she stepped in and rudely broke up one of these budding romances." If her mother's warnings seemed farfetched, the lesson of Lizzie Logan was enough to cool Ruthie on the idea of "playing with fire." Lizzie was seven years older than Ruthie, her idol, a pretty and popular girl whose farm lay just northeast of the Dennis property. Ruthie watched the progress of Lizzie's adolescence, her involvement with a local dandy named Will Chapman, and her subsequent exile to Grandview, New Jersey, where she apparently bore a child. Shortly thereafter, Lizzie married Johnnie Brown, and when Ruthie visited the Browns in Jersey City, she found her "once witty, laughing companion" defeated by life, "a somber, careworn creature whom I scarcely recognized." Lizzie's experience was enough to inhibit Ruthie around men, and she channeled her adolescent energy into her fledgling theatrical career.

While Mrs. Dennis bombarded theatrical agents with letters, the family relatives began to get wind of her scheme to put Ruthie on stage. They were incensed. No Christian girl, they protested, should entertain thoughts of a life in the theatre. Emma's sister and her husband, the affluent Alfred Northam Wrights of New Haven, insisted upon saving Ruthie from perdition by financing a term at the Dwight Moody School in Massachusetts. Though Mrs. Dennis was bent on stardom for her daughter, her own religious beliefs and respect for education forced her assent, not to mention the attractive prospect of one less mouth to feed. Ruthie dutifully packed, and in the fall of 1893 she became a resident of Reed Cottage on the campus of Northfield Girls' Seminary, under the watchful eye of the Reverend Mr. Moody.

Dwight Moody was the most famous revivalist of his day, one of the first of America's corporate evangelists who parlayed a passion for the Gospel into an empire of educational and missionary institutions. He preached the literal truth of the Scriptures and predicted the imminent bodily return of Jesus Christ, who would bring the final judgment of God on the world. Moody regarded the girls of Northfield Seminary with the same zeal as he did his converts, and at the beginning of each school term he personally welcomed new arrivals at the train depot.

A short distance from the train station, the Seminary was situated on the banks of the Connecticut River, near its sister Northfield Training School for missionaries, and the Mount Hermon School for Young Men. Ruthie found herself among hundreds of young girls at the seminary in a college-preparatory course that emphasized religious studies but also included composition, science, history, bookkeeping, and mathematics. Rules of conduct were strict. The faculty frowned on the sort of outdoor romps which Ruthie had come to love in the freedom of the farm, and she chafed under the confining "atmosphere of 'Christians.'" In a letter home from "way up here at the north end of nowhere," she wrote that she was doing her best to conform. "I don't know how much I've improved in knowledge but I know I have improved in obedience at any rate." In the next breath, she suggested that her mother write the principal, Miss Evelyn Hall, and inform her that Ruthie would be leaving before Christmas. Miss Hall would survive the news, Ruthie wrote impishly, "if she has not had a bad night-mare the night before."

Mrs. Dennis did not write the requested letter, but Ruthie did in fact leave before Christmas.

Toward the end of the fall term, Ruthie made an appointment to see the Reverend Moody, whom she had nicknamed "the vinegar cruet." She was troubled by the evangelist's insistence that theatres only stimulated and gratified "the most corrupt desires of the soul." Moody's views on dancing were only too well known. He equated dancing with the declines of entire civilizations and was fond of snorting, "The very idea of Noah dancing and playing cards in the ark, while the world was perishing!" Ruthie tried to set him straight. With a fourteen-year-old's tact she explained to the Reverend Moody that she was destined for a stage career, though she carefully avoided the mention of dancing. She told him that her mother had organized a dramatic club and had given her the plum role in its first play. "I just called my own (dancing) part 'exercises,'" she remembered, but Moody was outraged and began to lecture her on the theatre and its depravity. In the midst of his tirade Ruthie flounced from his office, packed her belongings, summoned a sled to the train depot, and fled to Pin Oaks, just in time for rehearsals of *The Old Homestead.*

The December 27, 1893, performance at Somerset Hall was the third presentation of *The Old Homestead* by the Pin Oaks Dramatic Club, and it was Ruthie's last amateur appearance. Soon her mother's efforts would bear fruit with Ruthie's professional debut in New York. Mrs. Dennis had organized the local dramatic club as a gift to her daughter, as a stopgap measure and vehicle for her talents until New York agents recognized her genius. Mrs. Dennis knew that Somerville was a dead end. Only three years earlier in Somerset Hall, when a group of skirt dancers began high-kicking, the audience had stampeded, *en masse,* from the hall. Ruthie deserved a more sophisticated audience, but in the interim *The Old Homestead* suited Emma Dennis' purpose. The play would give Ruthie a credit for her dossier, and the script itself echoed Mrs. Dennis' favorite themes. It emphasized temperance and allowed rural folk to thumb their noses at city slickers. Mrs. Dennis had adapted the script to her own use, changing a few names here and there. She called her own character Aunt Jerusha, instead of Matilda. Ruthie portrayed Whistling Joe, "the champion deadhead of America" —Happy Jack in the original version. In her most dramatic scene she discussed filial piety with her father, who portrayed Uncle Josh:

UNCLE JOSH: Do you ever think . . . ?

WHISTLING JOE: Think of what?

JOSH: Your mother. How she watched you all through the cares and dangers of your childhood; worked for you; prayed for you. I tell you, boy, you owe that mother more than you ever can repay.

In the years ahead, as Ruthie embarked upon her professional career, she had occasion to remember those words—with regret.

TWO

HURRYING PAST THE PICKLED CALVES

ONLY A SHORT train ride separated New York City from Pin Oaks farm, but during the winter of 1893–94 that distance carried Ruthie from her childhood into a career. She had just turned fifteen. Tall and lithe, she was more vivacious than pretty, with dark hair framing intelligent blue eyes, a fine, straight nose above a rosebud mouth. Her tomboyish ways had matured into a saucy wit, boundless energy, and devilment. Headstrong, Ruthie tested the very core of her mother's authority, and fierce battles alternated with ardent reconciliations. The two women were symbiotic. Ruthie supplied the talent and energy; her mother provided discipline and grit. Together they challenged the theatrical world of New York.

The theatre in 1894 meant Broadway as well as Buffalo Bill, the Opera and the circus, musical comedy, Coney Island, and curio halls. Highbrow and lowbrow mingled as the traditional, elitist audience for the arts moved over to make room for the middle-class consumer who had a few extra hours and money to spend. Popular entertainments aimed at a relatively unsophisticated audience gave birth to Ruthie Dennis' art. As Ruth St. Denis she aspired to the loftier echelons of fine art, but she remained a genius of lowbrow whose dance was born in dime museums, in outdoor spectacles, in the Delsarte movement, in variety and vaudeville. The period in which St. Denis' dance matured was the era of greatest expansion for American vaudeville, the mainstream of American popular entertainment, created by the converging rivulets of post-Civil War burlesque, minstrel shows, variety, riverboat shows, and honky-tonks. Vaudeville became the seedbed for America's early modern dance.

Ruthie arrived in New York during a rich period for American dance. Classical ballet flourished at the Metropolitan Opera with squadrons of ballerinas, preferably fleshy and foreign-born. The legitimate theatre, in transition between the era of stock companies and the new age of touring ensembles, lightened its fare and offered musical farces, each with its obligatory ballet spectacle or chorus line. Soloists of every possible stripe competed for jobs in these musicals, in private clubs or in the variety theatres. The dime museums where Ruthie got her start were the lowest rung of the theatrical ladder, but they catered to the solo dancer because other acts were too cumbersome for their tiny stages. With the development of the vaudeville syndicates, dancing girls found steadier work in tours to a network of American towns, and as the public appetite for dancing grew, dozens of Ruthie Dennises descended on New York to peddle their talents.

Ruthie and her mother moved into Miller's Hotel in Manhattan, which became their base for trips between Broadway and the farm. Advertised as a "Strictly Temperance House," Miller's Hotel catered to an intellectual clientele and was "recommended by educators throughout the country" especially for "families and ladies traveling alone or in parties." The proprietor, Mrs. Nancy Miller, was the same friend who had provided a mortgage for Pin Oaks farm, and she allowed credit on the Dennises' hotel bill until Ruthie could find a job.

After settling in their new quarters, mother and daughter sallied forth from the West Twenty-sixth Street hotel, turned onto Sixth Avenue, and spied Worth's Family Theatre and Museum. Like Miller's Hotel, Worth's Museum maintained a studied air of respectability, with "instructive, moral, and entertaining" amusements. "Professor" E. M. Worth had traveled the world gathering his collection of curios, rare coins, historical relics, and "living curiosities" such as a "human billiard ball." Inside the museum a "lecturer" guided the paying public through the dimly lit displays into the amusements hall which offered continuous variety acts and a "Grand Sacred Concert" on Sundays. The museum, argued its advertisements, "furnishes just what the moral and religious portion of the community wants, an unobjectionable place of amusement where every one can go and be highly entertained, instructed, and satisfied." Worth's also furnished Ruthie her first professional job as a skirt dancer for six performances a day.

During the week of January 29, 1894, "Ruth" made her debut at Worth's on a bill that included an equilibrist-juggler, an albino musician, and Lillie the Trick Dog. Ruthie's dance must have been satisfactory, for the museum hired her for an additional week, with grander billing as "The Only Ruth." The work was grueling, the surroundings unsavory. Ruthie remembered "hurrying by the triple-headed calves and other unspeakables in great glass jars filled with alcohol" to reach the stage, where she let loose with roll-overs, skin-the-cats, splits, and other acrobatics she had perfected by jumping off the Pin Oaks barn. Her specialty was "slow-splits" in which she "stood like a match and very slowly went down," tossing her long brown curls at the end of each musical phrase "with a little air of satisfaction which often brought a round of applause." If Ruthie was satisfied dancing six-a-day, Mrs. Dennis was more dubious, but as she wrote her husband, such entertainments were the only respectable outlets for middle-class dancing girls. "The museum is a 'museum,'" she wrote wryly, "but I guess it takes the respectable working classes for there is but one other place and that is the 'Opera House.'"

Reputation was a genuine concern for Mrs. Dennis as her daughter entered a profession that was next to prostitution in the popular mind. A dancing girl depended for her livelihood on a network of powerful males—agents, producers, club owners—who could be ruthless in exploiting young women financially, if not sexually. The press circulated reports of innocent girls lured into vice by unscrupulous theatrical agents, but a more common complaint was petty swindle. In a typical episode, reported by a theatrical magazine in 1895, two would-be producers offered bogus contracts to dancers, then absconded with their recruits' sizable wardrobe deposits. If a dancing girl managed to avoid such swindlers, she was certain to encounter the pawing patron or the theatrical powerbroker who expected sexual favors in return for employment. In the Metropolitan Opera's Vaudeville Club, where Ruthie performed in her early adolescence, private parlors were provided for tête-à-tête dalliances between boxholders and "artists of the female persuasion," and a cartoon of the period depicted a Vaudeville Club patron amusing himself with champagne and showgirl. In an effort to counteract this stereotype, some producers, such as F. F. Proctor, made a fetish of modesty in their female employees, but the general theatre climate of the 1890s was decidedly risky for a virginal farm girl.

Introduced into this world at a tender age, Ruthie developed an elaborate stratagem, a compound of opportunism and naïveté. When one powerful producer propositioned her, she "grew cold with fear," but uppermost in her mind was "Mother, and the money," and the thought that "all my ambitions had come to nothing." In this reaction lay the roots of the shrewd hypocrisy which underlay much of Ruth St. Denis' personal and professional life. All her life, St. Denis protested too much, wore her virginal purity as a badge even as she exploited her relationships. As a teenager she professed extreme reticence with men but managed to pose nude for a photographer, her "flutter of indecision" conquered by vanity and ambition. The photographer "made it all very artistic and plausible," she said, reflecting in her rationale the curious climate of the American arts.

The American attitude toward art is permeated with hypocrisy. Cultural historians have identified the origins of this attitude in a complex of native conditions—a political philosophy that equated art with luxury and privilege, a Puritan suspicion of sensory pleasures and nonutilitarian activities, a geographical isolation that bred conservatism. These conditions created a pervasive moralism. In Ruthie's day the theatre mirrored a self-conscious but curious public intent on amusing itself with minimal guilt, and popular entertainments justified themselves with elaborate rationales, ranging from Worth's Museum's "morally instructive pastimes" to the Delsarte movement's nascent dance disguised as "hygienic exercise."

These justifications became even more elaborate as women invaded the entertainment world on both sides of the footlights. Women in the audience covered themselves from stem to stern while their theatrical counterparts displayed trim ankles or, worse, the curvaceous legs that polite society referred to as "limbs." Bare feet were scandalous. The female form, particularly the dancing girl, became the focus of cultural insecurity and curiosity. "Everywhere it is woman, woman, woman; and every time it is elementary woman stripped of her externals!" enthused a reporter covering the 1893 World's Fair, which introduced the hootchy-kootchy that Little Egypt later made a household word at Coney Island. This fascination with women as entertainment commodities was linked with post-Civil War affluence or, as Thorstein Veblen phrased it, "conspicuous consumption" and the rise of the leisure class. Women became symbols of leisure and wealth, consumer objects to be adorned and displayed, as American vaudeville entered a period one historian called the years of "the Ascendant Female."

Not only were women displayed onstage, by the time Ruth Dennis made her debut at the Vaudeville Club the female audience was a new factor, leading one observer to grumble that "Pretty soon a chap will have to go home to be alone." Only women of dubious reputation had attended variety shows until the 1870s when Tony Pastor innovated "clean vaudeville" by attracting respectable female patrons with mild material and souvenir gewgaws. As ladies began to patronize high-class variety, the atmosphere of the theatre became even more self-conscious, with elaborate rationales required to justify the display of female bodies. Scantily clad women appeared as "living statues" or in tableaux that duplicated famous paintings or biblical episodes such as Susannah and the Elders. Ruth St. Denis matured as an artist in this climate. Her instinctive understanding of the American public's moralistic approach to entertainment helped her to shape a popular dance form, even as it encumbered her private life with guilt. Her bare-legged goddesses and her pious madonnas reflected a cultural, as well as personal preoccupation with female sexuality, a preoccupation that always sold theatre tickets. Hypocrisy, it seems, by another name was showmanship.

If Worth's Museum was a barely respectable beginning for her career, the Vaudeville Club in New York introduced Ruthie to the heady world of the wealthy and powerful. A remarkable marriage of highbrow and lowbrow, the Vaudeville Club opened in 1893 to satisfy the curiosity of Metropolitan Opera patrons who longed to sample the forbidden pleasures of the raucous music halls. Unable to risk scandal by stepping down to the Casino or even to Tony Pastor's, the opera patrons founded their own Vaudeville Club in the sanctity of the Opera House itself, much to the merriment of the popular press. Tongue in cheek, one reporter described the scene: "A thousand young men and women of this city, whose serious vocation in life it is to avoid death from ennui, have undertaken to prolong existence through the novel expedient of a variety show. Just why it is more amusing, or less wicked, to observe a young woman in house costume turn a somersault in a private theatre than to see the same performance at a concert hall is a distinction between right and wrong" that escaped him, he wrote. Another reporter from the *New York Dramatic Mirror* agreed, observing that "Between the cigarette smoke of the chappies, the fumes of the clubmen's liquor, and the starched condescension of the maids and matrons, there is an almost grotesque incongruity."

The incongruous Vaudeville Club offered Ruthie important connections which would further her stage career. One evening she danced before the club's glittering audience and rushed offstage, only to stumble into the arms of a distinguished gentleman who gallantly bent to kiss her hand. He was huge in stature, with a shock of carroty hair.

"He was my first real contact with a world I knew nothing about, a great social world that lay outside my experience but not outside my curiosity," St. Denis wrote in her memoirs. "His name, Stanford White, meant very little to me at that time." White, the prominent architect, had decorated the rooms of the Vaudeville Club and served on its board of directors. His fondness for showgirls, which ultimately caused his death in the notorious Evelyn Thaw affair, led him to dub the adolescent Ruthie his "Wild Flower." White wined and dined Ruthie, presented her with a bicycle and other gifts, loaned her money, and appointed various friends to keep an eye on her career. Their relationship, St. Denis insisted, was platonic. Her mother, always a formidable obstacle, managed to encourage White's largesse while maintaining a "subtle chill in the air," and Ruthie herself feigned naïveté. Undaunted, White took pleasure in promoting his Wild Flower's career and became the prototype for a series of avuncular figures in St. Denis' life, most of whom gave more than they received. On one occasion, after a late-night supper in White's hotel suite, Ruthie questioned her own behavior and motives: "How could Stanford possibly know what was in my mind? Perhaps he thought my naïveté was merely a clever blind. After all, I had accepted his help for many years . . . (and) he had a perfect right to assume that I would respond one day." Always plagued by guilt in these relationships, Ruthie looked back on her friendship with White and ruefully concluded, "I am a block of ice. That's what White always told me and now I can begin to realize a little what it cost him."

The valuable connections made in the Vaudeville Club led Ruthie to other odd jobs in the spring of 1894: a week at Hermann's Theatre; a job in White Plains, New York, for a salary of three dollars a day; a trip to Easton, Pennsylvania, as "one of four Spanish dancers." By late spring Ruthie secured an engagement at the Central Opera House Music Hall, earning a personal notice in the New York press. "Ruth, premiere danseuse, proved herself to be a kicker of the highest order and was deservedly encored," reported the *New York Clipper*. By summer these encores led her into the lucrative world of variety roof gardens.

Roof gardens became a staple feature of variety houses in the early 1890s as New York theatres converted from dramatic to variety fare. During the sweltering summer months these cool outdoor theatres catered to a family clientele. "Popper" and "mommer" brought their children. Pretty girls in summer gowns strolled in on the arms of young gents in linen suits, russet shoes, and broad-brimmed straw hats. Portly men lounged in wicker chairs, enjoying their favorite refreshment, and "while the breeze gently swept over them," an onlooker reported, "they drank the beer which foams, smoked the weed and were happy."

From sunset to midnight contented patrons enjoyed the showy ballets and solo variety acts that alternated on the roof-garden stages. This pleasant setting extended the theatrical season into the summer months and the late evening hours, a boon in employment for variety dancers. "In nearly all cases their wages have increased," reported the New York Sun, and "with the roof gardens competing against the regular variety houses, the performers have been able almost to make their own terms." Ruthie found that dancing was particularly in demand. She became a roof-garden regular, gradually distinguishing herself from the dozens of high-kickers, serpentine dancers, Trilby dancers, and skirt dancers on the stage. As "The Only Ruth" she appeared at the Madison Square Roof Garden in July of 1894, then at the American Theatre Roof Garden as "Ruth, Acrobatic Dancer." This latter engagement featured an athletic bill, with a contortionist, a juggler, and a female bicycle rider, but it was Ruthie who caught the critics' eye and established herself as "one of the very best acrobatic dancers on the stage."

Ruthie and other variety dancers of the 1890s must be considered among our earliest "modern dancers," for they were endlessly inventive in their search for a regenerative motor force for dance. The progress of dance during this period might be likened to the evolution of photography into film. By the late nineteenth century, American dance emphasized static pattern and completed pose. A popular variety act known as "living pictures" capitalized on this tendency by arranging models into familiar scenes and displaying them onstage inside immobile, ornate frames. Ballet spectacles also adopted a pictorial approach, using "human beings for pigments" in "compositions developed at wholesale rates." The ballet master of the day served as a field general, marshaling his troops, moving them in formation, or as one critic put it, "maneuvering dancers from tableaux to tableaux in nice juxtapositions that do not overstep the unity of the picture."

If dance had become static, early modern dancers such as Ruth Dennis needed a motional impulse, a reconnection to an *élan vital* which would animate choreographic form. Genevieve Stebbins, as Ruthie had seen, experimented with breath-rhythms and the spiral form with its torsional twist as an energizer for her statue-poses. Other variety dancers, for all their apparent triviality, explored the physics of motion—gravity, spatial illusion, the qualities of light—in a reflection of the larger cultural search for a dynamic fourth dimension. They disrupted linear time sequence and predictable spatial pattern with the human elements of asymmetry, dynamism, and surprise, and in so doing, created a modern dance.

Among Ruthie's peers on the variety stage were Amatti, whose "kaleidoscopic bicycle dance" added another motional dimension to the moving body. "Aerial ballets" in 1894 featured dancers suspended by wires on pulleys, their antics bathed in colored lights. With the development of electric stage lighting, Loie Fuller pioneered the "serpentine dance," which dominated variety dancing in the 1880s and 1890s. Clad in rippling silks, the serpentine dancer became a background for the play of moving lights, a clever inversion of the shadowgraph hand tricks which projected animated silhouettes onto a white screen. The popular Fuller imitator, Papinta, not only danced before an arrangement of mirrors which multiplied her moving image, but also danced upon a lighted glass trap door through which, unfortunately, she fell in 1895, temporarily ending her career. If the lighting effects often danced more than the dancer, these early creations shared an impulse toward multidimensional movement that marked the birth of modern dance.

In this inventive climate Ruthie developed the style and technique that served her during a fifty-year career as a matriarch of modern dance. She began as a skirt dancer, that category of variety dancer that also included the young Loie Fuller and Isadora Duncan. The skirt dancer, explained a dance historian of the period, "provided an outlet from the impasse into which dancing had been driven." She rediscovered movement flow by retaining the vocabulary of classical ballet, "the exchange, the pirouette, the balance," and adding "the grace of flowing drapery, the value of line, the simplicity and naturalness that were characteristic of Greek dance." The skirt dancer manipulated her petticoats, added acrobatics, and called the finished product Greek, Spanish, Egyptian, or Oriental, acquiring both the luster of exoticism and the respectability of a reference to civilizations past. Her skirt dance was a compromise "between the academical method of ballet and the grotesque step-dancing which appealed to the popular taste of the time."

Within the loose genre of skirt dancing, Ruthie explored every imaginable contortion that could please a paying customer and gradually developed a movement vocabulary of her own. Her greatest debt was to the Delsarte exercises that had developed her naturally flexible spine and taught her such "successive movements" as a jointless arm ripple that she added as a fillip to her routines. She specialized in twists of the torso and the swirl of draperies that became her stock-in-trade. She also nurtured the charisma and the theatrical know-how that informed her career by learning what pleased her audiences and the managers who controlled employment in the variety theatres.

Ruthie had found a reliable and influential theatrical agent, Mrs. E. L. Fernandez, whose own daughter Bijou became a famous stage star. Mrs. Fernandez helped Ruthie to master the good-old-boy network of theatre managers, dance directors, and talent scouts. In an early letter to her mother, Ruthie described the process by which she got a job: "Wednesday eve I got a call from Mrs. Fernandez to be at the New York Theatre on Thursday morning at 10 o'clock. So of course I went. I saw Mr. Lykens who is the man I danced for on the Olympia Roof garden. Well, he said, they, meaning the managers of the New York Theatre, wanted some ballet girls for the road." Lykens gave her a card to see Karl Marwig, the ballet master who was casting the show. "Well, I saw Marwig and also MacCormick, the man who gave me a trial on the Casino Roof. He remembered that, so he and Marwig had quite a reminiscing time about how they both knew me, some four or five years ago." With these connections, Ruthie graduated from variety roof gardens to the more sustained employment of touring roadshows. Her first major break was a cameo role in the touring production of *The Passing Show*.

During the summer of 1894 the Casino Theatre featured *The Passing Show*, Canary and Lederer's satirical review of the current New York theatre season. Billed as a "topical extravaganza burlesque," *The Passing Show* appealed to a theatre-wise audience, with inside jokes directed at the snooty Vaudeville Club and at current theatrical hits. With its topical slant, *The Passing Show* continually fed new routines into its format and borrowed from variety such popular acts as the toe dancing of La Petite Adelaide, one of Ruthie's rivals. On July 29, 1894, the directors of *The Passing Show* announced the acquisition of yet another novelty, La Blanche, a *danseuse gymnastique*. "It is asserted that she is the superior of all the many young women whose abilities run in the direction of placing their feet above their heads," reported the New

York *Times*, while the *Sun* clarified the newcomer's identity by reporting the following week that "Ruth LaBlanche has made a hit with her graceful dancing." Soon she became simply, "Ruth, Danseuse Acrobatique." Unlike La Petite Adelaide and the other variety performers who appeared as separate entr'actes in *The Passing Show*, Ruthie appeared as an integral part of the show in a scene titled "The Palace of Justice, Tempered with Mercy, etc." Little record remains of this early "eccentric dance" and its exotic setting, but it provides a tantalizing clue to one origin of the Hall of Judgment scene in St. Denis' later *Egypta*.

After touring with *The Passing Show*, Ruthie spent two years as a variety dancer in New York, returning now and again to the farm. She contributed her earnings to the family purse, but the Dennises' financial plight grew steadily worse. A prolonged legal battle over Pin Oaks had begun in 1891 when the family friend, Mrs. Miller, assumed payments on the farm and leased it to the Dennis family. While this maneuver eased their financial burden temporarily, the Dennises became unable even to meet their modest rental payments, and eventually they fought Mrs. Miller in court for repossession of the farm. Tom Dennis, who had stayed at the farm and cared for young Brother, was still unemployed, his fanciful inventions gathering dust in the United States Patent Office. He grew bitter about Ruthie's earnings, and letters from this period reflect his fears that his war pension would be siphoned to finance Ruthie's career. In the spring of 1896 the Dennises declared bankruptcy and sold their goods at auction. They moved to the Fort Greene area of Brooklyn, where Tom's older son already lived. This move signaled the beginning of the family's disintegration, for outside the stable precincts of Pin Oaks farm, the elder Dennises drifted apart while Ruthie pursued her career.

The uprooting and relocation were a terrible wrench for Ruthie, who was then seventeen. In her autobiography she wrote, "I did not know that anything could crush my soul as much as Brooklyn did. All my life the trees and fields had protected me from ugliness." The dour environs of the Brooklyn Navy Yard, where Tom Dennis finally found work as a machinist, became the family's new home, first in a residence on Kent Avenue, then on Willoughby near Jay Street, and later on DeKalb Avenue, where Mrs. Dennis opened a boardinghouse. The Navy Yard area teemed with working-class immigrants, particularly Irish, English, and Germans, whose accents Ruthie learned to mimic. Both the foreign- and native-born, drawn by jobs at the Navy Yard, lived in this neighborhood of rubble-littered lots, mazy alleyways, and a few brick-paved roads, with a red-light district along Sands Street, not far from the Dennises' Willoughby Avenue home. To Ruthie, Brooklyn was a horror. Throughout her diaries and journals, well into her later years, runs the refrain of Pin Oaks, her lost childhood, her Eden. She would return, would indeed own Pin Oaks again, but after 1896 her home was the theatre.

As a consolation for losing Pin Oaks, perhaps, her family enrolled Ruthie in the prestigious Packer Collegiate Institute, which still stands today in downtown Brooklyn. Its ivy-covered walls became a substitute Pin Oaks, as "Packer's came to mean to me a protection from the problems of home and the world." Ruthie enrolled in the fall of 1896 as a seventeen-year-old student in the third grade of the junior year academic program. Her subjects were composition, arithmetic, Latin and French, and the History of England and the United States; the yellowing *Semi-Quarterly Reports of Scholarship* at Packer still record Ruthie's high marks. She excelled in Latin and was admitted to the honors group in French. Her lifelong love of research and reading must have been nurtured in the school's excellent library, where students learned to use the library resources of the entire New York area. Ruthie probably made use of the Packer gymnasium and such extracurricular activities as the dramatic readings and *tableaux vivants* sponsored by the elocution teacher, Miss Helen K. Alt-Muller, who was a disciple of Delsarte. On one occasion Ruthie and the mother of a Packer classmate offered a joint recital, and Ruthie danced in imitation of Genevieve Stebbins, in Greek garb and bare feet. Just how the well-bred Packer coeds reacted to a showgirl for a schoolmate, or how the Dennises managed the thirty-five dollar tuition, are mysteries. Relatives or Stanford White may have helped pay the bill, and Ruthie herself earned extra money by posing for art students. She also worked as a cloak model for the Brooklyn firm of Abraham & Straus, but by the fall of 1898 she returned to the stage, joining the cast of the touring musical comedy *The Ballet Girl*.

The Edward Rice production of *The Ballet Girl* had premiered the previous Christmas at Manhattan Theatre in New York, opening to favorable press reviews. Typical of the light family fare of the 1890s, the musical comedy capitalized on the current enthusiasm for dancing girls. Its plot concerned the tangled love affairs of an artist, a Parisian ballerina, an American heiress, and a European noble, with plenty of "mirth and music, color and costume." Ruthie signed on as an acrobatic toe dancer, and she may have appeared in the play's Moorish ballet before she graduated to the role of "Gloria."

At nineteen, Ruthie had a half-decade of theatrical experience behind her, and her family must have felt she was mature enough to go on tour alone, for Mrs. Dennis remained in Brooklyn to look after her son. On her own for the first time, Ruthie described in letters home the typical life of a dancing girl on tour:

> You rise say at ten thirty, pack your things, eat your breakfast and catch an 11:30 train. Get into the next town (we did not have long runs I must say that) at 1:15 with a call for rehearsal at 2:30 sharp. Then you wash—take a short rest—and rush to the theatre there—between rehearsing and unpacking your theatre costume, etc. You stay until 4:30 or 5 P.M. Then back to the hotel where tired out you can either lie down, write or anything you feel like until 6 o'clock and from 6:30 until seven you may have one whole half hour to yourself . . . Then the last straw, after the show is all over—and you feel like carry-me-home-on-a-stretcher—you must pack all your different costumes and make up, etc., put them in a huge bundle and take down stairs to the wardrobe woman *then* you may go home and rest 11:45.

This dizzying routine left little time for socializing, but Ruthie began to form friendships with other members of the cast, including an attractive young man named Jack Hoey.

Ruthie and Jack became infatuated in Boston, tried to part in Worcester, broke off their romance in Norwich, and reunited in Montreal. They quarreled over his cigarette smoking and card-playing, but Ruthie managed to get him to church and wrote home that she planned to stay with Jack until she "straightened him out." The letters chronicling this road romance alarmed Mrs. Dennis, who repeatedly warned Ruthie not to allow Jack into her hotel room. From Lowell, Massachusetts, Ruthie replied that the girls in the next room had entertained men with whiskey and card-playing throughout one long night, and, in hysterics, she had called Jack to her room "for comfort and protection." She rationalized that "The damp, cold parlors close at 10 P.M.," explaining to her mother that with the cast always carousing, she could not get to sleep without a reassuring bedtime chat. "You see," she wrote, "this company is just like a little town wandering around the country, and each is dependent on the other . . . because in one night stands you are dead to the outside world." Unconvinced, Mrs. Dennis wrote immediately that she was on her way to join the tour. Ruthie telegraphed her not to come and promised that she had "prayed earnestly to be given the strength to resist evil." Apparently her prayers were answered. Crestfallen, she wrote that Jack Hoey had sent word that while he "admired her purity," he was no angel himself. "So," the ballet girl concluded, "this is where we *drop it, see?*"

Safely through this roadshow and early romance, Ruthie returned home and auditioned for a role in *A Runaway Girl*, a two-act musical farce produced by Augustin Daly. One of the most powerful figures in the American theatre, Daly was a drama critic and playwright turned producer, known for the extravagance of his productions, the severity of his discipline, and his skillful selection of actors. He had assembled a stellar stock company, both in London and in his own theatre in New York. In 1893 he became convinced that England's popular musical comedies could be imported for American audiences, and he added a series of musical farces to his dramatic repertoire at Daly's Theatre. One of these musicals, *The Geisha*, produced in 1896, featured the young dancer Isadora Duncan, who apparently was more fortunate than Ruthie Dennis. Ruthie's own mother had written the Daly company that year, only to be told there were no more jobs for dancers. Ruthie's luck was better in the spring of 1899. Daly hired her for the cast of *A Runaway Girl* as it began a cross-country tour. Ruthie signed on as "Folly, the Carnival Dancer," then added the role of an "English girl," and most important, only a couple of weeks into the tour, she began to understudy the speaking role of "Miss Creel."

Ruthie's elevation to the rank of understudy was a typical example of her own self-promotion and pluck. When *A Runaway Girl* played Boston, Ruthie spent a free evening at a competing play and remarked to her companion that she could "act better than that." Returning to *A Runaway Girl*, she approached the stage manager and inquired whom she should see about understudying a role. When he replied "The Guv'nor," Ruthie wrote Daly directly, and the producer allowed her to understudy and later assume the role of Miss Creel, the young and restless bride of an old fisherman. No sooner had Ruthie assumed the role than Daly died, having lived long enough to give Ruth St. Denis her first dramatic role—her first, that is, since *The Old Homestead.*

After touring with *A Runaway Girl,* Ruthie returned once again to Brooklyn and continued her dancing lessons. She studied Spanish technique with Karl Marwig, ballet with the Italian ballerina Ernestina Bossi, and *pointe* work with the famed Marie Bonfanti. From her agent, Mrs. Fernandez, she learned of an opening in a touring production of *Man in the Moon.* Hired as a chorus dancer, she found herself on a train bound for Baltimore. "I've got my bloomers on and my corsets off!" she gaily wrote her mother, whose own illness again prevented her from going along on the tour. For Ruthie, this job was familiar territory. An echo of *The Passing Show, Man in the Moon* was a comic revue of recent theatrical and sporting events, billed as a "spectacular fantasy in three acts." Dance numbers were plentiful, including an Orchid Ballet, a Cake Walk, a Four Seasons Ballet, a Jesters' Ballet, and an Expansion Ballet, which sounded suspiciously like glorified statue-posing: "In this ballet d'action designed by Karl Marwig," reported a reviewer in the New York *Times,* "the scene is a spacious hall of gold and white marble with mural decorations and statuary illustrating notable events in the history of this country," adding that the entire dancing troupe "is out of the common." Among the dancers in *Man in the Moon* were the durable Adelaide, no longer so petite, and Ruthie, who wasted no time in asking the stage manager to watch her rehearse a solo dance which she wanted to add to the show.

Ruthie also made new friends in the cast. Her favorite was C. P. Flockton, a character actor who wore a monocle, played the zither, wrote biblical plays, and referred to Ruthie as "Miss Montgomery, the Mystic Girl." This nickname is among the earliest evidence of Ruthie's interest in mysticism, though George Lederer, producer of *The Passing Show,* remembered that Ruthie was "crazy on the subject of the odd, the weird and the fantastic, and she read constantly." On the *Man in the Moon* tour Ruthie presented one actor friend with a set of essays by Ralph Waldo Emerson and she also studied Kant, but her taste ran to fictional romances. "These I devoured in great gulps because I never did read properly," St. Denis admitted. "My method from that day to this in reading books of any description has been to get at the story, see how it all came out, and then go back and begin all over again, if I like the book. If I did not I could congratulate myself on not having wasted any more time." As a choreographer, she also would "get at the story," and as she traveled and read and formed acquaintances, she absorbed the impressions that fed her art.

As she approached her twenty-first birthday, Ruthie felt restless, both in her personal life and her work. She had an enormous appetite for living. From Philadelphia she wrote of an evening on the town with members of the *Man in the Moon* cast. "Of course I did not drink—that stands for all time," she reassured her mother, "but everything else that came my way I took in." Inevitably she began to feel stirrings of independence, and her relationship with her mother began subtly to change. Still the object of her mother's intense ambition, Ruthie developed ambitions of her own, and she gradually assumed an almost maternal role in their complex relationship. When Mrs. Dennis wrote of her illness, longing for Ruthie's company, her daughter replied soothingly that she was sorry her mother suffered from insomnia and nerves. "If I was home we would have a nice talk—probably on faith, and bye and bye after much reasoning and arguing—you would feel a little better," Ruthie wrote, adding archly in her best Packer's French, "n'est ce pas—?"

As Mrs. Dennis' nervous instability increased, as her relationship with her husband deteriorated, she leaned more and more on Ruthie, who bridled under the strain. In one angry letter Ruthie threatened to withhold her confidences from her mother "because your anxiety crushes me. If you can only feel that I am going straight to perdition—then I must plod on my way *alone*." Ruthie felt exploited by her mother, just as she later did with women friends who were always "trying to get out of me what they should find in a man. My mother did the same thing—it gets down to a subtle essense [sic] of sex—without its honesty—and satisfaction—and so it makes for discord and great unhappiness."

Her unhappiness grew as she realized that she was almost twenty-one, without a lasting love relationship in her life. Her old boyfriend Clark Miller still hovered in the wings, writing long letters from Somerville and offering financial assistance to save Pin Oaks. Ruthie relied on Clark, valued his loyalty and stability, but their relationship lacked passion. "I did all I could to make him want me," she said, "but he never desired me. I used to beg him in my heart to hold me against the world but he never could or would." Ruthie wondered about men and physical passion. She decided that there were men "who really are greatly lovable and with whom passion works wonders and then there are other men in whom it only brings out the low and beastly." She knew that she was attractive to men and reveled in her own magnetic power. In a frank, almost deliberately provocative letter to her mother, she wrote that there had been men "who could scarcely have me come into the room where they were, without feeling that fine ether or magnetism which emanates from me," adding in frustration, "I am asking myself daily *how long* before it will come—"

As the century turned, Ruthie came of age. Restless, talented, troubled, she toyed with the idea of abandoning dancing for an acting career. She felt that her talents were wasted in musical farces, and in a prophetic letter written from the *Man in the Moon* tour, she said that she was destined for something more than "the kick, the bend, and the whirl":

> You know when I have danced my best, on several occasions people have been good enough to tell me that my dancing suggested something, they perhaps could not tell just what, but the fact that it meant a little more than the kick and the bend and the whirl— and as I watch La Petite Adelaide who is with us every night—and see how utterly senseless her dancing is, though immensely clever you understand, I feel almost that I'm not clever enough in that way to achieve her success—that line—because if I was something of a success in that line, I'm afraid it might be the end rather than the *beginning,* which I feel that to-day my life is.

Indeed that moment in 1900 was the beginning of a brighter career, for in a matter of days she would meet David Belasco.

THREE

FOXY QUILLER

"Foxy Quiller, the quintessence
of all human intelligence."
—FOXY QUILLER (IN CORSICA),
A POPULAR 1900 OPERETTA

RUTHIE MET David Belasco in the spring of 1900. Some strange al-
chemy forged a link between their disparate personalities: Belasco, the
powerful producer, almost priestly in his manner, with his black suits,
stand-up collars, and deferential air; Ruthie, at twenty-one a slapdash
Gibson Girl, her prematurely graying hair hastily arranged in a pompadour, her quick wit confident with youth. They met as Belasco organized the road company of his hit play *Zaza*, and as Belasco remembered
it their meeting took on Horatio Alger overtones: "One day a Brooklyn
girl about sixteen years old came to me with the familiar story," Belasco
recalled. "She was tall, thin, angular, very awkward, not at all
prepossessing, and her face was spotted with freckles. She said her
name was Ruth Dennis and that she was poor." The girl told him that
she wanted a career on the stage. "'I know I am not graceful, but I can
dance a little. I will do anything to get a start. Can't you help me?'"

Belasco studied "the mobile lines in her face and the changing light
in her eyes" and was struck "by the undeveloped possibilities in the
girl." He decided to hire her for the role of Adele, a "cafe concert girl"
in *Zaza*, and "once in my theatre, the energy and ambition of this girl
had no limit." Ruthie begged Belasco for a place to practice her dancing, and he lent her the stage of his theatre whenever it was not in use.
"Every morning after that she came to my old Republic Theatre and
practised alone. I never saw a girl with such a keen desire to succeed."

Belasco's memory of Ruth St. Denis' rise to stardom through pluck
and luck and his own generosity was a romantic but faulty account. By

the time Ruthie met Belasco she was past adolescence, already twenty-one, and a six-year veteran of the stage. She remembered actually auditioning for an assistant to the producer, and contrary to Belasco's belief, Ruthie practiced her dancing only at her mother's prodding. At least the essence of Belasco's story rings true: Ruthie was ambitious but undirected, and Belasco had a keen eye for "undeveloped possibilities." He admired Ruthie's zest, and she was intrigued by the "half-innocent, half-sinister personality" of D.B., as she came to call the director whose "almost oriental refinement of speech and gesture" was hypnotic for his followers. For four years Ruthie was a Belasco player, alternating among the casts of *Zaza, Madame DuBarry,* and *The Auctioneer,* learning the theatre trade from its resident genius.

By 1900 Belasco was in his prime as a producer, director, and adapter of plays. He had honed his theatrical style in the feverish atmosphere of gold-rush California, and he brought to Broadway melodrama in the guise of historical spectacle and domestic drama. The legendary Belasco "realism" was a pastiche of sentimentality and *fin-de-siècle* luxury, with the high color of tabloid scandal and the minute detail of the photograph. Belasco "thought in pictures," his major legacy to Ruth St. Denis. He orchestrated color, light, and crowd movement into realistic riots, thunderstorms, and battle scenes complete with galloping horses and booming cannon onstage. An antiques buff, Belasco prized historical accuracy in his plays. For his spectacle *Madame DuBarry* he imported a complete set of authentic Louis XV furnishings. Yet his forte, as one astute critic observed, was the hysterical rather than the historical, and in this he found a powerful ally in his protégée, Mrs. Leslie Carter.

Mrs. Carter had come to Belasco with scandal at her heels. The defendant in a lurid divorce suit, she was a pariah in Chicago high society, a desperate woman in need of a protector and a profession. Belasco recognized her undeveloped possibilities as an actress and groomed her for a stage career. After six years of intensive coaching, Mrs. Carter triumphed in Belasco's *Heart of Maryland,* and in 1899 *Zaza* made her a star. Mrs. Carter was Belasco's prize creation, the perfect exponent of his titillating but moralistic dramas that explored the lives of unconventional women.

Belasco was fascinated by aberrant womankind. Despite his clerical demeanor, he was a sensualist, with a private collection of pornography and a preoccupation with bizarre sexuality that extended to the subject matter of his plays. His heroine Zaza was a French prostitute, while

DuBarry was a milliner turned gambling-house shill who ultimately became mistress of the king of France. Belasco's heroines, in drama as well as in life, were unorthodox in their behavior, though they paid lip service to Victorian values. Thus for Zaza, the sight of her married lover's child was enough to turn her from the sinful life; similarly, the scandalous Mrs. Carter retained her married name for the stage, while Belasco himself appended a "Saint" to Ruthie Dennis' name. This apparent hypocrisy was an essential element of the Belasco woman's image. She was a sanctified vehicle for voyeurism. She allowed the theatregoer a glimpse of evil while reassuring him of the eventual triumph of good. In this image Ruth St. Denis found the roots of her own stage persona.

At twenty-one Ruth already had the courage, stamina, and the instinct for self-protection which Belasco warned were necessary equipment for a woman of the theatre. She also shared with Belasco a certain "ethical bluntness," a self-interest and singularity of purpose which the producer admired. "No man will ever hold her for long except through her mind," Belasco once said of Ruthie. "She's all brain." He meant it as a compliment.

Ruthie joined the cast of Belasco's Zaza in March 1900, just before the company sailed to London on tour. Her family was in a flurry of excitement over her first trip abroad, but as always, a major obstacle was money. Mrs. Dennis wrote a hurried note to Stanford White, who responded with a loan and promptly deputized a friend to keep an eye on Ruthie on the overseas voyage. On April 4 the steamship St. Paul left New York for Southampton with a cargo of scenery, costumes, and actors from two plays, Zaza, and the Casino Theatre's The American Beauty. The members of both casts fraternized on the voyage, and Ruthie conquered her seasickness long enough to join in impromptu concerts with the Casino dancing girls. She also formed a friendship with Eleanor (Nell) Stuart of Zaza, and when their ship docked at Southampton, the two girls traveled together by train to London.

Ruthie might have been Henry James's Daisy Miller, so complete were her wonder and innocence abroad. To her eyes the English countryside, with its quaint inns, thatched roofs, and rolling fields, appeared to be the pastoral set of a comic opera. She exulted in the greenery, unmarred by American advertising, and happily wrote home that "Lydia Pinkham, 'the kind you have always bought,' and Castoria doesn't stare at me from hedges." When they arrived in London, Ruthie and Nell searched for a hotel, found everything "ancient, dark, and dear," but finally settled in a room and set out to explore the city. "It seems to me that London fairly invites me to evil deeds," Ruthie wrote home romantically. "It offers so many dark and dismal alleys—such a lot of creaking stairways." Her Gothic imagination was stimulated further by a visit to the Tower of London. She also said a prayer in Westminster Abbey and visited Buckingham Palace where, wonder of wonders, a carriage rolled by with "a little old, fat woman in black" who turned out to be Queen Victoria. Ruthie watched in fascination as debutantes dressed in décolleté gowns arrived at the palace for the queen's "drawing-room." Somehow, just being there, watching, seemed to confer vicarious social prestige, and Ruthie felt a twinge of superiority to the snobbish adversaries of her childhood, now that she had "crossed the wide-wide ocean . . ."

Sightseeing gave way to long rehearsals as members of the *Zaza* cast prepared for the mid-April opening at the Garrick Theatre. Ruthie found herself involved in a theatrical operation vastly different from the helter-skelter world of variety and musical roadshows. Quality was the byword in a Belasco production. The director subjected his players to exhausting rehearsals until he was satisfied with each detail. He expected his company members to learn singing, dancing, fencing, and other dramatic skills that might be useful in a production, and he drilled minor actors as rigorously as his stars.

On the eve of the *Zaza* opening the cast spent seven hours in dress rehearsal, and Ruthie shared the general apprehension about the reception of the play. Preoccupied with the Boer War that spring, London theatregoers were subdued. To make matters worse, the Lord Chamberlain threatened to censor *Zaza's* racy plot. The threat proved idle, but the ensuing publicity attracted a glittering opening-night crowd. Edward and George, the future kings, joined the cheering for Mrs. Carter's pyrotechnics, and even the critics grudgingly admitted that this "false and flashy" play was a spectacular success, though one dissenter called it "eminently janitorious." Ruthie wrote home excitedly that the production was a hit, "tho it could have been otherwise because *Zaza* is a very decided play, nothing wishy-washy, and stranger things could have happened than that these Englishers wouldn't have liked it."

Ruthie's own part in *Zaza* was a small speaking role with a bit of singing and dancing, but she wanted more. She had in mind not only a solo dance for *Zaza* but also an appearance in a second Belasco play due to open in another London theatre. She wrote her parents about her careful strategy: "With the help of Nell, who is a great diplomat and spokesman, I approached Belasco and asked about dancing between my parts in *Zaza*. He was charming and said 'certainly I could.'" She then asked him if he would object to her composing a Japanese dance and calling it *Madame Butterfly* after his play which had been such a success in New York and was coming to London. "Then one more thing I spoke of—wasn't I the *bold thing*—*Madame Butterfly* is a Japanese play in one act, so it is preceded by another play of one act, so I says, says I, how would it be if I could do my *Madame Butterfly* dance between the acts."

Belasco agreed to consult Charles Frohman, the producer of his London staging of *Madame Butterfly*, and he told Ruthie to go ahead with selection of a Japanese costume and the choreography for the dance. Even though this dance apparently never materialized, Ruthie crowed with pleasure as she told her family of plans for her first Japanese dance. "The idea will, for a dancer, be rather novel," she explained, "and me—'foxy quiller'—calling it 'so & so in her *Madame Butterfly* dance,' will be decidedly novel."

As foxy and ambitious as Ruthie was, she also was introspective. Her growing interest in oriental mysticism was both a shrewd search for novelty and a quest for the self. One fed the other. Ruthie read British books on Japanese Buddhism, but as she meditated, her thoughts turned to exotic roles and costumes. She craved exposure to admiring audiences, but she also relished aloneness, when "no one is here to whom I must say what I don't think and then think what I don't say." In London Ruthie felt the beginnings of her lifelong tug-of-war between solitude and success, and perhaps both impulses led her to visit the Paris Exposition after *Zaza* closed in London.

Thousands upon thousands of visitors thronged to Paris that summer of 1900, for the Exposition, braving one of the worst heat waves in history to sample the pleasures of a culture poised on the cusp of the twentieth century. They were dazzled by what they saw: Tonkinese palaces, Chinese pagodas, and Khmer ruins in the Exposition's Colonial Section; the Maison de l'Art Nouveau, filled with fabrics, furniture, and decorative objects of a distinctive, curvilinear design; the Great Hall of Machines, with its whirring, metallic cacophony; the lively theatres along the banks of the Seine. The popular Palais de l'Électricité was a celebration of the achievements of science, a dancing fairyland of light made concrete in its carapace of electric light bulbs. The theme of this Exposition, its obsession, was that same dynamism that challenged all modernists, but a dynamism radically accelerated by science and applied technology. If energy was the motif of the fair, then dance seemed its natural expression. One American journalist suggested that the Paris Exposition was "nothing but one huge agglomeration of dancing." There were ballerinas at the Palais de la Danse, Egyptian belly dancers, Turkish dervishes, Cambodian and Spanish dancers, human channels for that energy expressed in the supreme symbol of the fair, the electric dynamo in its great gallery of machines.

For one visitor to Paris, the Bostonian Henry Adams, the Dynamo represented an entropic force that threatened the very foundations of civilized order. Adams felt that the new century teetered on a knife-edge between the Christian Virgin and the Dynamo, two kingdoms of force, the former representing Unity, the latter, Infinity and chaos. The same philosophical anxiety pervaded Ruth St. Denis' art. She spent her later years literally dancing Adams' Virgin, but in 1900, in the first flush of youthful vigor, she enjoyed the disturbing asymmetries of the fair. In the baroque buildings, exotic gardens, and decorative displays, she felt the lure of Art Nouveau, the quintessential style of the Exposition which she later incorporated into the style of her own dances.

Art Nouveau was a symbolic rendering of the forces of dynamism, an organic style that emphasized evocative line and decorative surface. The latest mode in 1900, Art Nouveau dominated the Paris fair. The central Maison de l'Art Nouveau displayed Tiffany glass, furniture, fabrics, and embroidery, more sumptuous in texture, color, and detail than the most costly Belasco production. The living embodiment of Art Nouveau, Loie Fuller, performed her Serpentine Dance at the Exposition in a tiny theatre equipped with its own electric dynamo. As Ruthie watched from the audience, Fuller created a calligraphy of undulating rhythms through the play of electric lights on swirling fabrics. In deference, perhaps, to the Japanese roots of Art Nouveau, Fuller shared her stage with the distinguished Japanese actress Sada Yacco, who appeared in a play and a Buddhist dance which one critic characterized as a "languorous evocation of Nirvana." Yacco's series of rhythmic poses "added motion to the poses one sees on Japanese fans or vases," creating a "series of tableaux to which the science and the discipline of the dance supply life and color." Before Ruthie's eyes the lessons of Genevieve Stebbins gained exotic dimension, and Sada Yacco joined Fuller as yet another mentor for St. Denis' later plastiques.

Her imagination fed by *japonaiserie,* Art Nouveau, Belasco, and Europe, a more cosmopolitan Ruthie returned to Brooklyn in the late summer of 1900. She came home to conflict. The elder Dennises, gradually going their separate ways, argued until Ruthie's father finally moved to Harrisburg, Pennsylvania, where he found temporary work in a machine factory. "Father was often away in those days," St. Denis remembered. "He and mother had drifted apart and were not very happy when they did meet." They met primarily to discuss money matters. The family existed on Ruthie's earnings, supplemented by Tom's odd jobs and pension and the slender income from Mrs. Dennis' boardinghouse. Mrs. Dennis kept strict accounts and reported to Ruthie that the majority of her stage salary went to pay household expenses, the remainder for her father's shoes and carfare. Humiliated by being on the dole from his daughter, Tom grew querulous, and the rift between father and daughter deepened. Ruthie, who had always been the hub of the family, now found herself the breadwinner as well, and her growing independence disturbed her aging parents. Mrs. Dennis warned Ruthie "not to be carried away with any high faluting [sic] ideas of being magnanimous," adding, "neither must you act from pride or false independence." Hardly independent, Ruthie still relied on her mother for personal and artistic guidance, though now she had ventured into the world beyond Brooklyn.

Both ambition and financial need led Ruthie to rejoin the Belasco company in the autumn of 1900 when the director revived *Zaza* for a cross-country tour. Belasco considered casting Ruthie as Madame Dufrene, the wronged wife of Zaza's lover, but Ruthie failed the audition. At the opening of the third act Madame Dufrene must sit quietly writing a letter, then, in one of Belasco's dramatic moments, pause motionless until her courier-maid answers the ringing of her bell. Ruthie simply could not sit still. She became the understudy for Madame Dufrene and returned to her old role as Adele.

This *Zaza* tour, which took Ruthie to the West Coast and back until the summer of 1901, gave her ample opportunity to study Belasco's theatrical techniques. He excelled in creating atmosphere. In the first act of *Zaza,* in the words of one critic, Belasco became "the painter in his most impressionistic manner, flinging splashes of humanity against a canvas. The filmy threads of broken dialogue," the minute direction of the dressing-room scene, were the "perfect combination of subliminal suggestion and concrete detail." This impressionism, which St. Denis' dances later reflected, also pervaded Belasco's lighting techniques. Light and shadow became dramatic elements, extensions of character. When Belasco trained his "baby spotlight" on Mrs. Carter, its colored filter highlighting her titian hair, she seemed ablaze with passion. Shrouded in shadow, she was the broken Zaza who sacrificed her lover for the sake of his family. Mrs. Carter herself became a model for Ruthie, who studied her acting style, her mannerisms, her mode of dress. In turn, the actress took notice of the novice, advising Ruthie on her *Zaza* costume and complimenting her singing voice. Ruthie was thrilled by these attentions and told her mother that Mrs. Carter was "a star of the first magnitude," adding modestly, "and I'm a scintillating satellite."

Star and satellite were destined to meet again in Belasco's production of *Madame DuBarry*, with rehearsals commencing at the close of the *Zaza* tour, but first Ruthie briefly joined the cast of another Belasco play, *The Auctioneer*, starring David Warfield. A caricaturist whose specialty was the immigrant Jew, Warfield was a member of Weber and Fields's burlesque company and had a repertory including a skillful imitation of Mrs. Leslie Carter. Belasco plucked him from burlesque and transformed him into a serious actor. Tailoring *The Auctioneer* to Warfield's talents, Belasco cast him as a Jewish peddler in a sentimental, rags-to-riches plot that recalled *The Old Homestead*. Ruthie appeared as Mandy in a small speaking role.

Ever the Foxy Quiller, clever and ambitious, Ruthie by now was wise in the ways of Belasco. She knew that the director watched for improvised bits that added color to a production. During an *Auctioneer* rehearsal, she began to giggle, and soon the entire cast was giggling along with her. Not at all annoyed, Belasco decided to keep the episode in the play, and the Giggling Girls became an *Auctioneer* feature, with Ruthie merrily leading the way.

The Auctioneer opened in New York at the Bijou Theatre on September 23, 1901, but after a few weeks, Belasco borrowed Ruthie for the cast of his historical spectacle *Madame DuBarry*, due to open Christmas Day at the Criterion Theatre. This time Ruthie won a substantial role. As Mlle. LeGrand, she portrayed one of a pair of Paris Opera dancers, the other being her old *Zaza* roommate, Nell Stuart. Together, the girls were courtesan-ballerinas, richly clothed in jewels and gowns of the Louis XV era, and in the first act Ruthie had the delicious experience of haughtily purchasing a hat from the humble shop-girl, Mrs. Leslie Carter. Ruthie also danced in the fourth act in a costume of blue feathers and appeared in a mob scene as a howling *sans culotte,* yelling with such conviction that Belasco made her leader of the mob that accompanied DuBarry to her death.

The story of *DuBarry,* with its depiction of an aristocracy doomed by the French Revolution, was fertile ground for Belasco's imagination. He invested $98,000 in the production. He reproduced a boudoir from the Palace of Versailles, with a bedside table actually used by the original DuBarry. From France came an authentic Louis XV bed with a stead of solid onyx and a spread trimmed with Russian sable. Even the first-act millinery shop was a replica of the original, for Belasco had done his homework, studying ancient advertising circulars for details of the shop where DuBarry had been employed. He also copied a Louis XV sedan chair with an overhead opening to accommodate Mrs. Carter's towering coiffure and he allowed his minor actresses, including Ruthie, to wear antique jewels from his own collection. *Madame Du-Barry* was Belasco's crowning achievement, the culmination of his relationship with Mrs. Carter and the apex of his own career. For Ruthie, *DuBarry* was an education in historical research and shrewd showmanship, the seed of her own appetite for lavish theatre.

When Belasco chose *DuBarry* as the opening production in his new Belasco Theatre in 1902, Ruthie resumed her role as Mlle. LeGrand but soon graduated to the role of Sophie Arnaud, Queen of the Opera, an acting-dancing part that eventually passed to her friend Pat Donar. Pat had become her closest confidante after Ruthie discovered, to her horror, that Nell Stuart was a "kept woman," and Pat kept Ruthie chaste company during the 1902 and 1903 *DuBarry* tours.

Touring with Belasco, Ruthie celebrated her twenty-fourth birthday in Boston, her twenty-fifth in St. Louis. Now well into early womanhood, she felt the gathering force of her own personality and talent but knew "that an awful restlessness was stirring me and that I had no deeply satisfying place to direct my energies." She sublimated her frustration through impromptu performances backstage. Clowning for the *DuBarry* cast, she imitated the stars of the play in the German, Irish, and Negro dialects acquired from her Brooklyn neighborhood. She passionately discussed philosophy with her beloved Pat and with Hamilton Revelle, the male lead in *DuBarry* who also became a close friend. Ruthie captivated her friends with her blend of lowbrow humor and

high-flown philosophy. Her earthy wit, a compound of backstage bawd-
iness and rural yarn, always undercut her pretensions to grandeur and
she was disarmingly direct, even when expounding the loftiest of ideas.

On the *DuBarry* tours she always looked slightly unraveled. In her
own words, she traveled "in a weary and besmudged state of looks": "I
never was very careful about my personal clothes and like the village
dress maker or the blacksmith's horse never properly shod," Ruth wrote
in an early draft of her autobiography. "So on these days of one-night
stands I arrived in a little traveling suit, skirts were long then, and we
wore shirt waists. My hair at twenty-three was beginning to be a little
grey." She wore her hair in a pompadour, "very hastily dressed, hair
pins always falling out, and Pat begging me to fix myself, some kind of
hat on top of this pompadour and my little hand bag. The skirt perhaps
needing a bit of attention as to the hem, and shoes which I despised
anyway, never given any attention, until they simply wore out and
would not do any longer."

Rushing from train to hotel to theatre, from Boston to Chicago and
San Francisco, Ruthie danced as Queen of the Opera, screamed as a
sans culotte, then changed into blue feathers for her fourth-act dance.
She grew bored. "Anything—anything—was the cry in those days to
keep my imagination and energies occupied." She studied the *DuBarry*
script in the hopes that Mrs. Carter might become indisposed. For a
time she was diverted by a new singing solo and subjected Pat to her
soprano trills, but the *DuBarry* tours remained drudgery.

On a spring evening in 1904 the *DuBarry* company arrived in
Buffalo, and Ruthie set out with Pat in search of a boardinghouse.
Passing by a local drugstore, Ruthie spied in its window a poster advertising Egyptian Deities cigarettes. It depicted the goddess Isis, solemn
and bare-breasted, seated beneath an imposing stone doorway inscribed
"No better Turkish cigarette can be made." Riveted by the poster,
Ruthie suddenly knew "that my destiny as a dancer had sprung alive
in that moment. I would become a rhythmic and impersonal instrument of spiritual revelation rather than a personal actress of comedy or
tragedy. I had never before known such an inward shock of rapture."

The cigarette poster, which became a permanent part of the St.
Denis mythology, was but the catalyst in a long-simmering process, a
trail of discovery that wound from *Egypt Through Centuries,* through
the Stebbins matinee, to books on Buddhism and the Paris fair. As a
catalytic icon, the poster was important—now Ruthie had a picture of

her vague yearnings—but a more significant moment in her life and career was the deeper epiphany she had experienced the previous summer.

During the summer of 1903, in a hiatus between the first *DuBarry* tour and its Belasco Theatre revival, Ruthie recuperated from her arduous travels in a brownstone apartment on Fiftieth Street in New York. It was a peaceful hideaway. On an idle afternoon she picked up her mother's copy of Mary Baker Eddy's *Science and Health with Key to the Scriptures* and for six weeks thereafter lost herself in the doctrines of Christian Science. St. Denis always called this summer of discovery her "Days of Peace." "My mother thought I was going mad and resented the whole experience," she said. "I remember saying to Mother —one day going downstairs—I looked up at her from the bottom step, she leaning over the top railing, 'Mother—I really don't care whether I ever dance again.'" All the tedious rehearsals, all the one-night stands, all the family conflicts faded as Ruthie studied Mrs. Eddy's philosophy of God as Infinite Mind. The "Scientific Statement of Being," so familiar to Christian Scientists, promised that "There is no life, truth, intelligence, nor substance in matter. All is infinite Mind and its infinite manifestation, for God is All-in-all." The Statement continued with a definition of the Spirit: "Spirit is immortal Truth; matter is mortal error. Spirit is the real and eternal; matter is the unreal and temporal. Spirit is God, and man is His image and likeness. Therefore man is not material; he is spiritual."

Schooled in her mother's distaste for drugs, sensitized by her preoccupation with sin, Ruthie eagerly responded to this Americanized mysticism which stressed the essential goodness of existence, a harmony demonstrable in human terms through physical healing. Ruth became a lifelong Christian Scientist, though the church twice rejected her for formal membership. "What do you suppose we split on?" she once quipped. "Hot water bottles and enemas!" Though she indulged in occasional medicines, she found in Christian Science a focus for her growing interest in mysticism.

Her "Days of Peace" also marked a moment of decision in her career, for by 1903 Ruthie realized that she was not destined to become the next Mrs. Leslie Carter. In a newspaper article on theatrical understudies, Ruthie's photograph appeared amid a galaxy of young hopefuls, but the story bore the melancholy message that "competition is so keen that there is little incentive to the advanced player to provide an opportunity for a less experienced if equally zealous rival." During a week-long revival of *Zaza* that winter, Ruthie finally won the Madame Dufrene role for her own, but after this short-lived glory she returned to the numbing *DuBarry* tour, still a bit player after three years on the road.

In her autobiography St. Denis claimed that Belasco wanted to make her a comedy star, with Stanford White picking up the tab, but Belasco himself insisted that he advised Ruthie to aim for a dancing career. "It was hard for her to put away the idea of acting," Belasco wrote, "but she finally agreed that I was right, and when the run of *DuBarry* ended we parted company." In fact, Belasco revived both *DuBarry* and *Zaza* in the fall of 1905, but Ruthie had gone her own way. She spent that autumn in a trivial musical, *Woodland,* which the New York *Tribune* critic summarized as a show "which will neither tax the intelligence nor stimulate the deeper laughter of the beholder, but which plentifully provides amusement of a more obvious sort and feasts the eye with color and the female form." Dancing and singing in the peacock chorus of *Woodland* was a far cry from the glory days of *DuBarry* and *Zaza,* but Ruthie considered her fall from fortune temporary. Foxy Quiller had ambitions even beyond Belasco.

She had an idea for an Egyptian dance. Inspired by the Egyptian Deities poster, Ruthie spent the last days of the *DuBarry* tour in local libraries along the route. She discovered *The Book of the Dead,* a translation of ancient vignettes and hymns from Egyptian funeral lore, and borrowed its Hall of Judgment myth as the scenario for her new dance. In this myth a deceased mortal submitted his heart for weighing on the scales of justice while reciting a confession before a divine jury. Ruthie followed this basic plot but substituted "Egypta, a suppositious goddess" of her own devising, in place of the mortal. In the course of her dance Egypta died, entered the underworld for judgment, and passing muster, ascended to the Elysian Fields.

As Ruthie outlined her dance, she planned for the curtain to rise on a darkened stage, with torch-bearing priests paying homage to the goddess, who descended from her shrine to dance the "Twelve Hours of the Day." With the end of the day and the dance, the goddess lay prostrate, while her soul, in the form of a mummy, journeyed to the underworld Judgment Hall where her confession earned her entry into the permanent dwelling place of the gods. This scenario suggested St. Denis' subsequent dance *Radha,* as well as Genevieve Stebbins' previous *Dance of Day*. This early *Egypta* also contained the essential elements of St. Denis' theatrical approach: the central female goddess who undergoes a test, the adoring acolytes who provide exotic atmosphere, the symbolic stage properties, the broad religious themes. Still wavering between acting and dancing, Ruthie called her creation "*Egypta,* an Egyptian play in one act, a pantomime without words . . . an epic dance typifying the life of man as revealed by the progress of the Sun in its journey through night and day."

As if to give reality to her vision, Ruthie paused in San Francisco on the *DuBarry* tour and had her photograph taken as Egypta. She wore a bolt of cloth wrapped about her slender body and on her head a vaguely oriental headdress, a jeweled headband with flower attached. Ribbons wrapped about her feet became her Egyptian dancing shoes. The young face in the photograph was intent, self-confident. So sure was Ruthie of her idea that in 1905 she submitted this first version of *Egypta* for copyright, but before she could produce the new dance, her attention turned to India.

Ruthie and her mother had come under the influence of Edmund Russell, an actor and Orientalist whose readings from *The Light of Asia,* the Buddhist poem by Sir Edwin Arnold, were much in demand for society gatherings. Russell was an odd one, an aesthete who affected flowing oriental robes and surrounded himself with coveys of young men. He fancied himself a high priest of the social set, offering lessons in deportment and Delsartean aesthetics, and he had the added panache of actually having traveled to India. The Dennis women shared with Russell a love of Delsarte and soon became infected with his orientalism. Russell loaned Ruthie books from his vast library and involved her in the Progressive Stage Society, which became an important influence at this juncture in her career.

Founded in New York in 1904, the Progressive Stage Society was organized for the purpose of "interesting the masses in the teachings and the art of great dramatists by producing modern social dramas of progressive tendencies, as well as the older classic dramas neglected by the commercial stage." Among its founding members were Henrietta Hovey, Edmund Russell's former wife who later taught Delsarte principles at Denishawn, and Grace Isabel Colbron, the writer who became St. Denis' ardent admirer. Many of the society members were socialists who denounced capitalist ownership of theatres and the irrelevancy of most plays to the pressing problems of modern life. The heroes of the

Progressive Stage Society were Hauptmann, Ibsen, Tolstoi, and Zola, whose plays were performed for a minimal admission fee, with seats distributed on a first-come, first-served basis. Despite its socialist slant, the society had a broader progressive purpose, the creation of "a stage with a nobler standard of art and a higher mission," a goal which attracted a wider spectrum of performers who felt that drama could uplift "the wage-workers, who need the education and inspiration that the right kind of stage could help to give them." Ruthie was apolitical but idealistic, and in 1905 she joined the Progressive Stage Society and appeared in its production of the sacred Sanskrit drama, *Sakuntala*, the work of the poet Kalidasa, translated into English and condensed into a three-act play.

The sole performance of *Sakuntala* occurred on June 18, 1905, at Madison Square Theatre in New York. Edmund Russell starred as King Dushyanta, and Ruthie appeared as Sanumati, a nymph, in the tale of a king's love for a flower maiden. N. F. Bhumgara, a Fifth Avenue merchant of oriental goods, supplied authentic costumes and décor, but in one critic's estimation, these costly effects suffered from the "Sixth Avenue darkies who were airily but sparingly clad in mosquito netting and draped about the place and over steam radiators to furnish Oriental atmosphere." More tolerant critics appreciated the sincerity of the venture which was significant to dance history as Ruth St. Denis' debut in an Indian dance. As Sanumati, Ruthie danced a solo before the fourth scene of *Sakuntala*, a dance which may have been an early version of *Radha*.

Radha, which brought Ruthie fame, began as an idea for a vaudeville dance. During the period of *Sakuntala* Ruthie decided to earn money for her masterwork, *Egypta*, by peddling several novelties to vaudeville producers. She had in mind something like the Indian dances she had seen the previous summer at Coney Island, where the world-famous durbar, or gathering of Indian potentates, was reproduced as an East Indian sideshow, complete with rajahs, snake-charmers, and nautch girls. Looking for information on India, Ruthie went to the Astor Library where, in true Belasco fashion, she researched her ideas. She read Pierre Loti's travelogue, *India*, which supplied to a generation of late-Victorians a vision of India as a lush and melancholy land of mystery. In *India* Ruthie found the romantic atmosphere she wanted for a temple dance, and in another book by a missionary she found the heroine for her new dance. "One day a dusty old volume was brought on speculation by the nice person at the desk," St. Denis recalled. "The book itself must have been over a hundred years old . . . As I read, my eye chanced to fall upon the word 'Radha' and, as we say, it rang a bell."

Ruthie had heard of the mythical maiden Radha in Edmund Russell's readings from *The Light of Asia*. She learned more about her in a series of books she owned, *Great Religions of the World*. In one volume of that series she found a suitable theme for her heroine to dance in A. C. Lyall's essay on Brahmanism. As Lyall wrote, "If a Hindoo be asked what is the object and ultimate good that he is striving to reach through religious rites, he will answer 'Liberation.' He must free his soul, the divine particle, from the bondage of the senses." Guided by this dramatic idea, Ruthie set about the creation of her temple dance.

"My first Indian dance was a jumble of everything I was aware of in Indian art," she said in her autobiography. Her awareness was limited. The India of *Radha* was an India pieced together from photographs, sideshows, and romantic literature. Though Ruthie envisioned her heroine as a chaste temple goddess, the Radha of Hindu legend is a milkmaid filled with desire for the handsome god Krishna, her earthly passion a symbol of desire for union with the Absolute. If this pining Radha seemed an unlikely temple idol, Ruthie cheerfully added to the inauthenticity of her dance by housing her Hindu goddess in a Jain temple, a stage set designed from a photograph. For her music she chose the ersatz oriental airs from Leo Delibes' opera *Lakmé*, itself based on a Pierre Loti tale. From these diverse sources she created her dance.

As *Radha* developed, it followed the early scenario for *Egypta*, with a few changes of character and plot. Again, a goddess sat upon a shrine, attended by worshiping priests. Descending, she danced a solo—Radha's "Five Senses" rather than Egypta's "Twelve Hours"—and overcoming earthly temptations, she returned to the sanctity of her shrine. *Radha* was *Egypta* simplified, and Ruthie believed that she could market the dance, along with other short solos, to the novelty-hungry producers in vaudeville.

One of Ruthie's most compelling qualities was her absolute belief in her own abilities. When she believed in an idea, others believed. During the autumn of 1905 she attracted a small company of Coney Island Indians, clerks from the Bhumgara store, and Columbia University students and friends of her brother's, an indiscriminate mix of Moslems and Hindus that turned her rehearsals into religious wars. Mrs. Dennis mediated these battles and also helped Ruthie to plot her choreography with salt and pepper shakers on the kitchen table. During rehearsals Patsy Donar played the piano, and even the Dennis men shared the excitement of creating *Radha*. Though Tom and Brother lived together in a bachelor flat uptown, they traveled down to Ruthie's each evening, and Brother took charge of the lighting design.

Ruthie's tiny New York apartment on Forty-second Street, between Eighth and Ninth Avenues, must have seemed the center of strange activity that autumn: streams of Indian visitors, arguments that lasted into the night, the smell of curry and incense, the sound of tinkling bells, the fall of dancing feet. Edmund Russell and entourage often stopped by to offer learned opinions, as did Jal Bhumgara, son of the Parsi merchant from the Progressive Stage Society. Old friends in Somerville got wind of Ruthie's work and wrote their encouragement, and church cronies of her mother's offered biblical counsel. This was an exciting period in Ruthie's life, a period also of frustration and doubt. Where would she find the money to produce her temple dance? The force of her will made miracles happen. Tom Dennis found a job and persuaded his employer to lend a hundred dollars toward Ruthie's dance. Mrs. Dennis' best friend, the impoverished but stagestruck Countess Ada de Lachau, dramatically donated her last twenty dollars. Most important, Pat Donar discovered an influential patron, Kate Dalliba, who offered her salon for the *Radha* premiere.

Writers, artists, and musicians mingled in Mrs. Dalliba's black-and-gold salon, where a showgirl might rub elbows with that most eminent of American poets, Edwin Markham. Indeed, Markham had provided an introduction for a volume of poetry written by Mrs. Dalliba's daughter, Gerda, a talented but undisciplined mystic whose poems spoke of Brahmanism and Buddhist nirvana. In one of her poems Gerda Dalliba declared, "I am a Hindoo though I pray no prayer/To any imaged Buddha," a mixed metaphor that applied to many of the artists who gathered in her mother's salon to speak reverently of an eclectic Eastern religion and art. Ruthie found a natural niche in this world of amateur orientalism. Perched atop a table draped with Indian cloth, her loyal Patsy at the piano, Ruthie performed *Radha* for the salon guests, and Mrs. Dalliba paid her fifty dollars and donated a larger sum for a proper set. Word of this private performance spread, and high society smelled success. Mrs. Stuyvesant Fish was next in line to champion *Radha*.

Mame Fish was an eccentric but powerful New York hostess who "fought for the bluebloods' right to raise a little hell now and then," the society chronicler Andrew Tully has noted. "Mrs. Astor's dinners gave you dull food and tedious conversation; Mame Fish's might produce a dancing girl in a floral cage on the backs of four glistening Africans." Ever on the lookout for novelty, Mrs. Fish invited Ruthie and her Hindus to dance in her mansion, though the press erroneously reported that the performers belonged to "one of the Southern tribes of American Indians"—"as if I were a Cherokee or a Sioux," Ruthie sniffed. After Mrs. Fish opened her doors, other invitations followed, and Ruthie also performed an early version of *Radha* for a party in the studio of the artist Rowland Hinton Perry. As glamorous as these events were, Ruthie wanted a theatrical engagement, and she and her mother made the rounds of producers, faces they had known for years, trying to sell her Indian idea. They finally found a buyer, Henry B. Harris, a young, independent producer still shy of forty years whose instinct for quality had made his Hudson Theatre a success. Harris liked *Radha* and believed in Ruthie. Though he had no immediate vehicle for the dance, he offered to rent Ruthie his theatre and to invite his fellow producers to a showcase performance of *Radha*.

Ruthie performed this showcase in January 1906, before the elite of New York's theatre managers who "strolled in, one after the other, laughing and joking among themselves, patting their expanded waistcoats, and smoking their inevitable cigars." After the performance of Ruthie's Indian number, "there was silence and they all filed out into the lobby and stood in a ring." What to do with this puzzling dance? Louis Weber finally broke the silence by agreeing to book *Radha* for a Sunday night smokers' concert. In Weber's estimation, *Radha* may have seemed "surefire Sunday stuff," for Sunday concerts posed a delicate problem for theatrical managers in 1906. The New York Sunday laws ostensibly forbade the moving of curtains, shifting of scenery, or the appearance of performers in costume on the Sabbath. Singing, reciting, and musical instruments were permitted, but dancing was strictly taboo. Most producers simply ignored the ban or camouflaged their variety shows as "Grand Sacred Concerts," but during the spring of 1906 authorities threatened to enforce the law. Perhaps Weber took on *Radha* because of its religious content, or he may have had an inkling that this dance by a Hindu goddess to French opera music, set in a Jain temple, would become theatrical history.

On the evening of January 28, 1906, the gents who had gathered for a good smoke and a leg show at the New York Theatre were puzzled by a new item on the bill. Was *Radha* a play? A dance? A minstrel show? As the first Hindu entered with his incense tray, an audience wag shouted in Negro dialect, "Who wants de Waitah?" and the raucous laughter faded only as the temple goddess began her earnest dance. She wore a gold jacket and trousers with an overskirt, but her feet and midriff were tantalizingly bare. She seemed serious, absorbed in her dance message, but her movements were enticing, especially when she fondled her own fingertips during the "Dance of the Five Senses." The curtain fell on an uneasy silence. *Radha*'s twin message—seduction, yet denial of the senses—was confusing but intriguing to the onlookers, and the New York Theatre extended Ruthie's engagement, trumpeting the return of the "Wonderful, mysterious, exquisite Radha."

After the New York Theatre, Ruthie moved on to Proctor's Twenty-third Street Theatre, where she performed two-a-day from mid-February to March. A program note advised, "The entire dance is done in bare feet." At Proctor's Ruthie shared the stage with a pugilist, a pair of trained monkeys, and a Shakespeare burlesque, then it was back to the New York Theatre for yet another "Return of the Exquisite Hindoo Ritual of the Senses." Though her audiences were receptive, the critic for *Variety* called Ruthie's dance "a virtual frost. A vaudeville audience will not stand the alleged Hindoo dances," he wrote, and "if anything is ever made of this act it must come from press work or through the semi-nudity of the woman."

Radha might have gone the way of all forgotten variety acts if New York society had not intervened. In the decade since the founding of the Vaudeville Club, the city's social elite had increased its appetite for theatrical amusements. Some prominent hostesses, including Mame Fish, regularly raided vaudeville to supply sensations for their guests. Other society matrons, spurred by do-gooder tendencies, scouted for meritorious variety acts that might be rescued and resurrected in a seemlier setting. *Radha* was natural prey. Not only was it a dance with a moral message, it also fed the ladies' fascination for things oriental.

Radha came on the American scene during the years of a popular groundswell of orientalism. Both a serious intellectual pursuit and a popular-culture phenomenon, orientalism was a phase in the greater

Ruthie in a dance in imitation of Genevieve Stebbins during her
Packer Collegiate Institute days.

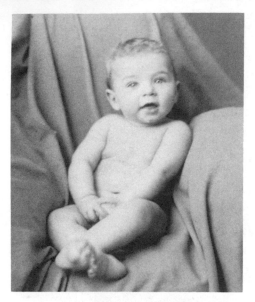

Baby Ruth, 1879.

Ruthie's family.

A solemn Ruthie, c. 1882.

Ruthie's mother, c. 1885.

Ruth Dennis (left of center) in
dame DuBarry, buying a hat from the
humble shopgirl, Mrs. Leslie Carter.

Genevieve Stebbins, the foremost American
exponent of the Delsarte method, and
Ruthie's model.

Already an actress,
young Ruthie in an imitation
of Paquerette.

"The Only Ruth" in her first professional engagement
as a skirt dancer at Worth's Museum, 1894.

Ruthie as a skirt dancer at the Casino Theatre
Roof Garden, c. 1895.

A rare photograph of Ruth in a ballet
costume, as a dancer in *Zaza*.

The Ballet of the Virgins from *Egypt Through Centuries* dazzled Ruthie.

The poster that inspired *Egypta* and *Radha.*

Ruth St. Denis and native Hindus in *Radha,* 1906.

The Dance of Taste" from *Radha*.

Ruth St. Denis in *Incense,* 1906.

cult of the exotic prevalent at the turn of the twentieth century. The roots of this fascination for the style, if not the substance, of the East might be traced back as far as colonial trade and shipping, on through the Eastern mystical influences on the American Transcendentalists, to the stimulus of increased contact between the Western and Eastern worlds, symbolized by travel literature and the world's fairs. Some scholars suggest that the American brand of orientalism represented a rejection of the fluctuating modern world, a retreat to the sacred societies of the East as primitive havens of spiritual order. At least one critic found in St. Denis' dancing "a universal rhythm beneath the broken chaos of our modern industrial world which shall infuse new joy and rhythmic harmony into our common life."

America's new cosmopolites in the early 1900s eagerly bought kimonos and Japanese prints, visited the Streets of Cairo at Coney Island, discussed the pros and cons of Buddhism, and sampled oriental literature. While scholars, spurred by the first translations into English of the *Sacred Books of the East,* pondered the *Bhagavad-Gita* and the *Qur'an,* laymen bought copies of such popularizations as a Delsartist's *Hindu Philosophy in a Nutshell.* Society balls adopted Japanese, Indian, and Chinese motifs, and even the most modest of American homes sported Japanese prints on their walls.

Japanese art had a head start in capturing the American imagination. Its foremost popularizer was Ernest Fenollosa, Chautauqua lecturer, art historian and curator at the Boston Museum of Fine Arts. India later received its due through the efforts of Ananda K. Coomaraswamy, who also used the Boston Museum as a base for spreading the gospel of Indian art in the years after World War I. Both lecturers were especially popular with female audiences, and women were the major purveyors of orientalism in America. "Women's clubs that have sipped tea over pretty much everything from Sun Worship to Mental Science generally fall back on Eastern lore for things to be enthusiastic about," explained a newspaper reporter in 1906, the year of *Radha's* premiere. One Orient enthusiast, Mrs. Orlando Rouland, heard about *Radha,* hurried over to Proctor's Theatre, held her breath through the trained monkeys until Ruthie appeared, then found her way backstage to the dancer's dressing room. "You know you don't belong in this dreadful environment!" she blurted, offering to arrange a matinee in a proper theatre with several of her friends as sponsors.

Prominent socialites joined Minnie Rouland as hostesses for the

March 22 matinee at the Hudson Theatre. Among them were Mrs. Charles C. Worthington, wife of the manufacturer, and Mrs. Adrian H. Joline and Mrs. Ben Ali Haggin, whose husbands were railroad magnates. More significant was the impressive array of artists' names on the invitation—Mrs. Eliot Norton, whose father-in-law was America's most prominent art historian; Mrs. Arthur Davies, wife of the painter; Mrs. Philip Conway Sawyer, whose husband had trained in Stanford White's architectural firm; and Mrs. Rouland herself, whose husband was a noted portraitist. Representing the intellectual elite of New York among the matinee sponsors were Mrs. Richard Watson Gilder, whose husband edited the influential *Century* magazine, and Mrs. Paul Leicester Ford, wife of the author-historian.

How did Ruthie, a mere variety dancer, manage such a stellar list of supporters? Her mentor, Stanford White, may have been instrumental in lining up backers, and Ruthie's own connections with the New York art world dated back to her mother's Eagleswood colony. A stronger bond among her supporters was their love for the Orient. Mrs. Alexander Tison and her husband had spent several years in Japan while he was law professor at the Imperial University of Tokyo. Another hostess, Mrs. Howard Mansfield, was married to the editor of a catalogue of works by James McNeill Whistler, whose paintings were influenced by Japanese prints. Each of these supporters saw in Ruthie's dancing a serious attempt to translate oriental principles into American art.

Greeting the guests that afternoon at the Hudson Theatre were Hindus in traditional garb who stood in the theatre foyer, serving tea and salaaming to the patrons. Inside the auditorium the air was thick with incense and steamy in the unseasonable March heat. Sweltering, the assembled guests sneezed and coughed politely through a twenty-three-minute musical prelude conducted by Harvey Worthington Loomis, a pianist and composer of comic operas who had written the music for the opening dance on the matinee, *The Incense*. Finally the lights dimmed for the appearance of the young dancer who billed herself, for the first time, as Ruth St. Denis.

From the folds of cashmere shawls hung upstage, she entered, bearing an incense tray in one hand, the other hand trailing through the air to mingle with the wafting smoke. She wore filmy white draperies, and her long fingers and bare feet were tipped with henna. Slowly she advanced toward her audience, swaying slightly, and deposited her tray downstage left, one hand spiraling upward as she fanned the smoke. She circled the incensor, then stopped on a musical climax and lifted the tray in a Statue of Liberty pose. She repeated this *puja* on the other side of the stage and crossed to stage center, facing her audience expectantly. The music began to course through her body. Leaning into one hip, her head inclined demurely, she lifted her arms in ever-rising ripples. She seemed to grow taller as she surrendered herself. Up and up her arms flowed, boneless, mesmeric, the disembodied essence of smoke itself. As her arms came to rest, she repeated the incense *puja*, then retreated into the backdrop of shawls and disappeared. In her wake she left traces of spiraling smoke.

Art Nouveau in dance, *The Incense* explored the evocative meaning of line. The undulating arm movement at the heart of the dance typified a Delsartean "successive movement" as described in Genevieve Stebbins' arm drill, "The Serpentine Series":

Raise arms sidewise level with shoulder, sink wrist, turn hand. Hand should now be well bent back on wrist, fingers to floor.
1. Bring wrist to shoulder.
2. Raise wrist until fingers touch shoulder.
3. Unbend arm, hand well back.
4. Repeat ascending lateral.
5. Repeat over head.
6. Repeat horizontal oblique.
7. Repeat ascending oblique.
8. Repeat front.
9. Repeat ascending front.
Finish at sides, then sink wrists to sides, hanging arms.

Nothing more than a Delsarte exercise refined by a keen artistic sensibility, *The Incense* became one of St. Denis' most enduring dances.

The same fascinating arm-play dominated the other new dance on the matinee, *The Cobras*, a street dance set in a noisy bazaar. St. Denis borrowed the idea for *The Cobras* from "The Streets of Delhi" at Coney Island, where she saw a snake charmer and hurried home to fashion snake-eyes from four hatpins which her father soldered to finger rings. With green stones glittering on each index and small finger, Ruthie pantomimed the coiling and hissing of two serpents, her arms gliding and darting in sinister foreplay. As the music, an excerpt from the *Lakmé* bazaar scene, culminated in a mad swirl of cymbals, St. Denis focused her hissing cobras on the Hudson Theatre audience. Several ladies swooned.

She closed her matinee with the popular *Radha*, by now a complete temple dance with an elaborate set and briefer costume. Underneath her gauzy skirt, her body swayed and spiraled, "as supple as a willow in the wind," rhapsodized Mrs. Ernest Fenollosa, who reviewed the matinee for her husband's magazine. "At last she is whirling like a bronze and silver cloud; until—a crash of instruments—she lies in a sobbing heap—and the lights are out!"

Her audience was agog. As one of the hostesses gushed after the matinee, "It's such fun to be in on something absolutely new—as this certainly is, for she has gotten it all up by herself, out of books and things. I believe she has never been abroad." Newspapers trumpeted St. Denis' success with such headlines as, "Yes, Society Did Gasp When Radha in Incense-Laden Air 'Threw Off the Bondage of the Earthly Senses,'" or the New York *Telegraph*'s more succinct, "At the Boom of the Drum Radha Kerflops." Everyone talked about *Radha*, wanted to see *Radha*, and hundreds were turned away from the subsequent public performances. Society invitations flooded St. Denis, who traveled to Boston to dance for Mrs. Jack Gardner at Fenway Court, then home to perform for the visiting Maharaja of Baroda at a reception-tea in the Bhumgara store. Charity organizations sought Ruthie for benefit programs, and the patrons of the Mary E. Walton Free Kindergarten invited her to perform at the Presbyterian Building, an invitation that was hastily withdrawn after church officials discovered that she danced in bare feet. Ernest Fenollosa and Mark Twain saw Ruthie dance, as did a beaming Stanford White who rushed backstage after a Waldorf-Astoria benefit to tell his Wild Flower how proud he was. It was their last embrace. Months later, White was dead, victim of the jealous husband of another of his protégées.

Ruthie heard about White's death in London, where she had gone in search of a wider audience. On the threshold of fame herself, she pondered White's dizzying life of pleasure, creativity, and notoriety, his destruction by "the very forces in which he sought to live." Soberly, she reflected on her own unfolding career. Five years earlier, at the beginning of her apprenticeship with Belasco, she had written, "I feel a force gathering within that one day when all is ready will make itself felt." That day had arrived, and Ruthie was ready.

RADHA

THE MYSTIC DANCE OF THE FIVE SENSES

CHOREOGRAPHY: Ruth St. Denis

MUSIC: Leo Delibes, *Lakmé* (Prelude, Mallika's Theme, dance music, The Forest interlude)

PREMIERE: (Private) Kate Dalliba salon, late 1905
(Public) New York Theatre, New York, January 28, 1906

———◆———

SETTING: The interior of a Hindu temple. The idol Radha sits upstage center on a pedestal shrouded with incense. Behind the idol is a golden background, bathed in amber light. To the side of the pedestal a temple caretaker, clad in *dhoti* and sacred thread, kneels in meditation.

SCENARIO: To the somber strains of a Brahman processional, temple priests enter from either side of the stage, bearing incense, flowers, sacred paste, and sacrificial food. As the music swells with the love theme from *Lakmé*, each priest approaches the idol in turn and offers his sacrifice, then kneels in the semi-circle to either side of Radha's shrine. The High Priest advances toward the idol. The music becomes ominous, trembles expectantly, then builds to a swift climax as the Priest salutes the idol, then joins the other priests.

The quiet of the temple dissolves in the dulcet strains of the love melody. The goddess, illuminated by a changing spotlight of blue, red, amber, and green, sits with arms and legs folded in the lotus position. She stirs to life, breathing deeply. Life courses through her body, and a faint smile caresses her lips. Her eyes flutter open, then gaze steadily. Her palms, folded in prayer, pivot into the form of a blossoming lotus. Unfolding her crossed legs, she rises from her pedestal and walks into the semi-circular space created by her watching priests. She accepts two strands of pearls from an acolyte and pauses, waiting for the musical cue for the "Dance of the Five Senses."

"The Dance of Sight"—The high note of a flute initiates the sensuous Persian dance music, with its tremolo refrain. Radha lifts a rope of pearls in each hand and revolves in place in a birdlike *bourrée*. Her posture is vertical, and she holds her pearls in oblong bunches, scarcely daring to unloose their loops. Obediently matching each musical phrase with its proper dance measure, she *bourrées* from side to side toward her watching priests, pausing occasionally with one leg lifted in gentle front *attitude*. Her dance concluded, she holds her pearls primly away from her body and exchanges them for circlets of bells offered by a priest.

"The Dance of Hearing"—Radha becomes playful as the "Rektah" dance music bounces and whirls. With a bell-loop in either hand, she stands in place, one knee bent, her weight thrust into the hip of her supporting leg. Her torso twitches off its vertical axis while her fluttering hands describe a semicircular path, extending from her sides to meet above her head. Her hands might be fireflies, her hips, a jaunty metronome. Moving toward her priests, she rocks from front to back leg like a hobby horse, then stops in a saucy pose with head flung back, one ear cocked to hear the final tinkle of the bells.

"The Dance of Smell"—Accepting a rope of marigolds, Radha moves in a series of simple steps and poses to the throbbing "Terana" dance music. The slow and measured melody suggests a pachyderm parade, but a twinkling sub-melody enlivens its plodding progression. To this livelier undercurrent, Radha revolves in *bourrée*, then waltzes from side to side to the statelier music. She twines her garland about her body as she waltzes and *bourrées* to her watching priests. Manipulating her garland, she loops it, bunches it, then in a pragmatic gesture, slings it over her shoulder. She is workmanlike, absorbed in her tasks. Her posture is upright until the final, dramatic pose when her curving body echoes the arc of the floral chain. Bending back, she trails the garland down the front of her arched body. One hand crushes blossoms to her face; the other clutches the flower chain to her thigh.

"The Dance of Taste"—Pressure accumulates in the music, again the "Terana" in minor key. Radha exchanges her flowers for a simple clay bowl. She sways, then brings the bowl to her lips, drinking deeply. The liquid flows into her body, and she abandons herself to an intoxicated whirling that culminates in a deep back bend. She almost loses her balance but recovers and sharply flings the bowl from her, then sinks to the ground in collapse.

"The Dance of Touch"—The music is the ingratiating "Mallika's Theme," with its steamy, hothouse aura. Kneeling, her skirt spread about her, Radha lifts one hand and caresses it with the other. She folds both hands to her ear in a sleepy-time gesture, then slides her hands down her body, outlining the curves of her own swaying form. Lifting her hands to her breastbone, she follows the line of her throat on under her chin with a scooping gesture that brings her fingertips to her lips in a final, voluptuous pose.

"The Delirium of the Senses"—The music becomes threatening, building to a *furioso,* as Radha rises and twitches her hips. Her skirt whips angrily from side to side. One elbow leads her into a spiral turn. Reversing directions, she turns restlessly until a nautch whirl possesses her. As she spins, one hand makes its own agitated rotation, then grasps her skirt, which she manipulates in a figure-eight swish. Suddenly falling to the ground, she writhes and trembles to a climax, then lies supine as darkness descends.

"The Renunciation of the Senses"—A faint light in the shape of a lotus blossom reveals a chastened Radha kneeling in meditation. To the sound of the love theme in minor key, she lifts her face to the light and her arms in supplication. From her bodice she draws a lotus blossom, and rising to the balls of her feet, she traces the outline of the flower on the floor, each step leading from the center of the lotus light to a petal point. The love theme swells in major key. Holding aloft the lotus blossom, Radha slowly steps backward to her shrine as the curtain lowers. The curtain rises once more on the temple scene, deserted now except for the idol, who sits in lotus position on her pedestal, lost in *samadhi,* or Self-realization.

Radha became the prototype for St. Denis' ballets, and the role became her stage persona: a virginal deity or queen who descended from the altar of purity, wrestled with evil, then returned to the peaceful sanctity of her throne. Many of her ballets followed this scenario, and even her shorter character dances were mutations of the solos in *Radha*. The *Nautch* derived from Radha's "Delirium of the Senses"; her dance of renunciation became the pattern for the Fugen-Bosatsu dance in *O-Mika*. The flower-rope dance reappeared in *Egypta*, as did the nautch-whirl and the temple ritual. *Radha* was the motherlode of St. Denis' future repertoire.

Not only did St. Denis work and rework the structure and themes of *Radha*, she used its basic gestural vocabulary as the scaffolding for her future dances. Essentially she employed the tools of the skirt dancer, a smattering of sentimentalized ballet—tippy-toe turns and waltz steps, simple *attitudes* and *dégagés*—embellished with the acrobatic antics of her supple arms and upper back. She combined these steps in brief movement phrases, punctuated by poses. The poses themselves suggested eclectic sources, both oriental icons and popular images of the late Victorian era.

In the "Dance of Hearing," Radha's pose on one leg, with one leg lifted and her torso twisted in opposition, suggested a dancing Shiva, an image she may have copied from Hindu books in the Astor Library. Her backbend pose in the "Dance of Smell" was a more contemporaneous image, a configuration from Art Nouveau iconography: the *femme fatale,* with head flung back, vulnerable upper body, half-closed eyes, parted lips. Finally, the source of the image of the enthroned Radha was the Egyptian Deities advertisement, with the goddess seated in meditation, her grave self-absorption both spiritually elevating and enticing.

A true Delsartean, St. Denis believed that each gesture and pose should objectify an inner emotional state, and *Radha* was an elaborate network of spatial and gestural symbols. In her copyrighted version of the dance, St. Denis specified that the "Renunciation of the Senses" should be danced on the balls of the feet, typifying the "ecstasy and joy which follow the renunciation of the senses, and the freedom from their illusion." Similarly, she organized each section of *Radha* around a symbolic motif.

St. Denis built her "Dance of the Five Senses" on a circular motif, "each circle emblematic of the Hindu cycle of reincarnation, the repetitive bondage of lives lived according to the senses." Circular floor-patterns, circular gestures and props echoed this symbolic theme, as did the cyclical structure of the entire ballet, the heaven-to-earth-to-heaven cycle of Radha's journey. For "The Delirium of the Senses" St. Denis envisioned a square floor pattern, "representing, according to the Buddhistic theology, the four-fold miseries of life," while the lotus design of the dance of renunciation suggested the ever-unfolding flower of the spirit.

Loaded with symbolism on paper, *Radha,* in actuality, was simple and symmetrical in design. St. Denis choreographed the dance with saltcellars on her kitchen table and she balanced her stage with equal rows of priests and democratically divided her attention between them. While the priests were her virtual audience, she acknowledged the actual theatre audience by keying her dance to front stage center, even to the point of walking backward to her upstage throne. This audience orientation created the illusion of a two-dimensional space, and it is helpful to think of *Radha* as a decorated surface. Many of its poses were in profile, rendering the dancer yet another decorative element in the overall stage design.

The set design for *Radha* became more elaborate with time. At first, St. Denis danced before a simple screen, with stereopticon lighting suggesting temple ruins. Later she acquired a reproduction of a Jain temple, a series of receding arches that carried the viewers' eyes toward Radha's distant throne in an echo of the centripetal force of the dance movement itself. Still later, St. Denis added a free-standing shrine that enclosed the meditating Radha, who could be seen dimly through the fretwork door. Her priests opened the door to begin the dance and closed the shrine when the dance ended.

As the set design became more elaborate, Radha's costume grew more brief. After the initial performances in New York, the original costume of dark body paint, beaded jacket, gold trousers, and gauze overskirt gave way to a flesh-colored, silk body suit covered with jeweled chains. The skirt, indispensable for the nautch whirling, became a stage property, handed to Radha by a priest just before the "Delirium of the Senses," and removed, without much ado, just after. On her first London tour Radha acquired a crown, and her costuming resembled European royalty crossed with kootch dancer, rather than the simpler Indian garb worn in the beginning.

The choreography for *Radha* also changed. St. Denis constantly improvised onstage, and in the filmed version of *Radha* in 1941, she added a flattened Egyptian walk between the solo sections, as well as head-isolations and other exotic embellishments. She varied the choreography for her priests, depending on how many Hindus she could assemble. In the film version two rows of priests enter from opposite sides of the stage in a ritual march faintly reminiscent of Martha Graham's *Primitive Mysteries*. The priests are clearly visible in the film during the transitions between Radha's dances, but during her solos only the hems of their saffron robes are visible in the film frames, because the male dancers were needed for another rehearsal during the filming.

Even as *Radha* evolved, the dance remained St. Denis' signature work. Its extraordinary appeal lay in its double message. It "borders on voluptuousness but it is chaste," wrote the eminent critic and librettist Hugo von Hofmannsthal. "It is consecrated to the senses, but it is higher." Reviews of *Radha* abounded in paradoxical comparisons. A British critic found the dance "athletic in its actuality and ascetic in its refinement," while a Boston *Herald* reviewer puzzled that "although her body is that of a woman divinely planned, there is no atmosphere of sex about her."

This mixed message stemmed from St. Denis' own stage personality and, by extension, from the quality of her gestures. The unvarnished practicality of her movements—the way she hoisted her flower-chain in *Radha*, the way she set down her tray in *Incense*, as any housemaid might do—was a powerful antidote to the farfetched exoticism of her dances. St. Denis, in the guise of Radha or any other deity, always retained a touch of the New Jersey farm girl, an Americanism as solid as her orientalism was ephemeral, which kept her dances from being too dangerously fey. This curious contradiction confounded her critics, though one writer found the source of *Radha*'s attraction to be its very ambiguity. The dance, he explained, appealed "to different persons in quite different ways. The casual idler or careless theatre-goer can find entertainment in its novel features. The artist interested in the study of the human form has ample opportunity for observation. Those who have been smitten with the somewhat prevalent microbe of orientalism will find much to their taste."

Radha could be viewed from multiple perspectives. As a study in exoticism, the dance had a surface sensuality and texture, a pictorial opulence, to sate the romantic appetite. Its atmosphere emanated all the heady perfume of Pierre Loti's India—the weird priestly rites, the flickering lights, the wafting incense and glowing jewels. As a morality tale, *Radha* focused on sensual indulgence but left no doubt as to the triumph of virtuous restraint. Moralists might enjoy its sensuality, secure in the knowledge that virtue would overcome vice.

As an exercise in eroticism *Radha* was a ritual orgasm, its heroine, the sort of *fin-de-siècle femme fatale* celebrated in the refrain of a popular song: "And you stole my heart/with your cunning heart/And the Egypt in your smile." This aspect of *Radha*, its dark, mysterious force, placed it in a tradition of erotic art which allied the dangerous female, luxury, and the lure of the senses in a powerful allegory. *Radha* had its antecedents in paintings such as Ingres' *Grand Odalisque*, which featured a voluptuous woman surrounded by symbolic objects: a censer (smell), font (hearing), and still-life fruit arrangement (taste). She caresses jewels and fabrics (touch) and gazes steadily at the viewer (sight). In analyzing this painting and the erotic tradition, John L. Connally, Jr., identified the erotic image as "that which is recognizable and desirable, but known to be unattainable, and therefore all the more desirable," a message which lay at the heart of Ruth St. Denis' *Radha* and helps to explain its enduring popularity.

FOUR

THE WORLD'S ENIGMA

The world's enigma solved in a girl!
Dance, Radha, in thy sacred ecstasy
Unveil to mortal eyes divinity.
　　　　　—MARGARET NOEL

ON AN EARLY winter afternoon in Germany in 1906, Ruth St. Denis sat down to lunch with the artistic elite of Berlin. Her host was Count Harry Graf Kessler, aesthete and diplomat, a quiet catalyst for the artistic ferment that made prewar Berlin the theatrical capital of Germany, if not the world. As artist, patron, and adviser, Count Kessler had a hand in almost every major career, from Max Reinhardt's pioneer work at the Deutsches Theatre to Hugo von Hofmannsthal's fecund partnership with Richard Strauss. St. Denis' dancing was the count's newest passion, and on November 18, 1906, he invited his friends to the posh Automobile Club to meet the young American whose dancing was the talk of the coffee-house crowd in Berlin.

That particular afternoon was a memorable one for Ruth. After a special matinee at the Theater des Westens in Charlottenburg, an affluent suburb of Berlin, her audience had crowded around the stage door to shout *"Wunderbar!"* as she made her way to a waiting car. Flushed with triumph, she traveled to the Automobile Club to meet Count Kessler's friends. It was an impressive gathering. Hofmannsthal was there, the "cold moonlight world" of his gaze fixed upon this young woman whom Kessler had told him was *"ein Wunder."* Kessler also had invited the artist Ludwig von Hoffman, the aging conductor Hans Richter, and Frank Wedekind, whose ironic plays shared with Hofmannsthal's writing an undercurrent of mysticism, their legacy from German Romanticism. The trend toward Realism in the German theatre was represented by the most illustrious guest of the afternoon, the playwright Gerhart Hauptmann, now at the crest of his career, whose dramatizations of social injustice had made him the "conscience of Germany." Most of these guests were mere names to Ruth, heroes she had known through the literature of the Progressive Stage Society. Now they had gathered to honor her, to meet the dancer whom a contemporary poet promised was "the world's enigma solved in a girl."

Far from the exotic creature they may have expected, the guest of honor proved to be a personality of "crystalline directness and normality," as another luncheon guest, Constance Smedley, recalled. "It was breath-taking to come into contact with anyone of such self-certainty." Smedley found Ruth's conversation "fresh and stimulating" but sensed that her "blissfully inevitable" candor was but the external shield for a private interior life. "She moved in a dual world," Smedley observed. "In all its human and material contacts, she was sanely and cheerfully normal; but with no sense of incongruity, she also lived and moved in an inner world of spiritual vision and insight and this was just as natural to her as the other."

With her characteristic mix of mystical rhetoric and slang, Ruth told the Berliners about her ideas. She knew that Berlin was a center of Egyptology and spoke eagerly of her own project, *Egypta*, rekindled by her recent researches in the London museums. As the count's friends pressed her with questions, she realized that the Germans probed dance, as they did the other arts, for philosophical and spiritual insights. To her new friends she was more than a glamorous dancer or an exotic novelty. "I was an artist in the deepest sense of the word and the subject of earnest and critical analysis."

In this stimulating climate of mutual respect, the first she had enjoyed since becoming a dancer, St. Denis clarified her own ideas and artistic philosophy. In the conversation of her new friends she sensed a provocative tension, conflicting definitions of art. "Words are like lotus flowers opening on the surface of the waters," wrote the Princess Marie von Thurn und Taxis, who met St. Denis at a similar luncheon. "We see the clear-cut shape of their luminous blossoms, but not the stalks and roots that plunge down below." The roots of St. Denis' luncheon conversation lay buried in the fertile soil of prewar Germany, a Germany of contradictory impulses that forged from its frictions the world's first truly modern culture. The surface culture, the official Germany of Kaiser Wilhelm II, blanketed Berlin with dreary architecture, overblown paintings of Prussian history, and smug drama at the Royal

Theatre. Yet underneath this facade stirred the spirit of modernism in the proletarian plays at the People's Theatre, the first forays into atonal music, the precursors of Bauhaus architecture, the earliest examples of Expressionist painting.

The modern temper, with its radical individualism, relative values, and emphasis on novelty and change, was foreign to St. Denis even though it was a logical derivation of her own Romanticism. By temperament and training Ruth was a Romantic. She believed that art linked the observer with the divine, that dance led the performer to God. In Europe she was more comfortable with practitioners of Art Nouveau or Jugendstil, devotees of Beauty, than she was with such early modernists as Richard Strauss, whose dissonant and introspective music puzzled her. Yet in Germany, even those artists and intellectuals who had retreated from Wilhelmian oppression into *fin-de-siècle* fantasies now seemed fragmented, fired by protest, as if the daydream world of Art Nouveau had ruptured from the force of its own internal pressures. Characterizing Germany's cultural climate in 1905, Hofmannsthal found "multiplicity and indeterminacy" everywhere, as each artist pursued the world's enigma in his individual way.

This emerging modern culture was cosmopolitan, cross-fertilized by Viennese intellectuals who added an elegant urbanity to Berlin's aggressive dynamism. If a single figure symbolized Germany in transition, it was Hofmannsthal, the Viennese poet who often worked in Berlin, where he became St. Denis' close friend. When he met Ruth in 1906, he had just begun the partnership with Richard Strauss that produced *Elektra* and *Der Rosenkavalier*. Behind him was the celebrated work of his youth, the solipsistic poetry based on Machian sensationalism, a theory of knowledge that defined the world through individual sensory perceptions. In a radical decision, Hofmannsthal rejected this earlier aestheticism and turned to a broader humanism expressed in drama and criticism. He "turned away from the attempt to capture the world in aesthetically perfect pictures," wrote the authors of *Wittgenstein's Vienna*, "and endeavored instead to convey an actual experience of life as it ought to be." The felt life, the immediacy, of St. Denis' dancing inspired Hofmannsthal's essay, "Die unvergleichliche Tanzerin" ("The Incomparable Dancer"), published in 1906 in *Die Zeit*. Hofmannsthal was struck by her "extraordinary immediacy," that "strict, almost jarring immediacy, this thing without comment, this great seriousness without a trace of the pedantic: all this creates about her the empty space which always surrounds extraordinary things." In the experiential nature of her art, Hofmannsthal detected the spirit of modernism and he felt that such dances would have been impossible "in an age less sophisticated, less complex than ours. I do not believe that anything like it would have been possible even a decade ago," he wrote, "nothing so thoroughly strange, so unashamed of its mysterious strangeness. It is not seeking for mediation, for being bridged over. It will have nothing to do with cultivation; it will not illustrate, will not elucidate. It presents us with something totally strange, without pretending to be ethnographic or sensational. It is there simply for the sake of its beauty."

For Hofmannsthal, St. Denis' art had all the lure of the Freudian subconscious, the strange logic of a dream. Her creation of an enclosed environment of mystery linked her with those modernists who believed in art for art's sake, the purity of aesthetic pleasure, though her dances were closer in atmosphere to the genteel decadence of paintings by Gustav Klimt than the passionate, psychological art of Egon Schiele. The sensual aspects of St. Denis' dancing were always subordinate to a transcendent purpose and she, like Hofmannsthal, believed that art must connect the real with the ideal.

At the core of Hofmannsthal's philosophy was a belief in "Praeexistenz," a near-Platonic belief in an ideal, suspended state of body and mind, akin to Nirvana, attainable in life. A word, or in St. Denis' case, a gesture, might catapult one into "Praeexistenz," and Hofmannsthal spoke reverently of "those little, yet so infinitely intensive gestures" with which St. Denis "sometimes threw her soul to the surface." If Hofmannsthal found ideal form in her dancing, his colleagues found their own interests and beliefs reflected in St. Denis' art. Max Reinhardt valued her theatrical genius, her Belasco-bred mastery of fabric, color, and light. Those Germans who admired the oblong silhouettes and sphinxlike attitudes of Klimtian Art Nouveau viewed *Radha* as a decorative surface, an ornate tapestry of poses. Devotees of the *feuilleton* or improvisational essay found in her *Cobras* the sparkle of café chatter, the allure of the unexpected, superb timing, and wit. One of the secrets of St. Denis' enduring popularity was her ability to reflect her viewers' own concerns, and in Germany artists and intellectuals welcomed her work as a resonator with their own.

One of St. Denis' American admirers had predicted her European success. Chicot (Epes W. Sargent), the sage critic for *Variety*, reviewed *Radha* in New York during the spring of 1906 and advised St. Denis to "profit by the experience of Isadora Duncan and take the act at once to Paris." Europe was the traditional proving ground for American artists, and other dancers before St. Denis had found receptive audiences and intelligent criticism abroad. Duncan, Loie Fuller, and Maud Allan had preceded St. Denis to England, France, and Germany; she, unlike them, would return home to nourish a new form of American dance.

St. Denis began her 1906 tour in London. Through the intercession of Henry B. Harris, who continued to guide her career, she signed a contract for a series of matinees in the new Aldwych Theatre in London. Fresh from her society successes in New York, she sailed for London in late May, armed with properties, costumes, and sets, as well as letters of introduction from her new contacts. Her mother and Patsy Donar accompanied her, and the Dennis men followed a few days later.

This was a homecoming for Tom Dennis, who had left his native Stourbridge as a boy. With Ruthie he made a pilgrimage to the Dennis' ancestral home, where an elderly aunt and her daughter still lived. Back in London, Ruth and her mother studied and sketched oriental artifacts at the British and South Kensington Museums and recruited Hindu extras for the dances from London's sizable Indian community. They also made shopping forays for more elaborate costumes, and Ruthie, gray now at twenty-seven, bought a black wig for street wear.

During these first pleasant days in London, word came of Mrs. Leslie Carter's remarriage, and Ruth rightly guessed that Belasco's anger would force the breakup of the partnership that had brought her to London six years earlier. The London of the *Zaza* tour, Victorian London in the throes of the Boer War, had become the gay social world of Edwardian England, with its rounds of charity benefits, hunting parties, palace teas, and balls dominated by the *bon vivant* Edward VII. The King and the peerage were powerful art patrons, and Ruth lost no time in presenting her letters of introduction.

One New York admirer, Dr. Holbrook Curtis, had given Ruth a letter for Consuelo, Duchess of Manchester. The exotic duchess, a Louisiana girl of Cuban parentage, was a widow who whiled away her hours with soirees featuring London's most fashionable artists. She received Ruth at Dr. Curtis' request and agreed to sponsor her in a series of private performances.

On the evening of July 20, 1906, Ruth danced in the duchess' home with the King himself in attendance. With the royal stamp of approval, she received invitations to dance for the American ambassador, White-law Reid, and for the visiting Maharaja of Kapurthala. Dr. Curtis had also given her a letter for the prominent painter, Sir Lawrence Alma-Tadema, and in his studio she danced for the equally prominent John Sargent. "Sir Laurence [sic] put lilies around the shrine and fixed beautiful curtains for the Hindoos to draw," Ruth remembered. That same summer the Earl of Lonsdale presented her in a stairstep series of garden parties. "He made a habit of lumping all his social obligations together and entertaining in a descending scale of social distinction," she observed, and on each successive evening her audience was less distinguished but more demonstrative.

As enchanted as she was by royalty, Ruth craved a genuine popular success in London, but her Aldwych matinees met with lukewarm response. Though the London *Times* critic found her performance of *Radha* "a new and strange experience—dancing that was charged with meaning," the box office told a gloomier story. The first matinee audience numbered only about 100 in a 1,100-seat theatre, and the receipts amounted to a paltry twenty-eight pounds. Solo dancing was not the box-office draw it would later become in London, and St. Denis, like Duncan before her, found her warmest appreciation in artistic and royal circles.

One of the audience members at the Aldwych matinees was Ruth's future agent, A. Braff, a blond and romantic Russian with excellent European connections in the theatre. Smitten by the dancer as well as the dance, "Braffie" went to work to secure engagements for St. Denis on the continent. But either through naïveté or double-dealing, Ruth also engaged the services of a second agent named Marinelli. In her memoirs she described Marinelli as "Monsieur X," an unwelcome intruder whose offers she indignantly refused, but her early diaries indicate that both Marinelli and Braff chased contracts for St. Denis, with her approval, before she finally settled on the Russian as her sole agent. Understandably, Marinelli was stung and he soon had his revenge.

During the London summer Ruth also met her musical conductor, M. A. W. Rodrigo, a Ceylonese who arranged several East tunes for the Aldwych performances, and just before the first matinee Loie Fuller summoned St. Denis to her London hotel. The famous dancer, who enjoyed a strong popular following in Europe, proposed that Ruth accompany her to Marseilles, where Fuller and a Japanese dancer, probably Sada Yacco, were scheduled to perform in an exhibition theatre. Fuller always had a canny eye for talent. Earlier she had persuaded the young Isadora Duncan to accompany her on a German tour, but Ruth declined her latest offer, probably because she was reluctant to become a Fuller protégée. "She was very urgent," Ruth recorded in her diary. "Mother and I had a long confab but on further consideration decided not to accept. She sent her man the next day to see if we had reconsidered."

After two months in London, Ruth finally received word from Braffie of an offer to play the Marigny Theatre in Paris, a second-rate variety house which her old friend Hamilton Revelle reassured her was "chic." The family at once made plans to depart London. Tom Dennis sailed home to New York and Patsy Donar stayed behind to appear in a London show, while Ruth traveled to Paris with a new entourage, including Revelle, Braffie, her mother and brother, and Hindus recruited from the London wharves. They were joined in Paris by Mabel Pollion, whose poem "To Ruth St. Denis, Dancing" appeared in that July's issue of *Theatre Magazine* under the pseudonym Margaret Noel. The daughter of a prominent New York family, her mother an artist, Mabel was among the first of many talented women attracted to St. Denis. In her poem she urged the dancer to "Throw off thy bondage/Teach us to be free!" and speculated that "Thy lithe body in that wondrous swirl/Of mystic loveliness by us be seen/The world's enigma solved in a girll", a forecast of the significance European admirers would attach to St. Denis' art.

The party arrived in Paris in high spirits, only to discover a horrendous betrayal. The rejected agent, Marinelli, had booked a rival *Radha* into the prestigious Olympia Theatre. With St. Denis' own Marigny engagement still a month away, the imposter's posters were everywhere, advertising "Radha, danseuse hindique" in both a *Radha* and a *Cobra* dance. Ruth might have anticipated this misfortune. Imposters were a time-honored tradition in the American theatre; once an act was a success in vaudeville, imitators mushroomed from coast to coast. St. Denis herself might have been considered an imitator by some Parisians, for the previous summer Mata Hari had appeared in Paris in bare feet and gold chains and "worked herself into a frenzy of worship" in a Brahman dance. But this Parisian Radha was Ruth's first, painful experience with direct imitation, and it was too early in her career for her to feel flattered.

After watching the Olympia act, Ruth engaged a lawyer to serve an injunction against the rival Radha, and she also took her battle to the press. The Paris edition of the New York *Herald* printed her dignified version of the Marinelli affair. In her letter to the editor, she appealed to the Parisians' national honor. "As an American girl I have been imposed on in a foreign country," she wrote, pointing out that the rival Radha had managed to steal her name and concept but not the execution of the dance itself. "Mine is the real and only 'Radha,' and I deserve to reap the fruits of my creation."

Apparently the public agreed, for the rival faded as Ruth set about orchestrating publicity for her own debut. In full Indian costume she rode in an open buggy through the Bois de Boulogne. She fed publicity to the Paris newspapers which promised "mysterious rituals of the Cult of Radha—tributes full of fervor which are rendered to the Goddess several times each year on the banks of the Ganges." The myths grew. An "interview" in *Le Journal* identified St. Denis as the offspring of a Brahman girl and an English officer, trained as a temple dancer and brought to Paris by a French officer who abandoned her there. This mixture of military dash and oriental mystery enhanced St. Denis' box-office appeal.

Other aspects of her Marigny preparations were less pleasant. The French Society of Authors and Composers prohibited her use of the *Lakmé* score on the grounds that highbrow music was unsuitable for the decadent art of dancing. Ruth was forced to find other ersatz Indian tunes. The rehearsals at the Marigny were disconcerting, with drunken stagehands who "made such a racket that I cried and the stage manager swore." On the eve of her debut, Ruth told her diary that "The whole experience has been a severe test and trial of our faith. It seemed as if all the error in the world, or rather in Paris rose up to block our path. Probably," she reasoned, "we have fought too much among ourselves and have not left enough for Divine Mind to do." She attended a meeting of Christian Scientists and found her strength renewed. "I am very thankful that in this awful city and theatre we have been able to bore through the darkness."

On August 31 she presented a press performance, then opened her act to the public the following evening. Dancing as "Miss Ruth" in the Marigny Revue, she found herself back in variety, among acts including a magician and an eccentric. Throughout the evening, coquettes promenaded through the audience, but the crowd fell silent as Ruth danced, "surely a good sign," she thought. The Parisian critics were enthusiastic. One described her *Cobras* in detail, comparing the sinister dance with "Baudelaire's poison": "The serpents are her undulating arms. They crawl languidly, they twist, they caress, they entwine, they smother . . . And the whole body of the dancer folds about, stretches, stands up erect; she's the divine animal protected by Shiva, that none would dare to strike. Her face has become drawn; her stare is steady, vitreous, cruel . . ."

"Let there be no mistake," another critic admonished his readers, Miss Ruth's dances were "not like those puerile but pompously advertised dances which have too often proved such a disappointment." As St. Denis' reputation grew, aristocratic Parisians such as the Rothschilds and artists including Loie Fuller stopped by the Marigny to catch her act. The management extended Ruth's contract for two weeks but she was relieved to leave the second-rate theatre when Braffie produced another contract for a series of performances at the Komische Oper in Berlin. Ruth paused in Paris long enough to be sketched by Rodin, then left for Berlin in the company of her mother and brother.

The Komische Oper contract worried Ruth. "I am afraid Braffie is not big enough to handle my show," she fretted. Though the Wintergarten, a huge amusements hall in Berlin, had extended a lucrative offer, Braffie preferred the prestige of the comic opera. Through October, Ruth performed in the opera *Lakmé*, dancing *Cobras* during its bazaar scene, and on alternate evenings she presented *Radha* and *Incense* between acts of such operas as *Carmen*, Anselm Gogl's *Zierpuppen*, and *Tales of Hoffmann*. In later years she loved to recall the squad of German officials who came backstage to inspect her scanty costume and body paint. "Well the morals of the German public are preserved," she wrote in her diary. "The 'government' preceded by Braff came to inspect my waistline! I turned and twisted evidently to their satisfaction, since I may continue to paint my tummy!"

Braff had chosen the opera engagement wisely, for in the audience were influential critics, artists, and intellectuals, including Ruth's new friend Hofmannsthal. In his review of *Radha*, he identified the paradox at the heart of St. Denis' art. "It goes to the limits of sensuality and yet it is chaste. It is entirely given up to the senses and yet signifies something higher. It is wild and yet subject to eternal laws." As he strolled with Ruth through the German countryside, discussing philosophy and Romantic poetry, Hofmannsthal discovered that this paradox extended to her personal life. She was a prude, but she craved sensual pleasures. On one occasion she told him that she disliked Swinburne's poetry because his intuitive "stream of being" was interrupted by sensuality. She did not explain, Hofmannsthal noted wryly, how she harmonized her pleasure in this pure stream of being with her own appetite for "lifeless objects like precious stones and rich garments."

Ruth's dualities fascinated Hofmannsthal, and he shared a proprietary interest in the dancer with his close friend Count Kessler. Both men had seen Isadora Duncan dance in Berlin in 1904, but when the count first saw St. Denis' *Radha,* he wrote Hofmannsthal that she achieved what Duncan merely attempted, "the fullest experience of purely sensual beauty, at once animal and mystical." Kessler asked for an introduction to Ruth, and he reported to Hofmannsthal that she was intelligent, beautiful, and high-spirited. The count became Ruth's most ardent German supporter.

A champion of modern art, Count Kessler had invited Gordon Craig to Germany in 1904, where the young theatrical designer left the imprint of his revolutionary ideas and, incidentally, began his relationship with Isadora Duncan. Kessler also commissioned the Belgian architect Henry van de Velde to decorate his Berlin apartment in the modish Jugendstil, the German equivalent of Art Nouveau, and at the count's recommendation Van de Velde became the director of the Weimar art institute that evolved into the Bauhaus. An artist himself, Kessler created a ballet scenario for Richard Strauss, but his forte was behind-the-scenes promotion. Then in his late thirties, tall and slim with penetrating eyes and a bushy mustache, the count was a dashing and influential protector for Ruth.

He invited her to breakfast with Gerhart Hauptmann and encouraged the playwright to create a pantomime for St. Denis. Kessler also asked Ludwig von Hoffman to sketch her, and when he heard that an imposter Radha would visit Vienna, he wrote to Hofmannsthal and urged him to expose the upstart in print. The count's most ambitious project for St. Denis resulted from an arranged meeting with Max Reinhardt, who asked Ruth to appear the following season in his intimate Kammerspielhaus.

Reinhardt had in mind for the 1907–8 season a production of Oscar Wilde's *Salomé,* with St. Denis as guest artist in the dancing role. *Salomé* was then in vogue; Richard Strauss had just completed his operatic version, and dancers from Maud Allan to Mata Hari used the music to plan their own *Salomé* dances. Ruth was intrigued by Salomé but objected to the Wilde version of the story, which relegated the dancing to a secondary role. Count Kessler agreed and urged Hofmannsthal to write a new poetic treatment, tailored to St. Denis' specifications.

In Kessler's correspondence with Hofmannsthal he outlined Ruth's idea for a more Biblical and allegorical *Salomé*, "primeval and Hebraic in tone." As usual, Ruth's concept stemmed from visual art, an old wood engraving she had seen in a Bible, with Herod, Herodias, and their guests seated around a table, watching Salomé dance. In this setting, Kessler wrote Hofmannsthal,

> immediately preceding the dance, a short, but highly dramatic and poetically compelling scene is needed, involving Herod and Herodias having brought Salomé to dance. In preparation for Salomé's entrance and the dance, the lights will gradually dim, so that the circle where she will dance becomes spotlighted. This takes place through some sort of "natural" occurrence, motivated in the scenery (moonlight through an opening or window, or something of the sort). Salomé's dance is now the important thing. She performs various dances, one after another, which make Herod wilder and wilder, until finally, in a raging frenzy, he gives the order. *During* the dance, the lights continue to grow dimmer, and the table gradually is completely dark, except the faces of the guests shine out of the darkness, until finally, only the distorted and twisted faces of Herod and Herodias are visible. They sit facing each other at either end of the table, at the relatively brightest spots. Out of this eerie darkness Herod utters the vow. Suddenly the curtain closes, and reopens to an atmosphere of haggard dawn, and Salomé enters with the head of John the Baptist.

In this proposal, St. Denis' choreographic approach is clear: her dependence on scenery and lighting for dramatic motivation, her pictorial approach to the dance scene, her manipulation of theatrical elements to focus on her own central role. She wanted Hofmannsthal to create a twenty-minute narrative to precede her solo dance. "The basic idea is, in any case, that the poetry remain throughout a frame for the dance," Kessler advised Hofmannsthal. "It seems to me that this project is perfect for you. The dance can and must be very strong poetically, captivating in beauty of language and tone, so that the dance blooms from it as a flower of poison."

For a time, it seems, Hofmannsthal worked with Ruth. "I've fallen into another type of collaboration with an improbable co-worker, the dancer St. Denis," he wrote his friend, Helene von Nostitz. "She's an intelligent and nice person and dances wonderfully, charming the audience with taste." Yet the *Salomé* project soon collapsed, perhaps because of personal friction. Ruth had become involved with Hofmannsthal's black-sheep brother-in-law, Hans Schlesinger, an artist based in Italy, whose interest in women was purely aesthetic. Both Hofmannsthal and Count Kessler recoiled at this liaison, and their friendship with Ruth became strained.

Ruth was drawn to creative, insubstantial men who flattered her with courtesies but posed no sexual threat, and she used their attentions as a potent weapon against her mother. Mrs. Dennis had accompanied Ruth this far on the tour. Each night she sat in the audience, then went backstage to offer cogent criticism. She was a perfectionist. On one occasion when Ruth's jeweled body suit seemed lackluster, Mrs. Dennis outlined each of the tiny, myriad jewels in black yarn so that they would "register." She carried Radha's crown from theatre to theatre, jealously guarding it in transit. Her frugality with Ruth's earnings was legendary. When ordering a meal, she would say to her companions, "If you're having soup, I'll have a spoon of yours." She was a strict taskmaster, the only person able to make Ruth rehearse. For such pains she expected absolute loyalty, and as Hans Schlesinger and other camp-followers appeared, Mrs. Dennis grew restive.

Mother and daughter quarreled constantly after leaving Berlin. St. Denis completed the Komische Oper contract, with an additional, lucrative month at the Wintergarten, then moved on to Eastern Europe. From the warmth of Berlin's intellectual circles, she came to the dreary theatres and lonely hotel rooms of strange cities in the dead of winter. Her funds were low and her mother threatened a nervous collapse. In a dark mood, Ruth found Prague that Christmas "unbearable" because of its "sinister Catholic atmosphere," and from Warsaw she telegraphed Braffie, who was in London, that her mother was very ill, her own financial situation, urgent. Mrs. Dennis decided to go home, and Ruth continued on in the company of her brother.

In Vienna once again St. Denis found solace in the company of the elite of a cultured city. Vienna in 1907 was "more than the capital of the Habsburg Empire," wrote one historian, "it was a state of mind. Two attitudes interacted in the outlook of most Viennese: lighthearted

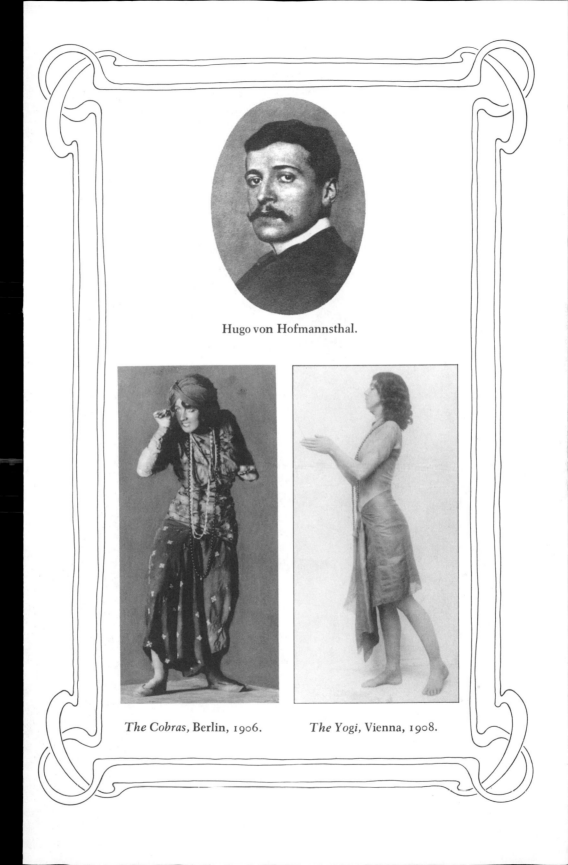

Hugo von Hofmannsthal.

The Cobras, Berlin, 1906.   *The Yogi,* Vienna, 1908.

The fashionable dancer, home from Europe, 1910.

St. Denis in "The Flower Arrangement" from *O-Mika,* 1913.

Ruth and Brother St. Denis in *O-Mika*.

Ted Shawn.

Ruth literally sits on a pedestal in this portrait with her husband, Ted Shawn.

Ruth St. Denis, Ted Shawn, and the first Denishawn company in Egyptian ballet from the Berkeley Greek Theatre pageant, 1915. Dancers, from left to right, are Vanda Hoff, Florence Andrews, Margaret Loomis, Carol Dempster, Shawn and St. Denis, Chula Monzon, Claire Niles, Yvonne Sinnard, and Ada Forman.

Ted shoots love arrows at Ruth in *The Garden of Kama,* their first joint choreography, 1915.

Ruth St. Denis as Egypta.

Ruth St. Denis as *Kuan Yin,* 1916.

enjoyment of the arts, or aestheticism, and indifference to political and social reform." This gay milieu brightened Ruth's mood. Though she was rumored to have had an affair with the brooding Expressionist painter Egon Schiele, then an art student, Ruth spent most of her leisure time among the members of the Habsburg aristocracy. Hofmannsthal introduced her to the Princess Kinsky, who sponsored her in a musical evening, and to Rilke's friend, the Princess Marie von Thurn und Taxis, who shared with Ruth a fascination with psychic phenomena and the occult. During one earnest conversation, the Princess Marie paid Ruth a compliment that she treasured all her life. "My dear child," said the elderly aristocrat, "there are two kinds of people in the world, those who are life-increasing and those who are life-decreasing. You are one of the life-bringers."

Renewed by Vienna, Ruth danced brilliantly. Her friends crowded the Ronacher Theatre and she remarked pertly in her diary, "House full. 'Pears to be the fashion over here." She acquired a new conductor-composer, Walter Meyrowitz, and as her act gained polish, her sponsors raised their ticket prices and still managed to fill the house. St. Denis combined "first-class material and perfect technique," wrote the critic for *Wiener Abendpost*, "with a wonderfully trained body, lithe and supple like a snake," and a "graceful and elegant command of all movements, down to those of her slender, nobly-formed fingers." Because of this, he concluded, "she doesn't confine herself to solemn, sacerdotal gesture; she can convey whirling ecstasy and meditative, dreamy tranquility with equally convincing power."

After a month in Vienna, Ruth traveled on to Düsseldorf, where she received "great appreciation. Letters, visits, etc. and manager wanted me to stay longer—the same tale everywhere." Her next stop, Hamburg, was less happy. During her two months there she found the Hansa Theatre vaudevillian in atmosphere and the audience filled with "heavy money-making people, without the enthusiasm of Berlin or the aristocracy of Vienna." Throughout that year, as she moved from her Berlin base to surrounding cities, Ruth grew bored with the grind of touring, bored with "solid and sodden Germans." Without the guidance of her mother, her standard program of *Radha, Incense,* and *Cobras* became sloppy until, her brother claimed, a dozen versions existed, and no one, not even Ruth, remembered the original dances.

In Budapest that Christmas, Ruth was depressed. Hans was there, small comfort. "It seems that I have been living other people's lives rather than my own," she wrote sadly in her diary. "Oh for a simple country farm house and a family and air." She missed her mother and longed for a family of her own. "I suppose this mood will pass." Though she meditated before each performance, her ennui infected her dancing, and she found it difficult to re-create the spiritual intensity of *Radha*, night after night. During a performance in Budapest she finally snapped. In mid-dance she began weeping hysterically, "I'm not a machine! I'm not a machine!" and Brother had to ring down the curtain.

Ruth needed a rest and a new artistic challenge. Freed from the watchful eye of her mother, she fled with Hans to Rome while her brother discreetly went his own way to Venice. "The eternal Game of Fire Playing was not so dangerous, it being Hans!" Ruth joked in her diary, "but that I could allow myself the adventurous joy of going alone with Hans to Rome! which I did—feeling not at all sinful—but quite courageous." After the couple left the Eternal City, Ruth decided that "Hans without Rome was devoid of interest," and she returned to the tour.

The Rome interlude restored her creative juices, and she returned to touring with two new dances. On February 9, 1908, in a special matinee at the Ronacher in Vienna, she performed *The Yogi*, her new solo composition. A pantomimic study of an Indian ascetic, the dance incorporated yoga exercises and reflected a passage in the *Bhagavad-Gita* which tells of the yogi

> *In a clean place setting up for himself*
> *A firm seat, not too high or too low*
> *Covered with kusha grass*
> *And an antelope skin and a cloth*
>
> *Pointing the mind toward one aim*
> *Ruling the motions of thoughts and sense*
> *Seated there, he should practice discipline*
> *For the purifying of the self.*

Austere and intense, the dance seemed to discipline all the disorder of St. Denis' personal life into her most powerful and distilled dance statement.

The curtain rose on an Indian forest. At center stage in a shaft of light lay a tiger-skin rug, and from the surrounding gloom glided a holy man in rags. He circled the rug and, depositing his bowl, sank into the cross-legged posture of meditation. Slowly he began a rhythmic rise and fall of breath. His arms extended from the torso to form a cross until his entire body folded forward, head resting between crossed ankles, hands before him on the ground. A breathless pause. In the distance the thin, high voice of a yogi chanted an invocation to Shiva. The holy man, listening, slowly rose to full height until he stood erect. At the cry "Shiva!" one arm staggered overhead, then another, and the yogi strode into the darkness, his arms upstretched to eternity.

This was a risky dance to present to the public. "It requires the most rigid control," Ruth said, "for there are but few gestures and these must have telling effect." The scaffolding of the dance was Delsartean, with the yogi's various postures and gestures suggesting his inward spiritual state and the progressive discipline of his body and mind. If her audience should fail to grasp this symbolism, then "the scene is painfully banal," she admitted. Far from banal, the dance was *"highest* art," by critical consensus, and Hofmannsthal wrote that *The Yogi* was "the most beautiful, intense thing I've ever seen in my life." He was equally moved by St. Denis' second new dance, *The Nautch*, which she substituted for *Incense* on her program at the Ronacher.

The Nautch was a savvy street dance, the happily vulgar display of a dancing girl. Her twitching hips, drumming feet, and provocative gestures were a corrupted form of Kathak dancing that began in the North Indian temples but progressed to the palaces and, eventually, to the streets. Ruth had seen nautch girls at Coney Island, and she added her own hijinks to their basic dance. To the accompaniment of hand drums and vocals, she entered and made a salaam or gesture of greeting. Casting aside her veil, she began to stamp her feet in accelerating rhythms, each measure of drumbeats shortened until her feet alternated in rapid succession. She ruffled her skirts in a figure-eight formation and, in an amplification of the climax of *Radha*, whirled in a spiraling turn. More footbeats, another salaam, then retreat.

Through the years St. Denis' *Nautch* evolved into a half-dozen different dances, named for their costume, setting or composer—the *Cadman Nautch*, the *Green Nautch*, the *Palace Nautch*, and others—but always the basic ingredients were Ruth's character acting, her head-isolations, enticing arms, skirt manipulations, whirling, drumming feet, and the tinkle of ankle bells.

This earliest *Nautch* in Vienna, performed in green gown and veil, must have been more lyrical than later versions, for one critic emphasized its "flowing, intricate movements." This lyricism vanished as Ruth aged and as she added theatrical touches, mumbling, begging *baksheesh* or alms, thumbing her nose rudely when refused. But her first *Nautch,* in Hofmannsthal's estimation, approached the classical perfection of Greek art in its intensity, rigor, sensuousness, and timing. For Hofmannsthal, St. Denis embodied the Greek ideal in theatre, a fusion of poetry, drama, and music that produced a social and religious experience for the audience. "She is a creature for whose existence we of the world cannot be thankful enough," he wrote. "She is absolutely unsentimental and as grandiose as Greek art."

Greek antiquity, and specifically the dancing of Isadora Duncan, was the yardstick most often used by German critics in evaluating St. Denis' dances, even when they disagreed. Even the most ordinary German press notices included fine distinctions between Ruth's subject matter and style, traditionalism versus classicism. The critic for Munich's *Allgemeine Zeitung* found her dances "the antithesis of that of Duncan, who was always more effective in theory than in practice." He felt that Duncan's art "was always more of an idea about art, which fit in with other modern stage ideas," while St. Denis' dancing stemmed from the "traditional school" exemplified by the Paris Opera, with "all too beautiful backdrops, light effects and background dancing." Another critic disagreed, describing St. Denis as "the living image of Greek sculpture" in a performance staged by the designer Mariano Fortuny in Berlin.

During this private showing in late 1907 at the Hohenzollern Museum for Arts and Crafts, Ruth modeled Fortuny's futuristic dress design, a single bolt of fabric approximately ten meters in length which converted into various costumes. In that peculiar mesh of modernism with antiquity, the Fortuny design resembled Greek drapery but also fulfilled the expectations of dress reformers. Ruth demonstrated the Fortuny design as a peignoir, a gown and train, a ballgown, and as a "fantasy costume." Moving to a cello accompaniment, she was "a living model of indescribable grace, posing, floating, dancing for the spectators." Hofmannsthal narrated this glorified fashion show and, indeed, continued the correspondent for the *Berliner Tageblatt,* "when the dancer appeared, clothed in the veiled gown, stepping in upon white sandaled feet, one could imagine her as a figure in a Hofmannsthal poem in the style of the Greek masters."

Comparisons with Greek art lent prestige to her work, and Ruth always was flattered by references to Isadora Duncan, but when she traveled to London during the summer of 1908, she found her work compared with that of another dancer, Maud Allan, whose version of *Salomé* had brought her spectacular success. Canadian-born and a resident of California, Allan had attended music school in Berlin and made her dance debut in Vienna in 1903. As Ruth planned a *Salomé* of her own, Allan brought her lurid but sentimental version to Munich, where government censors limited it to private subscription audiences. Ruth felt that Allan's dancing was derivative, and after seeing her London concert at the Palace Theatre wrote in her diary that Allan's dances consisted of "an adaptation of Isadora's Greek Spring rhythms, the costumes and actions of some of the German actresses in the part of Salomé, and a generous sprinkling of my arm movements during all of her numbers."

Allan was the sensation of London that season, and critics insisted on writing about St. Denis and Allan in tandem. When an article about *Radha* appeared under the headline, "Rival of Maud Allan to Appear," Ruth angrily wrote a letter to the editor of the London *Daily Express*. "The expression of thought by means of rhythmic movement constitutes the foundation of dancing and is infinite in its application," she wrote loftily. "Therefore the notion of one person working out a composition based on the laws of plastic harmony being a rival of another doing the same thing through the avenue of her own individuality is, if I may say so, absurd."

On this trip to London Ruth found a warmer reception than two years earlier. The climate for solo dancers had improved, stimulated by the rising popularity of Allan and Duncan and the proliferation of variety dance. The newspapers debated the relative merits of Fuller, Allan, Duncan, and the ballerinas Adeline Genée and Lydia Kyasht, all of whom appeared in London during St. Denis' stay in 1908. J. E. Crawford Flitch, who saw that London season and labeled it a "dance renaissance," found musicality, childlike charm, and spontaneity in Allan's "rapid sallies hither and thither, now a-tiptoe, now on bended knee," but not the fire and depth of Duncan's art. Flitch admired St. Denis, but where his German colleagues saw classical purity, he saw "somewhat limited, artificial and literal" symbolism. Her dancing "is symbolic but not in the large, suggestive way in which Isadora Duncan's dancing is symbolic," he explained. St. Denis' dancing "with some exceptions tends to be static, an affair of postures and poses, and in some cases these postures are more learned than beautiful." If the Germans revered St. Denis' "art of movement born of stillness," Flitch found it merely still and static, and he preferred her livelier *Nautch* where "for once she threw asceticism to the winds."

Critical tastes notwithstanding, at this stage in her career Ruth emphasized scholarship. She studied the Burlington House's Chinese exhibition and carefully noted the triple twist in the shoulders, torsos, and hips of its sculptured figures. She bought picture postcards of dancers from the South Kensington Museum's Indian collection, and her studiousness won her the appreciation of British artists and intellectuals, who, in 1908, were becoming aware of India's rich cultural heritage. In 1910 the critic Roger Fry wrote the classic defense of Indian art that became a turning point for British understanding of its colony's cultural wealth, and that same year Ananda K. Coomaraswamy, who became St. Denis' ally, founded the India Society in London. Already in 1908 a host of organizations devoted to interpreting Indian thought and customs—the Theosophical Society, the Vegetarian Society, the Society for Psychical Research—marked the advent of "a great reaction from the smug commercialism and materialism of the mid-Victorian epoch, and a preparation for the new universe of the twentieth century."

Ruth benefited from the fashion for things Indian, but her planned series of solo evening concerts still was a gamble. Dancers often performed matinee concerts for female audiences, but "whether the public will care for an evening of dancing or whether they will say in effect *toujours perdrix* remains to be seen," remarked one journalist in announcing St. Denis' London season. She had decided to risk her savings and reputation by renting the newly renovated La Scala Theatre for a concert series in October and November. Her program included the two new dances and the older trio combined in a complete East Indian suite. She opened her concerts with the devotional *Incense*, then quickened the pace with the colorful *Cobras* and *Nautch*. The intense *Yogi* provided a climax for the program, followed by the opulent *Radha*. In London St. Denis subtitled these dances the Purdah, the Street, the Palace, the Forest, and the Temple, indicating the more elaborate context for each dance created through setting, costumes, and supporting cast. With the memory of the temple dance lingering, the London *Times* critic wrote of St. Denis' "strong element of mysticism and religion" and only briefly mentioned her bare feet. The concerts were a modest success; St. Denis still was eclipsed by the more popular Maud Allan, until her loyal friends intervened.

Constance Smedley, who had become Ruth's devoted admirer in Berlin, was determined to keep the La Scala filled during her concert series. As founder of the worldwide lyceum club movement, Smedley was a natural organizer. She had excellent connections in London society and among artistic circles. Herself a playwright, she married the designer Maxwell Armfield in 1909, and together they founded the Cotswold and Greenleaf Players, devoted to a theatre of pastoral and joyous simplicity. The seed of the Cotswold Players was a mummers' play organized by Smedley that summer of 1908, with St. Denis a featured participant. "THE MUMMERS ARE ON THE ROAD," promised their playbill, with a list of poems, playlets, and mime sketches, "together with such odd DANCES, RHYMES, AND MERRY TRICKS as may happen." On the last two evenings in July, Smedley's vagabond players gathered on the Kensington end of Holland Road and proceeded to the courtyard of Armfield's studio just behind Holland Mews. Ruth appeared among the throng as a mysterious Eastern Princess who dropped a jeweled sandal along the road.

Smedley's circle of friends took up St. Denis' cause. They organized a dinner party to drum up interest in her concerts, and from this gathering came an illustrious committee of "Patrons of La Scala Theatre," with George Bernard Shaw and Rodin among its members. The committee staged a special St. Denis Gala, and through their efforts, Smedley wrote, "the stalls of the Scala were well-filled."

For the Gala, Ruth created a new dance, *A Shirabyoshi*, based on a story by Lafcadio Hearn. The dance may have had its roots in her earlier Japanese study for Belasco, and Hugo von Hofmannsthal probably suggested the text; several years earlier he had written an essay on Hearn and frequently mentioned him in his writing. As the dancing girl of Hearn's legend, Ruth performed before the mortuary tablet of her dead lover until a lamp brightened, symbol of her lover's pleasure in the dance. The London *Times* exhausted its polite superlatives in calling *A Shirabyoshi* "certainly one of the most interesting among the many impressive and beautiful things which this remarkable artist has to show," and Ruth left London in triumph.

After five months of English-speaking company and London conveniences, Ruth returned somewhat reluctantly to Germany. She performed engagements in Dresden, Bielefeld, and Weimar, and in the latter city danced a command performance for the Weimar court. After the program a committee of local businessmen and dignitaries offered to finance a school for St. Denis if she would make Germany her home. The offer was tempting. Weimar was the home of Goethe and Schiller, once the Athens of the empire, but Ruth may have sensed that this golden age of Romantic Germany was drawing to a close. Jugendstil was fading in favor of a bolder, raw Expressionism. The artistocratic elegance of the Habsburg and Hohenzollern world imploded with the psychological theories of Freud. War was on the horizon and Ruth already felt the "sinister thread" of militarism throughout German life. Her own brand of mysticism would have been outmoded in postwar Germany. By returning to an America virtually untouched by war, an America still innocent of modernism, she prolonged her popularity by another decade. Wisely, Ruth declined the Weimar offer and turned her thoughts toward home.

On the way to America she danced one last tour in England and Scotland, with a remunerative two-month engagement at the London Coliseum as headliner of a vaudeville bill that included a young juggler-comedian, W. C. Fields. These commercial engagements were necessary for her bank balance, but Ruth suffered indignities from vaudeville audiences impatient for technical tricks and virtuosity. During one performance at the Coliseum the audience in the sixpence gallery clapped through *Radha,* demonstrating their disapproval. The management had to lower the curtain in mid-dance. "A few persons who paid twelve cents admission didn't understand her act and were determined to break it up," explained the London correspondent for *Variety,* and "the people who were really enjoying Miss St. Denis did not know or understand what had happened. The management made a sad error when they permitted the gallery crowd to ruin the act of Miss St. Denis."

With her reputation and fortune made, and a wealth of experience behind her, Ruth sailed for New York in the summer of 1909. She never returned to Germany, but her friends did not forget. Twenty years after her departure and just before his death, Hofmannsthal wrote to her with fresh fervor: "I think never a month has passed, not even during war, without some vision, some recollection of yours passing through my brain . . . certainly the creature you were and every motion of your dances is going on living within me.

"You must understand," he went on, "I am living very much with

the shadows of human beings no more existing or not yet existing."
Looking back to the Germany of Goethe, forward to the modern age,
Hofmannsthal lived among his ghosts, while St. Denis, safely home,
danced on in the twilight adolescence of America.

FIVE

THE EGYPT IN YOUR SMILE

RUTH sailed home with Egypt on her mind. Since 1905 she had dreamed of producing her first choreographic idea, *Egypta*, and as she traveled through Europe she completed her research. In Berlin she met the eminent Egyptologist, Dr. Alan Gardiner, who remarked that he had never met a layman with so profound an instinct for archaeological science as St. Denis. She plied him with questions: "What did Egyptian priests wear? When did the kingship reach its apotheosis?, questions that were just information to me, they weren't even culture yet. They were just information, which like a squirrel I put in my pouch and just gathered and gathered." Dr. Gardiner arranged for Ruth to view papyri and other Egyptian artifacts, and in London she added to her backlog of notes and sketches through trips to the British Museum.

These were the years of exciting archaeological discoveries in the Valley of the Tombs of the Kings in Thebes. In 1887 an Egyptian peasant digging for compost unearthed ancient clay tablets in cuneiform, and this discovery of the Amarna Letters sparked the intensive archaeological explorations that captured the popular imagination. As Ruth danced in London in 1908 the newspapers recorded keen public interest in an Egyptian tomb discovered the previous year and thought to be the resting place of Akhenaten, the young Pharaoh married to Nefertiti. The London theatre took up the theme with a play set in Egypt, *False Gods*, which Ruth saw at His Majesty's Theatre just before she sailed home. She thrilled to its plot of religious heresy and regicide and memorized Beerbohm Tree's massive stage set, a great hall of receding columns which she copied for her own *Egypta* decor.

St. Denis came home to an America still infected with "the somewhat prevalent microbe of Orientalism," as one skeptic called it. In the years just before World War I, the public appetite for exotica peaked.

Ernest Fenollosa's Chautauqua lectures on Japan, the Japanese-influenced art of James McNeill Whistler and John La Farge, the exotic tales of Lafcadio Hearn, fed the vogue for japonaiserie. Other exotic cultures became the mode as Americans demanded eclectic oriental motifs in their entertainment, their literature, their homes and dress. Fashion magazines in 1913 advertised evening headdresses topped with Turkish plumes, afternoon frocks "in the Persian mode," Etruscan silverware, oriental tunics, Japanese opera bags, Chinese porcelains and pearls. "To an Oriental yellow pearls are choicer than white; to us the order is reversed; it is all a matter of longitude," *Vanity Fair* airily informed its readers in the sophisticated tone of the cosmopolite who considered the Orient a luxurious playground for sensual appetites.

The longitudinal boundaries of this idealized Orient were hazy at best. In the popular imagination the Orient stretched from the Atlantic to the Pacific Oceans, encompassing the Near and Far East from Africa to Japan. Indistinguishable in their exoticism, all oriental cultures were synonymous with sensuality, latent cruelty, and the bizarre. Their peoples were "pagan, not Christian; amoral not ethical; lazy rather than laboring; languid and never strenuous." This mythical Orient represented an inversion of American values, but it reflected a central preoccupation of the America of Robber Barons and great industrial fortunes: the Orient, above all, was a land of barbaric riches.

This stereotype generated scores of oriental plays on Broadway during the decade before World War I: Belasco's *The Darling of the Gods,* with its elaborate Japanese decor; *The Yellow Jacket,* based on ancient Chinese tales; Henry Savage's *The Sultan of Sulu,* set in the Philippines, and his Korean comic opera, *The Sho Gun.* Even the fledgling motion-picture industry offered oriental travelogues, including a popular Kinemacolor film of the Durbar coronation of Indian rajahs in 1912. These entertainments emphasized the texture and color of the East, and dance was an important part of the spectacle. *The Daughter of Heaven,* a Chinese extravaganza in 1912, introduced Violet Romer's "Dance of the Sacred Lotus," probably a St. Denis imitation, while the Algerian *Garden of Allah* the same year featured a chorus of Ouled Naïl dancers, several years in advance of St. Denis' own Algerian dances. The prototype of these exotic dances was *Salomé.* Richard Strauss's operatic version at the Metropolitan Opera in 1907 spawned dozens of dancing Salomés in vaudeville and the legitimate theatre, including Maud Allan, Gertrude Hoffman, and Mlle. Dazie, who undulated her veils in a Ziegfeld production before opening a school for Salomés on the roof garden of the New York Theatre.

Such pleasures took on the patina of respectability when allied with oriental scholarship. For his Egyptian costume fete in 1913, Louis Tiffany commissioned a decor from Joseph Lindon Smith, an artist who had recorded in meticulous drawings the treasures of the archaeological digs. Guests masqueraded as Egyptians, Greeks, Hindus, Syrians, and Romans. John D. Rockefeller came in the costume of a Persian prince, and Tiffany himself presided over the party in the guise of a turbaned Egyptian potentate. He engaged the New York Philharmonic Orchestra to play a score especially composed by Theodore Steinway and hired Ruth St. Denis as his featured attraction. As the entertainment began, four Nubian slaves entered with a flourish, carrying on their shoulders a rolled oriental rug. They salaamed and unrolled their priceless cargo, St. Denis, who performed a sinuous Egyptian dance. Resplendent in jewels, remote, seductive, she embodied the sentiments of a popular song, "The Egypt in Your Smile":

> All the Orient is in your smile
> Mysterious as the River Nile
> And you stole my heart
> With your cunning heart
> And the Egypt in your smile.

Famous and fashionable, St. Denis enjoyed the peak period of her solo career during the years between 1909 and World War I. With other dancers who bore the stamp of European approval—Isadora Duncan, Maud Allan, Loie Fuller, Adeline Genée, Anna Pavlova, and Mikhail Mordkin, St. Denis helped to pioneer a new form of American dance presentation, the legitimate theatre concert. Though early modern dance had developed in a public context of variety and vaudeville and in the private domain of society parties and matinees, St. Denis and her colleagues created a new role for dance independent of wealthy patrons and vaudeville circuits. On the strength of their reputations, they were able to fill the audiences of concert halls, though they returned to the popular stage now and again for larger salaries. Of these pioneers, St. Denis was the most influential in creating a new concert audience for American dance. Long after her colleagues had returned to the more comfortable climate of the European stage, St. Denis continued touring small-town America, drawing from its depths the audiences and dancers who would create the institutions of modern dance.

During Ruth's absence in Europe, trade magazines had kept her name alive with reports of her command performances before royalty and gossip about her tiffs with theatre managers. As she returned to New York in the fall of 1909, her American audience was primed and waiting, but she faced an uncertain future. "I don't know what Harris is going to do with me," she mused, but she needn't have worried. While she was away, Henry B. Harris had consolidated his position as one of the most powerful producers in America. In 1908 he completed the purchase of the Hudson Theatre, which he had managed until then. He also owned the Hackett Theatre, with seven stage stars and eleven productions under his management that season. Though he had been in the threatre business only five years, his fortuitous sponsorship of Charles Klein's hit play, The Lion and the Mouse, made him rich and allowed him the freedom to gamble. For a time he tried a supper theatre that failed, then converted that operation into the Fulton Theatre. He also planned a school for actresses, with classes in theatre history, voice culture, French and German, fencing and dance, and in 1909 he turned his attentions to Ruth St. Denis. Harris became Ruth's manager, booking her into legitimate theatres.

For her reappearance on the American stage, Harris scheduled his star for a series of matinees in the same theatre that launched her solo career. On the afternoon of November 16, 1909, at the Hudson Theatre, Ruth presented her original trio of dances, plus the Yogi and Nautch, new to American audiences. As the final curtain fell, she knew she was a success. She received nearly a dozen curtain calls, and the New York Times critic praised her dancing as "music in color and motion." Buoyed by her success, Harris sponsored her in an unprecedented and risky series of evening concerts, sure to attract both male and female patrons. "Monday night I play the nights!" Ruth gleefully recorded in her diary, and the New York Herald noted that the occasion was "one of the few times when a dancer has held the stage of a New York theatre as a regular evening attraction."

St. Denis always had star quality, that elusive genius that ignites onstage, but during her European tour she had acquired the accouterments of stardom, what her admirers called "class." She traveled now with an entourage that included, by one reporter's count, "one mother, one brother, one treasurer, twelve assorted Hindoos (guaranteed not to fade), diverse and sundry maids and secretaries." Her rippling arms were insured by Lloyd's of London. Her sets and costumes, refurbished abroad, were more costly and elaborate, her music, more sophisticated. Under the direction of Walter Meyrowitz, accompaniment for *The Nautch* now required four musicians onstage, while the simple cello melody for *The Yogi* swelled at its climax to a full-orchestra crescendo. For her touring program Ruth added a lantern-slide lecture on the Orient, delivered by a company member during the delays between her dances. Not only was her program more polished, her diverse solos now seemed unified by a progressively deepened spirituality, noted a Chicago critic who wrote that her art was "a consolation for almost an eternity of banal theatre."

The intensified spirituality of Ruth's dances reflected the growth in her spiritual life. By instinct and inheritance, she was a mystic who sought the direct experience of, and union with, God. Concerned with sin, she adopted the mystic's view of evil as an absence of Being or a false perspective on Reality, rather than as a vital force that vies with good. The genealogy of St. Denis' particular brand of mysticism can be traced through American Transcendentalism to the Swedenborgian mysticism of her parents' Eagleswood colony, to her explorations of Christian Science and, ultimately, Vedanta, the spiritual and philosophical background of Hinduism.

Americans of St. Denis' generation encountered Vedanta indirectly through the writings of European philosophers such as Schopenhauer or the American Transcendentalists, particularly Ralph Waldo Emerson, who studied the *Bhagavad-Gita* and the *Upanishads* in translation and adapted the Vedic concept of a universal spirit to his own definition of an Oversoul. A more direct introduction of Vedanta to the Western world came through a landmark event, the World Parliament of Religions at the World's Columbian Exposition in Chicago in 1893. One of the delegates to that convocation was an Indian swami, Vivekananda, whose flowing robes and yellow turban and clear exposition of Vedanta made him the popular favorite of the parliament. His subsequent lecture tours drew huge crowds from Baltimore to Brooklyn, where Ruth St. Denis' mother may have heard him speak.

Vivekananda adhered to the non-dualist school of Vedanta, as outlined by the sage Sankara, who emphasized the unqualified nature of Reality, the one pure Experience beyond the world of objects including the body and the mind. In preaching this ancient wisdom to Americans, Vivekananda encountered a welter of confusions. Bewildered by the varieties of popular mysticism, from spiritualism to Theosophy to Eastern thought, his listeners seemed unable to distinguish between serious spiritual doctrine and sham. They equated the Hindu religion with ritual immolation and occult sacrifice, and one Detroit matron demanded to know why Hindus sacrificed their female children to crocodiles. Vivekananda replied with gentle irony that perhaps females were more malleable, then went on to win his listeners' sympathies by stressing the validity of all religions as vehicles for reaching pure Experience. He institutionalized this belief by founding the Ramakrishna Mission, named for his own guru and dedicated to "the establishment of fellowship among the followers of different religions, knowing them all to be so many forms only of one undying Eternal Religion."

The non-sectarian nature of Vivekananda's approach appealed to Ruth. In 1908 in the company of Constance Smedley, she traveled from London to Surrey to meet Swami Paramananda, a disciple of Vivekananda and a member of the Ramakrishna Order. Then just twenty-five years old, Swami Paramananda already had begun perpetuating his master's teachings. "The central aim of Vedanta," he wrote, "is to bring all to one unifying understanding, yet to let each one follow his own particular form of faith." Swami Paramananda later settled in Boston, where he founded a spiritual center with a branch in California, and he published volumes of comparative literature, including a study of the Vedic influences on Emerson. As late as 1933 his Vedanta magazine, *The Message of the East,* still contained references to St. Denis, who was active in the Vedanta center in New York. Swami Paramananda was Ruth's initiator, the first authentic teacher of Vedanta she had encountered, though she had come across "a number of fake Yogi, trading on women's leisure and curiosity." Her meeting with the Swami marked the "beginning of a liberal spiritual education."

In the early days of her encounter with Vedanta, Ruth approached its doctrines through the prism of Christian Science. "The concentration of the mind upon one thought, the constant reiteration of that thought and ultimately complete belief in it—these are the cardinal principles of the two religions," she told a newspaper reporter in 1911. "The prayers of the Brahman are a series of declarations and denials. They deny evil and declare good and as the mind constantly dwells upon a single thought it ultimately comes not only to believe but to know the basic idea of that thought is a great truth." As she deepened her understanding of Vedanta, she realized that its doctrines involved more than the power of positive thinking, and in 1955 she declared that "Christian Science is the kindergarten of the higher Vedanta." In her late years Ruth carried with her two dog-eared books—a Bible, and an anthology of Sankara's writings.

From the beginning of her career, her dances reflected Hindu practices and Vedic concepts, from the puja ritual in *Incense* to the state of *samadhi,* or self-realization, depicted at the opening and close of *Radha.* St. Denis borrowed this meditative state from *Radha* and extended it into a full dance in *The Yogi,* her most rigorous philosophical exploration in dance and, surprisingly, a favorite among audiences and critics on her first American dance tour. One observer described *The Yogi* as "superficially the most simple and psychologically the most profound of her dances."

The 1909–10 tour took Ruth from New York to the Midwest and back along the East Coast, under the aegis of Henry Harris. After the initial Hudson Theatre performances, Harris booked Ruth into a Chicago theatre for two weeks of evening and matinee concerts during the Christmas season. As she prepared to depart New York, she received a telegram from Mrs. Potter Palmer, grande dame of Chicago society, asking that she perform free at a charity benefit. Mrs. Palmer shrewdly suggested that St. Denis would benefit from her own charitable contribution. "It would be a great kindness," she wrote, "and it would be good advertisement for you." Ruth accepted the invitation, and the ensuing publicity assured packed houses for her own performances at the Colonial Theatre.

A discerning eye in her Chicago audience might have noted a fair and aging "Hindu" among Ruth's supporting cast. Her father, finally persuaded to share in her growing fame, had come along on tour, though he refused to join his wife and son in adopting the St. Denis surname. Tom Dennis fussed with the lights backstage until union stagehands ejected him, then joined in the crowd scenes of his daughter's dances. His wife sat out front, taking notes; Brother St. Denis served as stage manager. The family was together again, reunited by Ruthie's prosperity. With her European profits, she had purchased a home on Staten Island for her father's use, and for her mother and herself she rented a studio on Fifty-seventh Street in Manhattan.

As her fame and fees increased, Ruth had problems with her company of Indians. One of her stage attendants, Mahomet Ismail, sued her on the grounds that he had invented her dances, but his suit was dismissed in court. Those Hindus who remained loyal to St. Denis were vegetarians who kept their own kind of kosher on tour. They refused to eat food that they considered unclean, and when their special food hampers accidentally were left behind in Chicago, they fasted for thirty-six hours on the way to Boston. They were labeled "colored" in Jim Crow America. In 1915 Ruth told a reporter that she did not dare book this early company south of the Mason-Dixon line because of the overt hostility of railway and streetcar conductors. Even in the North the Hindus could not stay at the same hotels as St. Denis or travel in her train compartment. One of the Indians decided to bolt and see America for himself, but Ruth was legally responsible for his whereabouts, having posted a bond in exchange for the Indians' visas. With the help of the Indian consul, she retrieved the deserter and kept her company in check long enough to finish the tour.

In Boston, St. Denis introduced a new dance, *The Lotus Pond,* set to languid music by Walter Meyrowitz. The setting was a Kashmiri garden. As the curtain rose the Rani (St. Denis) lay drowsing in the lazy warmth of summer, idly plucking lotus blossoms from the banks of the pond. In a sudden caprice she rose and danced about the garden, her yellow gown and green veil trailing behind her in the breeze. Her handmaidens watched, plaiting flower garlands. Bending over the pond, the Rani reached to pluck another blossom but disturbed a bumblebee that angrily buzzed around her veils. At once the tranquil atmosphere vanished. The music buzzed in agitated rhythms, as the Rani trembled and ran in fitful flight. As she fled she spied in the distance the approach of her beloved. Her mood changed to tender joy. She danced and twined blossoms in her hair until her beloved appeared onstage, playfully handing him a flower as the curtain fell.

The Lotus Pond was the first in a series of lyrical dances inspired by Isadora Duncan. Ruth may have modeled the dance on Duncan's *The Gallant, the Bee: Being His Visit to a Garden,* which Duncan performed during the 1898–99 season in New York, though Ruth claimed that she saw Duncan dance only twice, the first occasion being 1908 in London. On that occasion, Isadora evoked "visions of the morning of the world," Ruth remembered. "She was not only the spirit of true Greece in her effortless, exquisitely modulated rhythms, but she was the whole human race, moving in that joy and simplicity and childlike harmony."

Duncan, like St. Denis, was born to a willful, artistic mother and a creative but absentee father. She too began her career in American variety and danced for society gatherings, at one time performing a dance interpretation of the exotic *Rubaiyat* of Omar Khayyam. She appeared in Augustin Daly plays and solo recitals in New York, then traveled to London in 1899, where she presented concerts while St. Denis appeared with the London company of *Zaza*. Duncan also visited the Paris Exposition of 1900 and toured Germany, but unlike St. Denis, she made Europe her permanent home.

Both dancers belonged to a generation of American artists influenced by John Ruskin's essays on the morality of beauty and the Americanized mysticism of the Transcendentalists Emerson, Whitman, and Thoreau. While St. Denis studied Emerson's source, Vedanta, Isadora read Schopenhauer, who himself studied Vedanta and declared it the solace of his life. From this common intellectual heritage St. Denis and Duncan fashioned a rhetoric of Romanticism, but their ideas led them in different directions. They followed the polar paths of mysticism: one, seeking the Self in the Universe; the other, seeking the Universe in the Self. St. Denis, like Emerson, probed toward an unseen center, cultivating an interior space. Duncan, like Walt Whitman whom she admired, created an expanding consciousness that seemed to consume the cosmos. "Each movement," Duncan wrote, "reaches in long undulations to the heavens and becomes part of the eternal rhythm of the spheres." Isadora moved with centrifugal energy, from her solar plexus. Ruth moved centripetally, toward her soul and stillness.

Watching Duncan's outpouring of dance, Ruth marveled at her "coordination of all the inner nerves and muscles and rhythms and bloodstream and energies, all the unseen ones, and as they flowed outward into the body and the extremities we had a spectacle of 'The Dance.'" Duncan seemed to dance in capital letters; St. Denis moved in script. Isadora massed her body with an architectural sense of volume and weight, while Ruth dissipated her own weight and mass in favor of the linear flow of Art Nouveau. St. Denis embroidered her body onto the very surface of the space that Duncan boldly occupied.

Duncan turned to Greek sources while St. Denis explored the Orient, but they came to the common discovery that earned for them their role as matriarchs of American modern dance. They rediscovered an impetus for movement. Like other early moderns—Louis Sullivan with his organic architectural detail, Henri Bergson with his vitalist philosophy, William James with his psychological "stream of consciousness"—St. Denis and Duncan found a way to incorporate time values into their art. Nature was their model. "All the motions one needs to study for dancing can be found in nature," St. Denis declared. "Take the invisible motions of the clouds at sunset; one form melts into another, while one is almost unconscious of a change. No motion should be sharply abrupt. There must be no angles. A cat lies down in a series of curves." She found this idea echoed in photographs of Chinese dancers. "The slight sway of the hips, the lovely twist of the shoulders, gives us that cosmic movement which lies at the base of creation." St. Denis used this spiral of the torso and the arms in her own choreography, but because she lacked Duncan's spatial awareness, her spirals remained within her own body rather than catapulting her into space.

Duncan felt that the Greek style was inherently dynamic. The softly rounded figures of Greek bas-reliefs often stood with weight resting on the balls of the feet, as if ready for movement. Isadora herself spoke of the "seeds of movement," just as Walt Whitman wrote that "the profit of rhyme is that it drops seed of a sweeter and more luxuriant rhyme." Duncan felt that the "primary or fundamental movements of the new school of dance must have within them the seeds from which will evolve all other movements, each in turn to give birth to others in unending sequence of still higher and greater expressions, thoughts, and ideas." The emblem of this organicism in movement was the spiral form. Emerson used the spiral as a central metaphor for his thought, an emblem of the rising, never-ending chain of human aspiration for the divine. Genevieve Stebbins and, later, Isadora Duncan and Ruth St. Denis used the spiral form to create a modern dance expressive of ideal beauty. The spiral was inherently dynamic, inherently temporal. It was the type of modern dance.

In animating dance and extending it to a fourth dimension where space was allied with time, Duncan was more successful than St. Denis, more rigorous in her movement explorations, less prone to commercial pressures, more open to the dynamic model that music offered to dance. St. Denis never quite freed herself from a static, pictorial approach to movement. She did create a series of lyrical dances, culminating in the exquisite *Liebestraum* of 1922, and she experimented for a time with "music visualizations," the translation into movement of the structure of musical compositions. But the dictates of her own person-

ality and economic stringencies always drove her back to the more colorful, formulaic dancing for which she became famous. Privately, she
regarded Isadora as a symbol of all that she was not, a path-breaker
rather than a popularizer. "One of the bitterest disappointments of my
career," Ruth wrote in 1925, "is that I had to be an Indian—a Japanese
—a statue—a something or somebody else—before the public would give
me what I craved." She craved success, but she won it at a price. "The
'caviar to the many' is tragedy for the artist," she said. "My whole art
life has been a slow tragedy."

The Duncan-inspired *Lotus Pond* increased Ruth's touring repertoire
to six dances. She opened her programs with *Cobras* and *Incense,* followed by the lively *Nautch* and her new solo, then closed with the austere *Yogi* and the durable *Radha.* At each stop on her 1909–10 tour,
Ruth encountered enthusiastic audiences, and she demonstrated a new
maturity in her ability to control their attention. In Washington, when
two men began to laugh during *The Yogi,* another onlooker reported
that St. Denis managed to maintain her composure and keep her audience riveted on the barely perceptible movements of the dance. In
Plainfield, New Jersey, more than three hundred Somerville residents
traveled to the theatre by trolley to see the hometown girl who made
good. Little more than a decade had lapsed since Ruthie Dennis abandoned Pin Oaks with her family shamed by bankruptcy. Now she had
used her European earnings to repurchase the upper half of the farm
and with it, her self-respect. Nourished by appreciative audiences in
Baltimore, Philadelphia, and St. Louis, she traveled on to Cleveland
where a letter awaited her from Henry Harris, stating that he was
ready to produce *Egypta.*

When her tour closed in mid-spring, Ruth retreated to her father's
home on Staten Island to recuperate and to plan her Egyptian ballet.
This was her first attempt at a full-length dance production. Though
she claimed in her autobiography that she had only six weeks to prepare *Egypta,* her diary of June 29, 1910, indicates that she was busy
working on the ballet six months in advance of its December premiere.
She planned to use her earliest version of *Egypta,* the one-act dance
copyrighted in 1905, as the kernel of a much grander production. That
earliest dance dealt with *Egypta's* examination before the gods in the
Great Hall of Judgment and her depiction of the cycle of Egyptian history in the course of a single day, "The Dance of Day." To these original ideas Ruth added a palace dance, a scene on the banks of the River

Nile, and a temple dance reminiscent of *Radha*. She plagiarized herself for movement ideas, using the arm ripples of *Incense* for her river invocation, elements of *The Nautch* for her palace dance, and the rituals of *Radha* for her appearance as the goddess Isis.

Ruth gave these new dances Egyptian flavor by studying her European notes and illustrated texts, notably the works of E. A. Wallis Budge, curator of the British Museum's Egyptian section. She also borrowed details of dress and decor from James Henry Breasted's *History of Egypt* and J. Gardiner Wilkinson's *The Ancient Egyptians*. A woodcut illustration in the latter volume depicts women's garments similar to the costumes St. Denis wore in *Egypta*. From panels of Egyptian wall-carvings she devised a two-dimensional dance of profile poses for Egypta's attendants, one of the chief novelties of the production.

With the help of her mother, Ruth began organizing her ideas into a four-act dance. "Ruthie is a very good gatherer of materials," Mrs. St. Denis liked to say. "It's my job to put it all together." Mother and daughter collaborated on choreography in a process Ruth described in an interview in 1913:

> I rush in to Mother and tell her I have a new idea. She gasps and there is fearful turmoil all over the house in anticipation of what always happens. I get some one to play the piano; then I turn out all the drawers and get all the costumes together and sit down to think out the action and the pictures. The beginning and ending are the things that count most. The middle is usually rather fierce. From that on it is merely putting in detail and getting it to run smoothly with the music and originating the right scenery.

Ruth still thought in pictures, linking image to image, pose to pose. Music was a secondary consideration, and she asked only that her dance and the Meyrowitz music "run smoothly" together. As she choreographed *Egypta*, she enjoyed rehearsing before an invited audience, a practice ultimately vetoed by her mother who forced her to work alone. "Well, Ruthie, it's about eighty-five percent," she would say, "but we have to get the other fifteen percent before you open."

While Ruth choreographed for a newly recruited company of fifty supporting dancers and musicians, her brother designed the *Egypta* production. He created a light tower which shone a thousand-watt spotlight through colored lenses to suggest subtle gradations of atmosphere.

During the "Dance of Day" he modulated the lighting from the faint violet of dawn to the pale amber rays of sunrise to the white light of noon. For the "Festival of Ra" scene he created a sacred plain "so wonderfully lit that one could almost see the gray sands blowing about," sensational effects in the early days of electric stage lighting.

Ruth herself designed the *Egypta* costumes. Her basic attire was a transparent, ribbed tunic and a square-cut, black wig with jeweled headband. For her dance as Isis she wore diaphanous veils trimmed with gold and an elaborate headdress topped with horns and a lunar disk, similar to that depicted in E. A. Wallis Budge's study of the Egyptian gods. As the palace dancer Ruth bared her torso and wore only a wide Egyptian collar and halter, arm-bands, jeweled girdle, and transparent skirt of deep blue. In some photographs she substituted transparent cloth for the halter, and her breasts peeped from under her collar. Her red wig hung in braids tipped with gold beads, and fringe from her jeweled headband caressed each ear.

Each scene for *Egypta* had its own elaborate decor. For the opening scene on the banks of the Nile, a cyclorama painted with palm trees transformed the stage into a lush oasis. The temple set, copied from Beerbohm Tree's design for *False Gods,* was an imposing series of receding pillars. Belasco would have been proud. *Egypta* was opulent and expensive. Harris reportedly spent thirty thousand dollars on the production, including five hundred for the cyclorama and six hundred for the wigs alone. With a fortune riding on its reception, *Egypta* premiered on December 12, 1910, before a matinee audience at the New amsterdam Theatre in New York. It met with mixed success. The critics wrote gingerly of St. Denis' "thoughtful care in the preparation of her dances which were elaborately and tastefully staged," and agreed that while her own dancing was enchanting, her company of attendants seemed "anything but old Egyptian. They destroyed the very effect that she wished to produce. It was only when Miss St. Denis appeared upon the scene and all the others were quiet that the illusion was established and sustained."

Egypta, in its strengths and weaknesses, marked a critical juncture in Ruth's career. Essentially a solo artist, she tried with *Egypta* to expand her art across a larger landscape. Her model was the German theatre of Max Reinhardt, a fusion of dramatic dialogue, scenic design, lighting, music, and dance. Since 1905, when she copyrighted *Radha* as a "play without words," she had envisioned a new form of dance theatre which she described as "a sort of drama similar to pantomime, eliminating speech and leaving the natural motions that would accompany it. You get much the effect of when you listen to a play in a foreign language." This was dancing Delsarte, which worked for her shorter solos, but on the scale of *Egypta* her language proved too obscure, too static, for her audiences, and St. Denis lacked the proper balance among the artistic elements in her dance-dramas. "As plays they are only rudimentary," wrote one critic. "As spectacle they are imposing only at moments; dancing as generally understood is practically absent, the term being applied to a succession of poses, sinuous movements of body and limbs, and pantomime gestures." Yet, he conceded, "there is just now a cult for this sort of thing." St. Denis had her staunch supporters, including the influential Henry Harris, and the relative failure of *Egypta* left her only more determined to pursue her new form of dance theatre.

After only two weeks of matinee performances, Ruth dismantled *Egypta* and took it, piecemeal, on the road. Her touring program included three of the more portable and popular excerpts from *Egypta*—the "Dance of Day," the "Veil of Isis," and the palace dance—plus her standard East Indian solos. Just before she left on tour, one of her dancers mentioned that a prominent East Indian musician, Professor Inayat Khan, was lecturing at Columbia University. Ruth attended his lectures on the philosophy of Hindu music and persuaded the professor to join her company for the coast-to-coast tour. Another addition to her entourage was Emily Purkis, a costumer who later married Brother St. Denis.

During the spring of 1911 Ruth danced across the continent, from New York to Southern California, performing matinee and evening concerts in legitimate theatres. It was a grueling tour. In a single week she played one-night stands in Springfield, Milwaukee, Davenport and Des Moines, Kansas City and Topeka. Her Denver stay was almost a holiday, three luxurious days at the Broadway Theatre. In her audience was an impressionable, idealistic youth, a divinity student-turned-dancer, only nineteen years old. Ted Shawn saw before him a glamorous goddess who blended the two ideals most dear to his heart, divinity and dance. Watching St. Denis, he vowed that he too would become a "divine dancer," though he did not suspect that he would marry the high priestess herself. Three years intervened before their paths crossed again, as St. Denis traveled on West, Shawn, toward his own dance career.

Ruth reached San Francisco in early April. She performed at the Columbia Theatre where, a decade earlier, she had appeared with the touring company of *Zaza*. Just seven years earlier, on the *DuBarry* tour, she had paused to have her photograph taken as a young and earnest Egypta. Now she returned with the dance itself, or its fragments, to a city that always seemed sympathetic to her ideas. San Francisco, with its large oriental population and California climate of experimentation, was a hospitable home for varieties of mysticism. Even the clairvoyants and spiritualists had their own advertisement section in the San Francisco newspaper which reported that spring that a prominent matron, Mrs. Wickham Havens, had just completed the construction of her new East Indian mansion. Modeled on a Buddhist temple, the mansion included a marble altar flanked by incense burners where Ruth was invited to sit in the posture of Radha for christening ceremonies. She met the most important socialites and artists of San Francisco, including the playwright Richard Walton Tully, who took her on walking tours of Chinatown.

St. Denis dominated the newspaper pages during her two weeks in San Francisco. The society section reported on theatre parties of prominent citizens who returned to her concerts, night after night. The critic for *The Examiner* wrote several lengthy reviews, plus a full-page profile of the offstage St. Denis. He was astonished to find that the glamorous stage personality was only a gray-haired girl in sensible shoes who looked like "a school marm, a suffragette, or a rational clothes crank." She wore, he reported, the squarest, broadest shoes he had ever seen on the foot of a woman, but he was impressed with her intellect and sense of purpose. "I am trying to indicate the wonderful possibilities of the human body," she told him. "The art of dancing has become almost entirely objective. I am trying to make it subjective," a statement which became the credo of American modern dance.

From San Francisco Ruth traveled the length of California, performing one-night stands in small towns, until she settled in Los Angeles for a vacation at the end of the tour. She resumed voice lessons and took up the study of Japanese dance with a former geisha who lived in a Los Angeles suburb. Though this brief exposure was her first formal training in Japanese technique, St. Denis had seen Japanese drama and dancing, including the work of Sada Yacco, and she had created two Japanese dances of her own, *A Shirabyoshi* and her *Madame Butterfly* dance for Belasco. Japanese technique was torturous for a tall, loose-limbed farm girl, though Ruth struggled to emulate her teacher. "When I turned out my toes she turned hers in. When I straightened my knees she bent them. When I carried my head high, she perpetually drooped hers in that lovely line that I grew to watch forever after. With much pressing on my shoulders and much sagging of her own knees, she finally settled me in the classic mold, with knees bent, toes in, and eyes down. She was implacable."

Ruth learned that concentration of her energy was essential in mastering even the basics of Japanese technique. She applied her Delsartean theory of contraction and relaxation to her new Japanese technique. "The tendency of diffuseness of thought is toward relaxation," St. Denis wrote in 1913. "The trend of concentration is toward contraction. Japanese muscles are practically always contracted. Study the posture of the geisha. Her shoulders are drawn back, perhaps her face upturned in the similitude of trust, her fan fluttering its perfumed coquetries, but her muscles are taut as the rope that holds a straining ocean-liner at anchor." Ruth tried out her new Japanese postures on her California friends in a series of Japanese evenings hosted by her brother in Los Angeles.

In the midst of this California interlude, Ruth received a wire from Henry Harris, offering her a four-week vaudeville engagement in New York. She could not refuse. Vaudeville was anathema to her now that she had managed a tour of legitimate theatres, but Harris was still deeply in debt on her account. As headliner on a vaudeville bill, she could earn two thousand dollars per week, a portion of which would go to Harris as commission. She had only to perform a twenty-minute dance, rather than the full program required on concert tours. Ruth discussed the offer with her brother and asked him to consult with their mother, who always had the final word.

Brother wrote a long letter to Mrs. St. Denis, outlining the pros and cons of vaudeville and their debt to Harris. "Although I don't hold such a generous view toward Mr. Harris as Ruthie," he wrote, "on the other hand I don't hold with you and think that we owe him nothing. Setting aside the question of fairness or honesty, if we expect Mr. Harris to again back Ruth in some play or whatever manner the future may develop, we can hardly expect to have him for our manager only when the show is losing money." He reassured Mrs. St. Denis that the engagement was temporary. "We are not fooling ourselves about vaudeville." Reluctantly Mrs. St. Denis agreed, and Ruth returned home for two-a-day shows at Hammerstein's Victoria Theatre and Roof Garden during late July and early August.

The conflict between vaudeville and the legitimate stage was a persistent leitmotiv in St. Denis' career. She was a born lowbrow, her dance a product of Delsarte, dime museums, and variety, but she had high-art aspirations. The distinction between high and low art has become obscured in the pervasive mass culture of contemporary America, but in St. Denis' day the division was quite real. Vaudeville and "legit" were different worlds. Vaudeville paid better but "legit" had prestige. While a powerful syndicate controlled vaudeville, booking its artists with maximum efficiency, an individually booked concert tour was less reliable or remunerative. Concert tours also were more demanding, since the performer was responsible for an entire evening's entertainment rather than a single vaudeville act.

If vaudeville was less taxing, a dancer like St. Denis had to suffer the indignity of seeing her art quantified. Local vaudeville managers timed the duration of applause and the number of curtain calls for each act and sent reports to their New York offices. Artists were subjected to verbal abuse from house managers who stood in the wings and passed judgment—"Pep it up!" "That act stinks!" Legitimate concerts were far more dignified, but few concert managers had Henry Harris' entree to important theatres and few dancers had the box-office power to justify a concert tour. The *New York Clipper*, trade magazine for show people, carefully divided its touring performers into two separate listings: a Vaudeville Route List, and an "On the Road" listing for legitimate theatre performers. St. Denis' name belonged in the latter category. Her travel routes appeared alongside the schedules of touring plays and opera stars, and she enjoyed the prestige of association with Harris, who only handled legitimate theatre attractions. She had earned her highbrow status, and she guarded it jealously, for the distinction between high and low art went far deeper than mere prestige to the very nature of American art itself.

Irving Lowens, in his study of American music, identifies a basic schism in American art, a tension between "egalitarianism," or art that relies upon community, and "libertarianism," or art that caters to the few. A finer distinction, with regard to Ruth St. Denis' work, appears in Russel Nye's *The Unembarrassed Muse,* in which he characterizes popular art as confirming the experience of the majority, while fine art explores the new. St. Denis enjoyed the best of both worlds. Her dances confirmed Victorian values even as they explored new ground in movement and dramatic structure. She was a "class act" in vaudeville and a box-office draw in "legit." Janus-like, she maintained a delicate balance between high and low art, but her dance-dramas of the prewar period began to tip that balance. Too literal in their application of research, too loaded with message, too uneven in form, these dances baffled vaudeville patrons even as they excited a small coterie of admirers. During the 1912–14 period St. Denis experienced an erosion of her popular audience, her financial base. After seeing one of her dance-dramas, a critic declared that "the futurists, who have laid violent hands on art, at last have extended their influence to drama." Though her dances were hardly as experimental or radical as the Armory Show which introduced modern art to America just a month before the premiere of her *O-Mika*, St. Denis began to seem dangerously "arty." One observer of vaudeville praised the "artistic atmosphere" of St. Denis' dancing, but stated flatly, "It must be set down as hard fact that it fails utterly in its appeal to the regular patrons of vaudeville." Undeterred, Ruth continued her esoteric course, playing vaudeville long enough to repay Harris while continuing her experiments with the dance-drama form.

In the fall of 1911 Harris announced his season plans and stated that after St. Denis finished her vaudeville commitments, she would tour abroad "as far as India," while Richard Tully had been engaged to write a new play for Ruth. Tully, whose Hawaiian-flavored *Bird of Paradise* was a major hit at Daly's Theatre, had met Ruth as she toured the West Coast. They became fast friends. Tully may have been the "R" of St. Denis' autobiography, the married man she became infatuated with as they worked together on a new project, but the new Tully play never materialized and Ruth turned her attention to another project, two new dance-plays based on short stories by Lafcadio Hearn.

Several years earlier in London Ruth had based *A Shirabyoshi* on Hearn's tale of the same title, and she now turned to his collected stories, *Shadowings*, for material for another Japanese ballet. In that volume she found "A Legend of Fugen-Bosatsu," the story of a Japanese courtesan transformed into a goddess, and in the same book, in a listing of Japanese female names, she found her title, *O-Mika*, which means "new moon." Ruth envisioned *O-Mika* as a companion piece to a new Hindu ballet, *Bakawali*, based on another Hearn tale about a heavenly dancer who falls in love with a mortal. Both ballets incorporated the spoken word. Ruth commissioned Alice Elres to write dialogue for *Bakawali*, and for *O-Mika* she learned her Japanese lines phonetically from members of her troupe. Among her company members were Japanese, Indians, and Broadway actors, including Mogul Khan, who appeared with St. Denis for a decade, and Theodora DeCombe, who later distinguished herself in a supporting role to Maude Adams on Broadway. This company rehearsed, with Henry Harris' blessings, throughout the spring of 1912, preparatory to a May premiere.

On the morning of April 15, Ruth awoke to a headline in the New York *Times*: "Titanic Sinks Four Hours After Hitting Iceberg." By the next morning the banner headlines were black and bold as the scope of the tragedy became known: "866 RESCUED, PROBABLY 1250 PERISH; NOTED NAMES MISSING." Among the prominent passengers aboard the world's largest ocean liner on its maiden voyage were Mr and Mrs. John Jacob Astor, the painter Francis Millet, and Mr. and Mrs. Henry B. Harris. Mrs. Harris was safe, handed into the last lifeboat by her husband who gallantly relinquished his own seat to another woman. As the lifeboat drew away, Mrs. Harris watched in horror as her husband waved from the sinking deck. At the age of forty-six, Harris was dead. With him sank Ruth's hopes for a highbrow career, her financial security, her most valued professional friend.

The loss of Harris was a major blow. Ruth's family began to unravel, as it always did in crises. Her mother, who had warned against dependence on Harris, began to collapse under the strain and clung to Ruth, who responded by rebelling, on one occasion vanishing from the theatre and hiding in the home of acquaintances she barely knew. For a year she struggled to find society dates and odd jobs in vaudeville and tried to salvage her new dance-dramas. With the help of the Harris estate, after a long delay, she managed to present *O-Mika* and *Bakawali* on March 11, 1913, at the FultonTheatre in New York.

Bakawali, subtitled "A Hindu Love Tale of Indra's Heavenly Court," included four new dances, the "Dance of the Gold and Black Sari," which evolved into one of St. Denis' most popular solos; the "Jewel Dance Before the God of Heaven"; the "Dance in the Forest of Ceylon"; and the "Dance of the Blue Flame," which one critic suggested was a "pretty little imitation" of Loie Fuller's flame dance. Arthur Nevin wrote the musical score, and Joseph A. Physioc designed the set, which included a huge blue cyclorama lined with gauze and lighted from below to suggest the suspended, azure atmosphere of the heavens.

In the opening scene, a celestial dancer, Bakawali (St. Denis), fell in love with a mortal (Oswell Jackson) and sported with him on earth until fetched back to heaven in a wind chariot dispatched by the stern god Indra (Rex Tiffany). In the second scene as Bakawali underwent purification by fire, preparatory to appearing before Indra, she discovered that her lover, Taj, had foolishly followed her to heaven. Their dialogue, preserved in the scribbled marginalia on a copy of the score, included this exchange:

> BAKAWALI: You here! Alas what hast thou done? No mortal may come here and live again. Hast thou not seen what I have suffered? The agony of fire! But even yet more terrible the wrath of Indra when thou art discovered.
>
> TAJ: Nay then, I can but die. I could not let thee go. I hung upon thy chariot as they bore thee here.
>
> BAKAWALI: I can but bring great Indra in such a mood that he will pardon thee . . . perhaps the dance of dawn may win from him pardon . . .

As Bakawali approached Indra, who sat upon a golden lotus throne that appeared to float in the midnight sky, the great god thundered, "Thou has the odor of mortality about thee!" (When the actor fumbled this line in rehearsals, Mrs. St. Denis prompted from the audience, "That's where he says you smell bad, Ruthie.")

To appease Indra, Bakawali danced, and the choreography might have been suggested by Hearn's text in his short story:

> So she danced all those dances known in the courts of heaven, curving herself as flowers curve under a perfumed breeze, as water serpentines under the light, and she circled before them rapidly as a leaf-whirling wind, lightly as a bee, with myriad variations of delirious grace.

Beguiled by Bakawali's dance, Indra bestowed forgiveness, but his delight turned to rage as he discovered the presence of her lover. He pronounced a curse: for twelve years Bakawali should be frozen as stone from waist to feet. In the final forest scene Taj tenderly ministered to the immobile Bakawali for the prescribed dozen years, thus freeing her from the curse. As she came to life, she danced for joy.

Bakawali, with her symbolically frozen loins, was but one in a series of sexually repressed heroines portrayed by St. Denis. Tainted madonnas of the Belasco variety were a favorite persona, and there is a tantalizing hint that Belasco himself may have helped his former protégée refine both *Bakawali* and *O-Mika*. In one journalist's account of St. Denis' rehearsals, he mentioned a "well-known stage director who came in to polish dialogue."

Certainly *O-Mika* bore the Belasco stamp. In this Japanese dance-drama Ruth portrayed a courtesan, O-Mika, who became the incarnation of the Japanese goddess of mercy. The ballet opened with the vision of a Buddhist monk (Bunlaku Tokunaga) who learned that the goddess of mercy, Fugen-Bosatsu, might be seen incarnate in the courtesan O-Mika. Traveling to the Yoshiwara, or courtesan quarter, he found two samurai quarrelling over the favors of O-Mika. As she invited them inside her home to settle the dispute, the monk slipped in unnoticed and watched as O-Mika performed four dances: a ceremonial flower arrangement, a Chrysanthemum or Flower Hat dance, a spirited spear dance, and the slow and measured love dance of "A Thirteenth Century Poetess." At the close of these dances, she approached her samurai to choose between them, but meeting the eyes of the monk, she dropped her kimono and stood revealed in the raiment of the goddess of mercy. As she backed toward a niche and seated herself in the posture of Fugen-Bosatsu, the monk bowed at her feet while the samurai stood bewildered.

The sets for the ballet, designed by Soken Ito, included a forest scene, the interior of the courtesan's apartments, and large murals which flanked the proscenium arch of the stage, all rendered with exquisite detail. Robert H. Bowers wrote the score for O-Mika's dances. Ruth called *O-Mika* "little dramas with dancing interludes." The dances themselves were variations on the "transformation dances" then popular in vaudeville in which the performer shed a layer of costume with the beginning of each new routine. Ruth wore trousers and five kimonos of delicate crepe—salmon, violet, amber, rose, and green—layered under her embroidered cloak. She gradually shed each kimono until she wore a base garment of pale blue chiffon as Fugen-Bosatsu. Not only did her costumes signal each new dance, they also dictated choreography. The movements of the "Thirteenth Century Poetess" were slow and measured, she said, "owing to the fact that she must softly kick before her the long red trousers worn under her robe."

The Japanese garb proved restrictive for Ruth, who found the obi "as bad as the corset, all contrived allure." Still a dress-reformer, she preferred the freer costume of the samurai warrior, loose pajamas worn in an abandoned sword dance performed with Brother St. Denis. Ruth said the dance "showed the possibilities of the torso in its strange contradiction of rigidity and suppleness," but a critic found in her bold swordplay a suggestion of the emancipation of American women. "Here was no timidity or restraint, but breezy joyous exercise of boldness and muscle," the female critic enthused. "Women's deftness and agility were matched with man's strength and skill, without fear or favor." Another, perhaps more realistic, reviewer remarked that the sword dance was "a sort of Edmund Russell number, such as one has seen that entertainer extraordinary give on his aesthetic Thursday afternoons," suggesting that St. Denis' dance-dramas may have dated back to her days with the Progressive Stage Society.

Despite its inauthenticity, *O-Mika* won the approval of an audience of native Japanese. Invited to perform the dance before the Japan Society at the Hotel Astor, St. Denis charmed the Japanese with her costume and manner, her "air of refinement," though the critic for the *Japanese Times* questioned the vaudevillian antics of the samurai who fought over O-Mika, saying that their slapstick routine "smacked of a cheap show." Other reviewers echoed this criticism, and most of them found *O-Mika* and *Bakawali* merely static and boring, however beautiful. "It may be that Miss St. Denis will find a sufficient number of seekers after illumination along these lines to give her a profitable patronage," one critic wrote, "but it seems doubtful when one takes into consideration the multitude of places where, instead of merely being a looker on, anyone may personally participate in the intoxication of turkey trotting."

So long as Americans were content to sit and watch dancing as a remote and exotic spectacle, St. Denis was secure, but by 1912 Americans had discovered dancing for themselves. They turkey-trotted, tangoed, and bunny-hugged. Women, emancipated by the bicycle and bloomers, adopted ballroom dancing as a badge of liberation, and their antics shocked their more conservative countrymen who still questioned the propriety of the waltz. As *O-Mika* premiered in 1912, the New York *Tribune* printed a front-page report of the latest dancing scandal. "There have been turkey trotting and bunny hugging all winter in the capital smart set, introduced with considerable grace and no revolting features," the story explained, "but all agree that last night the freakish dance reached the limit of propriety." The young wife of a congressman, "as fascinating as she is bizarre," had appeared in a tube gown, smoking a cigarette, and "pirouetted across the ballroom floor clinging to her partner like a last bet on a lost cause."

The furor from the pulpit matched the frenzy of the dancing. This criticism was muted in more sophisticated cities but in the American heartland fundamentalist preachers warned their congregations that social dancing could lead to pregnancy, venereal disease, and to the ultimate decay of American society. One of the most popular documents supporting this position was Mordecai Ham's *The Modern Dance: A Historical and Analytical Treatment of the Subject,* published in Texas in 1916. With pseudoscientific methodology, Reverend Ham discussed the psychology of the dance craze, quoting from outraged physicians and social workers. His message was simple: Dancing was responsible for broken homes, illegitimate children, war, disease, and an entire catalogue of social ills. He told the story of Mrs. Edna Wagner, only thirty-two years old, who died after dancing the tango continuously for four hours, and the gent from South Carolina whose eye was poked out by the quill in his dancing partner's hat. Lurid subtitles in his text included "Men Must Fondle Girls' Feet" and "Undergarments Worn for Public View," and he included as a frontispiece a photograph of his baby daughters with the caption "Two Reasons Why I fight the dance." Ham's argument reflected the fears of war-era Americans who saw their familiar framework for behavior dissolving in the tinkle of ragtime and the thump of dancing feet.

All dancers labored under the opprobrium of the pulpit. The quintessential ballroom dancers of the day, Vernon and Irene Castle, went to great lengths to justify their art as hygienically, morally, and aesthetically useful. In her introduction to the Castles' text on modern dancing, Elisabeth Marbury tried a novel approach, agreeing with the clergy that certain dances were indeed vulgar. "Let us cooperate with our guardians of civic decency," she exhorted her readers, "and aid them constructively in the elimination of the coarse, the uncouth, the vulgar, and the vicious. Let us establish once and for all a standard of modern dancing which will demonstrate that these dances can be made graceful, artistic, charming, and above all, *refined*." Ruth St. Denis tried the same approach as social dancing preempted the appeal of her art. She joined in the fun, in a refined sort of way. In the summer of 1913 she appeared at the popular outdoor festival in Chicago's Ravinia Park. She was fifth choice for the job. When the Baroness Irmgard von Rottenthal, originally signed for a four-week appearance, cut her stay in half, Ravinia officials searched for a popular dancer as replacement. They tried to book the British ballerina Lydia Loupokova, the health faddist Lady Constance Stewart-Richardson, and vaudeville's Mlle. Dazie, but finally settled on St. Denis, who agreed to perform her high-toned dances outdoors, without scenery. She needed the work. She presented her Indian, Egyptian, and Japanese dances, plus a new solo, "The Rosebuds," to the "Amaryllis" tune she had warbled in *Madame DuBarry*. When the crowd politely applauded, she broke into an impromptu encore. Throwing a green veil over her Egyptian costume, she instructed the orchestra conductor to strike up a Victor Herbert tune and kicked up her heels in a stylish cakewalk-cum-tango. The crowd went wild and made her repeat it, and one critic said that the dance rescued her repertoire and reputation which were "somewhat sicklied over with the pale cast of pseudo-seriousness."

The Impromptu or *The Louis Quatorze Cakewalk* became a part of Ruth's repertoire, but she needed more popular dances on her programs to retain public interest. She decided to hire a ballroom dance team to share her concerts. In the spring of 1914 the ideal candidate appeared. Ted Shawn stopped by her studio for an audition and stayed to become her partner for life.

EGYPTA

CHOREOGRAPHY: Ruth St. Denis

MUSIC: Walter Meyrowitz

PREMIERE: New Amsterdam Theatre, New York, December 12, 1910

SCENE ONE: THE INVOCATION TO THE NILE

SETTING: The curtain rises on a tropical scene on the banks of the River Nile. It is dawn. A cyclorama painted with palm trees forms the backdrop for the river in the foreground, a broad wash of green fringed with hedges and bulrushes. From the gates of a temple upstage, a stairway leads down to the river banks, passing between two massive stone gods seated on thrones carved with hieroglyphs. Flowers float on the river, twine about trees, and adorn the gods and the singing maidens who fill the stairway as Egypta descends to worship.

SCENARIO: Egypta, wearing a transparent, ribbed tunic and black wig, descends the stairway, framed by two rows of chanting maidens. She carries a flower-chain in each arm and walks in undulating rhythms to the water's edge. She kneels, and as her maidens file past, she accepts food and gifts which she casts upon the waters. Bending low, her chest almost grazing the water, her face upturned toward the gods, Egypta begins her invocation to the Nile. She lifts her arms in sinuous ripples toward the heavens, suggesting the rising of the waters. As her arms spiral, she gradually rises from her knees to stand with her arms outstretched, palms upturned. She reascends the stairway and enters the temple gates.

SCENE TWO: THE FEAST OF ETERNITY

SETTING: A great banquet hall. Guests in festal garments sit on stools and chairs, sampling food and wine served by Nubian slaves. Tables laden with fruit and flowers surround the revelers.

SCENARIO: As the guests amuse themselves, eight dancers appear and perform a series of two-dimensional poses derived from Egyptian wall carvings. Theirs is a dance of shapes rather than volume, of decorative poses in flattened profile. As they conclude, a priest appears to address the assembled throng on the inevitability of death and the brevity of life: "Minister to the desire of thy heart," he admonishes the merrymakers, "for at length the day of lamentation shall come." To underscore his warning, a Nubian slave enters the dining hall, pulling behind him a mummy on a sled. He disappears with his eerie cargo, and the guests return to their amusement until four musicians appear with harp, tambourine, pipe, and lyre. They arrange themselves in profile attitudes, and from the rear of the stage a dancer enters between two curtains.

"The Tamboura"—The Palace Dancer wears a red wig, jeweled collar and girdle, and transparent skirt. She poses in profile, one leg lifted in gentle front *attitude,* her wrists drooping delicately over the lifted foot. She breaks into a quicksilver dance, flitting from posture to posture, moving primarily with her limbs rather than the volume of her body. As the dance concludes the guests resume their feast and the stage curtain closes.

SCENE THREE: THE MYSTERY OF ISIS

SETTING: A great temple of columns receding toward the focal point at center upstage, the throne of Isis, shrouded in gloom. There the goddess sits, wrapped in veils edged in heavy gold.

SCENARIO: Priests glide onstage, bearing votive lights. They make their obeisance to Isis, then quietly withdraw. The voice of a priest is heard offstage, chanting the praises of the goddess. He enters and offers incense, then prostrates at the idol's feet. She stirs. A shaft of light illumines her face and the delicate sweep of her lashes as she slowly comes to life. Isis lifts one hand in benediction. Stepping from her throne, she walks downstage, swaying. She assumes her identity as the goddess of the sky by lifting her veiling to expose the headdress of Hathor, with forked horns cradling the round disk of the moon. Underneath her veils she wears a straight, banded underslip covered with glistening bugle beads. She carries the bow and arrow of Neith, the great mother-goddess, and indicates with her veils the sweep of the skies, the sunrise, and the sorrows of Isis in her search for her dead consort, Osiris. Then she draws her veils about her and returns to the throne as gloom descends once more.

SCENE FOUR: THE PLAINS OF RA

SETTING: A gray expanse filled with mist and surrounded by rocky cliffs.

SCENARIO: In the pre-dawn hours dancers bend in the breeze, their draperies suggesting the swirling morning mist. They sway to and fro, circle aimlessly, then cluster, until the first faint rays of sunlight appear. Egypta sleeps upstage, on a stone slab. As the light reveals her presence, she rises and reaches her arms toward her life source, the sun.

"The Dance of Day"—Wearing a simple white, pleated tunic, Egypta mimes the life cycle of the Egyptian nation, using the metaphor of a twelve-hour day. She follows a floor pattern, an imaginary sun dial, with each activity occurring at a different hour on the dial. She dances the morning rhythms of peasants in their labors, sowing and reaping, her upper body bowed under an unseen weight. She mimes fishing, kneading bread, building, carrying water, all in profile postures. As the sun rises to noon, she depicts the pomp of kings, priests, artists, and musicians, the practice of archery by the military. The sun descends to late afternoon, and she mimes wars, alarums, invasions, until, in the lurid red light of the sinking sun, she falls stricken. The shifting mists reappear. It is dark. The moon begins to rise.

"The Dance of Night"—Egypta moves downstage to stand in a ghostly green light. In one hand she carries a small red heart. Behind her, the Great Hall of Judgment emerges from the greenish gloom. The great god Osiris sits upstage center, flanked by rows of judges, twenty-one to either side, painted in profile on staggered flats. In the foreground center is the

Great Scale of Justice. To one side stands Thoth, the scribe; on the other is Ammit, the Devourer of the Dead with the forequarters of a crocodile, and Anubis, the guide of the dead and examiner of the scales.

Horus, the hawk-headed Introducer of the Dead, steps forward and leads Egypta into the hall, taking her heart in his hand. He asks her to perform for the assembled gods. She dances a negative confession, addressing each sin to one of the forty-two gods: "I did not steal . . . I did not beat my slaves . . . I did not commit adultery . . . ," with Thoth keeping score. She completes her recitation and stands with her back to the gods, trembling, awaiting their verdict. Anubis places Egypta's heart on the scale. As it balances perfectly with the Feather of Justice, a great instrumental shout rings from the orchestra.

"The Golden Boat of Ra"—Egypta runs from the footlights through the knees of Osiris toward the backdrop which rises to reveal the Boat of Ra traveling toward the Elysian Fields. Egypta steps aboard as the curtain falls.

———◆———

Egypta is the most elusive of St. Denis' major ballets. Its score has vanished; it was never recorded on film. It survives only in photographs and the printed word, but traces of St. Denis' former dances are clearly discernible between the lines. Her lively dance in the Egyptian banquet hall recalled the "Rektah" dance of *Radha* and *The Nautch,* and the opening moments of "The Mystery of Isis" duplicated the priestly processional from *Radha.* For "The Invocation to the Nile" St. Denis used the arm ripples of *Incense,* and she borrowed the flower chains from Radha's "Dance of Smell." The source of her sun-worship ritual which opened the "Dance of Day" may have been a Genevieve Stebbins drill which instructed the Delsarte practitioner to

> 1. Place the backs of the hands on the forehead, fingers touching, while standing erect on both feet.
> 2. Extend the arms to the sides, palms down, while bowing the trunk and head; do not bend the knees. Be careful to have the arms and trunk form a cross; do not carry the arms too far behind.

3. Turn the hands and bring the arms above the head, hands in prayer form, palm to palm, while trunk has been lifting.

4. Again extend the arms sideways, trunk bowing.

5. Raise trunk as arms sweep above head to Position 3, which is the symbol of the flame, and henceforward will be named Flame Attitude.

6. Twist the trunk to the right, while holding Flame Attitude.

7. Extend arms sideways, bowing trunk in reverence to rising sun.

The drill was part of Stebbins' Eastern Temple Drill, adapted from various forms of oriental worship.

The scenario for "The Feast of Eternity" paralleled E. A. Wallis Budge's written descriptions of Egyptian banquet feasts for the dead. In *The Dwellers on the Nile* Budge described this ancient practice:

The guests arrayed in festal garments, with plenty of scented grease on their heads and (if women) flowers in their hair, sat on ebony and ivory stools or chairs, and ate course after course of meats, vegetables, and sweetmeats, and drank large quantities of beer sweetened with honey and wine . . . Among the selection of songs sung on such occasions was a dirge, the object of which was to remind the host and his guests that, however much they were enjoying themselves at that moment, the day would assuredly come when they must die; in some cases, to drive this lesson home into the minds of the company, the host had a mummy on a sledge drawn through the dining hall.

St. Denis excerpted portions of this description for her own program notes, and she followed Budge's description of the Hall of Judgment myth in *The Book of the Dead* down to the very names and positions of each participant and the procedure for weighing the heart of the accused.

St. Denis' efforts at historical accuracy may have been her undoing. *Egypta*, by most eyewitness accounts, was so loaded with symbolism, scenery, and ritual that its dance impulse barely survived. One critic characterized the production as "rather a solemn ritual of danceless dances," which serves as a fitting epitaph.

SIX

TEDRUTH

ONLY TED SHAWN could have persuaded Ruth St. Denis to accept a professional partnership and marriage. He was her match in ambition, narcissism, and idealism, if not in creative genius or chronology. He was just twenty-three years old to her thirty-five, the son of a Denver newspaperman and a mother descended from the Booth family of actors. Mary Lee Booth Shawn, like St. Denis' mother, produced amateur plays starring her own child, and eventually Teddy channeled his dramatic talent toward a career in evangelism. Deeply religious, he studied theology at the University of Denver until, in his junior year, he became partially paralyzed from a severe case of diphtheria. He turned to dance to restore his muscular control and began to affect the airs of an artist—flowing cravat, low collar, abstracted mien. "He was shy and reserved in those first days," Ruth remembered, "and his voice had a curious flat quality which manifested sadness." Charmed by this Young Werther, she felt that she might give him "a new willingness to life."

He came to her as acolyte to goddess, novice to master artist. He was looking for a job. In Denver he had studied dancing with Hazel Wallack, a product of the Metropolitan Opera Ballet who made Ted her partner for local performances and, was for a time, her fiancé. From Denver he drifted to Los Angeles, where he worked as a stenographer and formed a small dance company with another teacher, Norma Gould. Ted and Norma performed a popular series of "tango teas" in Los Angeles hotels, and before they left the fledgling film capital, Ted made a short film of period dances, *Dances of the Ages*, for the Edison Company. But these modest successes failed to satisfy his search for a blending of theatrical and spiritual values until he found what he was looking for in *The Making of Personality*, a book by Bliss Carman.

Carman was then poet-in-residence at the Triunian School of Personal Harmonizing in New Haven, Connecticut. With his companion, Mary Perry King, who directed the school, Carman advocated a philosophy of "Personal Harmonizing," rooted in the Delsartean idea of Triune man, the simultaneous cultivation of body, mind, and soul. In *The Making of Personality* Carman argued that dancing was an ideal vehicle for "bodily and emotional freedom and nervous relief as well as stimulus to expression within the limits of orderly beauty," and he praised Ruth St. Denis' efforts to create a dance that was physically, mentally, and spiritually nourishing. After reading Carman's book, Ted corresponded with the poet, and in 1914 he set out for New Haven, working his way East by performing ballroom dances with Norma Gould at stops along the route of the Santa Fe Railroad. Arriving at the Triunian School, Ted took a crash course in the principles that had shaped St. Denis' art—Delsarte, statue-posing, gymnastics, and natural movement such as yawning and deep-breathing. His teacher was Mary Perry King who had studied the Delsarte system with Henrietta Russell Hovey, the prominent Delsartist whose first husband was Ruthie Dennis' flamboyant friend Edmund Russell. Inevitably, this network of new acquaintances led Ted to the feet of the divine dancer herself. Through Brother St. Denis in New York City, Ted requested an interview with Ruth.

Their first meeting was memorable. Waiting expectantly for the exotic apparition he had once seen onstage, Ted was startled when a white-haired, slightly knock-kneed St. Denis strode into the room in dishabille, her hairpins awry, her hand extended in frank greeting. For her part, Ruth was taken with Ted's beauty. Six feet tall and beautifully proportioned, he might have been a model for Michelangelo's "David," his body all plush curves, his feet delicately arched. He wore the costume of a fierce Aztec warrior, but the face belonged to a teddy bear: chocolate brown eyes, chubby cheeks, petulant mouth. He was adorable, and talented, Ruth decided, as she watched him audition a spirited *Dagger Dance*. Her interest piqued, she began to probe his personality and unleashed a flood of talk that continued for fifty years.

They talked all that day, into the night. They shared pet theories and favorite authors, Emerson, Mary Baker Eddy, Delsarte. Each of Ted's previous female mentors—his mother, with her theatrical flair; his first dance partner, who nursed him back to health; the employer at a summer resort who exposed him to Christian Science; Mary Perry King, with her aesthetic theories—each of these women prepared Ted for an aspect of Ruth's multifaceted persona. He knew right away that she represented the pinnacle of his personal and professional aspirations. "I am a bit of driftwood tied up to your craft," he told her humbly in an early letter, and as they spoke that first evening, he paid homage to her genius. He told her of another evening in Denver when he first saw her perform and dedicated himself to a spiritual dance. He spoke eloquently, with the righteous intonations of a preacher. He had a way of saying "Ruth," with an elongated "u," that made her name sound holy, almost a prayer.

Ruth fell in love. Because she lived most intensely in her dreams and ideals, it was there that she loved most intensely. With Ted she shared a shining world, part poetry, part philosophy, and in small part, flattery. He listened to her dreams of a great temple of the dance, a universal school where purity of body, mind, and soul might fuse in artistic expression, and Ted vowed that he would make that dream tangible. They designed schools of dance, utopian colonies, entire systems of government in their heads. Ruth was exhilarated. She did not realize that her companion in dreams had his feet securely on the ground.

She invited Ted and his partner, Norma Gould, to join her for a concert tour of southeastern cities during that spring of 1914. The tour was designed to repay debts from *Bakawali* and *O-Mika,* and Ruth needed a ballroom team to broaden the popular appeal of her bill. Ted accepted with alacrity, but Norma, hurt by his abrupt transfer of affections, suffered a nervous breakdown and was replaced by one of St. Denis' backup dancers, Hilda Beyer. Ted taught Hilda his ballroom routines, and they also performed Greek and character dances he had choreographed. Ruth's numbers included her old East Indian solos and excerpts from *O-Mika,* plus a new solo, *The Scherzo Waltz,* which she choreographed to a piano composition by McNair Ilgenfritz. Gowned in rose-colored chiffon and matching turban, she simply danced, without oriental setting or theme, in the Duncanesque, lyrical vein she had begun with *The Lotus Pond* four years earlier.

They opened the tour on April 13 in Paducah, Kentucky. To celebrate, Ted gave Ruth his first gift, a copy of *The Gardener: Lyrics of Love and Life* by the Bengali poet Rabindranath Tagore. The next week, in Knoxville, he sent her his first bouquet of gladioli. Within two weeks, in Norfolk, he proposed marriage. Ruth was amused. Her road romances dated back to the days of Jack Hoey and *The Man in the Moon.* She had always attracted ardent suitors, but marriage was out of the question. She kept even her minor affairs strictly secret, to protect her public image as virginal goddess, and she suggested to Ted that they simply continue their *sub rosa* romance. He refused. She teased; he became furious. They quarreled and reconciled, on trains, backstage, sometimes even while dancing.

Ironically, they conducted their private drama in the public context of St. Denis' increasing feminism. During that spring, as American women agitated for the right to vote, Ruth performed a benefit for the National Women's Suffrage Association and a private concert for its convalescent president, Dr. Anna Shaw, as the feminist leader nursed a broken leg in her hotel room. In Delaware Ruth took a ride in an airplane, the first woman in Hanover County to attempt this daring feat. Through press interviews and publicity stunts, she cultivated the image of an unfettered "new woman." In such a context, marriage seemed an anachronism, and each of the marriages Ruth had known first-hand were failures, from her parents' to that of her childhood friend, Lizzie Logan. "Marriage," Ruth observed, was "an inventing law designed to keep two people together whether they wanted to stay together or not."

But Ted Shawn had one advantage. He came along at a time when Ruth's familiar landmarks were crumbling. She had yet to find a manager of the caliber of Henry B. Harris, though in 1914 she hired a press agent and advance man, Harry Bell, while her brother stayed on as general manager. Brother himself had recently married, and Ruth lost her claim to his undivided attention. More serious, her strongest emotional tie, to her mother, was severely strained. Mrs. St. Denis, whose emotional health always had been precarious, grew increasingly irrational that spring, with her husband living in Pennsylvania and her children on tour. Alone in New York, she wrote threatening letters. She manipulated Ruth's guilt and made her miserable until Ruth discovered that her mother had a new health problem, probably an addiction—to what, St. Denis never said, though after she committed her mother to a sanitarium in California, she alluded to this problem in a firm but loving letter. "For as long as I am able," she wrote her mother, "I shall see to it that the damnable stuff that is responsible for a large portion of this misery—*does not come near you.*"

Overwhelmed by family problems that spring, Ruth turned to her new young suitor for solace. More and more, she relied on her "Teddy Bumps," or as she also called him, "Boy." They took moonlit walks and talked philosophy. Ruth enjoyed a teacherly role. "I sometimes feel that

I want to—and can help you to attain your highest goals because of my position (such as it is) and influence," she told him, but warned that "only the spark of divine confidence in *truth* that I have nourished is of any *real* help to you." In truth, Ruth herself needed help. She needed a manager for her financial and emotional affairs, and she sometimes imagined that Ted's passion for her could make her problems vanish. "Dearest," she wrote him that July, "in some hours let us forget that there ever was a theatre in the world. Let me just be a woman— very simple and very willing—take me in your arms and let me look up into the blue—and forget—with you, with you."

She wrote him from Edgartown, Massachusetts, where she had retreated with her ailing mother, leaving Ted and Hilda to complete an engagement at Ravinia Park in Chicago, "I must do my duty for mother's sake," she insisted, but Ted wrote that he would die from the separation. As soon as the park engagement concluded, he hurried to Edgartown and confronted Mrs. St. Denis. In a four-hour contest of wills, they fought for possession of Ruth. Mrs. St. Denis, by then in her late sixties and in failing health, still impressed Ted with her argumentative powers, her dramatic range. She became, in succession, "a pathetic, broken old woman, a raging sea serpent, a roaring lion," Ted said, then finally capitulated by warning her daughter, "All right, Ruthie, I give my consent. But I warn you, he's no weakling." The battle decided, Ruth herself had misgivings, but Ted overcame her protests, and on August 13, 1914, they were married at the Aeolian Hall in New York City, with Brother and his wife Emily as witnesses. Ruth insisted that the word "obey" be stricken from the marriage vows, and she refused to wear a wedding ring, which she called a "symbol of bondage." They kept their marriage a secret, as they had their romance, and honeymooned at a Saratoga, New York, casino, where St. Denis' company performed the first engagement in a six-month, coast-to-coast concert tour.

The company, by then, had grown to five, including Ruth, Ted, and Hilda, a young dancer named Alice Martin, and Brother, who performed ballroom dances as René St. Denis. Other dancers joined them along the way: Evan-Burrows Fontaine, who auditioned an Egyptian routine in Chicago; Saidee Van Hoff, whom St. Denis spotted dancing for a charity ball in San Francisco; and a brother-sister team acquired from the floor show of a Los Angeles grille. As the company traveled from Canada and the northern states, down to Texas, then westward, the newlyweds struggled to find the proper balance in their relationship, both personally and professionally. Ted expected the fact of their marriage to make him a full partner to Ruth. She assumed that their teacher-pupil relationship would continue. They spent the next few years of their marriage in an elaborate tug-of-war, trying to harness two strong egos to a common yoke.

As their marriage evolved along its troubled course, a shadow marriage grew alongside, ultimately outlasting the actual union. This was the public St. Denis-Shawn marriage, a creation of publicity based on Ted's extravagant sentimentality, Ruth's shrewd appraisal of her own public role, and the public's own ideas about May-December marriages. This public marriage was an index to the actual relationship. Both partners aired their most pressing problems in print, in the guise of philosophical rumination, and they danced out their difficulties symbolically on the stage. Their duets chronicled a shifting relationship, from worshiper and idol to uneasy partners to soulmates joined on a spiritual plane.

Typically, in their early dances together Shawn was the ardent suitor, St. Denis, the prize. They established these roles in their first ballet together, an *Arabic Suite*, choreographed by Ted and premiered at Ravinia Park the June before their marriage. At the climax of their duet *Ourieda, a Romance of the Desert,* Ted enveloped Ruth in a white burnoose and whisked her away in the florid style that Rudolph Valentino, another ballroom dancer, would soon introduce to silent films. Ted and Ruth performed another new duet on the cross-country tour, their first joint choreography, *The Garden of Kama,* a love idyll set in the garden of a high-caste Indian family. As the Daughter of the House, Ruth resisted, then succumbed, to the love god Kama in his disguise as a humble fisherman. She wore a traditional Indian sari and arranged herself in decorative postures of yearning, strumming a lute and singing in her high, clear voice, "There is no breeze to cool the heat of love." As Kama, Ted again was the passionate pursuer, splendid in brown body paint and brief, bejeweled costume with pointed crown, his lush arabesques echoing the love darts drawn in his bow.

St. Denis' major new solo was *The Legend of the Peacock*, premiered at Ravinia Park just before the 1914–15 tour. The dance had its roots in an improvisation session in London five years earlier, as Ruth spontaneously imitated bird movements in response to a piano score being played by its composer, Edmund Roth. Using this material, she developed a bird dance along a traditional Moslem theme, the story of a rajah's favorite dancing girl who was poisoned by his jealous wife and doomed to inhabit the body of a peacock. In plumed headdress, brief bodice, and green lamé skirt with jeweled train, Ruth strutted in melancholy cadence, her head thrust forward, her arms folded as wings, her preening enhanced by an aquamarine spotlight. The dance was enormously successful on this tour and remained in St. Denis' personal repertoire for years. Somehow the *Peacock* symbolized the essence of St. Denis' public image—exotic beauty isolated in its own rituals.

Young Ted's image, both as an artist and as a man, was as yet unformed. Deeply sentimental and self-absorbed, he brooded about what Ruth called "dark fields in himself, of which I was instinctively afraid." Nor did he have the luxury of a private search for his own identity, for in marrying Ruth and choosing dance as a career, he invited public scrutiny of his innermost self. The press could not decide just who Ted Shawn was. On the 1914-15 tour, in the wake of the Russian ballet, critics labeled Ted "the American Mordkin," comparing him to Anna Pavlova's virile partner and shrilly debating Ted's masculinity in print. "It is well enough for a woman to be orchidaceous," sniffed a San Francisco critic, "but one dislikes it in a man." Defending Shawn, another writer argued that "There may be more than a trace of the effeminate about his appearance on the stage, but it could hardly be otherwise, for he is blessed with more than the common run of good looks and a form of perfect symmetry." Such was Ted's image of epicene beauty that when his marriage became public knowledge, leaked to the press by Ruth herself, the coast-to-coast headlines misidentified the lucky bridegroom as Paul Swan, a variety dancer known as "the most beautiful man in the world." Ted seethed, but when Hilda Beyer tried to set the record straight, she merely added a disconcerting note of opportunism to Ted's public image. "Teddy Shawn was very ambitious and expected to work up in the company," Hilda said sweetly in a newspaper interview, "but I guess he's just as surprised as any of us to work up to being the manager of 'the boss' so speedily. They just must have danced their way into each other's hearts." In the public view, Shawn was the golden boy married to a mature but still glamorous star. One reporter gossiped about "polite whisperings of their disparity in age, of the warm pursuit of the pluperfect Teddy by girly girls of teeny years, of Miss St. Denis' mental superiority and of her handsome husband chafing within the irksome bonds that bind," but admitted to his readers that the couple actually was lavish in mutual respect and praise.

They did try to make their marriage work. Buoyed by her first rush of tender love for Ted, Ruth was generous, as best she knew how. She promoted Ted to second billing as "premier danseur," encouraged his attempts at serious choreography, and relieved him of his lesser roles by hiring another ballroom team, Norwood and Mitchell. When the company played Evansville, Indiana, where Ted had lived briefly as a boy, Ruth modestly steered reporters his way, telling them that Ted was their best story. In Portland she allowed a number in her repertoire, the *Ruth St. Denis Mazurka,* to have its name changed to the *Denishawn Rose Mazurka,* as part of a publicity stunt and dance-naming contest sponsored by the theatre management. This symbolic cojoining of their surnames, Denishawn, ended any singularity that Ruth might have claimed. Though the dance of that name soon faded, Denishawn lived on as the name of the school and touring company that became the major dynasty of American modern dance. Ruth spent the remaining years of her marriage trying to extricate the Denis from Denishawn.

At the end of the tour, thanks to Ted's financial management, Ruth repaid her debts and had money to invest. They decided to establish an open-air dancing school in California, where they found themselves at the end of the tour. Before going East, Ted had taught in Los Angeles, and there they found a palatial estate originally built by the architect John Parkinson for his family. Located on a wooded hilltop overlooking the city, the Spanish-style mansion became the "Ruth St. Denis School of Dancing and Related Arts," or Denishawn, which opened its doors in the spring of 1915, with Ted as associate director. Indoors, a small studio accommodated some of Ruth's classes, and she also led moonlight yoga meditations on the outdoor dancing platform surrounded by eucalyptus trees where Ted taught pointe work, ballet, and ballroom dance. After classes the students splashed in the estate swimming pool, then ate their meals on wooden tables in the nearby rose arbor. It was an idyllic life, the most harmonious time of their marriage. "I think a hundred times during those early days of the school we would stop a moment," Ruth remembered, "and say to each other, 'we are happy and we've got just sense enough to know it.'"

The neighbors beyond the tree-lined walls thought the school was dangerously arty, and their worst suspicions were confirmed one afternoon when a dozen barefoot young ladies, their bathing suits barely covered by kimonos, raced from the school grounds into the streets in

Strutting in *Legend of the Peacock*.

Ruth St. Denis as a nautch dancer at Denishawn Theatre, Westlake Park.

Ruth St. Denis in *Dance of the Royal Ballet of Siam,*
performed in vaudeville, 1918.

Ruth St. Denis and Denishawn Dancers in a nautch dance at Denishawn Theatre, Westlake Park, c. 1918.

Ruth St. Denis in an East Indian dance, c. 1924.

St. Denis in chiton, the costume worn in her music visualizations, demonstrating
a pose from *Second Arabesque*.

Ruth St. Denis Concert Dancers in *Soaring*.

Final pose from *Sonata Pathétique,* Tokyo, 1925. Left to right, Jane Sherman, Ernestine Day, Grace Burroughs, Doris Humphrey, Edith James, Geordie Graham, Anne Douglas.

The Denishawn Company sails for Japan, 1925. St. Denis and Shawn, top. Left to right, Charles Weidman, Doris Humphrey, Geordie Graham (behind), June Hamilton Rhodes, Jane Sherman, Edith James, George Steares, Ernestine Day, Pauline Lawrence, Anne Douglas, unknown man, Ara Martin; kneeling front, Clifford Vaughan.

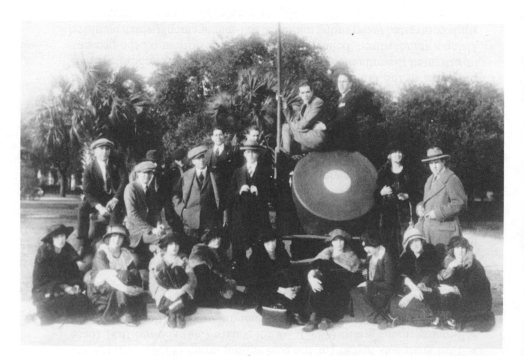

The Denishawn company on tour. St. Denis and Shawn are far right. Charles Weidman and Robert Gorham sit atop a cylindrical drum. Pearl Wheeler is fourth from left on front row.

hot pursuit of Piadh Morh, Denishawn's resident peacock. The press lavishly reported such capers, as well as St. Denis' community fence-mending, such as her choreography for a massive "pageant of childhood" sponsored that spring by the Los Angeles Board of Education. More than 6,500 children participated in the pageant, which took as its theme "Westward the Course of Empire," and St. Denis helped to organize them into great civilizations—the Greeks, the Romans, the Chinese—each with its characteristic national dance. All the city's schoolchildren came to Denishawn to audition for the pageant, which provided valuable publicity for the dancing school.

That June girls from California and nearby states responded to Denishawn's first summer catalogue and came to live in the school's dormitories. They studied the French, Italian, and Russian styles of classical ballet, character dancing, Greek and oriental dancing, dance history and philosophy, and plastiques and dramatic gesture based on the theories of François Delsarte. The Delsarte exercises were particularly important in developing America's first generation of modern dancers. The technique stressed the torso as a source of emotional expression and developed a flexible spine through its "successive" movements. Delsarte's Law of Reaction and Recoil led to a use of tension and relaxation which gave movement the dynamic richness that monotonal, flaccid ballet then lacked, as Shawn later wrote in his study of the Delsarte system.

The Denishawn barre typically began with stretching exercises, some with classical ballet "turnout" of the limbs and others with "Egyptian-style" feet parallel. The dancers then progressed to space-covering floor exercises and movement combinations, and the classes often concluded with students learning fragments from St. Denis' repertoire. Students paid a dollar per class or a steep five dollars for an hour of private instruction. Dancing teachers could take a course of seven lessons for fifteen dollars and learn such ballroom dances as the Shawn Step and Barcarolle, the Hawaiian Hesitation, and the Sea Gull Waltz.

Ted taught most of the technique classes, while Ruth sat before her students and "inspired" with a running monologue of philosophy, advice, and now and then, a demonstration from one of her dances. The Delsarte teacher was Henrietta Russell Hovey, whom Ted and Ruth had discovered living in Los Angeles. Invited to lunch, she demanded, upon arrival, "Well, which one of you is wearing the pants?" and stayed on to head a faculty that included Marion Kappes, who had studied at the Dalcroze Institute near Dresden and taught the Dalcroze system of music analysis through bodily movement.

The school was much more than a pastime or a money-making project for Ruth and Ted; it was the fulfillment of their own philosophy of art and education. They modeled the school on the utopian arts colonies of their own experience—St. Denis' Eagleswood heritage, and Shawn's ideas from the Triunian School of Personal Harmonizing. They adopted Bliss Carman's emphasis on fresh-air exercise as an antidote to the evils of modern life, a theory that Ruth's mother also had developed in her medical studies and in her early therapy at Dr. Jackson's water-cure. In addition to these influences, Denishawn drew upon the most advanced educational theories of the day, the work of G. Stanley Hall and John Dewey.

Shawn read Hall's 1911 study, *Educational Problems*, which stressed the interrelation of all fields of learning. Hall suggested, for example, that students might study history through a series of progressively more modern dances—an idea that Ted himself approximated in his early film, *Dances of the Ages*. Denishawn's broad curriculum and its title, "School of Dancing and Related Arts," echoed Hall's interdisciplinary approach. Hall also equated health with virtue and believed that intellectual development depended on physical training, giving dance the moral and intellectual justification that both Ted and Ruth needed. In his treatise on the "Value of Dancing and Pantomime," Hall deferred to Delsarte as a master theoretician in the field of expressive dance, and ultimately, Delsartean theory was the basis of Denishawn philosophy. When Delsarte taught that gesture was the mirror of inner emotional states, he established an axiom of American modern dance.

Denishawn also reflected the educational theories of John Dewey, who had established the world-famous Laboratory School at the University of Chicago, and was then educating a new generation of school teachers at Columbia University. Dewey described modern education as a process of growth, and Ted liked to employ Deweyian rhetoric in referring to himself as a "gardener" who "nourished" his student "plants." Also echoing Dewey, Ted felt that the teacher's responsibility was to create "the most friendly environment so that the seed or root will come to its finest flowering," and he designed Denishawn to nurture the intellectual, physical, and spiritual needs of each student.

Ruth called their system "the individuality system," which paradoxically, was no system at all. "We believe that to be one's best self is better than to achieve the cleverest imitation of some one else," she wrote in 1917, "and we seek by every possible means to discover the nature of the talent of each individual, the kind of dancing which each one does best." Each advanced student took a "diagnosis lesson," improvising with musical tempi and manipulating fabrics to demonstrate his level of dance ability. Shawn and St. Denis then prescribed a course of training and assigned specific dances which suited that student's temperament and talent. Even though Denishawn products later complained that they were taught to be Siamese, Javanese, Chinese—everything but themselves—their careers demonstrated that Denishawn also nurtured the individuality that was an essential element of modern dance.

As the summer of 1915 drew to a close, Ruth and Ted temporarily suspended the school and rented the estate to one of their students, the actress Lillian Gish. They resumed touring and took with them their most talented students, including two other Denishawn dancers destined for film careers: Margaret Loomis, then an eighteen-year-old Los Angeles debutante whose father was proprietor of the posh Angelus Hotel; and Carol Dempster, the dark and vivacious girl who became D. W. Griffith's inspiration in the early 1920s. Also on that first Denishawn concert tour was a young pianist and composer from San Francisco, Louis Horst, who came to Denishawn through his wife, Betty, a company dancer. Horst joined the tour in mid-October, planning to work two weeks as an accompanist, and stayed on as musical director for the next decade. Other members of that first Denishawn troupe were Florence Andrews, Claire Niles, Yvonne Sinnard, and Chula Monzon. Soloists were Margaret Loomis, whose *Lady Picking Mulberries* was used as a Denishawn classroom exercise; Saidee Van Hoff (variously, Vanderhoff and Vanda Hoff), whose seniority from the previous St. Denis tour earned her a featured role in Shawn's new Hawaiian dance; and Ada Forman, whose precise gestures, supple arms, and shapely feet led Ted to give her a Javanese solo.

Ada's new Javanese dance had a checkered history, typical of Shawn's choreography. When he choreographed his dance film in 1913, he created a dance to Hellenick's *Marche Indienne* and later rearranged it for Norma Gould as *Zuleika*. After he joined St. Denis, Shawn taught the same dance to Evan-Burrows Fontaine and called it *Danse Egyptienne*, then reworked the dance to add more difficult steps for another company dancer, Psychema (Winifred Faire). Psychema left St. Denis at the close of the 1915 season, and Shawn passed the dance on to Ada Forman, who performed it as *Danse Javanese* on the 1915–16 tour. When the unsuspecting Ada presented her solo on the Denishawn program in New York City, a critic for *Variety* accused her of stealing the dance from an exotic dancer then appearing in vaudeville, Lubowska, who was none other than St. Denis' old backup dancer, Psychema. Outraged, Shawn fired off a letter to *Variety*, detailing his version of the origins of the dance and defending his and Ada's integrity. Hardly had the dust settled when *Variety* printed yet another letter from Evan-Burrows Fontaine, claiming that she was the actual choreographer of the dance, and a companion letter from Brother St. Denis, supporting Miss Fontaine's claim.

This minor scandal underscored an important new element in Ruth's artistic life, Ted's gradual domination of her career and his growing friction with her brother. After this initial Denishawn tour, Brother went his own way, briefly touring with his own small company of dancers before settling down as a petroleum engineer and retail merchant. Ted took over Brother's duties as stage manager and he also choreographed most of the new material for the supporting dancers in the company. His choreographic sensibility was perfectly suited to the public appetite for novelty and the demands of touring. Like the newsreels and travelogues he adored, his dances were quick, colorful, and episodic, and if Ruth liked to spend months choreographing her productions, Ted turned out dances on demand.

Typical of his early efforts was the new Hawaiian number on the 1915–16 concert tour. Performed in grass skirts by Saidee Vanderhoff, Shawn, and the Denishawn dancers, the new dance duplicated a hula routine that the company had seen in the Hawaiian village of the Panama-Pacific Exposition in San Francisco during the previous tour. Unlike the other dances on the Denishawn program, which were carefully supervised by Louis Horst, the Hawaiian number used recorded music and one observer complained that the victrola "ran down and wheezed" in mid-hula. Ted also created a series of "nature rhythms" for the tour—impressionistic dances such as *Sunrise* and *Dragon Fly*— which implemented Mary Perry King's natural body movements. He opened the program with a solo for himself, a dance interpretation of the twenty-third Psalm, and closed with a series of "modern" or popular divertissements, including a *Baseball Dance* in which Claire Niles pitched, ran the bases, struck out, and umpired, all in time to sprightly music.

Ted choreographed all the popular numbers, except for Ruth's *Impromptu*, a reworking of the cakewalk-cum-tango she had spontaneously created the previous year at Ravinia Park. Originally, the dance had been a delightful bit of improvisational foolery, a mimicry of Negro high-stepping and the sultry tango, to a Victor Herbert tune, "Al Fresco." Now *The Impromptu* lost its punch, amid so many other comic dances. Ruth broadened its comedy to burlesque and added imitations of the other dances on her program. This was a time-honored ploy in vaudeville, and St. Denis herself had shared vaudeville bills with Bedini and Arthur, a comic team that burlesqued her dances. Now she parodied herself. The audience loved Ruth burlesquing the *Baseball Dance*, Ruth aping the hula and tripping over her own tango, but in many ways *The Impromptu* and this tour marked an erosion of St. Denis' artistic sensibility.

She had been touring the United States and Europe for a decade now and could rightfully claim to be America's modern dance pioneer. For many Americans, Ruth St. Denis was their introduction to performing dance. No other native-born dancer of major reputation crisscrossed the country as St. Denis did, year after year, developing audiences and future dancers. When she appeared in Duluth in November 1915, the local critic reported that only the ubiquitous Anna Pavlova and Adeline Genée had preceded her there. Another critic wrote that St. Denis' dancing defied analysis, "for criticism infers study and comparative comment, and in these matters who is there to study, and who is there to compare?" Ruth braved deplorable touring conditions, cramped railway cars, filthy dressing rooms, fire-trap theatres, and sometimes physical danger. On the 1915–16 tour, near Laramie, Wyoming, an armed bandit boarded her train and passed his hat among the passengers. Harry Bell, Ruth's advance man and publicist, had in his pocket the Denishawn payroll which he slipped to the dancer next to him, who stuffed it in her muff. The gallant bandit did not search the ladies, and Denishawn's box office receipts were saved.

This tour marked a subtle shift in St. Denis' public image, from mere performer to Pioneer. She was on her way to becoming the "Miss Ruth" of legend. Though she was only thirty-seven years old, critics mentioned admiringly that "Miss St. Denis still possesses complete control of her physical powers," and they tried to analyze her staying power, the secret of her still-flourishing career. In the patriotic tone prevalent during those early war years, one critic wrote that in her dances "she sounds the first faint murmurings of an American art that is struggling to voice itself. All of her numbers have an originality and a spirit that is entirely of this country." Ruth herself adopted this patriotic rhetoric in promoting Denishawn as "representative of the spirit of America and fitting the American need much better than any imposed foreign system." Though the school's faculty used foreign techniques such as classical ballet, Ruth explained that "we are not restrained by them when it is either necessary or desirable to do free, unique, or individual things. The whole Renaissance of the Dance is due to America and American artists," due that is, to Isadora Duncan and Ruth St. Denis.

In keeping with her growing awareness of her own historical role, St. Denis jealously guarded her position. She bridled when critics compared her work with the Russian ballet, which in its color, exoticism, and eclecticism, bore some resemblance to her own art. When a writer for the Boston *Transcript* reviewed her Egyptian dance and suggested that Nijinsky had invented the Egyptian style of two-dimensional movement in his *L'Après-midi d'un Faune,* Ruth hastily dispatched a letter, pointing out that her 1910 *Egypta* predated Nijinsky's *Faune* by two years. She added archly that she herself might have inspired the Russians, as her agent A. Braff had traveled to Russia in 1908 with photographs and press clippings of her dances.

Her growing reputation as an American dance pioneer coincided with her first overwhelming popular success. That winter, as the Denishawn company continued its concert tour on the East Coast, a booking agent for the Orpheum circuit, George Gottlieb, sat in on the Denishawn matinees. He selected several numbers from the concert repertoire, focusing on St. Denis' solos, and put together a vaudeville program for B. F. Keith's new Palace Theatre in New York. Ruth had not appeared in vaudeville since her 1913 tour to repay debts on *Bakawali* and *O-Mika,* and she undertook the Palace engagement reluctantly, fearful that her art again would be misunderstood. On the eve of the Palace opening, the *New York Clipper* still warned that among arty circles, "St. Denis is a star, but it is a question whether vaudeville patrons want this." They wanted it, and more. The company played to sold-out houses, and as many as five thousand patrons were turned away on a single evening of the week-long run. Keith's immediately bought off Ruth's other commitments and signed her to an exclusive contract for a series of vaudeville performances through May. Explaining her popular success, one highbrow critic enthused that "The psychological moment for great dancing has arrived, and the public has been educated to understand what it is all about," while another pointed to St. Denis' triumph as "an educational example of the actual advancement in vaudeville." Vaudeville had not changed; St. Denis had. Her repertoire, now dominated by Ted's brief comic dances, was more accessible to a mass audience, and Ruth herself no longer seemed so remote, so meditative or cerebral. In her newest solo, she literally let down her hair.

The Spirit of the Sea, her most popular dance on this tour, was the culmination of her Art Nouveau-inspired solos. Just as the painters and craftsmen of Art Nouveau had been obsessed with the sensual qualities of women's flowing hair, Ruth loosed her own white tresses for the first time onstage and wore blue-green and white veils of tulle that extended the swirling lines of her hair. Brother designed a large blue cyclorama with a background row of lights protected from audience view by a line of waves about two feet high.

As the Sea Spirit, St. Denis lay on her stomach, facing the audience, her feet touching the background row of lights. Streaming from her in all directions were her aqua and white veils. Bathed in Brother's blue-green lighting, she swayed on the floor, her body ebbing and flowing, then very slowly rose and with widespread arms suggested the infinite horizons and bottomless depths of the sea, all to the billowing *Sea Pieces* by Edward MacDowell. An updated version of Loie Fuller's Serpentine routine, the *Sea* solo was an enormous success and stayed in Ruth's repertoire until 1923, when she encapsulated it in a larger *Spirit of the Sea* that featured Ted Shawn as a fisher boy with attendant Denishawn sea maidens. In this expanded version Ruth placed Ted on a rock, prone and pining for his lost sea spirit, in an echo of Nijinsky's final erotic pose in *L'Après-midi d'un Faune.*

After their huge success in vaudeville, Ruth and Ted headed home with fattened purse to reopen the Los Angeles school for its second summer session. They offered a twelve-week course, with seven weekly classes, two hours of craft work such as fabric dyeing, five hours of systematic reading each week, two private lessons with St. Denis during the summer, and room and board, all for a five-hundred-dollar fee. Among the new recruits was the fourteen-year-old Margaret Severn, a child performer of some renown, who arrived from the East Coast, chaperoned by her mother. From California came Lillian Powell, herself a former student of a Denishawn teacher, Gertrude Moore;

Florence Andrews, who later became Florence O'Denishawn in the Ziegfeld Follies; and, most significant, a shy but intense girl of twenty-two, Martha Graham. The daughter of a Santa Barbara physician, Martha was then a student at the Cumnock School of Expression in Los Angeles, where she studied dramatics, art history, and physical training. The last summer before her graduation she came to Denishawn where Ruth remembered her as "exceedingly shy and quiet, with the same fascinating, homely face that she has today. Most of the time in my class she sat very still and listened." It was Ted who discerned in Martha the dramatic fire behind her diffidence and she quickly became his protégée.

This was an exciting summer at Denishawn, for Ruth had received an invitation to perform at the Greek Theatre of the University of California at Berkeley, the first dancer so honored. She decided to employ the entire school in producing a dance pageant of Egypt, Greece, and India, similar to that mounted the previous summer for the school children of Los Angeles. The Denishawn students, electrified by the prospect of actual performing, went to work dyeing, stenciling, and sewing the 450 costumes required for the pageant, while the advanced students learned new dances, many of which were expansions of earlier St. Denis solos. In addition to her students Ruth recruited almost one hundred dancers from the classes of the summer session of the University of California.

With scarcely a month to stage the pageant, Ruth went into seclusion with Ted and emerged with a three-part production, each of its parallel segments depicting the daily life of an ancient civilization and its spiritual beliefs: "Egypt," essentially a reworking of the "Dance of Day" and "Dance of Night" from *Egypta*; "Greece," a Bacchic feast and dance version of the myth of Orpheus and Eurydice; and "India," the story of a couple traveling through successive lives until attaining Samadhi, or Self-realization, incorporating *Incense* and bits of St. Denis' other East Indian dances. For each of these segments the broad walk before the Greek Theatre stage was transformed into a river—the Nile, the Styx, the Ganges. In the orchestra pit Louis Horst conducted the San Francisco Symphony in a patchwork score of pieces by Walter Meyrowitz, Arthur Nevin, and the Comtesse Ada de Lachau, an old friend of Ruth's mother and one of the earliest backers of *Radha* who wrote the music for the pageant's Greek duet. Margaret Loomis and Florence Andrews had featured roles in the pageant and Martha Graham appeared briefly in "Egypt" as one of the "Dancers with Triangles." The Temple Priest and "Tender of the Burning Ghat" was the same Mogul Khan who had been with St. Denis since *Radha* and was now married to her personal maid, Mary. Ruth appeared as various deities, with Ted as her consort, but their most memorable duet from the Berkeley pageant was *Tillers of the Soil,* a dance for two Egyptian peasants.

The stage lights rose on their two curved bodies in silhouette, kneeling and facing each other with heads overlapping. Rising, they whirled abruptly at some imagined noise, then side by side began their daily toil. He wore only a length of cloth about his hips, his head clean-shaven. She wore a long, sacklike garment with a scarf tied about her head. Together they formed a rudimentary plow, he grasping a forked branch, she hoisting the attached rope over her shoulder. After the plowing he sowed grain and she followed, reaping and depositing the grain in her cradled arm. Their movements were cadenced, with pauses that suggested time immemorial. They moved in profile, their bodies flattened two-dimensionally. Their walking was footsore, weighty with fatigue. He scattered seed. She harvested it. She herded animals while he speared a fish with his staff. Their labors completed, they gathered their daily food and departed, the man with a protective arm about his mate who rested her weary head on his shoulder.

This moving duet remained in the St. Denis-Shawn repertoire for years. With minimal means the two dancers suggested a universal story of labor and love. This was the only one of their duets that was filmed and the extant version, filmed in the early 1950s when both dancers were past sixty years old, still illuminates important differences in St. Denis' and Shawn's dance styles. She creates a character of whole cloth, a peasant woman both gentle and sturdy whose ungraceful, earth-rooted walk suggests a harmony with nature that has a grace all its own. Her movements incorporate dramatic motivation so that she becomes her role. Shawn assumes his role. He seems to be dancing even while he creates his character. When he spears his fish we notice the arabesque that provides the thrust for his movement. His posture is more vertical, more balletic than St. Denis', and even in his hieroglyphic poses he seems more "correctly placed" technically, but less convincing dramatically. Ruth could walk like an old sack, while Ted seemed the *danseur noble.*

In the midst of the Berkeley pageant preparations, Ruth suffered through the most difficult period of her relationship with her family. Her mother was then a patient at the Pasadena Sanitarium near Los Angeles and in disturbing letters she begged her daughter, "for God's sake do something besides writing me love letters—do something to release me or I'll go mad." Ruth arranged a furlough so that her mother might visit with her father, but when she refused to return to the sanitarium there was an ugly scene in which she was returned by force. That spring Ruth filed suit in a Los Angeles court to be made guardian of both her parents. She was given custody of her mother, but her father challenged the suit and that autumn won his case. At issue was Tom's expenditure of funds to develop his inventions which still lay dormant in the United States Patent Office. Entrepreneurs, knowing of his famous daughter, encouraged Tom to pay them to develop his designs and Tom schemed to siphon Ruthie's money to finance his dreams. When he tried to dip into a pension that Ruth had established for her mother during their days in London, St. Denis filed suit. The court agreed with her that her father had been ill-advised but ruled that he was mentally competent to manage his own affairs, denying her guardianship. Throughout the hearing Tom charmed the assembled witnesses and reporters. He said he was willing to go hungry to perfect his latest idea, a lightweight gasoline engine, and insisted, "I don't want charity from anyone." An embarrassed Ruth explained to the press, "Ever since I have been dancing I've helped dad and mother and I want to go on trying to make them comfortable all the rest of my life, but even the reputed salary of a dancer cannot go on forever paying fees on patent applications and other lawsuits." Her father, proud, feisty, and still dreaming, finally became a resident of a home for Civil War veterans in Sawtelle, near Los Angeles, where he died in 1918. His wife improved with treatment at the sanitarium and moved into an apartment of her own in Long Beach, where she lived on until 1931, attended by a faithful nurse and enjoying cordial relations with Ruth.

The *Dance Pageant of Egypt, Greece, and India* opened at the Berkeley Greek Theatre on July 29, 1916, and was repeated at the Panama California International Exposition in San Diego, again in Los Angeles and Santa Barbara, before Ted and Ruth took excerpts on the road. While the school remained open with Denishawn's resident manager, Edwinna Hamilton, and Gertrude Moore of the faculty, the company resumed touring on the Orpheum circuit in fulfillment of contractual obligations left over from the previous season in vaudeville. As they toured, Ruth and Ted discussed the future of Denishawn. The school had been born in the shadow of war, opening its doors in the spring of 1915 as German submarines sank the ocean liner *Lusitania*, straining the official United States policy of neutrality. Now, as Ruth and Ted moved north in the winter of 1916–17, bold newspaper headlines announced incident after incident in the growing submarine warfare. Traveling by train to Duluth, where they were due to open on Easter Sunday, they heard on Good Friday that Congress had declared war on Germany. Ruth was afraid but believed that "step by step Divine Wisdom is leading me through this world nightmare." She worried that Ted would enlist in the army, leaving her to bear the burden of Denishawn alone, but privately she worried even more about Ted's reluctance to enlist. He told her that he feared not so much being killed as "being changed," a reference perhaps to his fears for survival as an artist.

Ted had a growing reputation as a dancer and an expanding empire to protect. He was a clever and hard-working administrator, and the Denishawn school had a burgeoning enrollment. Hollywood studios sent their stars to Denishawn, and D. W. Griffith required his actresses to attend twice-weekly sessions to learn emotional expression through movement. In addition to Dorothy and Lillian Gish, Denishawn trained Florence Vidor, Ina Claire, Ruth Chatterton, Louise Glaum, Mabel Normand, and Louise Brooks, among others who created a language of silent film gesture based solidly on Delsarte. Sometimes the movies borrowed Denishawn dancers and made them stars, as in the case of Carol Dempster, and Denishawn students appeared as dancers in such movies as *The Victoria Cross, Night Life in Hollywood,* and Griffith's monumental *Intolerance.* After St. Denis choreographed the Babylonian dances for *Intolerance,* she herself developed a yen for the movies but apparently she appeared only once, in a small role as the Duchess of Marlborough in the 1946 Paramount film *Kitty.*

Hollywood was one lucrative source of revenue for Denishawn, but another was its sizable out-of-state enrollment. Ted and Ruth were their own best publicists, and wherever they toured, they scouted for students and promoted Denishawn. The image they projected was that of a finishing school, where well-bred and carefully chaperoned young ladies might acquire charm and grace. To this end, they made a short film of school activities—"Papa" Shawn and "Miss Ruth" sitting down to tea, Denishawn students posing primly in yoga class and splashing in the pool after handing their wraps to a turbaned servant—and this film became part of their touring programs. In just two years, Denishawn outgrew its Los Angeles estate, necessitating a move to larger quarters near Westlake Park while a new outdoor theatre was under construction in the suburb of Eagle Rock. Ruth fought the move and the school expansion. She argued that Denishawn was a "seven-month's child, born before it was ready mentally, and it has growed like Topsy." The point of the school and their teaching, she believed, "was to pass on our principles to the students—and either we teach in a pure spirit of charity or we make money. Our *business* as yet is in the theatre. Our teaching should be a duty and a pleasure." Ted saw it differently. He was a born businessman. She was a born artist.

Despite her protests, Denishawn expanded, and that summer of 1917 a brainy and talented dancing teacher in her early twenties arrived from Oak Park, Illinois. Doris Humphrey signed up for Denishawn's summer session and eagerly awaited her private lesson with "Miss Ruth." When the time came, St. Denis watched her dance and asked, "What do you do?" When Doris answered, "I teach," Ruth replied, "You shouldn't be teaching, you should be dancing," and Doris stayed on to become her protégée and Denishawn's leading dancer. Another newcomer was Pearl Wheeler, a less talented dancer who became Ruth's close personal companion and, in time, a brilliant costume designer for Denishawn. The expanded school curriculum that summer included Louis Horst's courses in counterpoint, harmony, and theory and history of music, which were destined to influence the future course of St. Denis' career.

On the stage of the new Denishawn Dance Theatre in Eagle Rock, the advanced students of the school performed Monday night concerts and a weekly children's matinee. The inaugural performance in the four hundred-seat outdoor theatre was a benefit for the American Red Cross. The audience sat on three sides of the extended apron stage, an unusual design in those days, and the sense of intimacy was heightened when servants brought refreshments to the characters of the dance-drama onstage, then continued into the audience, serving everyone spiced sherbet, betelnut, and sweetmeat paste.

With the relocation of the school, Ted and Ruth bought a bungalow in Eagle Rock, their first permanent home, and christened it "Tedruth," a name more suggestive of domestic harmony than was the case. Ted longed for a normal family life, and at Tedruth, amid the luxuriant flowers and pepper trees, he pressured Ruth to become pregnant before it was too late. At thirty-eight, the thought of babies horrified her, as did the cozy atmosphere of life in the California sun. "I had a sick feeling that something inside of me was being let down and down and down," she wrote in her autobiography. "At parties or musical evenings I was treated as something of a unique personality, a charming friend, someone who brought a little heightening of life to the occasion. I had stood for something high and something powerful and now I was merely one of them. I knew this could not last forever."

Ted tried to make her happy, tried to prolong their first romance by sending her flowers and gifts and by annually celebrating a host of sentimental occasions—their first appearance together in Paducah, Kentucky, their "'versary" dates on the thirteenth of each month. He also began compiling a two-volume book about her career, his ultimate tribute of love. He was still her devoted servant and often signed his letters with a self-portrait, a tiny figure salaaming to his queen, but Ted wanted more than the residue of his wife's success. He wanted equal billing on tour and equal recognition for his more-than-equal efforts in the school. Ruth was proud of his growing confidence and skill, but she also knew that Ted would never be her equal in performance magic. Ted assumed roles; she had the power to transform them. Her dancing blazed with intelligence, charm, and spiritual conviction, and she made her audiences feel that they were involved in a remarkable experience. Ruth knew her powers, and she felt that she had earned her star billing through hard work and God-given genius. She resented Ted's demands and felt trapped by the twin institutions of marriage and Denishawn. She could never be "merely one of them."

Groping for escape, she indulged in minor affairs with men of two types: fatherly confidantes in the Clark Miller mold and boyish artists like her own Ted. These liaisons consisted primarily of stolen glances, furtive love letters, and surreptitious meetings in the moonlight, all in an atmosphere of utmost secrecy. Whatever guilt Ruth felt was alleviated by Ted's own peccadilloes, crushes he developed on two successive young men after the disturbing discovery of "dark fields" in himself. The adolescent tone of his and Ruth's extramarital affairs was typified by a diary passage written by St. Denis about one of her admirers: "Do not go away—do not leave me—if I am weak—then be thou my strength?" She appended a telling phrase: "Since I may not speak to him—I must dance my need and speak sometimes to the world." She was searching for fuel for her art. She believed that since *O-Mika* and *Bakawali*—since just before meeting Ted—she had not created a single first-rate dance. She decided to retire from dancing and give some thought to an acting or singing career, a plan aborted when, shortly after Christmas, Ted received a summons from his local draft board. Before he could be drafted, he enlisted in the Army Ambulance Corps and was stationed at Camp Kearney near San Diego. He put the school's affairs in order, and Ruth embarked on a tour to promote Liberty Bonds.

This was Ruth's first tour without Ted and the company in four years, and freedom was sweet. She took with her only Denishawn's principal dancer, Margaret Loomis, and its musical director, Louis Horst. They traveled the Majestic vaudeville circuit from Texas up to Canada, then back down the West Coast, performing six numbers on each vaudeville bill—two solos for Maggie and four for Ruth. Without Ted's managerial skills, it was a difficult tour. In Waco the stage backdrop failed to arrive, and they danced on a bare stage with "bad music, bad lights, and a loose floor cloth," but farther south in San Antonio, Ruth proudly reported, they broke the Majestic Theatre house record previously held by a fortune-teller, "La Mar—the Girl with the Thousand Eyes." Ruth joked that "Even high art seems occasionally to have a little drawing power," but in Dallas, where their program competed with a Mardi Gras ball, she saw only "four people and a dog out front." Worse yet, in Galveston when the curtain rose on her Japanese dance, she heard a "groan of disappointment" from the audience of soldiers, while a heckler shouted, "That's rotten!" She danced on, gritting her teeth "a trifle nervously" and told Ted, "I held on that I was dancing for God and for you."

Actually, she was dancing for herself. On this tour she began to experiment with "music visualizations," musical scores made visible through movement, a concept derived from the Dalcroze techniques taught at Denishawn. With Louis Horst, who already had improved her musical taste, she rehearsed new dances—a Siamese solo, an unfinished Herodiade, and a *Dance from an Egyptian Frieze* that became part of her repertoire, though the audience favorite remained a romantic solo that Ted had created to a Dwight Fiske melody, "The Moon of Love Waltz."

She was happier on this tour, and she allowed her weight to balloon to 152 pounds. She read her *Science and Health* and gossiped with

Maggie; her placidity must have disturbed Ted. He wrote her anxious letters from his army camp, and she responded cruelly, "I am getting my peace and as surely *you will get your fame.*" She went on, "Because I have felt less restraint—have been more peaceful—done my work more uniformly well—and am better poised—on this tour does that mean that I have loved you less?" Ted, who was trying to keep the school going by commuting to Los Angeles on weekends, reminded her of her responsibilities to Denishawn. He had told her when he joined the army that he planned to close the school after the coming summer, leaving Ruth free to pursue her own plans, but now he talked of keeping the school open through the fall. Ruth responded angrily, "I cannot any longer be attached or sucked into other people's stronger plans." Ted promised that she might have most of the summer free.

With the close of her tour, she returned to Los Angeles for the summer, where she appeared in a five-week run of *The Light of Asia,* a dramatization of the same Buddhist text that Edmund Russell had read to her during her *Radha* days. This was a Theosophical version of that text, produced at the Krotona Theosophical Institute's stadium in Hollywood. The play starred Walter Hampden, an actor well known for his Hamlets, in the role of the Buddha, Prince Siddhartha. As the vision of his wife Yashodara, St. Denis appeared in a dance scene, described by the Los Angeles *Times* as "a noble and altogether beautiful performance." St. Denis was also listed as choreographer, though Doris Humphrey helped her create the dance for the vision scene and appeared with other Denishawn dancers in a nautch during the play.

Freed from the pressure of teaching, Ruth felt renewed tenderness for Ted, and she wrote him that summer of "the sweetness and peace that have been mine since your dear love has stilled the wild tossing that filled the vacuum in my heart." She agreed to perform an entertainment for the Officers' Training School at Camp Kearney and in the fall she agreed, reluctantly, to tour the lucrative Pantages circuit in vaudeville. "Truly if you had not been taken by the government," she wrote Ted, "I would not let myself be taken again on a tour. My heart again cries for peace and center, but it will enable me to do those temporary things that I otherwise could not do. And yet," she asked, "is making money the best thing that I do?" For a fee close to twenty-five hundred dollars she performed weekly engagements with a group of four Denishawn dancers, including Doris and Pearl. Their route led them from the West to East Coast and back again. Their repertoire included a new Siamese dance for full company, the *Dance of the Royal Ballet of Siam;* a solo for Ruth, *Theodora,* with St. Denis as the Byzantine empress, moving in tiny skimming steps and hieratic poses before a mosaic backdrop designed by Maxwell Armfield; and a new group work, *The Spirit of Democracy* or *Triumph of the Allies,* set to Chopin's *Revolutionary Étude.*

The latter ballet opened with St. Denis sitting onstage as a brooding Spirit of Democracy. Lifting her eyes she gazed at far horizons, then stood and moved restlessly, without direction. Suddenly she spied a sinister object on the horizon. With the help of lighting effects, this unseen menace appeared to grow into a blaze of destructive fire whose first victim, Belgium, stumbled onstage to seek shelter at Democracy's feet. Staggered by the onslaught, Democracy called to her allies who bent with determination to the task of destroying the enemy. The dancers lined up and mimed hand grenade maneuvers and bayonet drill. In a running, leaping finale they celebrated victory and peace, a climax deflated in Washington where the Keith's Theatre appended a Pathe News Pictorial titled *The Fight Is On!*

The Spirit of Democracy was one of Ruth's earliest attempts to translate the emotional qualities of music into group movement, and she wanted to continue to work in this vein, an impossibility while touring vaudeville. She was weary and wrote Ted, "I want to touch fundamentals again." Each evening, she told him, her dancers "lead me on—hang on me the gorgeous robe—I sit motionless for the curtain to go —and then like a marionette I begin—and go through the motions—no honestly dear—I do more than that—I dance, but wouldn't you get tired after a while if nobody answered you back?" She longed for solitude, for a "white room" of her own where she might renew her creative energies. Her malaise went beyond mere personal problems to the heart of her creativity. "Just as people are sick internally and after prayer and fasting return to their former working harmony of body, so artists grow sick in spirit," Ruth wrote, and they "have to be bled or nourished or rested until their capacity to reflect beauty has been washed clean of fears." The fear that sickened her was a nameless fear that assumed many forms: fear of losing Ted, fear of losing her own genius, even fear of going mad. "I saw what happened to my mother before me, what demons of darkness she had fought so bravely, so insistently," Ruth wrote, "and yet in her they had not been destroyed at their roots. And in spite of all the loving and interested help I had received, it seemed that my roots were still undestroyed and that they kept putting forth their enervating and poisonous branches, reaching out into all my activities. Not so much fear of any one thing but just fear in the abstract, a latent terrible possibility that lay at the bottom of consciousness like a sediment in water, ready to color every action at the slightest calling forth." She decided to retire, at least from vaudeville.

She wrote Ted of her decision, and as soon as the Armistice was declared, he hurried to Detroit where she was appearing with her dancers and tried to change her mind. For several weeks they argued about Denishawn, their careers, their marriage, and for the first of many times, they "agreed to disagree." Ted returned to Los Angeles and disposed of the Denishawn properties at Westlake Park. He opened his own small studio, with only Martha Graham and a new pianist, Pauline Lawrence, to assist him. Ruth announced her retirement from vaudeville and planned her own group of concert dancers to implement some new ideas she shared with Doris Humphrey. Tedruth continued to be home base.

On November 8, 1919, Tedruth burned to the ground. Ruth had lit a gas heater in the bathroom, then stepped out of doors, and moments later the entire building was in flames. She managed to salvage a trunk of photographs and an East Indian rug. Ted frantically tried to save their priceless costuming library, the trunk of costly kimonos from O-Mika, their oriental wall hangings and valuable scrapbooks, all lost. They found their fifteenth-century Japanese temple gong melted.

That night Ruth wrote in her diary, "Little Tedruth is in ashes. And now my soul is naked and I can see it and can tell how spotted and soiled it was. Who shall deliver me from the body of this continuous death? Is there any one final renunciation that can free us?" She sensed that her marriage, like Tedruth, lay in ashes.

THE SPIRIT OF THE SEA

GROUP DANCE

CHOREOGRAPHY: Ruth St. Denis

MUSIC: Roy S. Stoughton

DECOR: Robert Law Studios

PREMIERE: October 15, 1923, Apollo Theatre, Atlantic City, New Jersey

———◆———

SETTING: A blue cyclorama forms the background of this seashore scene. At the left is a curved projection of rock on which the Fisher Boy stands and later lies as he receives the embrace of the Sea Spirit. A large fish net and sea shells lie near the rock. Blue-green lights bathe the stage.

SCENARIO: The curtain rises on a slow-moving Dance of the Sand Nymphs, who enter carrying long strands of kelp which they manipulate in plastique figures to a drowsy, murmuring passage in the music. A trio of the nymphs suddenly runs offstage and returns with the Fisher Boy (Ted Shawn), who plays with them in a dance full of little phrases and quick playful turns. Laughing, he tosses his net over the group and tows them to the rock, where they escape. He pretends to be cross and sulk; they coax him into good humor. He chases them until, weary of their play, they stretch out on the beach in attitudes of abandonment. The Fisher Boy leans against the rock, chuckling at the girls.

The lights dim as evening comes. The Sand Nymphs try to tempt the Fisher Boy to resume their play, but he resists. To an undecided and fretful passage in the music the girls coax him as he climbs upon the large rock to watch the moon rise over the sea. Reluctantly, the Sand Nymphs leave the stage, the lights deepening in the silence of early evening.

The Fisher Boy sits crouched, holding his knees, watching the ocean line at the back of the stage. The music is meditative. On the opening note of her theme the Sea Spirit (St. Denis) lifts her head slowly into the moonlight which lightens her silver hair. She lies on her stomach at the back of the stage, swathed in green veilings with streamers flowing from her shoulders. For the first few measures of music she moves with a deep, swinging motion of her shoulders and torso. Then she rises and stretches her arms, revealing her flowing draperies. With a heavy and sombre rhythm she ripples her arms in the motion of an unbroken wave as she moves toward the footlights, then turns her back on the audience and moves away, trailing her long draperies.

She begins her "broken wave movement," consisting of short phrases, each one higher than the last until in a climax she throws her draperies toward the sky, then allows them to "trickle" down to the stage. After repeating this sequence until she reaches the rear of the stage she performs a playful "fish dance" with upward spurts of energy and sinuous swimming motions. At the conclusion of this dance she sees the Fisher Boy.

The Sea Spirit gazes at the Fisher Boy in a childlike way, then performs another phrase of her fish dance for his amusement. He bends forward from his rock to watch her movements. The dance trails off and a new note in the music suggests a love motif borne on a deep sea rhythm. The Sea Spirit moves across the stage, trailing her draperies, and forms a crescent under his rock, her body arched, head thrown back, hair streaming. He leans toward her for a kiss. She tries to hold him to her but realizes he cannot join her in the sea and sadly she turns, moving to the back of the stage once again. She begins her "broken wave movement" again and with the crash of a chord reaches the crest of a wave, then turns her back and slowly disappears into the sea. Unable to resist her allure, the Fisher Boy jumps from his rock in pursuit of the Sea Spirit and is drowned.

This condensation of St. Denis' choreographic notes for *Spirit of the Sea* is faithful to her original idea, with one exception. She planned to end the dance with the disappearance of the Sea Spirit. The melodramatic drowning of the Fisher Boy was a later addition and may have been Ted Shawn's idea.

The Spirit of the Sea was the happiest blending of St. Denis' own choreographic skill with Denishawn theatricality. A magnified version of her earlier solo, the group dance contained the essential elements of St. Denis' style: the manipulation of draperies, charming little group dances, the mortal male's pursuit of the ethereal female, her arm ripples expanded into an entire dance on a vast scale. Havelock Ellis once referred to *The Spirit of the Sea* in solo form in describing the St. Denis dances he loved best. He preferred those dances with the slowest, broadest movements because it was then that St. Denis transcended prettiness and sentimentality to convey a cosmic force.

SEVEN

MUSIC MADE VISIBLE

WITH HER RETIREMENT from vaudeville and her growing separation from Ted, Ruth turned her attention toward a new interest, music. She always called herself "an eye dancer, not an ear dancer." She was quite rhythmic and sensitive to melodic line, but her taste in music did not match her meticulous attention to costuming, lighting, and scenery. Ordinarily she made dances, then found music to fit, as she suggested in a letter to Ted about a new dance she had choreographed: "You might show the forest plastique to someone on the chance of their thinking of a forest or pastoral symphony of some kind," Ruth wrote. "The music should be very beautiful and help me out." Music, to St. Denis, was atmosphere, scenery, a complementary background rather than an integral part of the dance.

Like other variety dancers, Ruth choreographed her early works to borrowed bits of opera ballet music and to tunes commissioned from her accompanists. Classical music was considered taboo for the inferior art of dancing. Ruth was most comfortable with a simple percussion accompaniment, and she attempted to find authentic native music for her oriental dances. For one of her early *Radha* tours she engaged Professor Inayat Khan to play Indian ragas, but for her more lyric dances she relied on minor American composers such as Harvey Worthington Loomis, a Brooklyn-born composer of musical pantomimes, children's music, and comic operas. Loomis wrote the music for *Incense,* and St. Denis used excerpts from the Delibes opera *Lakmé* for her *Radha* and *Cobras.* When she took these dances to Paris in 1906, the society of French composers vetoed her use of *Lakmé* and she resorted to a journeyman musician who rearranged and disguised the score. Isadora Duncan encountered the same prejudices but persisted in her use of music by Beethoven, Chopin, and Bach, while Maud Allan popularized the lighter classics such as Mendelssohn's *Spring Song*. St. Denis had less sophisticated taste in Western classical music until Louis Horst joined Denishawn. At his urging she began to use Schubert, Debussy, and Gluck, and she worked in tandem with the musically gifted Doris Humphrey, who helped her choreograph dances as early as 1918. Another impetus to Ruth's growing interest in music was the addition of Dalcroze studies to the curriculum of Denishawn.

Émile Jaques-Dalcroze was a Swiss composer who evolved a system of musical training based on rhythmic movement. In 1910 he organized an institute for rhythmical training in Hellerau, Germany, and subsequently established Dalcroze institutes in his native Geneva, London, Paris, and Berlin. Dalcroze isolated key elements of musical structure—tempo, dynamics, duration, metrical pattern, pitch, and so on—and taught these concepts through a system of rhythmic exercises called "Eurhythmics." To do was to learn, Dalcroze theorized, much as John Dewey and G. Stanley Hall suggested in their own pragmatic educational theories. A Dalcroze student might learn musical accents, for example, by marching and stamping on the "Pop!" of *Pop Goes the Weasel,* or study polyrhythms by running while a pianist played a walking rhythm. Or, to learn dissociation, just as one hand at the piano might play *forte* to the other hand's *piano,* the student contracted certain muscles while relaxing others. Dalcroze devised an entire chart of music and movement equivalents that included musical pitch translated into the position and direction of gestures in space, musical intensity of sound equated with muscular intensity, and musical counterpoint equated with oppositional movements. He applied his theories to choreography for movement choirs, and in 1914 in Geneva organized a rhythmic choir to interpret orchestral symphonies in movement.

Though Dalcroze designed his exercises to teach the structure of music through movement, a generation of "interpretive dancers" adopted his methods to analyze movement itself. In Germany Mary Wigman studied the Dalcroze method, and Marie Rambert brought the technique to Diaghilev's Ballet Russe. In America interpretive dancers added Dalcroze to their Delsarte technique. The Delsarte system, with its elaborate charts of gesture, proved of limited use for early modern dancers. Because Delsarte focused on the emotional content of gesture for the individual body or bodies grouped into tableaux, his system, as popularly applied to dance, was essentially static and pictorial. Its spatial implications were confined to the area immediately surrounding the body—how an arm stretched overhead might suggest triumph, for example—while the Dalcroze system offered a dynamic base that extended movement through time, into space.

In 1912 Dalcroze wrote a remarkable essay, "How to Revive Dancing," which summarized the concerns of early modern dance. He defined dancing as "the art of expressing emotion by means of rhythmic bodily movements," and he dismissed the moribund art of opera ballet as musically ignorant. Even the interpretive dancing of the Isadora Duncan variety was merely decorative, "reproducing the attitudes of Greek statues, and by no means asserting the personality of the dancer." Dalcroze found no structure, no logic, in these interpretive dances. "They operate in space without order of sequence; they are never led up to, they occur at haphazard; they are not the inevitable product of nuances of feeling dictated by the music; finally, they fail to interpret the mentalities of contemporary human beings." In theatrical dancing, Dalcroze charged, "Plastic polyrhythm is unknown. The art of contrasting movements and attitudes is still in an embryonic stage. The simultaneous execution of slow movements with the same movements at double, triple, or quadruple speed has never been attempted." St. Denis decided to attempt such a dance.

She denied that the Dalcroze system was the primary inspiration for the "music visualizations" she began choreographing in 1917, though she admitted that both shared a common principle, the understanding of music through movement. Rather, she mentioned the experience of watching Isadora Duncan perform to Schubert's *Unfinished Symphony* and realizing that "she stopped when the music became too complicated and compromised by making one of her unforgettably noble gestures in complete disregard of the music." Dalcroze had observed this same license (or lack of pedantry) in Duncan, noting that "she rarely walks in time to an *adagio*, almost invariably adding involuntarily one or more steps to the number prescribed by the musical phrase. This arises from her inability to control the transfer of weight of the body from one leg to another in all its variations of pace." Both Dalcroze and St. Denis wondered if a more precise rendering of music might not be achieved.

Ruth gathered several of her former Denishawn students and began experimenting with music visualizations, which she defined as "the scientific translation into bodily action of the rhythmic, melodic, and harmonic structure of a musical composition, without intention to 'interpret' or reveal any hidden meaning apprehended by the dancer." With Doris Humphrey as her assistant, and Claire Niles, a Delsarte enthusiast, as her principal dancer, Ruth analyzed piano compositions and translated their structural values into dance. Listening to Louis Horst and, later, Ann Thompson or Everett Olive at the piano, she instantly conceived a mental picture of the mood conveyed by a piece of music. Doris helped her refine that picture into appropriate movement. They studied time values and rhythmic patterns and devised quick movements for eighth notes and sustained gestures for whole notes. They considered dynamics, muting muscular energy during *pianissimo* passages, and choreographing forceful gestures to match each crash of chords. Ruth even considered the spatial implications of a given score and mirrored the rise and fall of melody with the rise and fall of the dancers' bodies relative to the stage plane.

The dances that resulted were similar in construction. Balletic movements, *pas de bourrées* and arabesques, blended with running steps, natural skips, and hops. These movements coalesced in decorative tableaux that drooped in emulation of Delsartean "decomposing" or relaxation exercises before being reabsorbed into the movement flow. Often the girls linked arms, held each other lightly about the waist, or allowed their arms to pulse airily to the music, a vestige of the time-beating gestures that accompanied Dalcroze drills. They used scarves to extend their movements into space or, conversely, to create a luxuriously draped frame for the body's stationary "plastique" or sculptural posing. Pearl Wheeler designed two basic costumes to insure depersonalized uniformity in the ensemble—a silk chiffon shift worn over a leotard, or simply the leotard itself, a "fleshing," dipped into a tea solution to give it a neutral flesh tone and worn with a blond wig that equalized the dancers' appearance. Throughout, the atmosphere of the dances was disciplined and well bred, the very image St. Denis had wanted to project through Denishawn.

One of her first music visualizations was a sprightly, sunny dance for three girls—Doris Humphrey, Claire Niles, and Betty May—to Claude Debussy's *Second Arabesque in G Major* for piano. Using both the Dalcroze and Delsarte methods, she created a series of classical Greek poses connected by swift running steps, a pony trot, hops and swings to the tripping triplets of the main theme. Her extensive annotation of the dance mentions "wreathed arms" intertwined in the fashion of Greek maidens and "vase arms" gently arched overhead. The dancers' movements echoed the architectural structure of the score. They paused on each musical rest, and when the music indicated a repeat, they repeated their previous movement phrase. When the triplets played in treble clef descended to the bass, the dancers changed from lyric arm gestures to vigorous leg swings. When the notes cascaded like a waterfall, they ran toward the audience, following the downward rake of the stage, then reversed directions upstage as the piano notes ascended. The groupings were Delsartean—an initial moving frieze in profile, a final pose with hands crossed at the breastbone and heads demurely inclined—and St. Denis followed Delsarte's dictum that physical motivations should be expressed by the "physical zone" or lower body. "A joyous, lyric dance like *Second Arabesque* should radiate physical joy, just sheer animal spirits," she wrote, "and therefore the feet and legs, space-covering in their activity, should be the instruments of expression."

In a prodigious surge of creativity, Ruth choreographed more than thirty music visualizations and by December 1919, she had assembled a touring repertoire for a company of nine dancers, similar in concept to the Isadora Duncan Dancers, the six disciples of Duncan who performed throughout the United States in the period during and after World War I. The repertoire of the Ruth St. Denis Concert Dancers also included two works by Doris Humphrey, in addition to those she created in collaboration with St. Denis, and two of Ted Shawn's visualizations of Bach inventions, originally designed as a Denishawn classroom exercise in counterpoint.

While Ted toured vaudeville with students from his own school, Ruth took her concert dancers on a West Coast tour that eventually wound its way across country to the southern states by December 1920. It was a shoestring operation. June Hamilton Rhodes, daughter of the Denishawn manager Edwinna Hamilton, went along as company manager, while Harry Bell provided scattered bookings. The musical direction was haphazard. Louis Horst stayed with Ted, and Ruth employed a dozen accompanists, including chief pianist Everett Olive, Pauline Lawrence, Mischa Levitski, Howard Brockway, Clarence Adler, George Copeland, Katherine Goodson, Henry Souvaine, Olga Steeb, Mana-Zucca, and Richard Buhlig. Harry Bell advised Ruth that she did not need to travel with a string quartet. "This would not have been true before the Duncans went out," he wrote, "but now the public realizes that a pianist amply fills the bill of a good artist." Sometimes different pianists performed successive movements of the same composition during a dance, and St. Denis always used her own accompanist, Ann Thompson, for her solos. Ruth performed only in the California cities, with Ted as an occasional guest, but primarily the tour was a group effort, with no stars, no elaborate scenery or costumes. Many of the concerts were society dates, with sponsors such as the Junior League. For five months the Concert Dancers toured the West Coast, then after summer vacation regrouped and continued touring southeastward as far as Little Rock, Arkansas, where in January 1921 the money and the bookings ran out.

If the Ruth St. Denis Concert Dancers were a financial failure, they garnered lavish praise from critics who called their music visualizations "a departure from established tradition," "art so extremely new as to seem, at times, incredulous," and in the words of the Atlanta *Constitution,* dances that "opened a new world." A typical program on the tour included two dozen dances, with an initial section of short solos climaxing in the Humphrey–St. Denis visualization of Beethoven's *Sonata Pathétique* for full company; a filler section of songs performed by tenor Ellis Rhodes, with some dance accompaniment; and a final section of solo and group dances culminating in the sparkling *Valse Brillante.* When Ruth performed, she usually occupied the favored second and next-to-last positions on the program, with a saucy new version of the *Nautch,* her *Greek Veil Plastique* patterned on Genevieve Stebbins' *Dance of Day* and performed in Fortuny veil, or one of her newer solos such as *Kuan Yin,* a plastique depiction of the Chinese goddess of mercy to Erik Satie's *Gymnopédie #3.*

As Kuan Yin, St. Denis stood in a blue light at center stage, wearing weighted chiffon robes with a floor-length swatch of gold lamé draped over her tall crown and descending to the stage. The dance consisted of drapery manipulations and decorative poses, detailed in St. Denis' dance notes, which began: "Walk forward—back through veil. Bend forward in pity. Hands in teaching attitude. Hands in prayer. Take veil in right hand, wrap around right wrist. Pose right hand then left." This was vintage St. Denis, sculptural and still, in marked contrast to the livelier music visualizations for her dancers.

The *Sonata Pathétique* was a visualization of the first movement of Beethoven's Opus 13 in C Minor. Six girls followed the bass and antiphonal melodies, while Doris Humphrey represented the major melodic themes. Ruth had observed that "where there is an emotional expression, even the dynamics of a large group never equal the force of one individual's emotional capacity," a compositional idea later reversed in Humphrey's mature work but suitable for St. Denis' romantic sensibility. They used this idea to dramatic advantage in *Sonata Pathétique*, contrasting Doris' solo movement with that of the ensemble. Denishawn dancer Jane Sherman remembered that the dance "seemed to be about the leader of a small army in some vague battle that ended in victory, albeit with casualties," a suggestion that elements of the dance may have derived from Ruth's earlier *Spirit of Democracy*, but here the drama was submerged in the mathematical equation of music to movement. In a program note St. Denis wrote, "In all visualization there must be a constant compromise between the spirit and the form, and it is always a matter of taste and not of scientific argument as to whether to choose the emotional content of a chord as against the mathematical arrangement of the figures relative to the notes." In *Sonata Pathétique* emotional content had the edge. One admirer, writing to Ruth decades after seeing the dance, still remembered the emotional impact of the opening *gravé*, when the dancers "massed in one corner, their backs to the audience, their arms up, their fingers fluttering in seeming supplication," a tableau made all the more effective by strong lighting from the wings that cast the dancers' shadows on the backdrop.

The repertoire also included scarf dances in the Loie Fuller mode, with volumes of heavy silk manipulated in spiraling arcs or spreading balloons, as they were in Denishawn classroom exercises. Doris displayed her mastery of this technique in her own *Scarf Dance*, choreographed to Cécile Chaminade's *Valse Caprice in D Flat*. She used five yards of Spanish silk to fashion a narrow streamer. Flinging her scarf overhead in elongated arcs, leaping through a hoop of hovering fabric, she created her own silken skywriting, enhanced by simple dance steps.

Doris also helped Ruth to choreograph an audience favorite on the tour, *Soaring*, a visualization of Schumann's *Aufschwung: Fantasiestücke*. In this dance four girls grasped each corner of a huge silken square, with Doris underneath at center. As the quartet skipped to and fro, then knelt, the scarf ballooned like a parachute and descended, in approximation of the variations in dynamics and pitch of the score. Doris was the centerpiece of picturesque formations, such as the "flower-step," where she emerged from a chrysalis of silk, unfolding her arms like petals. The dancers wore blond bobbed wigs and flesh-colored leotards or "soaring suits," while varicolored lights suggested wind, wave, and cloud. To Ruth's chagrin, during their last concert in Little Rock, her dancers had to add stockings and garters to their soaring suits at the request of municipal authorities, an absurdity that symbolized the defeat of her dream of a pure music visualization in dance.

Ruth came home from the tour emotionally and physically exhausted. She consulted Christian Science practitioners for a variety of ailments and took refuge in the company of a small circle of friends who met on Thursday evenings to discuss philosophy, poetry, and art. Among them was a young actor, Craig Ward, with whom she developed a romance. They collaborated on a program of dance and poetry and performed a series of concerts in California cities. Ruth took along several of her dancers and retained *Second Arabesque* from her concert repertoire, but the focus of the tour was Craig's poetry reading and Ruth's dancing. As he read from Tagore's *The Gardener*, the volume that had been Ted's first gift to her, Ruth improvised to its lush romanticism: "When I go alone at night to my love tryst/birds do not sing, the wind does not stir/the houses on both sides of the street stand silent." Ted did not stand silent; he joined the tour. He performed a Siamese suite with his wife, a Chinese dance of his own, and their old Egyptian numbers, but he did not participate in the poetry-dance duets.

Though Ruth was discreet as always, Craig Ward boasted of their liaison, and rumors spread through the dance world that Ruth and Ted would divorce. Ted reassured their friends that their marriage was solid, but he and Ruth remained separated for a period of three years. During those years, 1919 to 1922, they toured with their own separate companies and reassessed their relationship. As early as the war Ted had intimated to Ruth that he was attracted to both sexes, but she told herself that his brief affairs were normal outlets for an artistic nature. She told the press as much. Her interviews during this period are filled with ruminations on the androgynous nature of the artist. In her diary in early 1920 she wrote about her separation from Ted and his newest male friend: "Ted now has his own studio and a friend who believes in him and who gives him what I could not—and if it were not for Ted's real affection for me—causing him to wonder constantly if he is doing the right thing—he would be quite happy I believe." She mused on the causes of the separation. "I am older than Ted—I have been acknowledged an artist by the world before he is, and I have a most uncompromising critical spirit. I have assumed since the first that in matters of art I knew best." Blaming Ted's ambition for their rift, she concluded bitterly, "I am the one person in the world that is bar (at present) to his feeling of supremacy."

Ted himself was deeply troubled during this period and looked to his ideal of marriage for personal salvation. He desperately wanted a marriage based on sexual fidelity and swore that he would purge his own sex life of wanderings. He was riddled with jealousy. When Ruth wrote him about her flirtation with a fatherly game warden in Yosemite National Park, or, more innocently, mentioned her violinist by his first name in a letter, Ted despaired. Ruth defended herself. "What you want and will perhaps not be at peace until you get it is the complete control sexually of every thought, impulse, and act of my life. Perhaps," she warned, "you will force me to a final choice. I think you make a hell for yourself that is unnecessary. Much of you still is a boy."

Yet she manipulated his insecurity, confessing to each romance in lavish detail. After the discovery of one new beau, she wrote Ted of her "sense of pride and conquest and thrills, like a child with a new toy who did not quite know how the damn thing was going to behave— whether she would keep it or wouldn't, whether it was good for her or not." Her candor only deepened Ted's despair. So absorbed was she in her own romantic dreams, that his outrage genuinely surprised her. "I do not expect you to get to where you will never be jealous of me," she wrote. "To the world and to you I am a sinner whereas to myself—I am a puzzle and a problem." She wished that Ted had a wife without her own "rovingness and indecisions, where your abnormalities—if you had any—would at least be your private affairs. With a reasonable wife you would have had children which would have further taken up your affectionate nature but still leaving your individual life fairly free." She begged Ted to consider an open marriage, based on mutual affection but individual freedom, an idea she knew was contrary to "a perfectly tremendous weight of tradition and public opinion" in 1920, but "If it turns out that I love my work more than my capacity to love humanly, then I was made so and cannot help it. My kind of loyalty is all I can give." She was willing to be tolerant. "If the love that I can and do give you cannot satisfy your spirit, then you can still look for another channel to supply to you what I lack and so complete the full circle of your love."

In letter after letter, they argued about marriage and their most personal problems. Those letters that were too sensitive, or too pressing, to be entrusted to the mails were hand-delivered by Ruth's confidante and courier, Pearl Wheeler. Ruth also sent letters to her lovers by Pearl, and on one such mission Pearl was involved in a tragic automobile accident that left her face permanently scarred.

Though their personal life was turbulent and destructive, Ted and Ruth put on a proud public face. In the summer of 1919 they jointly appeared in a production of *Miriam, Sister of Moses,* a dramatization of Hebrew history written by Ruth's old friend from London, Constance Smedley, and her husband, the stage designer Maxwell Armfield. The British couple had come to the United States during the war and immediately traveled West to Denishawn, where St. Denis commissioned sets from Armfield for her *Spirit of Democracy* and *Theodora.* During that early visit Smedley showed the Hebrew play to Ruth, who liked it but "hesitated to risk her supreme position in the world of dance by competing in a new field," though she was intrigued by Smedley's concept of rhythmic drama, later developed in her Greenleaf Rhythmic Plays. "Drama proceeds from the roots of dance and music as well as speech," Smedley believed, and she choreographed the rhythmic structure of her plays as carefully as if they were dances. Ruth finally consented to appear in the title role of *Miriam, Sister of Moses* after the war when Smedley and Armfield were invited to join the summer drama faculty at the University of California and stage the play in the prestigious Berkeley Greek Theatre.

Ted choreographed the dances for the play and reluctantly took the role of Moses, his first venture into professional acting. He was not a success. Ill at ease and overweight from his fallow period in the army, he was, by his own admission, "unsatisfactory." The critics focused their rave reviews on Ruth. "She is gifted with a voice of unusual quality and a superbly responsive physique," rhapsodized the critic for the *Christian Science Monitor.* "The present writer, watching her, could not remember having seen half a dozen of the leading actresses of America or indeed of Europe who could surpass her in natural grace or individual appeal." Other writers noticed her mastery of Smedley's concept of rhythmic drama. "In countless places throughout a long and tedious part she fused a fine rhythmic sense," Frederic McConnell wrote in *The Drama.* "Emotion found translation not in pantomime, but in a vast rhythmic understanding of human feeling. Miss St. Denis can remain still and yet not be static."

The play was an embarrassing experience for Ted, who found more pleasure in his own projects than in riding Ruth's coattails. The years of their separation were painful years of personal and artistic growth, "when the foundations of my life were being washed away," Ted said. Now in his late twenties, with the army and Denishawn behind him, he devoted himself to teaching in his Ted Shawn Studio and tried to regain his own dancing form. He studied the Delsarte system and Spanish dance technique and continued the explorations of religious dance he had begun during the war. He also produced vaudeville acts for the Pantages circuit. While Ruth toured with her concert dancers, Ted sent Lillian Powell and other students into vaudeville with a fairy-tale extravaganza, *Julnar of the Sea,* and he also revived his Bacchic *Mystères Dionysiaques,* previously performed in the Denishawn Dance Theatre.

Ted himself toured vaudeville with Martha Graham and a small company in the exotic *Xochitl,* a dance spectacle based on the Toltec legend of an emperor's lust for a dancing maiden. Ted commissioned a score from Homer Grunn, an expert on southwestern Indian music, and scenery and costumes from Francisco Cornejo, an authority on Aztec-Toltec art. The dance exploited Martha's dramatic passion, and the climactic, clawing duet between drunken emperor and protesting maiden won Ted raves for the virility and dynamism of his choreography, performed mostly on half-toe and stylized in the manner of Aztec reliefs. *Xochitl* was a triumph for Ted. For the first time he heard his work labeled "original," and critics lauded *Xochitl* as "the first native American ballet."

During 1921 Ted continued to create dances on native American themes, and he refined his musical taste under the supervision of Louis Horst, who accompanied him on a transcontinental tour. Ted also took along Martha Graham, Dorothea Bowen, Betty May, and Charles Weidman, and from Los Angeles to New York, critics found his performing much improved. "Ted Shawn is immense," wrote a Minnesota critic. "What he was in vaudeville not so many seasons ago doesn't matter. What matters is that he has since worked at his art, perfecting it, until now his dancing has attained nearly as high a point of aesthetic excellence as even Ruth St. Denis could wish." Though he had not escaped from Ruth's shadow, Ted felt a growing sense of confidence in his own artistic and managerial powers. He wrote Ruth that he had finally won Horst's respect through his cool handling of financial crises on the tour, and he also mentioned Louis' "very sweet friendship" with

Martha Graham. Ted developed a close friendship of his own with Robert Gorham, who danced the role of the emperor in *Xochitl* until he was injured and replaced by a talented newcomer, Charles Weidman.

By the time he reached New York at the end of his 1921 tour, Ted had repaid a thirty-five-hundred-dollar backlog of debt, shed his excess weight, and regained his self-confidence. He decided to open a New York branch of his school with Martha Graham as his assistant. "She is hen-brained in some ways," Ted said of Martha, but he overlooked her volatile temper and her unorthodox romance with Louis and paid her thirty-five dollars a week to teach classes and keep the studio accounts. Always persuasive, Ted convinced the manager of an apartment building in Manhattan to give him living quarters and a studio plus her own secretarial help in exchange for a modest fee.

"It is the opportunity of a lifetime for us to get a foothold here in New York without expense to us," Ted wrote Ruth, trying to win her approval for a revival of Denishawn. "I thought it better to call this the New York branch of Denishawn than to just say Ted Shawn was teaching and again further the idea that you and I had separated in any way. Furthermore in all the publicity we are stating that you will be here in person later on." To avoid adverse publicity, Ruth acquiesced, but Gertrude Moore, who managed the California studio, was furious. She felt that Ted's New York branch killed the California school, and for several years, until the West Coast Denishawn closed in 1924, the rivalry between the branches was intense.

On opposite coasts, Ruth and Ted spent their first Christmas apart in 1921, and Ruth wrote bitterly in her diary, "This day I am unmarried to you, Ted." He himself grew tired of their endless turmoil and wrote her, "We are building on sand and merely prolonging something that otherwise must be a clean break." Yet the divorce never came. A tenuous thread bound them together and grew in strength as Ted developed his own artistry—the bond of their work. Ruth was, above all, a professional of the theatre with instincts as profound as a Bernhardt or Duse, and she was willing to share her expertise with Ted, in spite of their personal differences. She demonstrated that professionalism and a certain compassion in a letter she wrote Ted when his spirits were at lowest ebb. Overweight and depressed, he was planning his 1921 tour and wrote her for advice on a set of publicity photographs. She examined them and replied, "This is your first big advertising signal. You need to take another set of photographs, and face more 3/4 with action in the face and the wig a little more uniform by pushing it out a little bit and the tape not quite so far down on the eyes." She appended a sketch. She advised him to tauten his chin by lifting his face in front-views and told him to wear a stiff buckram-backed stomacher. "You need a higher waistline to give breadth to your shoulders and narrowness to your hips. And don't worry about your weight," she added, "when the time comes, you'll be fine." In a single page of prose she reshaped him into a perfect physical specimen, and a grateful Ted replied, "Who in the whole world could give me such splendid criticism, so keen, so searching, so absolutely true?" He knew that only Ruth could, and she knew that she would.

In New York, Ted's troupe performed a fateful matinee at the Apollo Theatre on December 2, 1921. As if to convince their friends that their marriage was sound, Ted lavishly dedicated the program to "Ruth St. Denis, High Priestess of the Dance, my beloved wife, my loyal comrade, my patient guru." The impresario Daniel Mayer attended the concert and afterward offered Ted a contract for the following season, with the suggestion that he ask his "loyal comrade" to join him. Ted was ecstatic. A Mayer contract meant solid bookings, financial security and prestige, and he set to work at once to persuade Ruth to join him in reviving both the Denishawn company and school.

Their negotiations were prolonged and tedious. Since as early as 1920, Ruth had privately contemplated a "comeback" in her diaries, and she was tempted by the Mayer offer. She admired Daniel Mayer, whose clients had included Pavlova, Paderewski, and Caruso. She knew that he was a first-rate manager and that she, of all artists, needed management, "otherwise I appear to wander about rather futilely giving out little sprints of ideas, but never really settling down to a purpose." Ruth agreed to rejoin Ted on several conditions. She insisted on a separate studio for herself in New York and the freedom to lead her own personal life. Ted was vehemently opposed to both requests but acquiesced to salvage their dance partnership. Ruth also demanded top billing, a bitter blow to Ted who felt he had earned equal status, but when the publicity brochures were printed they advertised, "Ruth St. Denis with Ted Shawn and the Denishawn Dancers," each name in progressively smaller print.

They also negotiated personnel. Now that her favorite, Doris Humphrey, had gone her own way into vaudeville, Ruth wanted "our three little stars," Dorothea Bowen, Marjorie Peterson, and Betty Horst, to accompany them on the London leg of the tour. Ted wanted, and got, Martha Graham. Ruth then decided that Betty Horst was too fat and rejected her, much to Ted's dismay, for Louis Horst, apparently trying to revive his own marriage, had agreed to go to London for expenses only, if Betty were taken along as a dancer. Ted reminded Ruth that "Betty May, Martha, and Pearl and the other three are all inclined to be heavy," and to save Louis' salary, he added Betty Horst to the roster.

With personnel matters settled, there were still questions of itinerary and repertoire. Ted originally planned the first part of the tour, a month of concert appearances in Virginia and the Carolinas, to raise traveling money for a month of vaudeville in London, but Ruth asked that the proceeds from the southern tour be used for the financially ailing school in California. They compromised and agreed to split the proceeds. On other matters their differences in opinion were illuminating. Ted was a shrewd merchandiser of talent; Ruth fought for her own artistry. She objected to the original plan of opening the tour in New York without a preparatory period on the road, and she asked that her Chinese solo, *Kuan Yin,* open the touring program as an invocation. Ted objected, "It's so much more dignified and theatrically impressive if the first number can be by others of the company, holding you back as the supreme thing to be arrived at." Ruth prevailed, and in February 1922 she met with Ted in Greensburg, Pennsylvania, and signed a three-year contract with Mayer, then returned to the West Coast to prepare for the tour.

She had no illusions that the lucrative Mayer tours would be a high-art enterprise, even though they were concert bookings. "We are offering this now, really, more as a theatrical performance than as a strict concert," she wrote Ted, "and therefore we will have to buck all of the Russian and other companies which I am not afraid of IF everything we do is technically as well as artistically as perfect as we can make it." There was scant time for perfection. With only two months to prepare, Ted feverishly planned the tour routes, assembled publicity materials, planned orchestrations with Louis, and raised money for the London fares. Meanwhile he rehearsed Charles Weidman, Martha Graham, and Betty May in New York, while Dorothea Bowen taught Pearl Wheeler the ensemble work in California. The hastily assembled repertoire included *Xochitl,* with Ruth replacing Martha in the lead, the old

Egyptian dances, a Siamese duet, Ted's Spanish numbers, and among Ruth's dances, a new and profound pair of solos, *Brahms Waltz* and *Liebestraum*.

The solo to Brahms's *Waltz No. 15, Op. 29* was a simple sequence of swooping waltz steps and walking steps on half-toe with dramatic undertones, as indicated in St. Denis' dance notes: "Run diagonally to right. With weight on right, throw head back and push arms down at either side. Recover slowly, bringing arms in front. Accent three last notes with wrist." In performance she appeared barefoot, in pale blue chiffon with a scarf of the same fabric draped over both arms and across her back. Stately and tall, she waltzed in a pink spotlight, her arms paddling the air as if it were liquid, or patting imaginary stairsteps to indicate accented notes. As she waltzed she arched her upper body and back, exposing an expanse of vulnerable white throat, a configuration popularized in Art Nouveau and common to the dances of Isadora Duncan. At the end of the *Brahms Waltz* she came to center stage and barely paused as the music faded into the strains of Liszt's *Liebestraum*, which became one of her greatest solos.

The lighting shifted from pink to blue, the mood, to tender sorrow. On the opening notes of the melody, her throat inclined forward, her shoulders slightly drooped, her arms came nearer her body, and the soft ball of one foot caressed the stage to suggest the more intimate sphere of *Liebestraum*, a dance of unrequited love. In three-quarters profile, with her head inclined over one ear, she danced a question-and-answer pattern of search and rejection. She used breath-rhythms to underscore the ebb and flow of the dance, and Louis Horst noted that St. Denis breathed with all her body in these waltzes, "and this inspiration and expiration, this 'breath,' is what so likens these dances to an unheard song." She reached with yearning arms into her dancing space, then focused inward on her turns, as if aware that her search for love was in vain. With one last gesture she reached toward an unseen figure in the wings, then, rebuffed, walked slowly offstage, her body resisting the pull of her fate. *Liebestraum* often left her audience in tears.

The genesis of *Liebestraum* was an idealized love affair with a young composer who was part of Ruth's California circle, and as she rejoined Denishawn, she reluctantly parted from her new friend. She avoided Ted during their month in Virginia and the Carolinas and kept company with Pearl Wheeler as they sailed for London in May. Also on board the ship were Betty May, Dorothea Bowen, Charles Weidman,

Louis Horst, and Martha Graham, made miserable by the presence of Betty Horst, and Ted, excited about his first trip abroad. They arrived in London for a June 4 opening at the Coliseum, the huge vaudeville arena where Ruth had appeared as a soloist thirteen years earlier. Then she had endured taunts from the peanut gallery; now she earned the approval of the London public and press with dances that, ironically, she considered inferior to her first works. "To be sure, I had the Japanese, the Egyptian, and the *Peacock*," she wrote, "but these were not the products of that austere and great beauty of which my soul had dreamed. These were not properly the fruit of twelve (sic) years."

The London critics greeted St. Denis warmly and treated the Denishawn company as nothing more than an extravagant setting for her homecoming. "Miss St. Denis' dancing is always delightful, and her present program is as good as any that she has given before in this country," was all the London *Times* had to say about the program. The dance establishment welcomed Ruth as an old friend. Adeline Genée, presiding over the Dance Circle, invited Ruth and Ted to speak at a dinner in their honor, and Frank Crowninshield, Condé Nast, Marie Dressler, and other celebrities crowded their dressing room to pay compliments after each performance. They were invited to the home of Havelock Ellis, the writer and philosopher whose *Psychology of Sex* was one of Ted's favorite books, and they also met Edward Carpenter, the mystic whose writings Ruth admired. In her free time Ruth escaped to her old haunts, the Egyptian and Indian collections of the British and South Kensington museums, and she rediscovered two long-time friends, Kate Dalliba, who lent her salon for the first performance of *Radha,* and Braffie, Ruth's former manager, aging now but still hoping to manage another St. Denis tour.

After vaudeville engagements in Manchester and Bristol, Ruth and Ted made a brief side trip to Paris where they saw the Diaghilev Ballet Russe. Ruth admired the technical proficiency of the company ballerina, Tamara Karsavina, but felt she could not compare with the "human hummingbird" she so admired, Anna Pavlova. From Paris Ruth and Ted sailed home where they had a summer job awaiting them at an arts center in Peterboro, New Hampshire. Mariarden was an arts colony in the New Hampshire hills, founded by Guy Currier, a wealthy corporation lawyer, and his wife, Marie, a former actress who had studied dancing with St. Denis. The Curriers assembled a faculty of distinguished artists, including the actor and stage director Richard

Bennett, the playwright Stuart Walker, and Grace Ripley, director of the Boylston Studio of Costume and Design in Boston, who for a season had taught at the West Coast Denishawn. Children came from all parts of the country to Mariarden, where they donned Greek togas and imbibed the Mariarden formula of health and culture. The Curriers contacted Ted just before the London tour and asked that he teach dancing twice weekly in exchange for a portion of each student's tuition plus a rent-free house and studio. During the summer of 1922 he commuted weekends from New York Denishawn and installed Ruth in the Mariarden cabin, where she worked on her repertoire for the upcoming Mayer tours and taught an occasional children's class. Among her students were the Braggiotti sisters, Berthe and Francesca, who later founded one of the first Denishawn school franchises in Boston.

As she always did, Ruth absorbed the creative essence of the artists around her. She renewed her acquaintance with Joseph Lindon Smith, the artist and student of Egyptian archaeology who a decade earlier had created the decor for Louis Tiffany's Egyptian fete. She also developed an enduring friendship with the composer Sol Cohen, then in residence at the MacDowell colony across the valley from Mariarden. Good company, peace, and privacy lifted Ruth's spirits and gave her time to ponder the commitment she had made to Denishawn.

The Mayer contract was even more binding than her marriage contract. Ahead of her lay three years of forced togetherness with Ted and the institution they had spawned. This time, she vowed, her individual art would survive. The public marriage would guide Denishawn—Papa Shawn and Miss Ruth, shoulder to shoulder in public but free to pursue their private lives. Ted reluctantly agreed and wrote her, "Your old slogan, 'Shoulder to shoulder' is absolutely right—looking together into the infinite and walking that way—and not me gazing idolatrously into your eyes."

Dramatically, he promised her, "I have severed my umbilical cord from you—and I shall never again be your child—either I die, or grow strong to be thy mate."

EIGHT

THE DENISHAWN EMPIRE

DENISHAWN WAS more than a mere touring company or a dancing school. During the Mayer years, 1922 to 1925, it became a major cultural institution and franchise, with authorized branch schools in a dozen American cities; there were a Denishawn magazine, Denishawn films, and a touring company that eventually performed in every state in the union as well as Canada and Cuba. Denishawn dances were distributed nationally to teachers through a Normal school course by mail and a series of choreographic notes published by G. Schirmer, Inc. The Ampico piano roll company distributed rolls of Denishawn technique classes, recital dances and music visualizations. For an entire generation of Americans, Denishawn symbolized highbrow dance at its most accessible, colorful, and spectacular.

The Denishawn style was a happy hybrid, a blending of Ruth St. Denis' romanticism with Ted Shawn's sentimentality, her exoticism and his eye for the vernacular. With its repertoire of more than sixty ballets, the Denishawn touring company exported dances of almost every picturesque culture—Spanish, Greek, Javanese, Chinese, Siamese, American Indian, Aztec, Japanese, Egyptian—and of every dance style —ballet softened by bare feet, ballroom dances, music visualizations, native dances, Loie Fulleresque experiments with draperies and light, lyrical dances of the Isadora Duncan variety, St. Denis' own distinctive Orientalia, and Shawn's ventures into Americana. Denishawn was both a travelogue to distant lands and a catalogue of American modern dance to date, yet for all its strange beauty and surface variety, the Denishawn repertoire offered a fairly narrow range of familiar characters and themes. Most of the dances developed the simple premise of boy-pursues-girl, in various exotic guises. Most of the dances were solos packaged in layers of color, costuming, and scenery, and even in the group dances the Denishawn corps often functioned as decorative background. Only a few of the dances were abstract, and even those had their dramatic vignettes or submerged stories that revealed Denishawn's roots in vaudeville and silent film.

Ted's work dominated the repertoire, with two of his ballets for every one of Ruth's. Ted liked simple stories told in broad outlines, and many of his dances were cartoons: *The Crapshooter* (1924), with its strutting gambler; *Betty's Music Box* (1922), with its trio of beruffled maids who prissed in a pink spotlight and exchanged gossip; his *Cuadro Flamenco* (1923), with a stereotypical Spanish spitfire pursued by a panting bullfighter. Ted even borrowed from minstrel shows to create a *Juba Dance* (1921). He had a feel for society in his dances, a sense of human interaction missing from Ruth's more stylized, allegorical ballets, and he gave the Denishawners more opportunity to dance. Some of his choreography for the Mayer tours was genuinely new. He had studied Spanish dancing with Ortega in New York, and in 1923 he traveled to Spain for more study. His new Spanish ballets featured intricate heel rhythms and authentic touches of flamenco, but much of his choreography was recycled from previous works.

St. Denis' begging for *baksheesh* from her *Nautch* reappeared in Shawn's gypsy dance, *Maria-Mari*, choreographed in 1922 and later performed by Geordie Graham, Martha's sister. For Charles Weidman Ted created *Danse Americaine* (1923), a solo for a blustering dandy who shot craps, played baseball, and pursued pretty girls. He lifted the baseball portion of the solo from Claire Niles' old *Baseball Dance,* and later took the craps episode from *Danse Americaine* and expanded it into *The Crapshooter,* a spin-off solo for Charles. Ted also reworked Ruth's wartime *Spirit of Democracy* into a postwar version, *Revolutionary Étude,* choreographed to the same Chopin piano score. He eliminated the St. Denis-Democracy figure and made himself a symbolic Figure of Revolt, incorporating in his role the entire corps of struggling nations depicted in Ruth's work. Clad in tatters, Ted mimed his struggles before a moving backdrop of two Denishawn dancers who represented a wall of fire, their red scarves flicking like tongues of flame. They performed *Revolutionary Étude* on each of the three Mayer tours.

Ted also remade his first duet with Ruth, *Arabic Suite,* into a complete ballet, *The Vision of the Aissoua* (1924), adding dancing girls and a chorus of Bedouins to its basic cloak-and-swagger romance. Actually, *The Vision of the Aissoua* was much the same ballet as *Cuadro Flamenco,* but in an Algerian setting. Instead of brandishing a bullfighter's cape, Ted flourished a scimitar in the Algerian ballet, and Ruth was the same aloof but alluring seductress in a *danse du ventre* similar in tone to her *Cuadro Flamenco* solo. The Denishawn Dancers, onlookers in both, contributed appropriate gasps, applause, and an occasional group dance.

Ruth's contribution to the repertoire also was an accumulation of past dances—her *Greek Veil Plastique* and Chinese *Kuan Yin,* her durable Egyptian and Japanese dances, her music visualizations, and the *Spirit of the Sea* solo reworked into a group dance. She also revived the *Three Apsarases,* the celestial dancers' court dance from *Bakawali,* as a trio for May Lynn, Betty May, and Martha Graham. One of Ruth's most fortuitous revivals for herself was the *Dance of the Black and Gold Sari,* also from *Bakawali.* In its 1913 form the solo was *Dance of the Gold and Black Sari,* a seductive dance performed by Bakawali for her mortal lover, but in 1921 St. Denis exchanged the Arthur Nevin score for Roy Stoughton's *In the Palace of the Rajah* from his *East Indian Suite.* She also domesticated the content of the dance, turning it into a clever fabric display with undertones of shrewd salesmanship.

The dance began as St. Denis walked pertly onstage, with the sari draped over her arms. She wore a short blouse or *choli,* an underskirt, a black wig, gold jewelry, and ankle bells. In the course of the dance she wrapped the sari around her, pleated it, tucked it into her skirts, all the while stamping out nautch rhythms with decorative hand gestures and chattering in ersatz Hindi. The intricacy of her maneuvers is evident in this excerpt from her choreographic notes for *Black and Gold Sari:* "*Rond de jambe* with right foot to back of trailing tail. Take sari in the right hand. Slide left hand along edge towards the end and hold sari overhead by turning under left arm, running to right and back in semicircle to the center. Make tent of sari over the eyes and end with short vamp, coming forward." Her agility and stamina, at the age of forty-plus, are also suggested in another excerpt from these notes: "Nineteen steady Nautch turns to the right, starting with body bent low to right, right hand holding sari to hip, left hand straight out in back. Gradually come up straight, placing the left hand to the hip and right arm out straight." *The Dance of the Black and Gold Sari* was one of the most popular numbers on the first and third Mayer tours, and in 1927 was still being performed, with a change of costume, as *The Dance of the Red and Gold Saree.*

The first Mayer tour began in October 1922, with performances in smaller towns in upstate New York before the big opening October 9 at the Selwyn Theatre in New York City. This was Ruth's first appearance in New York in almost four years, and the New York *Times* reviewer treated the occasion as a solo triumph. He praised the Belascoesque realism and fine detail of her dances, as distinguished from those of other "interpretive" dancers. "Always in Miss St. Denis' work," he wrote, "there was direct, definite fancy and gesture, none of your picking daisies off bare boards or drinking from fountains of canvas drops. She gave atmospheric illusion in lighting effects, the glint and caress of rare fabrics, realistic study in movement and background . . ." He added in passing that St. Denis was "ably assisted" by Ted Shawn and the Denishawn Dancers.

As the Denishawn company performed its matinees at the Selwyn, further uptown at Carnegie Hall Isadora Duncan created a stir with her revolutionary dances and spirited curtain speeches. Fresh from a tour of revolutionary Russia, with her new Russian husband in tow, Duncan performed her militant *Marche Slav,* then berated her American audiences for failing to provide her with the school she had sought in war-torn Russia: "Why will America not reach out a hand to Russia as I have given my hand?" she demanded—fighting words in 1920s America, then in the throes of its own Red Scare and witch hunt for Bolshevik sympathizers. Isadora eventually was hounded from America, and the episode made a deep impression on Ruth, who was more sensitive than ever to adverse publicity, more keenly aware of the need to guard her own personal and professional reputation.

This sensitivity to public approval was an important aspect of the public image Ruth fashioned for herself as the matriarch of Denishawn. As Miss Ruth, model for her students and dancers, she cultivated an ever-virginal image of Olympian spirituality, intelligence, and charm, with an emphasis on good manners. The myth was often at odds with reality. "She had all the mystery, all the magic," remembered Martha Graham, "but she had no concern for being a correct 'lady.' She could eat peanuts on a street car. She could do anything and did. She had real, old Irish wit, sometimes stinging." She favored *double entendres,* told on herself. "Isadora relieved women of the use of the corset," she said with a wink, "but with my bare midriff I was responsible for the separation of church and state." She was still beautiful at forty-three but was careless about her own grooming and Ted constantly pressured her to glamorize her appearance and refine her manner in public. To the press Ruth and Ted stressed their solidarity, the wholesome atmosphere of Denishawn, the careful chaperoning of their female dancers, and the happy camaraderie of Denishawn life.

In creating this myth, Ted was Ruth's eager ally. Socially insecure, he harbored resentment about social snubs. On one early tour he and Ruth attended a postperformance party where Ted danced with a titled aristocrat, and the next day, waiting for their train, Ted and Ruth strolled on a lawn in a posh residential neighborhood, only to be shooed away by a butler. "You dance with a duchess one night and you get chased off someone's lawn the next," Ted said ruefully of his life as a dancer. Denishawn gave him the opportunity to be Papa Shawn, pater-familias, respectable authority figure. On the first leg of the Mayer tour he left London with a complete tailor-made outfit, cutaway, waistcoat, striped trousers, top hat, and cane. He was the direct link with the dancers, keeper of the purse, arbiter of casting, and most of the Denishawners felt closer to Papa than to the more distant Miss Ruth.

On tour Ted required his female dancers to attend parties hosted by his university social fraternity, Sigma Phi Epsilon, and at least one Denishawner resented being delivered to these parties with great fanfare, only to be dumped there and left to the mercy of pawing fraternity boys. The same dancer sensed a touch of hypocrisy in Miss Ruth and Papa Shawn. Though they delivered lofty lectures on philosophy, morality, and art to their dancers, when Christmastime came around they presented them not with the books they eagerly anticipated, but with identical tin lunchboxes, suitable for schoolchildren. Other Denishawners denied any hypocrisy in their leaders, especially Miss Ruth. "She did not always live up to the standards she had for herself," said Anna Austin, "but who does?"

Many of the Denishawners, particularly the students, revered Miss Ruth. Eager for her approval, they occasionally bore the brunt of her tart tongue. Ruth was a woman of immense verbal skill, impatient with others' failings. She often spoke her mind with devastating results. Once, traveling by train to some engagement on tour, she passed Martha Graham's sister Geordie in the coach car and paused to ask, "Why don't you give up dancing, dear? You're never going to make it," or words to that effect. She did not even realize that she left Geordie

Graham, a devoted company member and perfectionist, deeply hurt by her blunt analysis.

Miss Ruth was never deliberately cruel, as Papa Shawn could be on occasion, and with Denishawners she respected and admired, such as Doris Humphrey, she could be a generous teacher and friend. Ruth was far more comfortable than Ted in her role as goddess surrounded by Denishawn acolytes. "She acted all the time, she couldn't get away from it," remembered one of Denishawn's composer-conductors. "She would come into a room and everyone would look at her. She had a magnetism, of a rough sort. She was not what I would call a very highly refined person. Ted tried to be. That was his mistake. He was never a genuinely natural person. She was at all times. Her natural self was an actress."

From New York, Ted and Ruth and their Denishawn Dancers traveled to the South, then west as far as Denver, back across the continent to the East and South again, then north to Canada before returning to New York in April of 1923. Louis Horst went along as music director, playing the piano and conducting an instrumental quartet of piano, violin (John Froling), cello (Peter Kleynenberg), and flute (Augusto Scalzi). The press notices often mentioned the high quality of the musical accompaniment. Also included in the Denishawn entourage were a business representative, treasurer, electrician, carpenter, properties manager, wardrobe mistress, and wardrobe assistant. The nine Denishawn Dancers on this first Mayer tour were Martha Graham, Betty May, Lenore Scheffer, Julia Bennett, May Lynn, Louise Brooks, Peggy Taylor, Charles Weidman, and Paul Mathis.

Ruth had suggested the inclusion of Paul Mathis just before the tour began and Ted, suspicious at first about another young boy of Ruth's choosing, eventually agreed that "Paul has the true Denishawn spirit and except for actual physical height is a much better dancer in every way (than the other boys), save the few physical stunts." Paul was short in stature but a natural athlete, and his coming to Denishawn was a typical story. At the age of sixteen, never having studied dance, he saw Ruth and Ted perform in Philadelphia during the Denishawn vaudeville tour of 1917. Smitten, he went backstage to pay his respects but was blocked by a recalcitrant doorman, then rescued by Pearl Wheeler, who took him to see Ted and Ruth. They invited Paul to take classes at the California Denishawn, and after overcoming his parents' objections, he studied in the school and later became a Denishawn

Dancer. During the first Mayer tour Ted decided that Paul was too short to dance with him onstage and replaced him with Robert Gorham, who had left Ted's previous touring company to pursue a degree at the University of Virginia. Paul left the company to become one of the most valuable teachers at New York Denishawn.

Pearl Wheeler, who became known as the dragon-guardian of Miss Ruth's door, also went along on that first Mayer tour. Since the Liberty Bond tour of 1918–19, Ruth and Pearl had been close friends. Ruth enjoyed Pearl's little personal attentions and admired her immense skill in costuming and decor. For the first Mayer tour Pearl created splendid Spanish costumes with authentic detail painstakingly copied from photographs, and she assumed responsibility for the music visualization costumes of delicate "Denishawn crepe" and the bulkier masks and costumes for the oriental dances. She was thorough. When Ruth requested advice on costuming, Pearl would reply with careful notes and figures and accompanying swatches of fabric. She was absolutely devoted to Ruth, whose brilliance seemed to fill a void in her own self-esteem. Pearl once sent Ruth the following poem:

> I have no education
> I just grew up like a weed
> Then, out of my life went ambition,
> The very thing that we need.
> I know not why I'm lonely
> I know not why I cry
> But sometimes in all my sadness,
> I hear a voice that I know
> And then, like a spark through the heavens
> My sadness, all seems to go.

When Ted complained about Pearl's devotion to her, Ruth replied, "The reason I turn to Pearl as I do is quite obvious and reasonable. She is at least in relation to myself a negative person—she loves me—as she would love a child—something to care for and see grow under her hands. What to you would be a burden she does easily and gladly. I need someone to think for me," Ruth continued, "so that I can put my whole mind on other things. Then when I am sane and dressed and want love and communion, I turn to you."

Pearl's Spanish costumes furbished Ted's new *Spanish Suite*, which most critics mentioned as the most popular ballet on the first Mayer tour. Premiered on the trip through the South just prior to the tour, the *Spanish Suite* originally included a solo for Martha Graham. In London, Martha joined Ted in the smoldering duet, with Ted reassuring Ruth, "I dare not, nor want to, put as much sex into the dance with Martha as I would with you." Now with Ruth in shape again for the main Mayer tour, Ted gave her Martha's roles and made the *Spanish Suite* as sexy as possible. Ruth opened with a solo, *Danza Espagñol*, with much winking and smirking to music by Granados, followed by Ted's sultry *Tango* and their duet, *Malagueña*. A Chicago critic found the whole Spanish suite distasteful, with Ruth "rather too intimately friendly with the audience," and Ted, in his "Valentino visualization," slack-jawed and altogether un-Spanish, but the audience loved it, and Ruth added a new dimension to her image. Her photographs in Spanish costume on the Denishawn publicity posters were considered so provocative that in Louisville, Kentucky, the Board of Public Safety suppressed the posters and threatened to censor the entire Denishawn program.

With the close of the first Mayer tour, Ted sailed for Spain in search of greater authenticity for his Spanish dances, while Ruth vacationed in Charleston, South Carolina, then returned to the Mariarden colony for the summer. When Ted returned from Europe he joined Ruth at Mariarden, where a small group of Denishawn dancers also was in residence. They planned the dances for the next Mayer tour and performed a program at the University of Virginia, while Ted made frequent trips back to New York to supervise the Denishawn school.

While the Denishawn Dancers traveled on tour, the main Denishawn school in New York groomed fresh recruits for the company. The school operated in a house on West Twenty-eighth Street in Manhattan, with an uptown studio at Carnegie Hall. The director of New York Denishawn was Katharane Edson, an accomplished Delsartean who had studied with Mrs. Henrietta Hovey and also with Andreas Pavley and Serge Oukrainsky of Anna Pavlova's ballet. She supervised a wide array of dance classes. Ruth and Ted lectured and taught at Denishawn between tours, and the school offered classes in Indian, Japanese, Algerian, Javanese, and Egyptian styles, theatrical makeup, music visualizations, and the handling of draperies. Elsa Findlay, who later spent her career with the Cleveland Institute of Music, taught Dalcroze Eurhythmics at New York Denishawn, and Paul Mathis taught classical ballet. Prospective students auditioned for Ruth and Ted on tour or sent their photographs to the school, where the Denishawn faculty kept on the lookout for good dance material, particularly males. One scholarship student came to Denishawn in May 1924, after his photograph was selected from dozens of applicants, and with only six months' training he became a member of the Denishawn touring company. "He's the best material in a long time," Ted told Ruth, "tall, well built, masculine, and not too good looking." The Denishawn schools trained not only dancers, but teachers, who returned to their communities and established Denishawn branches in Boston, Kansas City, San Francisco, Minneapolis, Dallas, and other cities.

Among the new Denishawn Dancers for the second Mayer tour were Ernestine Day, Margaret Dickinson, Lefa LaVine, Martha Hardy, Theresa Sadowska, George Steares, John Messersmith, and Stuart Mackall. Most important, after two years in vaudeville, Doris Humphrey returned to Denishawn, bringing with her Pauline Lawrence, the former Denishawn pianist, who had accompanied Doris as her music director. Regaining Doris compensated somewhat for the loss of Martha Graham, who at the close of the first Mayer tour left Denishawn to perform in the Greenwich Village Follies and pursue her own solo career. Many of Martha's roles had reverted to St. Denis after her reunion with Shawn and though she regained *Xochitl*, Martha found herself more often merely a member of the Denishawn corps. When she left Denishawn, her sister Geordie took some of her roles, and Doris Humphrey immediately won several new solos in the repertoire, which was the most unified in Denishawn history.

The program for the second Mayer tour was condensed from almost thirty short numbers to several lengthy dance-dramas and a few divertissements. For their new dances Ruth and Ted used only the music of American composers, including Edward MacDowell, Charles Tomlinson Griffes, Louis Moreau Gottschalk, and Charles Wakefield Cadman, who was widely known for his *From the Land of the Sky-blue Water*. Ruth used a Cadman score for her revised *Nautch*. The composer found a native melody, *Minstrel of Kashmira*, in a book by Ratan Devi, *Thirty Indian Songs*, and he fashioned it into a cheerful air that was more Western in character, livelier and less hypnotic, than a traditional Indian nautch. St. Denis' new *Street* or *Cadman Nautch*, also called *Green Nautch*, combined five basic techniques taught at the Denishawn school: head-isolations punctuated by raised eyebrows;

characteristic gestures such as the opening salaam or bow; fabric manip- ulations including the use of the *chuddah* or head scarf as a frame for the face and accent for the eyes; nautch turns that slowly gathered ve- locity; and alternating foot-beats of progressively shorter duration, ac- cented by a gesture of dragging one foot behind the other, "done with a saggy dip of the front knee and the dragging of the ball of the foot behind," with a concluding stamp. This *Nautch* had a dreamy, poetic air, as opposed to the more coquettish nature of her earlier *Nautches*. She specified soft adjustments of weight and "even, quick, quiet rhythms." Throughout the dance her posture hinted at seduction, with her head lowered and chin tucked under so that her eyes gazed from under her lashes, her chest withheld and pelvis thrust forward. In per- formance she wore one of two basic nautch skirts: a single, fifteen-yard "Marwari skirt" of satin that whirled and rippled with her nautch turns, or "Delhi skirts," a hundred yards or more of thin cotton muslin edged in gold or silver braid, layered into skirts and hung from the same waist band. She always wore a short blouse, a colorful ob- long or square head scarf edged in braid, massive dangling earrings, bracelets, and layers of ankle bells. The *Cadman Nautch* became St. Denis' standard nautch solo. She performed it for more than thirty years, though as she aged, its dramatic elements, mugging, Hindu gib- berish, and raised eyebrows, gradually dominated its dance values.

Ruth also used the work of American composer Charles Tomlinson Griffes for her major new production in the repertoire, *Ishtar of the Seven Gates*. An elaborate Babylonian ballet, *Ishtar* was as much the culmination of her Orientalia as Ted's new *Cuadro Flamenco* was the summation of his choreographic style. The two new ballets were totally different, though each boasted the lavish decor made possible by reve- nues from the Mayer tours. *Cuadro Flamenco* was vaudevillian in its essence, from the sight gags, such as chairs pulled from beneath un- suspecting señoritas, to the gay cantina atmosphere. The simple story line, with its bullfighter wooing a tempestuous Spanish dancer by offer- ing her a bundle of shawls, offered the opportunity for sumptuous dis- plays of fabric and color. Ted had brought home trunks of gorgeous Spanish costumes. In Seville he bought a complete bullfighter's outfit from a torero who was superstitious about a small tear in one of the pant legs, and he also found a voluminous white skirt for Ruth with a low-cut bodice of a deep wine hue. She added a costly Spanish shawl given her by her friend, the singer Amelita Galli-Curci. The Denishawn Dancers, laden with ruffles, combs, shawls, and flowers, performed an authentic sevillanas, a lively dance of Seville, stamping their feet and playing castanets. Ted mimed a bullfight, and Ruth's solo was a haughty Spanish routine, more flirtatious than flamenco, with skirt-ruffling kicks and provocative backbends.

Cuadro Flamenco was far removed in atmosphere from *Ishtar of the Seven Gates,* Ruth's first major dance-drama since *Bakawali* and *O-Mika.* She read every book on Babylonian history that she could find, including Margaret Horton Potter's *Ishtar of Babylon* and Morris Jastrow's *Civilization of Babylonia and Assyria.* She found the research the most difficult of her career because of the scarcity of sources. "Chinese? You've got a living art form," she told an interviewer. "Egyptian? That was easy. Hindu—a pushover if you're in the mood to study Hindu, but when you come to that Babylonian stuff—very little. I got down to coins the size of your thumb to find a little headdress or a particular action." She based her dance on the ancient myth of the descent into Hades by the goddess Ishtar, mother goddess of fertility. The dance followed Ishtar's descent from her shrine, through each of seven gates where she was progressively stripped of her jewels, before arriving in Hades. There she plucked the black veil of death from her lover Tammuz and, rescuing him, reascended to her shrine, reclaiming her jewels along the way. Ruth was Ishtar and Ted, Tammuz. Doris portrayed the Queen of the Underworld, a juicy dramatic role that she vastly preferred to the sugary solos given her by Ted. The Robert Law Studios concocted a magnificent and versatile decor for *Ishtar,* a single set that served both as an atmosphere of underworld decadence and an opulent setting for a deity.

Though Ruth felt that she had finally created another masterpiece in *Ishtar,* a Minnesota critic panned the ballet as uninteresting and pretentious. "It is a marvel of lighting, color, and elaborate detail," he conceded, "and undoubtedly it would have created a real sensation in the days before Cecil B. DeMille inserted a little Babylonian orgy into every film picture of American home life." The review underscored an important fact of Denishawn life in the 1920s. Hollywood was a strong competitor, and Denishawn could not match the movies' pageantry in opulence or scale and still maintain its mobility as a touring company.

Another significant competitor during the Mayer years was Russian ballet. In its wartime tours of the United States, the Ballets Russes of Serge Diaghilev had established a standard for dancing and spectacle that became the yardstick by which every touring dance company was judged. Denishawn followed the Ballets Russes by a season in London, and on the Mayer tours it often followed in the footsteps of Anna Pavlova and Adolph Bolm, who toured the United States with their own groups, or the Pavley-Oukrainsky Ballet, founded by two veterans of the Pavlova tours. Denishawn's reviews compared favorably with the Russians'. One passionate Pennsylvania critic, his heart divided between Pavlova and St. Denis, finally decided in favor of Ruth, "though she sometimes stoops to tricks that register well at the box office."

The box office was doing splendidly on the Mayer tours, and Ruth and Ted made a good deal of money, as much as $200,000 in a single season's receipts. Twenty percent went to Daniel Mayer's commission, and much of the rest reverted to Denishawn productions—$1,200 paid to Charles Wakefield Cadman for the *Feather of the Dawn* score alone, thousands more for the *Ishtar* set. Even more went into the Denishawn schools, as Ted negotiated to purchase the Steinway Building in New York as a permanent home for Denishawn. Even so, Ted and Ruth did not get rich. The institution they had spawned grew like hydra, with ten new debts for every one paid. Ruth was a constant worry to Ted in this regard. She simply had no sense of money; Ted, her mother, or Brother had always handled her earnings for her. She spent whatever she had impulsively, and Ted watched her carefully to make sure that her appetite for fabrics and authentic properties did not get out of hand.

Ted had his own appreciation for fine quality, and when he had the money and time he was capable of producing a superb ballet like *The Feather of the Dawn*. Taken on the second and third Mayer tours, *The Feather of the Dawn* was a Hopi Indian ballet based on the legend that held it auspicious if a feather blown into the air at dawn was wafted away by the breeze. Ted made this legend into a spectacular dance, with native rituals including a Corn Grinding Dance, an Eagle and Wolf Dance, and a Dance of the Corn Maiden. The setting was an entire adobe building, with two roof levels and a ground-floor interior. Earle Franke, who created the set, also designed the costumes which included authentic beaded moccasins, Hopi baskets, and masks copied from originals in the Smithsonian Institution. Ted's major solo in the ballet was an *Eagle Dance*. He wore on his arms huge, feathered wings, and a costume consisting of a pair of brief trunks, moccasins, Hopi jewelry, and a black pageboy wig with head band. His dance was one of the finest he ever created, with complex footwork and soaring leaps brought back to the earth in a rooted pose on half-toe, with knees flexed, torso cantilevered back, and wings widespread. Ruth greatly admired *The Feather of the Dawn,* and Ted himself thought it rivaled anything of the Russians'.

The second Mayer tour was as punishing as the first, an endless chain of one-night stands. In a single week in 1924 Denishawn played Saginaw, Michigan; Lima and Zanesville, Ohio; Newark, New Jersey; and Greensburg and Altoona, Pennsylvania. Doris Humphrey recalled that the company members boarded trains in the wee hours of the morning, covered with layers of body paint, bone-weary, but "Not so Miss Ruth. She had the energy of four people. Looking fresh and glowing, she would roam the aisles for dancers who were awake enough to listen to her crop of ideas and dreams, of which she had a fresh supply every morning." Friends of Ruth's always said the same thing: at any hour of the day or night they found her alive, vibrant with ideas, and always scribbling, scribbling, scribbling. She wrote a good deal of poetry. She confided her innermost thoughts to her diary and also penned pages and pages of philosophical and spiritual essays on the nature of love, sin, art, and humankind. A major influence on her thinking during this period was P. D. Ouspensky's *Tertium Organum: A Key to the Enigmas of the World,* translated by her friend, Claude Bragdon.

Bragdon was an architect, Theosophist, and the designer of Walter Hampden's theatrical productions. Through Hampden, who had appeared in the West Coast *Light of Asia,* Bragdon met Ruth. They enjoyed an instantaneous rapport. With his blunt head, close-cropped hair and round, sad eyes, Bragdon did not particularly look like a mystic, but he and Ruth had read all the same books—Mabel Collins' Theosophical tracts, books about Delsarte, Max Müller's *Sacred Books of the East.* They became part of a circle of friends that included the composer Roy Harris, the novelists Owen Wister and Zona Gale, and Norman Bel Geddes, who had designed but never executed a theatre for the first California Denishawn. Ruth and her friends often gathered in the home of Walter Kirkpatrick Brice, a world traveler and philanthropist who enjoyed having his dinner guests dress in oriental robes from his collection. The dinner conversation ran to esoteric themes, and from Bragdon, Ruth learned about Ouspensky's *Tertium Organum.*

Tertium Organum was the second major book published by the Russian mathematician and philosopher. *The Fourth Dimension,* published

in 1909, established his reputation as an important theorist in the field
of mathematics. *Tertium Organum* followed in 1912, but it was not
until 1920 that an English-language version became available through
the translation jointly undertaken by Nicholas Bessaraboff and Claude
Bragdon. In *Tertium Organum* Ouspensky offered a new vision of the
universe, a fourth-dimensional reality in which time became only the
movement of consciousness (psychic life) upon a higher space. Time
thus served as the fourth dimension of space, and the familiar three-
dimensional world of height, breadth, and length was revealed as only
a partial and inaccurate perception of a unity lying beyond the limits of
ordinary ways of seeing. Other thinkers during this period, including
Albert Einstein, explored the concept of a fourth dimension, but in
Ouspensky's version, one entered this dimension through a heightened
intuition or sensitized psyche. In his fourth-dimensional reality, Ouspensky found infinity, wholeness, vitality, and timelessness, an Eternal
Now, which demanded a new mathematics and system of logic. In con-
structing his argument he bitterly attacked positivism, the philosophical
approach that adopted the method of experimental science, as "how to"
philosophy, handy in dealing with questions of how phenomena operate under given conditions, but useless in questioning those givens, particularly time, space, and causality. Ouspensky's greatest contribution
in *Tertium Organum* was his exposure of man's habits of perception.
In one graphic illustration he constructed an imaginary one-dimen-
sional, linear world, then a two-dimensional world of flat planes, to
demonstrate how the dimensionality of the world depends upon the development of consciousness. His description of a higher, fourth-dimensional reality was less precise, though no less intriguing to those readers
in the early 1920s who agreed with a New York *Times* book reviewer
that Ouspensky brought "conceptual clarity to the field of the occult."

St. Denis did not pretend to follow all the nuances of Ouspensky's
argument, but she responded eagerly to his discussion of art as an instrument capable of penetrating to a higher reality. "The phenomenal
world is merely a means for the artist," Ouspensky wrote, "just as colors
are for the painter, and sounds for the musician—a means for the understanding of the noumenal world and for the expression of that understanding. At the present stage of our development we possess nothing
so powerful, as an instrument of knowledge of the world of causes, as
art." Ruth underlined that passage in her copy of *Tertium Organum*
and another which asserted, "In art it is necessary to study 'occultism'—

the hidden side of life. The artist must be a clairvoyant; he must see that which others do not see." Ruth felt that those words confirmed her philosophy of art, and she was particularly struck by Ouspensky's description of the motionless, matterless, holistic nature of a higher reality which, she felt, confirmed her experience. In dancing Ruth often felt stillness in motion, a state of equilibrium achieved through movement, and those moments were the closest to God she ever got. She was most free while dancing, most orderly, most clear, and in Ouspensky's work she found words for her experience.

In a lecture she gave in the 1930s, "God Geometrizes," she tried to express the impact of Ouspensky's work on her view of dance. If, she reasoned, "the line, the curve, the sphere, the spiral and other forms are the geometric blocks from which our objective world is evolved," then Ouspensky's arguments "lead to the borders of a new order of thinking . . . As yet the Dance has been more or less content and delightfully content with obeying the reactive laws of rhythm and the objective beauty of design without bothering its head about looking deeper into the cause or changes of these rhythms and designs. These have their root in our very three dimensional viewpoint itself." She waded in deeper: "It will be felt, rather than intellectually conceived that the nearer we get to Truth, the less we will dance. The fourth dimension may cut our legs from under us, as it were, leaving us contemplating the universe from a mount of perfection, without movement." She cloaked these remarks in witticisms, quipping at one point, "I realize that I am a long way out to sea—yet I have to swim out as far as I can hoping that someone will eventually send me a boat in which to get back to shore." But this philosophical question was very real for Ruth St. Denis, as it was for major thinkers such as Ralph Waldo Emerson, who reasoned that the highest form of communication was silence. Throughout her career of creating dances, in her most private moments, in her diaries, in the rehearsal room alone, Ruth pondered the still-point of perfection and its implications for the artist. She tried to create dances that explored the question. Her most successful attempt, *White Jade* (1926), was an exquisite study in balance, harmony, and stillness in which she seemed to "contemplate the universe from a mount of perfection," but in the very success of *White Jade* lay its failure. In 1927 St. Denis was forced to remove the dance from her Ziegfeld Follies repertoire because, in the opinion of the management, the dance did not move enough to maintain audience interest.

During the Mayer years, however, Ruth used her ideas from Ouspensky in creating works for her "synchoric orchestra," an expansion of her music visualizations into dance interpretations of orchestral symphonies. Most of these studies were confined to the Denishawn school and never reached the stage. The earliest, a visualization of Schubert's *Unfinished Symphony*, occurred about 1921 in the California branch of Denishawn. Ruth chose the Schubert work because it was relatively short and because the score was available to her in California. She used fifty dancers, each representing an instrument, though not maintaining an exact one-to-one correspondence. She envisioned this dance orchestra as a tool for exposing the mathematical principles underlying dance, so that a higher form of expression might be evolved from those principles. At about the same time, Claude Bragdon was involved in experiments of his own, also influenced by Ouspensky. He attempted to create "color-music, the organization of color and light into an emotional language, just as music is sound thus organized." To this end he constructed a "color organ" and conducted experiments in a laboratory supplied him by his friend Kirk Brice. Bragdon's equations of colors with human emotions, his charts identifying red as a physical color, blue as a spiritual color, and so on, had their echo in St. Denis' color dances in later years, including her *Color Study of the Madonna*.

As Ruth and Ted traveled with the Denishawn Dancers, they occasionally took turns reading from Ouspensky's books to their assembled dancers. On one occasion Ruth reported, "The children were engrossed and asked many questions. We spoke of the four-dimensional body, and Ted said, 'Now listen. Let's get this thing straight, and not let our brains go around in meaningless circles. Ouspensky says that the perfect body of man . . . exists now in four dimensions. If this is so, and the intersecting time-divisions of our senses are removed, we can not only see the perfect body which exists now, but . . . it's along these lines that the future dance, with its geometric patterns based on a greater understanding of our fourth-dimensional life, will be of the greatest value.'"

For Ruth, these were the heady moments of the Denishawn tour, but there were as many moments of fatigue, drudgery, and tedium. At the end of the second Mayer tour, after eight months of crisscrossing the continent, Ruth retreated to a rest cure at the Battle Creek Sanitarium in Michigan. For several weeks she attended lectures and participated in a regimen of "biologic training" designed to "harmonize oneself with life." The sanitarium reminded Ruth of her mother's water-cure in up-state New York and she wrote happily, "I am a vegetable that is being well washed."

While Ruth visited the sanitarium in May of 1924, Ted went his own way to New York. Their marriage was not doing well. Though the demands of touring had eliminated most of their extramarital flirtations, Ruth and Ted found little solace in each other's company. They came close to separating again, and the Mayer contract was the only bond that prevented a complete break. The strongest aspect of their marriage, their spiritual and intellectual relationship, suffered as Denishawn grew in prestige and power. Most of their arguments during this period were related to the fortunes of the Denishawn school. In the summer of 1924, as Ted negotiated in New York for the Steinway Building as a permanent home for Denishawn, he wrote Ruth a new set of demands. He asked that she agree to a fundamental principle, "your own being convinced that if you find you want to experiment with that portion of your life which is not free in marriage—you will make a clean break first." He specified three alternatives: a mutually exclusive marriage, in which case Ted would continue bearing the burden of the school; Ruth taking control of the school in Ted's absence; or a termination of Denishawn, with each of them pursuing his own independent career. "God help me," Ruth told her diary, "I may be wrong but it seems to me that Ted's worst fault is self-righteousness. He is so pure and so sure, so complacent and faintly superior. Perhaps I do deserve it all, I don't know. I try to be really loving, to praise him, to nurse him, to sustain him—none of which so far as I can honestly see he gives to me." She was in Los Angeles that summer, after a vacation to Colorado with her brother's family, and she took the opportunity to assess the fortunes of the West Coast school. She itemized the school salaries in a letter to Ted and reported that there was "too much overhead for the amount of business done," but she praised the school staff, particularly director Hazel Krans and Nina Garrett, of whom she said, "Artistically speaking, she is a class A teacher, one of the best I have ever seen." Ruth argued for a continuation of California Denishawn, pointing out that 75 percent of the school's revenues was going to support the New York branch, but Ted favored closing the Los Angeles school. He had some ambitious new ideas for the New York operation, one of which was a high-quality magazine espousing the Denishawn ideals. He toyed with titles, *The Denishawn Dancer* and *The Deni-*

shawn Dance Arts Magazine, before settling on the simpler *Denishawn Magazine.*

A quarterly review devoted to the art of dance, *The Denishawn Magazine* made its debut in the fall of 1924, with Ruth and Ted listed as founders and editors, and as associate editors June Hamilton Rhodes and Katharane Edson, who had just been named national director of all the Denishawn schools. Handsomely designed, the magazine featured original art work by Bernice Oehler, including a wide border around the cover with sketches of St. Denis and Shawn dances. Inside the magazine were lavish photographs of Ruth and Ted standing shoulder to shoulder, a class of dancers in black wool bathing suits being taught by Miss Ruth, who wore a flowing summer dress and hat, a partially nude photograph of Ted, and publicity shots from the Mayer tours. Ruth wrote the lead article, "The Dance as Life Experience," which began, "I see men and women dancing rhythmically and in joy, on a hilltop bathed in the saffron rays of a setting sun," and continuing with Ouspenskian observations on "the Eternal Now of the Dance." In the midst of this reverie Ruth inserted a wistful note that reflected her concerns about her career: "The spectacle of a singer or dancer or actor continuing on the stage in parts too young for him is tragic enough," Ruth wrote, "but still more tragic is the situation of the artist who, in his maturity, having grown to the most interesting and beautiful stage of his consciousness, is forced to withdraw from his active career because of the childish demand of the public for mere youth."

As she toured, Ruth felt her age, forty-five. She hoped that the third Mayer tour, which began in October 1924, would be her last. Already she was making plans for a year of "external freedom from entanglements." In California that summer she had resumed her singing lessons, and she secretly cherished hopes of a singing career. She sang for her friend Galli-Curci who told her, "With a month's study you can beat Mary Garden," then a singer of renown. Encouraged, Ruth continued to practice her singing as she traveled on the third and final Mayer tour. This tour took the Denishawn company on a circle of the continent, from New York northwest and to California, then southeast and back up to Ohio and New York again. Twelve dancers made the tour, with Ruth Austin, Lenore Hellekson, and Howle Fisher among the new additions. Doris remained the principal soloist, and she was allowed to perform her own composition, a *Scherzo Waltz* solo. The big new Denishawn number was *The Vision of the Aissoua,* Ruth and

Ted's Arabic ballet, and Ruth created a new set of *Schubert Waltzes* for herself.

This music visualization of various waltzes by Schubert was a joyous, delicate dance, with Ruth costumed in a pale pink georgette gown worn over tea-colored fleshings. Her blond wig was dressed high in loose curls. She began the dance at center stage, spinning gently on the ball of one foot with the other in a "Greek arabesque" with softened line. More spins and swaying *pas de basque*, heavy skips that she called the "Duncan step," and circular waltzing steps completed the dance. The arms often "visualized" the music, with "little tossing movements" of the fingers and small circles of the hands at the wrist, or a visual approximation of pitch as in, "Run right and catch the high note with the left hand high." The arms also pressed the atmosphere in opposition to the thrust of the body, indicated in this note: "Run diagonally right two steps, and leap softly on the right foot, bending the left sharply at the knee, throwing the upper body and head back and pressing the hands palms down at the sides." The *Scherzo Waltzes* were full of dynamic richness, nuances of withheld or apportioned weight. In the words of one of her conductors, St. Denis "rode the music." A 1925 film of the *Scherzo Waltzes* shows St. Denis in her prime, with stately, upright body and billowing arms, her head and eyes following the path of her revolving waltz. She ends with a gesture of surrender from Art Nouveau, wrist to forehead of back-flung head.

Ruth and Ted also performed a new *Balinese Fantasy* and Ruth choreographed her own Balinese solos from this material. Her notes on Balinese style reveal the importance of facial expression and dramatic embellishments on a few basic body positions and movements of the arms and head. She specified "a feeling of childlikeness" for one of the solos that began, "*Seated on the box*, expression is cat-that-has-eaten-the-cream, corners of the mouth are up. *As you spring* into first pose, chin up, look over the shoulder and the chin is out in turns, with much squatting, and a smile." St. Denis explained that the basic facial expression was a dead pan "to impress your audience with the idea that behind your gesture, something tremendous is going on. Generally, eyes are down, and the feeling is that one's own face is a mask. The projection by the mask face is an impersonal emotion. Because the Buddha plays such an enormous part in the influence of the arts of the East, it is well to remember that the habitual expression of his face is with the eyes three-quarters closed, showing a vision of the inner and outer world." St. Denis annotated her dances for teaching purposes, and they are only a rough guide to her actual performances. She was notorious for improvising onstage.

The third Mayer tour, completed in April 1925, extended Denishawn's record for travel to more than 556 concert performances in over 293 cities before a cumulative audience that surpassed the one-million mark. Denishawn left in its wake a more sophisticated dance audience, a sprinkling of dance schools, and a memory of strange beauty that bloomed in the imaginations of those spectators who filled the opera houses, high school auditoriums, music halls, and amphitheatres, night after night. A Texas critic tried to encompass in words the scope of Denishawn magic: "Here is the eloquent gesture, the technique that does not protrude, chaste miming and elemental struggles, heroic figures, and vague dream fancies, the essence of all religions expressed in the worship of beauty, the evolution of ideas and the triumph of good over evil forces that shines through the dramatized legends." Denishawn was multidimensional, a decorative surface that transported the viewer through space and time to distant cultures and deep into occult dreams.

As the kernel of those dreams, Ruth felt buried within layers of institution, much as her solos were embedded in the larger Denishawn spectacles. Of the Denishawn school, she said in later years, "It cut across my personal career, period." Of the company itself, she had mixed feelings. Denishawn extended her performing years and brought her to the apex of her career, but Ruth always thought of herself as a solo artist. "Every creative artist is an entire institution in himself," she once said. "The rotating of his life and expression is in reality a complete circle. He instinctively refuses to be a part, merely one cell of a larger organization which suppresses the functioning of his entire consciousness." Denishawn, she felt, suppressed her individual art, so it was something of an irony that in early 1925 the Denishawn company received an invitation to tour the Orient. Ruth, who had introduced a brand of oriental dancing to America, had always wanted to journey to the countries of her dances' origins. But she wanted to go alone.

In her diary she wrote, "I have been looking forward at the end of this three years' contract to a great period of rest and peace, a period of calling my soul my own, of directing certain of my own affairs in my own way and having time and leisure to let the spirit well up in my consciousness into new and beautiful patterns. Now, in a moment, this whole concept seemed to be swept away, and still another period of hurrying and confusion to be contracted for again." A tour to the Orient meant exhausting travel under primitive conditions, extremes of climate, performances in the most inadequate of theatres, but the Orient also meant color, texture, smells, philosophies, and dances that Ruth knew only from books. She knew that this was her only chance to go, and she said yes.

NINE

THE ORIENT AND BEYOND

As THE STEAMSHIP *President Jefferson* sailed from Seattle to Yokohama in the late summer of 1925, Ruth sat on deck, listening to Ted read aloud from Walt Whitman's poems. Suddenly she burst into tears, "full of the knowledge, with great sadness, that I too am a Whitman—I have felt as great and as deeply as he has—but I have not spoken. I have not acted it out. I have allowed life to bind and circumscribe my actions and expression, as though I have been cut off from sources of power by my own cowardice and stupidity." This voyage through the Orient, through Japan, China, Malaya, Burma, India, Ceylon, Indonesia, Indo-China, and the Philippines, was also an inner voyage. With her endless self-criticism, Ruth spent the next fifteen months probing the sources of her weariness, her creative malaise, as her dreams of the Orient collided with its reality.

Her preparations for the trip were, as usual, hasty. The Denishawn company finished its third Mayer tour in early April, with a brief recess before regrouping to perform a summer concert at the Lewisohn Stadium in New York. That left only a few months to prepare for the Orient. A major problem was the Denishawn school. Ruth and Ted debated closing the New York branch but decided to leave a skeletal staff of Ted's stepmother, Mabel Shawn, and Hazel Krans from the California school. Another pressing concern was musical direction. Just after the third Mayer tour concluded, Louis Horst announced that he was leaving Denishawn after a decade as its musical director to study composition in Vienna. He later joined forces with Martha Graham. Ruth and Ted were stunned and Ruth privately felt that when Louis left, following Martha by a year or so, "the signal was given for the dissolution of Denishawn."

Searching for a conductor-composer, Ruth and Ted approached several candidates and finally settled on Clifford Vaughan, a pianist and organist trained at the Philadelphia Conservatory of Music. Then in his early thirties, soft-spoken and courteous, Vaughan went to work on the Denishawn repertoire. He composed the music for *A Legend of Pelée*, Ruth's new dramatic solo, on the train from New York to Seattle, their port of embarkation. "They weren't great compositions," Vaughan said of his Denishawn scores. "They were written to illustrate the dances. Musicianship was a secondary consideration." Vaughan played the pit piano and conducted a pickup orchestra on tour, and throughout the Orient he listened to native music and translated its rhythms into compositions adapted to Western instruments. He kept company with the Denishawn carpenter-electrician, Stanley Frazier, and with Brother St. Denis, whom Ted had invited along as stage manager. Brother, known to his friends as Buzz, had pursued a career in geology and petroleum engineering in Wyoming since parting company with Ruth and Ted in the early days of their marriage. He still knew more about stage lighting and sets and more about Ruth's temperament than anyone. He agreed to rejoin Denishawn for the oriental tour, leaving his wife and two children in California for the duration.

Ruth and Ted also hired June Hamilton Rhodes, who had been with them in the early California days, as their company manager for the tour. June was a tiny blond dynamo, opinionated and bossy, and she clashed with the no-nonsense Brother St. Denis. "June insists on having her finger into *everything* and thinks she has to show a man how to put a color in a lamp," Buzz complained in his travel diary. "Then she will fly over and tie a couple of strings on a baton (already being properly done by Stanley or a stage hand), then she will fly out front and tell Ruth something about the light that she already knows, then after it's over she will tell how hard she worked, conveying the impression to the unsuspecting that she is doing everybody's work. The funny part of it," he puzzled, "is that most of the time apparently Ruth and Ted take it all in." Ruth was easily influenced by her closest companions, and on this trip she allied herself with Pearl Wheeler, who fed her dreams and reported company intrigues. Pearl was no longer dancing, as she had in the early days of Denishawn. Gray-haired now, defensive, fiercely protective of Ruth, Pearl supervised the vast array of Denishawn costumes and wigs. Her brilliant costume designs were so intrinsic to Ruth's works that Pearl might have been credited as co-choreographer. On the oriental tour she created new costumes and oversaw the dancers' ironing and minor repairs. A dour taskmaster, she specialized in snide remarks and orchestrated Ruth's approval or disapproval of various protégés.

Twelve dancers made the trip to the Orient: Doris Humphrey, who took along her mother, to their mutual regret; Pauline Lawrence, rehearsal pianist and dancer, who with Charles Weidman formed a close-knit trio with Doris; the sensitive Geordie Graham, with her sad eyes and thoughtful nature, now dancing Martha's role in *Xochitl;* Anne Douglas, a dainty oriental type; the handsome George Steares, who was not a very good dancer, and Ernestine Day, an attractive brunette who was. The three newcomers were Jane Sherman, an intelligent girl of seventeen who had studied for several years at the New York Denishawn school; Edith James, a self-contained young woman from Arizona; and Mary Howry, an early Denishawn student who wanted to specialize in Javanese dancing. In addition, Grace Burroughs, a teacher, and Ara Martin, who helped Shawn with his secretarial work, paid their own way and appeared in full-company ballets.

On the morning of August 19, 1925, the company scrambled on deck as the *President Jefferson* steamed into Yokohama Harbor. Ahead, the mountains, shrouded in clouds, seemed to rise steeply from the sea itself. Fishing boats crowded the harbor, but the atmosphere was serene. Japan barely noticed the arrival of Denishawn. Ruth was fascinated by the rickshaws lining the dock and tried to take a ride to the customs house, which was only a short walk away. When she climbed in and signaled her destination the rickshaw driver unceremoniously dumped her out. "We later surmised that the fare would not have been large enough for him to bother, but I had to smile," Buzz noted with some satisfaction. "Ruth St. Denis was the same to the coolie as anybody else, but I'm sure Ruth didn't feel that way. Everybody had to laugh." After customs, the company boarded a train for Tokyo where a swarm of press photographers and a committee of performers from the Imperial Theatre gave Denishawn its official welcome to Japan. The company rode to the Imperial Hotel in a rickshaw caravan, then visited the hotel roof garden as guests of the manager of the theatre. Ruth readied herself for some authentic Japanese entertainment. To her surprise, their host offered for their enjoyment the latest movie from Hollywood, "an hour and a half of the most vulgar, cheap, sexy, obvious display of our national sins that we had ever seen," she shuddered. This was her first encounter with a recurring phenomenon in the Orient: the American visitor longing for the spiritual essence of the East, the Oriental, eager to please, purveying the material pleasures of Jazz Age America.

On opening night at the Imperial Theatre Ruth was apprehensive. Dance was a highly developed art in Japan, with discriminating audiences and critics. She had not dared to bring her Japanese dances to Tokyo but she was uncertain how her *Greek Veil Plastique, Black and Gold Sari, Waltz and Liebestraum,* and other ethnic dances would fare. The members of the audience, mostly Japanese with a sprinkling of Americans, constantly came and went, snapping photographs, destroying her concentration. They responded coolly to her dances and she went back to the hotel, heartsick. After the first week in Tokyo, however, the audiences and critics began to acquire a taste for Denishawn. Their change of heart may have had something to do with a change of program. Every five days the company performed an entirely new program in Tokyo. Each of the four Denishawn programs brought to the Orient featured a major work and a series of divertissements. Ruth and Ted had carefully pruned much of the Orientalia from their programs, substituting Americana and music visualizations. In Tokyo their opening program included a mixture of lyric and dramatic solos and the Algerian *Vision of the Aissoua.* The Japanese seemed to prefer Denishawn's subtle, dreamy, and poetic dances, especially the music visualizations, and the second week's more popular program featured the evocative *Spirit of the Sea* and a gentle new solo of Ruth's, *The Queen of Heaven: A Study of the Madonna,* substituted for her more vulgar *Legend of Pelée.*

A Legend of Pelée, Hawaiian goddess of fire, was another of Ruth's solos based on the premise of a costume. She designed a gray silk tent that fitted over her head and descended to completely cover the stage, with small holes through which scarves could be flicked, representing tongues of flame. Thus transformed into a volcano, Ruth mimed an elaborate tale of love, jealousy, and destruction by manipulating her silk draperies, "rumbling" her arms underneath and ultimately "erupting" into a great flinging of scarves. She probably got her idea for the dance from a book about the 1902 eruption of Mount Pelée in Martinique, written by her friend John Lovell, but the dance was tedious, Ruth disliked performing it, and it represented the nadir of her art. Muffled in costume, she danced a metaphor of her submersion in Denishawn theatricality.

Pelée disappeared from the Tokyo program for the rest of the month-long stay and the Japanese critics warmed to Denishawn. Most of the writers compared the company with earlier visits by Anna Pavlova, whom they considered a representative of old-fashioned European ballet. As one critic wrote, "We have never been so moved as by the dancing of Denishawn. When Miss Anna Pavlova came we admired her technical skill, but these artists bring us a spiritual and physical beauty of dance, a more elemental and vital thing to dance than mere skill." Denishawn was modern but devoted to beauty and more than one critic expressed surprise that such an exquisite art could come from materialistic America. Anti-American sentiment was rampant in Japan, with relations between the two nations strained by American immigration policies. Denishawn conquered the Japanese prejudices. One writer reported that his Japanese friends had declined to see the company, feeling that modern dancing as depicted in American films was sensational and vulgar. The writer admitted that he went to see Denishawn with the same misgivings but left "amazed at my ignorance of what real dancing can be. A stage draped in black velvet, a perfect little orchestra led by a delightful pianist and violinist, and then Miss St. Denis. We are told that she has been dancing for many years, in fact when I was quite young I remember her name being spoken of as a great artist, and that was many years ago. At the present day she looks like a girl in her teens. Her figure is perfect, and so is her dancing."

One of the critics who most admired Denishawn, Natsuya Mitsuyoshi, introduced Ruth and Ted to Matsumoto Koshiro, leading actor at the Imperial Theatre. During the company's stay in Tokyo Koshiro offered daily classes in Japanese dance technique to Ruth and Ted and the Denishawn dancers, and Ted secured rights to Koshiro's ballet-drama *Momiji Gari*. Ruth and Ted also visited the music museum at the Imperial Palace where they examined costumes of the Bugaku, musical instruments, rare books, and properties. At times, in the midst of such treasures, in the ancient Buddhist temples, or in the Nō dramas that lasted for hours in the temple theatres, Ruth began to recover some basic sense of herself. For a moment her weariness, problems, and preoccupations faded and her strong instincts for beauty came to the fore. She drank in textures, colors, and sounds and allowed her feelings to merge with the Japanese art around her. In the midst of a Nō drama she reported, "Two women [men, but dressed as women] have entered. They are in gorgeous red brocade kimonos. They stand a long while, the chorus chants, and the drums clack and the high flute gives long, drawn-out notes. We do not understand; we can only feel. What a strange, archaic form of long-gone-by beliefs and emotions." The tempo of Japanese art was her own.

During their month in Tokyo the company attended the Kabuki theatre, a geisha party at a riverside teahouse, luncheons and dinners in private homes, and tours of famous shrines. They were photographed everywhere. Just after they arrived, Ted and Ruth took the girls downtown to a major department store and had them oufitted in summer kimonos. Ruth tried the same publicity ploy she had used in Paris twenty years earlier, parading her kimono-clad dancers down the street and into their rickshaws. To their embarrassment, they later learned that they had purchased bathing kimonos. At least Ruth's instincts for publicity were sound. Throughout the Orient she posed for photographs, in temples, before the Taj Mahal, on camelback, compiling a dossier for future use. Ruth was extraordinarily photogenic. She had a trick of looking upward, toward "eleven o'clock," that smoothed her neck and showed her facial bones to advantage and, as Delsarte advised, projected a spiritual countenance.

The kimono episode did not daunt the Denishawners' passion for shopping. They bought lacquered boxes in Japan, silks and ivory in China, brass gongs and uncut stones in Burma, rugs in India, batiks in Java, and exotic birds and monkeys in Singapore. Pearl was the most gifted bargainer among them. "She takes up the piece of cloth or braid or jewel that she wants," Ruth wrote in wonder, "and upon asking the price immediately offers from one quarter to a third of the asking price. This figure she keeps on repeating in carrying tones until the merchant falls under a kind of hypnosis—and usually gives in!" With Pearl in the vanguard, Ruth spent every cent she had. "I have the financial morals of a goldfish," she confessed. "I can resist everything but temptation." She developed a passion for exotic birds and in Singapore indulged her "parrotinitis," as Buzz called it. At one point the Denishawn company traveled with sixteen birds in its entourage, including Ruth's beloved new pet, a cockatoo she named Dada. She rationalized her spending as a business expense. With Ted she picked up accessories for costumes, a complete stage set in Peking, and props and wigs from the Imperial Theatre in Tokyo. Everything was relatively cheap, and compulsive shopping became the company pastime in the few hours between rehearsals and evenings in the theatre.

Reluctantly they left Tokyo by train in late September and moved southward along the length of Japan, performing in almost a dozen cities before sailing up the Yellow Sea into Manchuria and China. Travel within China was treacherous. Warring factions conducted midnight raids on the railway tracks under the noses of troops of the young republic. "The annual 'war' is on," Ruth reported in her diary, "and some 'general' from the north is attacking some 'general'—all small g's—from the south, so the railroads are uncertain." She pondered the state of her own nerves. "Strange dead period when I do not feel anything. My outer self travels—dances—shops and goes eagerly and willingly to see the various sights, but the inner me remains motionless in a curious detached dry state."

In early November the company finally reached Peking, where Mary Ferguson, director of the Peking Society of Fine Arts, met them at the Chien Mein gate. Miss Ferguson became an indispensable guide, arranging the purchase of Chinese stage sets, introducing the Denishawn company to prominent artists in Peking. She had them to a luncheon in her home on that first afternoon and after lunch Ruth and her brother immediately began sightseeing. They visited the Forbidden City or palace quarter of the Imperial residence, fully opened to the public only that year when the deposed heir to the throne requested of the republic that he be allowed to move to Tientsin. Buzz was impressed by the Forbidden City with its series of terraces, expanses of glazed tile and marble balustrades, pervaded by an atmosphere "so weird," he said, that it could only be understood by being there.

Later with Ted, Doris, and Charles they visited the Temple of Heaven, the shrine of the national religion of Imperial China. With a hired car and an interpreter they drove to the walled park three miles from Peking and entered through a series of gates, past an ornate building used by the emperor in fasting before religious rites. In the heart of the compound they came upon the outdoor Altar of Heaven, three circular terraces of dazzling white marble stacked concentrically like a flat wedding cake, two hundred feet in diameter, and surrounded by a circular wall and buildings roofed with tiles of ultramarine. It is one of the simplest and most profound architectural spaces in the world, and Ruth felt herself drawn to the very center of the altar where she stood with her arms raised toward the heavens, feeling "for an instant of time the descending rays from the invisible Sun of Life, pouring into my spirit." Something about the conjunction of art and nature, white marble and glazed tiles set in a grove of trees, woke her dormant muse. She had an idea for a dance. "To worship the four elements of earth, air, fire, and water," she reflected, "out of which is fashioned an exquisite thing—this Woman of Jade!" Translating her experience into art, she created her finest solo dance, *White Jade,* completed at the end of the oriental tour.

After three days of performances in Peking, the company traveled to Tientsin and boarded a steamer for the trip to Shanghai, where they were due to perform at the Olympic Theatre. Buzz described the journey: four days and nights on a crowded boat, its decks littered with Chinese passengers, the air thick with the smell of opium. When they reached Shanghai, the company stayed in a hotel in the French district of that divided city of concessions. With its large department stores, asphalt streets and expensive estates, Shanghai seemed almost European, save for its mixture of exotic nationalities. Here, as elsewhere in the Orient, the Denishawn tour was as much a journey through colonial empires as through Asia itself. In Singapore the company found English universally spoken. They found Tientsin a thoroughly Anglicized city. The Dutch influence so pervaded Java that Buzz reported, "The part of Java we see is a European country, with a lot of native Javanese residents, their color and their sarongs seem about all that is left." Their hosts throughout the tour were embassy personnel, native aristocrats, foreigners, or fellow artists, and only rarely did they encounter the daily lives of the native population. Within this circumscribed world of their travels was the even smaller world of Denishawn itself.

It was, on the surface, a harmonious company, a family ruled by Papa Shawn and inspired by Miss Ruth, distant parents who traveled deluxe while the company went second-class. In an effort to feel closer to her dancers, Ruth instituted a series of philosophical evenings. On Thursday nights the dancers gathered in Ruth's or Ted's room to listen to readings from *Tertium Organum,* with appropriate discussion. According to Doris Humphrey, Ruth also tried playing mother hen, instituting a bed check on her Denishawn wards and insisting that they wear extra underpants when riding camelback. Even though preoccupied with her own problems, Ruth was the figurative center of Denishawn. Jane Sherman wrote home about an evening at an Indian beach when "Ted, Brother, and us girls all played around Miss Ruth as though there wasn't another person on earth." As the youngest member of the Denishawn family, Jane was still in awe of Miss Ruth, who asked her once to vigorously towel-dry her back in a Japanese bath. "She should only have known," Jane wrote, "how much courage it required for me to touch her so roughly!" Inevitably, the young dancer grew disillusioned. "It is nervy for me to say so," she wrote her mother, "but I suspect Miss Ruth has no honest-to-goodness brains. She is a good medium for the artistic force and she has a true artistic instinct (tho lately I think it's getting a little blurred by too much emphasis on costumes). But in other ways she actually seems stupid, whereas Ted is clever but has to use his wits in ways that are not quite straight. Miss Ruth also seems to be too easily influenced by those about her."

Her eighteen-year-old's assessment was not too wide of the mark. Ruth was impractical and easily influenced, but rather than stupid, self-preoccupied and depressed. "My experiencer is working fine, but my realizer is all worn out," was one of her favorite sayings in the Orient. "Is it merely the natural and mortal course of things that at forty-five I am tired and more or less incapable of emotion," she asked herself. "Is it that I am merely in a (long!) period of negative living in a circumstance which is no longer my natural element of creativeness?" She questioned the point of her artistic life, which seemed an endless round of payment and debt. "We work like dogs a whole winter to pay off the debts we accumulated during the summer. We operate on the illusion that we are popular—that we are a success—when we are not. In a word, we don't pay! The only money we actually make is in vaudeville."

She was middle-aged. Her spiritual energy seemed dry. Pearl understood this, as she understood Ruth's need to consider artistic alternatives. When Ruth had an idea for lecture-concerts that would present the dances of many nations with their history and philosophy, Pearl supported and amplified the idea. She herself suggested that *Ishtar of the Seven Gates* might be made into a movie, with the actual dance as prologue. When Ruth told her of her vision of a dance called *White Jade*, Pearl helped her plan its costume and decor. Pearl understood Ruth's need for beauty and she lovingly prepared her dressing rooms, placing a bit of tapestry on the wall or a rug on the floor to cushion the effect of bare and often inadequate quarters.

Ruth also relied on her brother, and on this tour they shared many a conversation in the early hours of the morning aboard ships or trains. Brother was an intelligent if unpolished man of forty, proud, shrewd, and straightforward. On the oriental tour he supervised all the baggage, which increased in direct proportion to the frenzy of shopping, and he set up all the stages, including one he had to build from scratch in Java. He appeared in several dances, including *Cuadro Flamenco* and *Boston Fancy*. He even did a bit of advance booking in the absence of Asway Strok, the Russian resident of Singapore who booked the oriental tour from month to month. Brother had little time left for socializing, though he managed to meet with representatives of the petroleum industry throughout the Orient. He was devoted to Ruth, but not blindly. He did not share her passion for philosophy, but he was willing to listen and to let her occupy the limelight. He was, perhaps, the best friend she ever had.

The company spent Christmas Day in Rangoon, Burma, where they were fulfilling a ten-day engagement at the Excelsior Theatre. Rangoon was hot and filthy, filled with great black crows who scavenged the refuse thrown into its alleyways. June Rhodes managed to find a scraggly Christmas tree, "one of the only sixteen Christmas trees in Burma," boasted a Denishawn publicity release. They decorated it with tinsel balls and a cardboard angel. "It's hard to realize it's Christmas," Ruth wrote, "with the smell of incense and curry in the air and fly-catching lizards running over the white walls of our rooms!" In Rangoon the Denishawn company broke with protocol and accepted an invitation from one of the native *nouveau riche,* an opium dealer and smuggler who gave them a magnificent banquet and party. Though the local police commissioner advised them against going and Asway Strok worried that Rangoon society would be shocked, "We came to the Orient to see what we could see and not be bothered about our reputation," Buzz said, "so old Strok came along himself and I noticed he seemed to have a pretty good time."

In Rangoon they saw a good deal of native dancing. Through a government official and his American wife, Ruth and Ted saw the Burmese "Pwe" or dance-drama in private homes and in public performances in the seedier districts on the outskirts of the city. Through their hosts they also met U Po Sein, the most revered actor-dancer of Burma, who gave Ted private lessons. Ruth found the Burmese dancing the finest she had seen, technically difficult with its squats, vertical jumps and S-curved arms and its rhythmic subtleties, almost like American jazz. Later in Singapore she choreographed with Doris *A Burmese Yein Pwe*, accompanied at its premiere by native musical instruments purchased in Rangoon.

On the threshold of India, Ruth felt spiritually renewed. "Last night in bed, reading *Tertium Organum* again, I felt a curious, strong conviction about the fact of conscious being, as independent of brain," she wrote, "and I suddenly felt that another self, her glorious consciousness was now intact, and always would be, and a feel of relaxing stole over me. Some curious inner strain let go." On the train from Calcutta to Bombay she spent a harmonious evening with Ted, like old times. Ted reminded her that *Radha* premiered on that very evening, twenty years ago in New York. They went on to talk nostalgically about art and life, their marriage and careers. Ted took advantage of Ruth's receptivity to press his case for equality in their relationship, equal billing and equal artistic recognition "after twelve years of service." Though Ruth had always been reluctant to concede these points because she considered herself the superior artist, she admitted in her diary, "Ted is easily the greatest male dancer in the world today. His character or personality dances are not in my opinion as good as his lyric or plastiques," but she took into account "his splendid intelligence, charm, and great singleness of purpose. He is broad in his vision of artistic possibilities. Perhaps," she mused, "at last a real partnership."

On this trip—as always—Ted had been busy choreographing new ballets and devising new schemes for the school back home. On shipboard from Seattle to Yokohama he finished a book on *The American Ballet* and began another. From his meticulous notes on native dances he encountered throughout the Orient, he wrote *Gods Who Dance,* published in 1929. He also prepared publicity releases for American newspapers and course outlines for the New York Denishawn as he toured. During his train conversation with Ruth, he told her of his plan for a Greater Denishawn, a colony of the arts, with a theatre to be designed by Claude Bragdon, a dormitory and cafeteria, a vocational school, a roof garden, a temple for Ruth's religious ideas, and a business operation to be managed by June Hamilton Rhodes. Captivated by the grandeur of the plan, Ruth agreed to work for Greater Denishawn. She felt it might offer her the opportunity to create quality dances at her leisure. She forgot, for a moment, her antipathy to institutions. She forgot the past.

Doris Humphrey, who knew Ruth better than any of the Denishawn dancers, was startled when she first heard of these plans and wrote home that she was surprised to see Miss Ruth cooperating "because she has wanted to break away, at least for a year." Ruth regretted her promises to Ted almost as soon as they were made. She knew that his arguments were sensible, that a permanent home for Denishawn was more practical than a network of rented studios, but "for some reason deep down in me," she wrote, "I do not want it built." After their conversation she had crawled "back into my little lower narrow bunk of a bed and lay there thinking after the lights were out. I cannot overcome my instinct that this is wrong; but if it leads to a *real* partnership I will be content."

India loomed larger in Ruth's imagination than any other country on the oriental tour. On her first free morning in Calcutta she eagerly set out to explore the land that had occupied her creative thoughts for the last quarter of a century. As she walked through the teeming streets she thought of Swami Paramananda, who had introduced her to the spiritual heritage of India. With Pearl she headed down the long avenue that led to the bathing ghats on the river, where a festival of the goddess Saraswati had attracted throngs of Hindus. On either side of the avenue stretched a queue of lepers, cripples, the poor and the diseased, their bony hands thrust forward in hopes of *baksheesh*. Ruth was deeply horrified. She returned to her hotel room and sat motionless for an hour. "I am beginning to see that the India I have adored since my first reading of the *Light of Asia* no longer exists," she wrote in her diary, "or rather it exists now for me much more intensely in the depth of my own spirit than in the poor huddled beggars lining the roadsides. If twenty years before I had seen any such sight there would have been no *Radha* and perhaps no career."

In Calcutta, Ruth performed for her first Indian audience, with great success. Among her admirers in the audience was Rabindranath Tagore, the Bengali poet and Nobel laureate in literature, who came backstage to invite her to teach in his Visva-Bharati or World University, where scholars and artists from around the world gathered to share ideas. Ruth knew Tagore's work, which had formed the basis of one of her earlier poetry-dances, and when the poet visited the United States in 1930 they presented a joint recital in New York.

During that first Calcutta engagement Ruth had the courage to perform two of her Indian dances, the *Dance of the Black and Gold Sari* and the *Nautch*, which she had tested on a Rangoon audience with some success. Her audiences at the Empire Theatre in Calcutta greeted the *Nautch* with roars for an encore and in India it became the most popular dance in the Denishawn repertoire, along with *Black and Gold Sari*. Just why the *Nautch* struck such a responsive chord with Indian

Miss Ruth and Papa Shawn in fancy dress clothes, London, 1922.

Ted Shawn as the Fisher Boy and Ruth St. Denis as the Sea Spirit in *Spirit of the Sea.*

St. Denis and Shawn (center) with students at Mariarden colony. Martha Graham leans against tree with Pearl Wheeler second from right.

Shawn and St. Denis in *Tillers of the Soil*.

Ruth in one of her most famous dances, *Liebestraum*.

Ruth, the actress, in *Miriam, Sister of Moses*.

Ted Shawn's ballet *Cuadro Flamenco*. Left to right, Ted Shawn, Martha Hardy, Pauline Lawrence, George Steares, Louise Brooks, Anne Douglas, Charles Weidman, Ruth St. Denis as La Gitana, Lenore Scheffer, Doris Humphrey, J. Roy Busclark, an unidentified girl, Theresa Sadowska, and Robert Gorham.

Ruth St. Denis (center) in *Ishtar of the Seven Gates*. Doris Humphrey sits left and Ted Shawn lies on bier, right, with company members on second Mayer tour.

Ruth, wearing the jewels Ted gave her, in *Josephine and Hippolyte*, 1929.

audiences is connected with the politics of colonialism and nationalism. Historically, Indian dancing was a sacred activity, with the *devidassi* or dancing girls of the temple performing only for the gods, rather than for spectators. As dancing moved into the royal courts and became allied with concubinage, the art degenerated in technique and prestige until, by the 1920s, nautch dances were performed primarily by prostitutes. The British ruling class disdained the nautch. La Meri, the American ethnic dancer who toured India in the 1930s, remembered that British women did not approve of white Western women performing Indian dances and requested that she omit hers from her program. St. Denis, on the other hand, benefited from this class conflict.

Ted Shawn reported that the native Indians in the audience cheered the loudest and longest for Ruth's Indian dances and so crowded the subsequent performances in Calcutta that an additional section of seats had to be allotted to them. He reasoned that their enthusiasm was a natural response to Ruth's superiority to the native nautch dancers, her "having a richness and purity beyond the conception of these native women and having a beauty and charm of person not possessed by them . . ." Other onlookers suggested, a trace more cynically, that the natives may have been merely titillated by the spectacle of a Western woman in Indian dress performing a dance done only by harlots, but Nala Najan, an Indian dancer born in America, supported Shawn's view. He regarded St. Denis as a champion of traditional Indian dance. "She opened the door," he said. "The Indians saw that a woman could dance and be respectable at the same time. Indian dance was looked down upon by the upper class and was relegated to a certain class of women. This changed after Miss Ruth went there." Ruth claimed credit in subsequent years for leading the revival in Indian dance which dated from the mid-1920s but Rukmini Devi, a major figure in that renaissance, insists that the credit belongs to Anna Pavlova. Whatever the cause, native Indian dancing began its ascendancy after the visit of Denishawn, and Ruth realized why when she finally saw a native nautch dance in a Quetta bazaar. Two female impersonators in full nautch regalia shuffled their feet, wiggled their hips, and twirled listlessly. Ruth had to admit that her nautch was more authentic.

Quetta, near the Afghan border, was a mountain-station outpost of British India (present-day Pakistan), where nomads herded goats alongside the railroad tracks that cut deep into the desert and Baluchistan mountains. The Denishawn company spent three nights in Quetta, per-

forming for an audience of British soldiers. Leaving by train for Lahore, Ruth stayed up late to watch the moon rise and conceived an idea
for a new dance. She would call it *India*: "India, old, dying, ragged,
homeless, wandering, blind, lame, sick, and deformed—dreaming of
other inner worlds, trying to think through to reality—existing, invisi-
bly, perfectly, timelessly, beautifully in the midst of shadows, wars, disease and death. India, very very old and eternally young, because thinking on Eternity gives youth that is ever at its noon." She would begin
the dance in rags which would be removed by the ministrations of a
yogi, "then India, beautiful, intact, radiant, still vital, clad in red and
gold, would rise, moving harmoniously to the rhythm of song and chorus." The dance became *The Spirit of India* and her description of it
reflected the reconciliation of Ruth's spiritual vision of India and its
material reality. Near Calcutta she had visited the monastery of Ramakrishna on the banks of the Ganges at Belur Math. There she saw
the *samadhi* or burial shrine of Ramakrishna and Vivekananda. It was
a day of peace. In the quiet of the monastery, surrounded by yellow-
robed monks and worshiping pilgrims, Ruth felt "the heart of spiritual
India subtly pulsing around us," and she knew that her India lived
other than in her imagination.

This trip through India was a trip through Ruth's past. Everywhere
she found reminders of her beginnings as an artist. In Cawnpore a con-
jurer came to her hotel room and performed his "mango trick," producing from beneath a dirty handkerchief a flourishing mango tree. To
Ruth's astonishment, he told her, after some conversation, that he had
belonged to the troupe of jugglers and snake charmers who performed
in the East Indian village at Coney Island in 1904. On another occasion in Bombay, Ruth discovered that the Gaekwar of Baroda was in
her audience. After the performance they reminisced about the afternoon in 1906 when a very young Ruthie Dennis danced her *Incense* at
the Bhumgara Store reception honoring the American visit of the
young Gaekwar.

Through Lahore, Cawnpore, and Lucknow in northern India, Ruth
sensed the cultural differences between the Mogul- and Persian-
influenced North and the graceful Bengali culture of East India. In the
north Ruth saw Moslem mosques and shrines, and in Agra, with Ted,
she visited the most renowned of Mogul marvels, the Taj Mahal. "*It is
before us, waiting for the sun*," she wrote in her journal just before a
daybreak visit to that most perfect of monuments to love. "Dearest and

I stood at that dawn hour near the great entrance gate and wept in each other's arms," Ruth wrote, "over the beauty and pathos of that dream in marble." When the other Denishawn dancers arrived in mid-morning they were disconcerted to find Papa Shawn and Miss Ruth, already there, in native garb, posing for photographers.

Inside the Taj Mahal, in the burial vault, the great domed ceiling sucks visitors' voices into a whirlpool of ghostly echoes, as if the dead were whispering their own epitaphs. Ruth stood in that space and, at Brother's suggestion, began to sing. Never had she heard her own voice sound so sweet and pure as in its echo. "Pearly, who has *always* believed in me said, 'Now you have heard your own voice,'" Ruth wrote, "which was true and not true. I knew only too well what unearthly beauty that marvelous dome gave to my poor tone."

During her travels through India, Ruth could not help noticing the "sullen natives" who bridled under British rule. A strong spirit of nationalism was stirring in India, gathering force under the leadership of Mohandas Gandhi whose famous salt march in defiance of British taxes was only four years hence. Ruth was an ardent admirer of Gandhi, and in Bombay she reported an argument with an Indian acquaintance, Ruth "hotly defending the influence and power of Gandhi," her friend "defending Ford, with his tractors, as the saviour of India." The movement for independence was exacerbating centuries-old tension between Moslem and Hindu. One afternoon in Calcutta as Ruth and Pearl shopped for fabrics, the shopkeeper shooed them from his premises and closed his doors with a clatter. Warned that a Moslem-Hindu riot was under way, Pearl and Ruth escaped safely to their hotel.

In the midst of this political turmoil Old India, its fortunes fading, lived on in the person of His Exalted Highness, the Nizam of Hyderabad, richest and most powerful independent ruler in India. He brought his entire entourage of wives to the rickety British Cinema Theatre in Secunderabad, where Denishawn performed in late April of 1926. His Sereneness insisted on sitting backstage just behind Stan Frazier, who was running the lights. On the other side of the backstage area, just behind Brother St. Denis and the spotlight, sat the Nizam's chattering wives in purdah, with a special veiled box for the Pasha Begum and her attendants. Denishawn dancers dashing by in their revealing Soaring suits, Buzz mumbling his colorful epithets, the glamorous St. Denis drenched in perspiration, did not faze His Exalted Highness. He came every night in the same dusty linen jacket, tennis shoes, and stubbly beard. After the final performance, the Nizam received Ted, resplendent in evening clothes, and Ruth in her best evening gown. "Visions of emeralds and diamonds, necklaces and eardrops, as tokens of appreciation floated before my excited gaze," Ruth remembered. She presented the Nizam with bound copies of *The Denishawn Magazine* and in return the richest man in the world presented her with an autographed copy of his book of poems.

Before leaving India the Denishawn company traveled southward through the temple country of Tamil Nadu, with a week of performances in Madras. In nearby Adyar Ruth and Ted visited the Theosophical Society international headquarters, then continued on a tour of the Tamil temples. At the famed Meenakshi Temple in Madura a group of *devidassi* or temple dancers gave a special performance for Denishawn. Ruth explored the temple, devoted to the Hindu god Shiva and his consort Meenakshi, and felt herself drawn out of the twentieth century into "the orbits of a mentality that refuses to take account of the earth's turnings." In the depths of the temple, amid dancing shadows cast by candlelight, the very architectural detail of the temple seemed to dance. Ruth saw "elephants parading solemnly through corridors and disappearing into the distance. Through an archway, for a moment, we see a lily tank of blue lotuses scintillating in the sunshine; now that fades. We go underground, where only a few pilgrims penetrate; and here is a kind of awful silence. And now time does seem to be dead." For two hours she lived in the suspended world of Indian history and Hindu religion. When she emerged from the temple and felt time recapturing her, she bade good-bye to India.

By boat the Denishawn company traveled to Colombo, Ceylon, and enjoyed the tropical terrain, with its lush vegetation, palm, rubber, and coconut trees and saturated rice fields. For a week they performed in the Colombo Public Hall, then made a side-trip to Kandy, a resort city in the hills and center of Singhalese religious festivals. By luck they arrived in the midst of a festival in celebration of the birthday of the Buddha. The Temple of Buddha's Tooth, visible from the dancers' hotel, was the focal point of an elaborate procession, with musicians, singers, villagers with lighted torches and an elephant with painted tusks bearing a gold and crystal shrine housing the sacred relic. Masked "devil dancers" performed their rituals of exorcism. Ted hired the most talented troupe to teach his male dancers their complicated rhythms and steps, later adapted to Denishawn's *Singhalese Devil Dance*.

Back in Colombo, where the audiences were sparse but enthusiastic, Ruth wrote on the closing night of their engagement, "We are grateful that tonight in the theatre there was even a larger house than at the beginning. It encourages us. Our faith which never really goes out needs sometimes new fuel to keep its light burning." The company was dispirited. Traveling from boat to train to theatre and back, they rarely had sufficient rest. They subsisted on canned food whenever the local cuisine was questionable and drank boiled tea. Several of the dancers, including Ruth, had been ill with a variety of ailments that ranged from mild heat rash to the enervating dengue fever. Ruth worried that the girls in the company were becoming bored. Though the younger dancers attracted young English businessmen and beaux from the consulates, "the older ones like Doris find it all rather dreary in spite of all the interest of traveling and playing and sightseeing," Ruth wrote. "After all we are like people on an island—or in a boat—and can't get off." As the tour wore on, tempers flared. After a series of fierce arguments Doris' mother packed her bags and returned home. June Rhodes also left to negotiate the United States tour for the coming winter. Ted and Ruth fought over Pearl and Pearl fought with everyone. Since coming to the Orient nine months earlier, the Denishawn company had danced every night not spent on a train or boat. Now Ted announced a month's vacation in Singapore.

When they reached Singapore after a seven days' voyage from Colombo, Ruth and Ted took advantage of the hiatus to plan their ballets for the upcoming United States tour. Their repertoire would be a travelogue of oriental cities visited and artists met—*Momiji Gari* based on Matsumoto Koshiro's work; the *Singhalese Devil Dance* learned from the dancers in Ceylon; Ruth's *Spirit of India* and *White Jade* and a replica of a dance performed by Mei-lan Fan in Peking, *General Wu Says Farewell to His Wife*. The latter dance was finished so quickly that the Denishawn company premiered it in Singapore, with choreography credited to Ruth, along with Ruth and Doris' new *Burmese Yein Pwe*.

The *Yein Pwe* was a re-creation of a typical Burmese festival of dance, song, and dialogue, with George Steares and Charles Weidman as clowns and Doris Humphrey leading a quartet of dancing girls. Doris' solo was fiendishly difficult, as is suggested in Ruth's choreographic notes: "Start upstage center. Burmese semi-squat position with hands flat on side at breasts, elbows well back. Starting with right foot take three steps and side backward, flip kick: the left hand makes a small downward, outward circle into position about at the hip—the right hand makes small upward, outward circle, the hand flipping into position about at right ear with palm up." That was only the first sequence of steps in a complicated solo of hops, stamps, deep *pliés,* and fluttering fan work, all executed in a costume with long hobble skirt and tight jacket. The choreography called for Doris literally to lose her footing at the conclusion of the dance: "Jump into low squatting position, and on last chord, slide feet from underneath. The end pose is with both feet extended straight forward, body in upright sitting position, parasols at either side, elbows bent." Doris and the girls first had to learn how to walk in their Burmese skirts, let alone dance.

In Singapore Ruth suffered a bout with dengue fever and spent several days recovering at the Adelphi Hotel. Sitting on her private veranda, she looked across the hotel lawn toward the harbor that lay between Singapore and the distant Indonesian islands. "Clouds hanging over harbor," she wrote, "softly pink, like flamingos' wings. A yellow moon is full and serene. Those flame-blossomed trees like we had in our hotel courtyard in Secunderabad line the boulevard. Between me and the ship riding quietly at anchor in the bay, on the waterfront there are large green lawns for tennis, and both the English and the Chinese play football. The Chinese generally win, they tell me!" She rested and wrote poetry, a sure sign that she was gaining emotional strength.

Before they left Singapore Asway Strok, the temperamental and peripatetic booking agent for the tour, rejoined them after representing another artist for a short season in China and Japan. Strok booked Denishawn into Java during late July and early August. Though the Javanese sponsor, the Kunstkring or Art Circle, advised him not to book more than a week of performances, Strok stubbornly extended the Denishawn stay to five weeks. The houses were so empty in Soerbaja that a series of small Javanese towns was added to the tour. On one stop, the outdoor theatre had no stage and Buzz had to order fifty bamboo poles to erect a scaffolding to support the black velvet cyclorama. After a disheartening month, the company moved on to equally dispiriting stops in Saigon, Hong Kong, and Manila, a disappointing and insipid city, Ruth said. She took refuge in her reading of *Tertium Organum,* the *Bhagavad-Gita,* and the works of Mary Baker Eddy. "There is nobody out front," she wrote during a performance in Saigon. "We are going through one of our usual depressed and puzzling moods. A moment ago—resting before the opening, I entered again into the inner place of the Most High—where God is everywhere present in equal intensity." She wondered how she might sustain that peace.

A side trip to Phnom Penh revived her spirits. By automobile over near-impassable roads Ruth and Ted journeyed to the Cambodian capital six and a half hours from Saigon. They arrived on the evening of a celebration in honor of the King of Cambodia's birthday. Cambodian dancers performed a mesmeric dance, their feet beating rhythmically, their knees bent in deep *plié,* their hands dancing a lively story, heads immobile under heavy crowns. Ruth and Ted watched, fascinated, with suffocating blankets over their legs to discourage the ferocious mosquitoes. They returned to Saigon, covered with insect bites but elated, as they always were when they saw fine dancing.

It was a relief to leave Saigon for China and Japan, Denishawn's final stops on the oriental tour. The company brought with them new dances acquired during their travels and some of the Orientalia they had omitted from their earlier programs—Ted's *Japanese Spear Dance* and Ruth's *Kuan Yin* or Chinese goddess of mercy. The critics and audiences responded even more enthusiastically than a year before. "Their dance is the admiration of the Japanese," wrote one critic in sayonara. "We ask the Japanese dancers whenever they are inclined to take on a foreign style to follow the example of the Denishawn dancers who are sympathetic to true Oriental souls."

In Tokyo, between performances, Ruth had begun work on her new dance idea, *White Jade.* Her starting point was its costume. On the day she began work she stood in her dressing room while Pearl pinned endless yards of chiffon around her. Through a mouthful of pins Pearl gave orders while Ruth twisted and turned, complaining all the while that the fabric was too bunchy or too long. Pearl added weights to the hem of the skirt, streamlining it into sculptural folds, and she attached a pearl headdress, purchased in Shanghai, to a sturdy buckram base. Prints of the Chinese goddess of mercy lay strewn around the floor. Gazing at them, Ruth tried various mudras, a gesture of benediction, a pose of blessing. She invited Clifford Vaughan to help her work. She had asked him for a score that would be both delicate and rhythmic, pervaded by "a feeling of cool white porcelain." With nothing more to guide him, Vaughan delivered an atmospheric but unobtrusive composition with a simple and sweet melody. He helped Ruth rehearse and suggested several gestures that might complement certain passages in the score. From this process emerged St. Denis' *White Jade,* the finest treasure she brought back from the Orient. The dance was the fruit of a year of self-examination, a year of creative stimuli. In choreographing *White Jade* Ruth returned to what she knew best, a solo dance created from the stuff of her innermost feelings.

Sailing home on the *Korea Maru* in November, Ruth evaluated her experience in the Orient. "It has all been very interesting but very hard," she wrote in her travel diary. "I look old and tired. It has been a horrendous task." The Orient had not offered any new truths. "I went on a long journey thinking that I should find some new thing under the sun," she continued, "but I find that I already knew love and duty, impulse and dreams, and what I found was what I had already felt, dressed in strange garments and speaking strange tongues, but outwardly the same."

She had made one self-discovery. "When I am dancing—when I am at any time expressing reality, I am nearer reality and in a more harmonious state of being than at any other time. I find a real escape from the limited sense of life that I ordinarily have. Human relationships are suspended and the sense of age." She went halfway around the world to discover that home was wherever and whenever she happened to be dancing.

WHITE JADE

CHOREOGRAPHY: Ruth St. Denis

COSTUME: Pearl Wheeler

MUSIC: Clifford Vaughan. Originally scored for two flutes, two oboes, one clarinet, two first violins, two second violins and violas, two cellos, two triangles, and a piano.

PREMIERE: December 6, 1926, Philharmonic Auditorium, Los Angeles

---

SETTING: The Chinese goddess of mercy, Kuan-Yin, sits stage center on a low, red-lacquered base. She wears filmy white draperies wrapped about her body and a mantilla of the same material, covering her headdress of pearls and extending to the floor. In one hand she holds a lotus branch. From her wrist hangs a pearl and white-tasselled Buddhist rosary. She is illuminated by a blue-white light.

Behind her stretches a Coromandel screen, lavishly painted with blossoms and temple scenes. To either side of her pedestal is a white lotus plant in a square container placed on a small, black-lacquered stand. At the base of one plant is a small bottle; at the base of the other is a tiny basket containing a carved fish. Each plant gently curves toward the central goddess.

SCENARIO: Kuan-Yin sits with straight back, her left leg folded beneath her, her right leg slightly outstretched so that the elevated knee supports her right hand which is draped over it in a restful pose. In the other hand she holds a lotus branch, symbolizing the undeveloped but living spiritual consciousness. With flexed elbow she rests the lotus against her left shoulder. Her eyes are closed in meditation.

The music begins, mysterious, aloof, sweetly exotic. Stirring, Kuan-Yin moves one hand in a gesture of benediction, palm forward, fingers slightly curved. Her body is immobile, a sculptural mass. Only the arms and hands move in delicate, rococo gestures. She then shifts her weight onto her left hip, folding her legs to the right, her torso slightly twisted toward them. She brings the lotus branch across her chest to rest it against the other shoulder and inclines her head away.

Placing her lotus branch on her pedestal, she rises and steps forward, turning in profile. She lifts her hands in prayer position, then cups them to form an unfolding lotus.

To the tinkle of the piano, the trill of the flute, she crosses to the table on her left, takes the tiny bottle symbolizing the waters of life and draws both arms toward her body, one held horizontally across her midriff, its hand supporting the elbow of her vertical right arm. In this pose she bends to her left side, pouring from the bottle held in her right hand. Returning upright, she replaces the bottle on its stand and crosses to stage right.

From the second table she takes the small basket containing a fish, symbol of fertility. Holding it, she sways slightly like a flickering candle flame, then replaces the fish in its basket, sets them on the table and returns to center stage.

She stands facing the audience, folding her arms inward so that they are obscured in the folds of her gown. Sinking to her pedestal, she draws her legs into the lotus position. Her eyes close once more in meditation.

White Jade was a study in stillness. "In the opening scene what the audience responded to without in the least analyzing it was the held vibrations of the body," St. Denis said. "I am not just standing there. I am dancing." Her ability to concentrate her energy, to hold it in suspension, made *White Jade* the most refined of her oriental solos, the simplest yet the most profound.

The impersonal nature of the dance was enhanced by its costume and setting. The stage suggested whiteness, simplicity. Her draperies massed St. Denis' body into a flowing, sculptural form, a neutral background against which each gesture appeared in relief. Each movement was made deliberately yet serenely, with just enough weight behind the gesture to indicate the texture of porcelain, its smoothness and coolness, its delicacy. St. Denis went beyond mere representational gesture into abstraction. When she poured the waters of life, her body itself became an emptying vessel. When her hands mimed an opening lotus blossom, her entire body seemed to open and unfold, her spirit to flow outward.

Even in her later years when, unable to sit, St. Denis danced *White Jade* from a standing position, her audiences found the dance a deeply moving experience. *White Jade* took the viewer beyond externals to essences. It accomplished what Isadora Duncan dreamed of in a dance called "The light falling on white flowers": "A dance that would be a subtle translation of the light and the whiteness. So pure, so strong, that people would say: it is a soul that we see moving, a soul that has reached the light and found the whiteness."

St. Denis herself described the dance in a poem she wrote, *White Jade*:

> *I am Kuan Yin on the Altar of Heaven.*
> *Around me are the elements of nature, earth, air, fire,*
> *   water, and ether.*
> *I gaze upon the outer world of mountains, seas and plains.*
> *I listen to the music of the stars, the low murmur of*
> *   waters, the soundless humming of the silent air.*
> *In me are the elements of the Tao.*
> *My breath is the rhythmic evidence of unseen life.*
> *I move to the rhythm of the Drums of Heaven.*
> *My feet are weaving out the measure of Eternity.*
> *And the God of Joy flows forth in endless patterns*
> *   of my Cosmic Dance.*
> *My body is the living temple of all Gods.*
> *The God of Truth is in my upright spine.*
> *The God of Love is in my heart's rhythmic beat.*
> *The God of Wisdom lives in my conceiving mind.*
> *The God of Beauty is revealed in my harmonious being.*
> *I am Kuan Yin, the Merciful, the Compassionate.*
> *All men and women and children and all beasts, all*
> *   creeping creatures and all flying things*
> *   receive my love.*
> *For I am Kuan Yin, the Mother Merciful, who hears and*
> *   answers prayer.*

I AM A BELEAGUERED CITY

MONEY ALWAYS helped. When their tours went well, when they had money to feed their dreams, Ruth and Ted drew together. In the three years following the oriental tour they made and spent more money than ever before. They took their oriental booty on a triumphal tour, culminating in sold-out concerts at the prestigious Carnegie Hall. They built Denishawn House in New York City. They used their influence to persuade newspapers to hire dance critics. They entertained celebrities: Amelia Earhart, Theodore Dreiser, the sculptor George Grey Barnard, Rabindranath Tagore visiting from Calcutta. But the reality of the Great Depression ended their dreams and as America slid into economic collapse, Denishawn disintegrated from internal stress and Ruth and Ted parted, emotionally and financially bankrupt.

The future seemed propitious as they returned home from the Orient. On their most recent wedding anniversary Ruth had written in her diary, "Twelve years married to the most intelligent and dearest boy in the world!" Persuaded by Ted's arguments, she had agreed to support the concept of Greater Denishawn. With their profits from the Orient they purchased two pieces of property immediately adjacent to land Ruth already owned in the Bronx. They paid a contractor to begin construction of a Moorish mansion to include living quarters and a spacious studio. A thirty-thousand-dollar mortgage financed the entire project. With such a debt they could not afford to be idle, and ten days after their ship docked on the West Coast they began an American tour under the sponsorship of Arthur Judson. They chose the Judson contract over Daniel Mayer's because it was only a sixteen-week commitment. "Like the Orient contract it seemed it was the easiest thing to do," Ruth reproached herself, "but in my heart it seems always that I take the easiest way, that the hard way would be to face poverty and obstacles to again speak my own soul."

Except for *White Jade* Ruth took mostly older solos on the Judson tour, including *Greek Veil Plastique* and *Dance of the Black and Gold Sari,* though she choreographed a popular new group work, *In the Bunnia Bazaar.* This was nothing more than a glorified setting for her *Nautch.* The scene was an Indian bazaar filled with sari vendors, idlers chewing betel nut, beggars, women bearing bundles on their heads, and a bird-seller displaying Ruth's beloved cockatoo Dada. The Denishawn Dancers in brown body paint, Indian head veils, short blouses and gold-bordered skirts, performed a simple version of *The Nautch,* followed by Ruth's famous solo.

The Judson tour lasted from December 1926 through early April of the following year. From Los Angeles to New York the company toured four alternating programs, each with a section of music visualizations and a section of divertissements, Orientalia, or major group works. The heart of the repertoire was the new oriental dances, grouped together as "Gleanings from the Buddha-Fields." These were samples of the native dances of Cambodia, Japan, China, Java, and Burma, set in a sumptuous context of silks, native jewelry, brass, baskets, and plush rugs. An audience favorite was *General Wu Says Farewell to His Wife,* an adaptation of the dance-drama performed by Meilan Fan and his company for Denishawn in Peking. This was one of the few full ballets in the Denishawn repertoire in which neither Ted nor Ruth appeared. Charles Weidman was the General and Anne Douglas his wife in a story of battle, love, and suicide. George Steares portrayed a property man in the Chinese mode. Clad in black, he moved furniture about the stage to form imaginary objects and with a wave of a leafy wand suggested a willow tree, much to the audience's delight. The stage setting was three richly embroidered satin panels as backdrops with paper lanterns overhead. Clifford Vaughan wrote the score, which incorporated authentic Chinese instruments.

Ruth's new material for the tour included *White Jade* and *A Javanese Court Dancer,* choreographed to a Clifford Vaughan score that approximated the music of a gamelan orchestra. In Java she had seen a *serimpi,* or royal dancer, in a Wayang Wong dance festival. Her interpretation of that dance was little more than a stylized walk. Wearing a tight, floor-length sarong and trailing a batik stole, she moved with ladylike bearing, torso erect, hips tilted forward, knees bent. With each step she struck the floor with her heel, then swiveled the foot outward in a ceremonious gait. Calmly progressing across the stage, she rippled her arms and manipulated her trailing scarf. Her elastic arms and fingers appeared double-jointed as she stood with arms akimbo, fingers doubled back almost to her wrists. This Javanese dance, with its slow but steady energy level and its subtle shifts of weight, was technically the most difficult of her dances, Ruth said. Yet Jane Sherman observed that despite its beauty and fascination, the dance lacked the theatrical-spiritual impact of other St. Denis solos. The dance did not come from within. It was a technical exercise.

Ted scored a major triumph with his *Cosmic Dance of Siva*, which electrified his American audiences as it had in the Orient. As the Hindu sculpture of Nataraja or the dancing Siva, he wore only body paint, brief trunks, and a towering crown and stood on a pedestal within a huge upright metal ring that haloed his entire body. Moving in plastique, he mimed five cosmic stages: creation, preservation, destruction, reincarnation, and salvation. The dynamics of the solo ranged from still balances on half-toe to violent twists of the torso and furious stamping of the feet, all confined within the hoop that represented the container of the universe. At thirty-six, Ted was more agile than Ruth and more virtuosic, and critics devoted almost as much space to his dancing as to Ruth's.

The Judson tour concluded with four unprecedented dance concerts at a sold-out Carnegie Hall in New York. The *Times* reviewer praised the "exceptional richness and beauty" of the program which was "more elaborate than even metropolitan audiences have come to expect." The cheering audience brought the company back for bow after bow until Ruth raised her hand and gestured for silence. Thanking the audience for its enthusiasm, she asked them to join her in supporting Greater Denishawn. She summarized the history of the school and outlined her hopes for a temple for religious dance. Warming to her subject, she spoke of a new fusion of philosophy, religion, and art, of a dance for all people in all walks of life. She never once mentioned Ted Shawn, who stood fuming in the wings, and he never forgave her.

The professional rivalry between Ruth and Ted never abated. Ruth told of an incident at the start of the tour when Ted read a press notice titled "Ruth St. Denis Dances" and raged, "Where was *I* last night? I see how this season is going to be!" She wrote in her diary, "I felt only pity, that he is still the victim of such fear." Even in his old age, after he suffered a heart attack, Ted lamented to his friend La Meri that he had been eagerly awaiting the day when Ruth would retire and he could still dance—an ambition that went unfulfilled until St. Denis died in 1968, leaving Shawn to survive her by three years. Ted fought for every scrap of publicity, every bit of praise. Ruth did nothing. Self-absorbed and enchanted with her own ideas, she generated publicity and praise. Ted bitterly resented it. Clifford Vaughan remembered that Ted had no sense of humor whenever public praise was at stake. On the oriental tour, in Jakarta, Vaughan was invited on the stage for a bow. Simultaneously an usher brought a huge wreath down the aisle, stepped onstage, and thrust it into the arms of the startled musician. "Miss Ruth could laugh it off, but Ted never got over it," Vaughan said. Ruth's assumption of superiority, echoed by the public and press, exacerbated Ted's resentment. He found her patronizing, and she was. "The whole institution of Denishawn has held together and developed because of Ted's loyal, intelligent efforts," Ruth wrote in her diary during the Judson tour. "He has been wonderful, progressing steadily from year to year, overcoming many people's first aversion or downright antagonism to his art and personality. As 'my child' I am proud of his expanding talents—his steadying character—his dear lovable heart. I am ever and ever grateful for our love and work together. But I feel that I am intended to do other and better things."

Despite their fundamental rivalry, Ruth and Ted were close during the Judson tour. Pearl had remained in California, much to Ted's relief, and Brother St. Denis had returned to his own family. Ruth and Ted spent their spare hours together, planning the structure of Greater Denishawn. After the close of the tour they went their separate ways for the summer but stayed in touch through chatty and loving letters. "Miss Ruth has no plans, purposely," Doris Humphrey wrote her mother. "She's been managed and planned for on such a rigid schedule for so many years that for a few months she's going to luxuriate in doing what she pleases. Ted, being a planner by instinct, has every moment of the summer laid out for himself." While Ted traveled among the Denishawn schools, Ruth did some teaching and enjoyed her New York friends. She appeared in a Players' Club production of *Julius Caesar*, staged by her friend Norman Bel Geddes at the New Amsterdam Theatre that June. Members of the club, all distinguished actors, writers, musicians, and artists, assumed minor as well as major roles in the play. Ruth was part of a Roman mob that included among its bloodthirsty rabble such notables as Basil Rathbone, Edgar Lee Masters, and Don Marquis.

Too soon the summer was over and Ruth faced the prospect of another tour, this one the most remunerative and least palatable of her career. She and Ted had signed a contract with George Wintz to appear as headliners in his road company of the Ziegfeld Follies. With nine of their Denishawn Dancers they would perform as many as nine times per week, mostly one-night stands, throughout the United States, Canada, and Cuba, for a period of nine months beginning that September. They agreed to this punishing tour for one reason only: their salary of thirty-five hundred dollars per week, most of which was earmarked for the new Denishawn House. Doris Humphrey and Charles Weidman stayed behind to keep the New York school operating and a nucleus of Denishawn Dancers and new recruits joined Ruth and Ted on the tour. One of them was Estelle Dennis, whom Ruth called her "muchly namesake." Estelle marveled that Miss Ruth, now nearing fifty, managed to stay energetic on the grinding tour. Her secret was catnaps. Traveling or backstage, she instantly dozed whenever she got a chance. In one city on the tour, the local mayor asked to meet St. Denis and was led backstage, only to find the famous dancer curled up on a trunk, sound asleep. She had the energy of a young woman, but even that proved insufficient on the Follies tour.

Through the fall of 1927 they played small theatres in Ohio, Alabama, Louisiana, Tennessee, and Texas, traveling with the Follies company of comedians, variety artists, and show girls. The tour seemed a mockery of everything Ruth held dear. "This kind of life seems to have killed all possible sense of beauty," she wrote in her diary. "I can't start anything with any sense of expression. Our life is so hideously broken up into petty patterns of rising before dawn, of bad food, of stupid reporters, of endless smell, horrible stage doors and dressing rooms. The hours in the performance almost compensate. Then we feel lovely moments when we dance." Whenever she performed *White Jade* she entered a meditative state that renewed her spirit, but in *Pelée*, her *Nautch* and *Red and Gold Saree* she relied more and more on mugging, ruffling her skirts and accelerating her musical tempi to make her audiences respond. "I am lazy!" Ruth wrote in her diary. "Instead of forging ahead with the work that I ought to do, I spend my hours devising means to escape it, and no one loves me enough to make me do the finishing and hard work I ought to do. Ted said tonight out on the stage—'You need Mother.'—and I agreed, more heartily than he realized."

She despised the boisterous atmosphere of the Follies and its exploitation of women. Standing backstage one evening, waiting to go on in her *Nautch*, she noticed "a Strokish person, standing by Wintz, looking me up and down. 'Very, very nice,' said the Voice of the World, patronizingly, comfortably considering the future box office. It suddenly struck me," she wrote, "that the Voice of the World was money (what else?), coming through those coarse lips." When they reached Sweetwater, Texas, Wintz drew her aside and told her that *White Jade* would have to go, that it did not have enough pep for a Follies program and it puzzled her audiences. "It was casting pearls before swine," she wrote despairingly in her diary. "My pride would want me to stop and go home, but I realize that if people have not the culture and interest to come when I am inspired, but only where the Follies bring them, then they get what they deserve—a ghost of beauty."

With *White Jade* taken from her repertoire, she was entirely dispirited, and the critics noticed. After a Dallas reviewer expressed mild reservations about her performance, Ruth spent a sleepless night, searching her soul. "Must I endure drudgery and early jumps and bad food and filthy dressing rooms—must I be humiliated as well? Do I deserve it? Really, very sincerely, perhaps I do. Have I followed the path of least resistance? Have I neglected my own work because it was easier to do? Have I allowed my own temperament to so starve for lack of food that I have no more beauty? How did I get into this and how can I get out of it?" She retraced in her own mind the steps along the path that had led to this abyss. Even in the Orient, she said, she felt she was "just part of a show." Before that, during the Mayer years, she had sacrificed her own art to the rush of touring schedules, the audience appetite for novelty, the demands of the school. Even in the early days of Denishawn she had allowed her own vision of carefully crafted, epic ballets to slip from her grasp. With the exception of her music visualizations, she had compromised her artistic integrity. The end point of her reflection was her marriage, Ted's marathon struggle with her mother in 1914. "The strange, unresolved feeling persists after all these years, I did the disloyal thing to you, beloved mother, and to my art. Is it nearly finished?" she asked in torment. "Have I paid enough?"

The essence of her differences with Ted never seemed clearer than during a discussion they had shared a week earlier on the tour. It was one of their typical arguments, conducted with elaborate courtesy and theatricality in a hotel room in Beaumont, Texas. June Hamilton Rhodes sat nearby, pen poised to capture the words of Miss Ruth and Papa Shawn for dissemination to the Denishawn family. Ruth, in rose negligee, her white hair loose, sat before a breakfast tray. Opposite her, sharing coffee and rolls, was Ted in a mulberry Japanese kimono, his hair tousled, his "eyes intensely brown with concentration." Their topic of discussion was "the individual versus the institution." In reality they were discussing themselves and Denishawn.

Ted argued for the necessity of institutions which provide a secure financial base and an organized buffer between the artist and the necessary tasks of life. "My concept of institution is that it is merely the structure or set of tools by which you achieve your purpose," he said. He and Ruth would be free to create "only when we own outright the buildings for our own living, our school and theatre, and when we have some source of money which does not necessitate our traveling around the country on one-night stands, tired, sleepless, nervously exhausted." Ruth disagreed. "We will achieve this institution only by giving, in vulgar parlance, the public what it wants. Then we no longer discuss the production of art, but of entertainment. The energy needed to give one's time to the accumulation of money often exhausts one's equipment and when the money is earned it will be too late to utilize it for art."

Listening to Ted's enumeration of the characteristics of the ideal institution, Ruth protested, "There is a vital thing you leave out and that is the stimulus of the unknown. I like to keep the feeling that I have waked up this morning with an inspiration for a ballet and I do not know how big nor what shape nor to what heights it may lead me. Institutions can only preserve already crystallized ideas. As soon as they become crystallized they have already shed themselves from the creative spirit." Creator and preserver, romantic and realist, they brought together in their diverse points of view the complete creative process of the performing artist. Like the Yin and Yang of the Denishawn emblem, they were complementary halves of a whole, but, tragically, each aspired to become the other.

After her night of self-examination, Ruth gathered her courage and told Ted that after the completion of the Follies tour she would spend a sabbatical year in Europe alone. For a year Greater Denishawn would have to thrive, or fail, without her. Germany symbolized the flowering of her art, the acceptance of her work by artists and intellectuals, and she dispatched June Rhodes to Germany to book performances for the 1928 season. To strengthen her resolve, she announced her plans to John Martin, new dance critic for the New York *Times*, who wrote in a January column that St. Denis intended to spend the coming year abroad. Curiously, her decision brought her even closer to Ted who despite, or because of, his "sense of loss" began to woo her as in earlier days. He was solicitous and attentive and on one memorable afternoon in San Antonio gave her one of his handsomest gifts.

It was October and San Antonio, that graceful Texas city with a Mexican heart, lingered in the last, ripe days of an Indian summer. Despite a busy performing schedule with the Follies, the Denishawn company managed to visit a ranch, where they ate barbecue and watched bronco riders, and in the city itself browsed through some of its antique shops. In one, Ruth and Ted paused to visit with the proprietor, a small, dark-haired woman with strange dark eyes, dressed all in black velvet. She showed them to a table with a reading lamp and brought for their inspection a set of jewelry, said to have been a gift from Napoleon to the Empress Josephine. Fingering the exquisite tiara, necklace, earrings, and bracelet, the dealer began to intone their history when Ruth cried, "I can't stand it! They are too lovely!" and snatching off her hat, began to don the jewelry. "I can't describe the sensation they gave to me. I had on no makeup, my hair was flat and undressed, yet some spirit of Beauty did rise in me," she said. "I did look for an instant beautiful. I glanced in the mirror that stood on the table. I was another person." Ted also noticed the transformation. For the first time since the Chinese Altar of Heaven, Ruth looked luminous, ethereal. He did not hesitate. He bought the entire set of jewelry for her and later re-named their duet *Valse Directoire, Josephine and Hippolyte*, with Ruth wearing the jewels as part of her costume. Denishawn publicity materials capitalized on audience sentiment by identifying the jewels as an "anniversary present."

That same week in Texas, in Corpus Christi, Ruth and Ted met a man who was destined to play a major role in the drama of their partnership and marriage. Fred Beckman was young, slim, handsome, and utterly charming, a Jay Gatsby figure of uncertain background and personal mystery. They met him on the beach. Ted was bewitched. When they left Corpus Christi, Ruth and Ted promised Fred that they would find some place for him in the Denishawn operation. Ruth wrote Fred a few weeks later and seemed to condone Ted's interest in him. "I am so glad that avenues of communication between you and Ted have opened up, that perhaps you may, anyway, play together!" she wrote him. "Teddy needs play so badly. He has borne a great responsibility, really beyond his years, yet few persons ever reach his inner life, ever play with him (mostly we don't have time) to release both the fun and beauty that waits to be released in his nature." Yet by Christmas, when Fred had written that he was coming to join them, Ruth wrote, "It is a terrible test. There may be some gossip—me going to Europe—Fred being much in evidence. As for me, I think a good deal, I don't feel much." As if to brace for the coming cataclysm, she added, "I've always known that there are tides of life, ebb and flow that go on underneath the surface."

That Christmas she and Ted took four days off from the tour and returned to New York where the new Denishawn House was waiting. Pearl had come to New York to furnish the house and it was ready for their arrival. As their taxi approached Van Cortlandt Park in the Bronx, their excitement grew. At 67 Stevenson Street they jumped out and ran back a few feet to get a better view. It was a handsome house of Moorish style with arched doorways and tiled roof. A gateway opened into a walled garden and beyond, a gallery led into the house. Ted and Ruth dashed inside. "My, but it looks big! We clung together for a moment—at last our home!" On the ground floor was storage space for scenery, costumes, and Denishawn records and files, a laundry room and a costume workshop. The second floor housed a sixty-by-forty-foot studio, offices, a dining room and reception area, and twin bedrooms and baths for Ted and Ruth. A tower stairway led to a library and roof terrace which afforded a view of the nearby park and Jerome Reservoir. The roof terrace was the scene of many an emotional storm in years ahead, but that Christmas Ruth and Ted could feel only glee. "We ran like excited children all over from cellar storage to roof with a trail of friends behind us." Gazing at their new home, Ruth remarked, "Every brick a one-night stand."

While they were in New York, Ted and Ruth tended to "the children," as they called their Denishawn dancers and students. They met with Doris Humphrey, who was managing the Denishawn school. Doris had a following of her own among the students. She was an excellent teacher, with a head full of choreographic ideas. She wanted more freedom to try out her own work. Ruth described their tense confrontation, "Doris feeling her freedom and wanting more of it, Teddy filled with fear and resentment, I hovering anxiously between the two of them and finally being overcome, quite, by Ted's manner toward Doris. We ended with nothing settled." Later on the Follies tour, when Doris and Charles sent them notices of their recital in New York, Ted was deeply depressed and "only after a half hour of earnest talk did he begin to emerge from the cloud of fear," Ruth said.

After their Christmas holiday they rejoined the Follies in time to play the Teatro Nacional in Havana, Cuba, a novel stop on the tour. "Well, this is a gala time!" Ruth wrote in her diary. "We're going to the Casino to gamble!" Fred had joined the tour as their personal representative and "his coming has made us all gayer," she reported. Fred knew how to flatter, how to draw Ruth and Ted into lively debate, how to soothe their egos. He was a good listener. Ted thrived on his attentions. He would dance his heart out for Fred, who watched from the wings. "My intuitions tell me," Ruth wrote in her diary, "that Ted has fallen deeply in love with Fred and that he feels that he is finding his authentic soul. You can imagine what this is doing to me, crushing my heart beyond endurance."

But the more Ted opened himself to love, the more he reached out to Ruth. He told her that he understood her past peccadilloes, that for the first time he understood her idea of an open marriage. After one of their long talks Ruth wrote in her diary, "Ted is so earnest and so boyish, so naughty and full of ego and the next moment so lovable and sincere, I love him so. Perhaps after a period of going apart we can adjust our temperaments better than we now do." But any hope of better rapport with Ted eroded when Ruth herself became involved with Fred. She felt herself succumbing to his charm during the spring of the Follies tour, though she resisted out of loyalty to Ted. "But there are limits to my emotional endurance," she told herself. "I am starved for tenderness and beauty and a love relationship." She began to exchange secret letters with Fred, little scraps of poetry and bits of advice. Fred developed a litany of pet names for Ruth—Madonna, Shanti, Mrs. Boss, Goddess, Medea, Precious Person. "One day—as all things wanted badly enough come true—we will really be alone," he wrote her, "alone where I might be that which you see in me, not what I am, a worshipper at your feet, waiting to serve." Theirs was an idealized affair and a closely guarded secret. "There is a great mystery here that we should love as we do," Fred told her, and Ruth wondered in later years, "What was it in him—he so avowedly a homosexual—that attracted me? Was I secretly hoping and longing for the same kind of experience that he has given Ted? Was I trying to love Ted through Fred?" The motivations and cross-currents of manipulation among this trio were complex indeed and forceful enough to destroy a marriage and an institution. Though Fred was but the catalyst for the dissolution of Denishawn, he was a talented *agent provocateur*.

The center could not hold. Ted discovered one of Ruth's letters to Fred. Ruth summoned Pearl to join her on the tour. June Rhodes returned from Germany with the crushing news that the St. Denis name no longer had drawing power in Europe. From the Denishawn school in New York came rumbles of dissatisfaction from Doris and Charles. With the close of the Follies tour—aptly named—Ruth and Ted hurried to New York for a final confrontation.

They called a meeting at Denishawn House for the purpose of discussing Greater Denishawn. In attendance were Fred, their manager Margerie Lyon, Hazel Krans, who taught children's classes, Doris Humphrey, and the school secretary, Olga Frye, along with Ruth and Ted. Ruth opened the meeting by outlining their plans for Greater Denishawn. She asked those present to form a board of directors for the implementation of the Plan which included a future dormitory, a theatre already designed by Claude Bragdon, and additional studios to be constructed on adjacent land they had already purchased. She enumerated the financial sacrifices that had made the Plan possible, the oriental tour, the Judson tour, the year in the Follies. Ted continued the presentation by discussing the new policies that would govern Greater Denishawn. He mentioned a committee of censors who would be appointed to hear evidence in cases of immoral behavior among the students—the faculty and staff, presumably, were exempt. According to Doris, whose autobiography included the only detailed published account of the meeting, Ruth then added that the school would establish a quota system for Jewish students.

Ruth was vaguely anti-Semitic, particularly in the case of the powerful Jewish managers who were so influential in the theatre, but she never mentioned in any of her writings a quota system or anti-Semitic policy in Denishawn. Several of her friends and protégés were Jewish, including Klarna Pinska, who became her ally when Denishawn dissolved. Her only mention of anti-Semitism was an entry in her diary in which she told of defending a Denishawn dancer whom Ted alleged was undermining the school because of her Jewishness. Ruth might well have approved of a quota system as part of public policy, however. She was fearful of public opinion. In the early 1950s she posted a disclaimer on her studio door, disavowing any Communist ties, though she continued to consort with theatrical personalities of left-wing political persuasion. She did not display any sort of bigotry·in her private behavior and Doris said of the Greater Denishawn meeting, "This was the first time I had heard either director express a racial prejudice, and I was shocked."

Doris' shock turned to anger when Ted demanded that she and Charles join the Ziegfeld Follies for a season to raise further money for Greater Denishawn. Doris refused and bluntly told Ruth, in particular, that her own performance in the Follies was a disgrace. Ruth burst into tears and defended herself, even though she knew the charge was true. Later in her diary she wrote, "Well our first Directors' meeting apparently ended in failure. Doris, for whom it was largely held, was it seemed to us in a negative, criticizing, carping mood, maintaining her right, with little or no faith in our judgment, to adjust her artistic priorities. So as it stands she will not be with us again. As far as we could judge Doris sits in a self-imposed judgment upon our acts."

But Doris' opinion was important to Ruth and she knew that the loss of Charles Weidman, Pauline Lawrence, and the other dancers who would follow meant irreparable damage to Denishawn. She wrote Doris a letter, asking her understanding. She apologized for lowering her performing standards. "I have given many 'shows' that had neither spirit nor charm," she admitted. "I was tired and harassed with keeping the wolf from the door." She reminded Doris of their days together in the Ruth St. Denis Concert company and pointed out that the company "cost me personally over five thousand dollars which was paid for by money earned in vaudeville." She concluded, "All life is a compromise. I do sincerely the best I can under the circumstances of the moment."

Doris' reply was gentle and loving. She called their separation a painful but natural process. Her decade with Denishawn "directed my life, and I will never forget the debt I owe you in vision, encouragement and development in every direction. We agree on the goal," she said, "we only disagree on the path and that gives us some basis of spiritual understanding." She offered to fulfill her promise to perform with Denishawn in the upcoming Lewisohn Stadium concert and offered to contribute two new works of her own, *Air for the G String* and *Grieg Con-*

certo, a suggestion that Ted angrily refused. Ted considered Doris a traitor to Denishawn, as he still harbored resentment against Martha Graham, but Ruth wrote Doris in a final letter, "don't let either of us let pride stand in the way of a friendly interchange."

It was a wounded Denishawn that performed in the Lewisohn Stadium in August 1928. Of the company that performed in the stadium before the oriental tour in 1925, only Ernestine Day, Anne Douglas, and George Steares remained. Geordie Graham had gone, following Martha, and now Doris, Charles, Pauline, Jane Sherman, and others. Anna Austin, Estelle Dennis, Gertrude Gerrish, and Lester Shafer remained from the Follies tour, and personnel from the school filled in. The Braggiotti sisters returned from the Boston branch of Denishawn to appear in Ruth's new ballet, *The Lamp.*

Ruth had returned from the Orient with the feeling that her future work should be universal, rather than specifically oriental. Perhaps she realized that her own Orientalia could never match the authentic native dances of the East. She began to choreograph "metaphysical" ballets, the first of which was *The Lamp,* based on her own poem of the same title and on the drawings of William Blake. "All art is autobiographical," Ruth had remarked in the Orient, and *The Lamp* was an appropriate metaphor for the current conflicts in her life and career. It depicted a struggle between the forces of Life and Death and their transformation by Wisdom. "We are overwhelmed and yet we still believe./We are dying and yet we still live./We run to and fro and bewail the hour of our birth/Since it has led us to this wall," Ruth wrote in her poem, but "there upon the high horizon of the Soul/Appears the night Lamp of Eternity./The dreadful darkness is illuminated." The ballet opened on a joyous scene with dancers frolicking before the figure of a Woman with a Lamp (St. Denis) who stood at the top of pyramidal steps. Progessively the dancers froze in their plastique as a Figure of Death (Ted Shawn) approached from an upper corner of the stage. Mowing down figures in his path, spreading terror and destruction, Death came to the foot of the steps and directed the lowering of a great veil over the bodies strewn on stage. The Woman with a Lamp called the survivors to her steps to light their torches, then dispatched them to the corners of the veil, where they began a concerted effort to lift its weight. As the veil ballooned into the air, obscuring the Figure of Death, he shed his death mask and black robes and transformed himself into a Figure of Life, concluding the ballet with a series of duet dances and groupings around the Lamp Bearer, reminiscent of the groupings in the drawings of William Blake. The music was Franz Liszt's brooding and extravagant tone poem, *Les Préludes* performed by the New York Philharmonic Orchestra, and an unidentified critic for the New York *Times* remarked that Ruth's apocalyptic ballet "leans much more strongly toward the mysticism of Blake, upon whom she has patterned her movement and costuming, than it does toward that of Lamartine, who inspired the music of Liszt." He concluded that St. Denis had succeeded in "creating unmistakable mood and many moments of visual beauty."

The reviewer presumably was John Martin, new dance critic for the *Times*, who acquired his job as an indirect result of pressure applied to his publication by Ruth and Ted. Ted was particularly eloquent in his arguments that general assignment writers, sports writers, even music critics were ill-equipped to analyze the art of dance. The prestige of Denishawn and the growing number of independent dance concerts in New York led the *Times* to engage its first full-time dance critic in 1927. Shortly after his review of the Lewisohn program, Martin wrote a major Sunday piece in the *Times* that marked a turning point in St. Denis' career. He began by way of a historical overview of the "romantic revolution" that spawned the "aesthetic" dancing of Isadora Duncan and Ruth St. Denis who gave a quality of feeling to dance where before there had been nothing but skill. But the principle underlying that aesthetic dancing, he wrote, "has become weak and artificial in contrast to what has grown up in our hearts and minds since the war." He distinguished between art and aestheticism, the aesthete demanding the sensation of pleasure from contact with beauty, the artist seeking truth. St. Denis' aestheticism was outmoded, he wrote. "How one would rejoice to see her bid a happy adieu to the old aestheticism; to watch her lay away in camphor balls all the veils and scarfs and garlands, and pack in chests the lyres and spears and torches, along with the pleasant tunes of Liszt and Chopin and Moskowski, which has for so long been the trimmings of Denishawn dancing." He exempted St. Denis' oriental solos from his argument and stressed that St. Denis herself was far from passé: "Her beauty of line, her instinctive sense of style, her incomparable hands which seem like thinking organisms in themselves, are only externals to the glowing idealism and the inner spirit which mark her as the outstanding figure of her art today."

Ruth read Martin's essay and noted in her diary that it was a "quite understanding notice," though she rejected his arguments. He had urged her to perform "something ugly—searingly, searchingly ugly," when she had dedicated her entire career to the quest for beauty. The fledgling modern dance that Martin so admired—the early dances of Martha Graham, Doris Humphrey's *Life of the Bee*—were foreign to Ruth's nature. Stripped of Denishawn exoticism and decorativeness, they focused on psychological and social struggles or on human movement itself, rather than a transcendent ideal. "To discover that the body can be moved in several different ways and that it is more natural to move in such a way or in such a rhythm is in the end but examining the words of a sentence, the means of the dance," Ruth protested, "and not at all its end which is Joy and Beauty and the evocation of Life." Why mire oneself in the struggles of the ego when Truth could be beheld? Ruth's dances often included elements of struggle but her focus rested on a higher, transcendent truth—Radha in meditation on her throne, Kuan-Yin at the still point of silence, the Woman with the Lamp on her stairway, shedding light. She did not understand the deliberate ugliness, force, and dissonance of her "children's" revolt, their deliberate grounding of the soaring balloon of the spirit, but she tried to understand. She continued to attend their concerts and she kept an open mind. By 1933 she wrote a loving and congratulatory letter to Charles and Doris on the occasion of one of their independent concerts.

She was slower to appreciate the early work of Martha Graham which was angular, forceful, and rhythmic, but she warmed to Graham's Americana, particularly *American Document*, with its spoken text and its themes of Puritanism and lust within a native American context. As it developed, Graham's work had many similarities to St. Denis': central female figures of great mystery and power, themes of sexual repression, inherent theatricality, an imaginative use of stage props. In 1937 Ruth and Martha met in a much-heralded rapprochement. The occasion was the summer dance workshop and festival at Bennington College. Ruth watched Martha teach a class, which she later noted was "a magnificent example of body building and strengthening but extremely ugly and hard, one phase and a very necessary phase of preparation for the dance." She wondered why "There is no rhythmic response taught—no melodic line taught—no hands nor head nor facial" expression. But after the class and a performance that reunited St. Denis, Graham, Humphrey, and Weidman in a survey of modern dance, Ruth and Martha met in a public embrace, which John

Martin was quick to note in his New York *Times* column. "Dear John," Ruth wrote the critic in 1955, "It took a long time for you to raise me to be a modern dancer."

Without the creative lifeblood of its best students and dancers, Denishawn struggled on during the late 1920s. Among the mainstays of the school after 1928 were Evelyn Latour, Anna Austin, and Klarna Pinska. In the fall of 1928, just after John Martin's suggestion that aesthetic dance was passé, Ruth and Ted expanded the school that was the major stronghold of aesthetic dancing in America. They added a new studio and dormitory on land adjacent to Denishawn House and announced additional classes in ballet, plastique, Dalcroze Eurhythmics, piano, voice, and French with supervised reading. Their brochure advertised sixteen spaces in the dormitory where "pupils can be accommodated under guidance of a kindly House Mother, offering them the rare opportunity of being in the atmosphere of Denishawn House."

The atmosphere of Denishawn House was glamorous in those last days, Klarna Pinska remembered. On an evening one might find Sol Cohen or Alexander Alexay at the piano, the lights dimmed and blue, Ruth reading poetry while several of her dancers—she called them "acolytes"—improvised "in rather a Byzantine fashion." By day the mansion was the scene of endless costume fittings, photography sessions, hurried conferences about dances, publicity, finances, and travel itineraries, and in every corner, countless scenes of personal drama. The main players were four, in various combinations: Ruth, Ted, Pearl, and Fred. While Ruth and Ted fought the last battles of their marriage, Fred served as pawn, go-between, and adviser, and Pearl protected Ruth and primed her ear. Had it been a dance, it might have been Jose Limon's *Moor's Pavane,* a four-way struggle of jealousy and deceit tempered with love.

Ruth's relationship with Pearl had always been that of goddess and devotee. Pearl made all her costumes, helped to supervise her productions, and even served as a personal maid. As she nursed Ruth through her difficulties with Fred and Ted, Pearl began to demand her undivided devotion. "Pearly is trying to get out of me what she should find in a man," Ruth realized. "My mother did the same thing." In a letter to Ted she confessed that "This business of Pearl in my life has been for years an unsolved problem because she objectified a character problem in myself—a none-facing of facts, as my mother would say—a blurred and unmet element of getting something for nothing." Pearl had martyred herself to Ruth. "She is stifled as an individual in her work and life generally and is not fulfilled emotionally—this is what my selfishness has done," Ruth said. "I have let Pearl devote her heart and energies to my affairs when all the time I knew I could not respond in the whole-hearted affection that she craved." With much anguish on both sides, the friends parted in 1933, with a financial settlement for Pearl arranged through Ruth's lawyer. Pearl relocated in California where she had her own dance company and school. Ruth sent her money on occasion and in the 1950s, when she purchased land near Hemet, California, Ruth wrote Pearl that she would always have a home with her.

The disentanglement from Fred was as costly for Ruth and Ted, though Fred himself emerged unscathed. After Denishawn House dissolved and Ruth and Ted went their separate ways in the early 1930s, Fred married the daughter of one of the wealthiest investment brokers in the United States and became a successful businessman himself in New Jersey.

As for Ruth and Ted, their marriage deteriorated to the point that they discussed divorce. Fred was not the only complicating factor. Ruth turned to a series of youthful companions, male secretaries, even her own musicians and students. These crushes were brief, messy, and, on more than one occasion, expensive, as Ruth sent them packing with a check. Ted rarely stayed at Denishawn after 1928. He built his own studio in Westport, Connecticut, which became his base of operations. He was only thirty-seven years old, still in his performing prime. He made two solo tours of Europe, with great success, and toured the United States with remnants of the Denishawn Dancers in 1931–32. Between tours he returned to New York, helped with the Lewisohn summer concerts, and contributed what he could to Denishawn. On one of his European trips, he received a letter from Ruth, asking for a divorce. He opposed the idea and told her he had finally found a center in his work, as she had in hers. Ruth wanted a divorce, though she asked herself, "What do I hope to gain? Well, spiritual freedom and honesty. It will release us both from what has become a bind—we go bankrupt in order to start business again." She consulted an attorney in 1931 but decided against filing for divorce, though the question came up over a period of years, whenever Ruth met a new lover or felt the urge to be completely free. In 1947 she shocked Ted by again asking for a divorce. He appealed to her sense of history and to the myth that their marriage had become. "An action of this kind, considering we are both famous people, is going to cause a lot of unnecessary talk which cannot but injure many innocent bystanders," he wrote her. "It will damage your great work, and surely the need for physical, legal union with some other man is not so strong that you would contemplate an action which might easily completely destroy this great work into which you have put so many years of your life, and is the result of your maturest spiritual powers." They never divorced, but after 1931 they did not live together again.

Their marriage ended against the backdrop of financial ruin for Denishawn. The school and property taxes drained every cent they were able to earn through touring. With an abbreviated version of the Denishawn Dancers, Ruth and Ted performed dates along the East Coast during the winter of 1928–29 and Ted continued the tour alone while Ruth went to the West Coast that spring. While she was in California she performed a solo concert at the Figueroa Playhouse in Los Angeles and premiered a new dance, *A Tagore Poem*, which she called "a prose poem of movement." The dance began with Ruth in a sari, seated onstage, an Indian veena stretched across her lap. After some stroking of the veena strings, an attendant removed the musical instrument and Ruth rose to perform a dance of drapery-manipulation, stepping over her sari train, gathering it in one hand, tossing it behind her. This dance had the same little hidden drama as most of St. Denis' solos. Toward the end of the dance, her notes suggest, she walked downstage on four big beats of the Moore-Koopmore music, head alert "as though looking over a balcony; left hand rising higher each step, as though saluting someone in the street below. On the fourth step left hand is raised very high, then sudden drop on left knee, hands together in salaam;" then withdrawing, she gathered her sari train "as in disappointment." This passage of the dance echoed the lines of a Tagore poem which inspired the dance, "It was midday when you went away." The poem may have been read simultaneously with the dance. Ruth had wanted to create a dance interpretation of Tagore's poetry since she visited his university in Calcutta in 1926, and when the poet himself visited New York in 1930 he joined St. Denis in a duet recital of poetry and dance at the Broadway Theatre.

After Ruth returned home from California, she and Ted undertook a duet tour in the fall of 1929 in hopes of earning eight thousand dollars for the Denishawn school's annual operating expenses. They failed to earn anywhere near that much, and knowledgeable critics complained that their duet repertoire consisted of excessively sentimental, dated works that were recycled with new titles. "They scarcely do credit to artists of the calibre of their creators, in spite of the fact that the audience responded vigorously," a New York critic wrote. The death of Daniel Mayer, who had continued to book their tours, the dawning Depression, and the decline in Ruth's drawing power at the box office, all contributed to a steady erosion of performing dates and income.

The Lewisohn concerts remained lucrative, though they could not underwrite the cost of the school. For five summers, 1925 and 1928 through 1931, Ruth and Ted and the Denishawn Dancers appeared in the outdoor concerts at the stadium on the grounds of City College of New York. On a temporary stage erected over the middle of the playing field, they danced before thousands of spectators who arrived hours before the concerts to secure the best vantage point. Of necessity, the Denishawn concerts emphasized spectacle. For the third stadium concert, in 1929, Ted choreographed a music visualization of Honegger's *Pacific-231* for male dancers only, a foretaste of the all-male company he founded after the dissolution of Denishawn. That same year Ruth performed a Cambodian solo, *Bas-relief Figure from Angkor-Wat*, and expanded it into a full-company ballet the following summer at the stadium.

During these years Ruth and Ted often planned the stadium programs by correspondence. In the early summer of 1929, with the stadium concert less than two months away, Ruth wrote Ted from Yosemite National Park, where she was vacationing with her brother's family. She outlined the stadium program of fifteen dances, the longest of which was a twelve-minute group dance, and suggested a new love duet for herself and Ted. "I saw us entering from opposite sides, both as young and fresh as we could be," she wrote, describing the new duet she had in mind. "Our first gesture is of a high recognition. We stand well apart, gazing at each other, and then with first our right, then left hands we salute each other. Then in a very light rhythm, with great freedom and beauty of bodily motion we begin to dance near and around each other, a little like *Gold and Silver Waltz* but not so set, costumes much more exquisite and unearthly in color and a greater feeling of a prose poem, where you do things and then I do them, always with a joyous, tender looking at each other and a slow coming nearer." She concluded by specifying "a plastique in the center, very delicate, then more free rhythm carrying the recharged ecstasy of the plastique to the very circumference of the stage, then a final running together—a sense of meeting together with an upward gesture—does this sound like anything?" Apparently it did not, or the time was too short, for the 1929 stadium concert had no new love duet. For their three nights' work that summer, Ruth and Ted received a little over eight thousand dollars. Of that amount, almost half went for production expenses, leaving little to cover their overdue taxes and bills. They made a great deal of money, but never enough. Most of what they made reverted to their productions.

The mortgages on the Denishawn House and dormitory amounted to well over thirty thousand dollars. Monthly payments and taxes exceeded the revenues generated by school tuition, and the future of Denishawn was in doubt. Ruth wanted Ted to take over completely, leaving her free to work alone. "If Teddy does not take the school," she wrote in her diary, "then there will be no school, for I cannot carry it. The next period of my life must be given to regaining the path of my own destiny which was suggested by *Radha* and the early days of my work." Ted, however, was an astute businessman and he knew that the end of Denishawn was near. He suggested to Ruth that they take bankruptcy, resolve their backlog of bills, and start their careers anew, separately.

Ruth resisted the idea of bankruptcy because it was a humiliating reminder of her earlier loss of Pin Oaks Farm and because it was her nature to dig in her heels in times of duress. She also had nowhere else to go. In 1931, with the help of a lawyer, she reorganized New York Denishawn as the Ruth St. Denis School of Dancing and its Related Arts. She cut the school staff, tried to rent rooms in the Denishawn dormitory and dissolved all the Denishawn branch activities. Ted was supportive and helpful in these efforts. At his suggestion, she incorporated the school to protect them both from personal liability. She wrote begging letters to acquaintances, asking for financial help. Intermittently, she worked. In 1931 she offered herself on the lecture circuit, with three stock speeches, "The Future of the Dance in America," "The Philosophy and Dance of the Orient," and a plea for "putting the arts back among the people" titled "The Community Dance Studio." She organized school recitals and choreographed a musical comedy, *Singapore*, in 1932. The same year she was named Dance Department Director for the Chicago World's Fair. She planned an ambitious *Ballet of the States,* with "prize girls" from each state to be chosen to participate, but the fair directors vetoed the project as too expensive.

She also published her first book, a collection of her poetry entitled *Lotus Light.* They were mostly love poems, mystical poems about Beauty and Truth. Several were dedicated to "B.B." or Best Beloved, Ruth's pet name for Ted, and at least one was written for one of her young companions. They were transparently autobiographical. Her friend Ruth Harwood illustrated one of the poems with a drawing of two male figures kneeling before an illumined goddess. "Now that between you two/I am slain upon the altar,/You may find a God to worship/In my resurrected self," was the poem's cryptic message. They were not very good poems. As William Rose Benét observed in the *Saturday Review of Literature,* "As a poet, Ruth St. Denis is a marvelous dancer."

The more desperate her financial situation became, the more ambitious her schemes. In 1933 she conceived a plan called "Friends of the Dance," an incorporated society formed for "the purpose of revealing the relationship between Spiritual Consciousness and its expression in terms of Rhythm, Form, Color and Tone." The society would sponsor the formation of a national ballet company drawn from the forty-eight United States. Each society member would contribute two dollars per month, with one hundred dollars from each institutional member such as museums and clubs. Listed as directors in the papers of incorporation were Ruth, Edmund Dill Scott, Helen E. Gordon, Katherine P. Nichols, and Catherine M. Buchal. The organization never existed beyond paper.

Ruth also wrote governmental agencies in Washington, D.C., seeking federal aid in meeting the mortgage payments on Denishawn, but she found that the Denishawn debt exceeded federal limits for eligibility. "The whole institution is falling to pieces," she wrote in her diary just after a school concert in 1933. John Martin, in reviewing that concert, blasted the students' work as "sadly inept and amateurish," and wrote that "Even after one has made due obeisance to Miss St. Denis' great contribution to American dancing and her glamorous and magnetic presence on the stage, it is still difficult to excuse the presentation as a professional entertainment of what is in fact a school performance." Ruth agreed with his evaluation. "My recital, personally, was a great success. The children were not good. It was the last lesson for me. I must stand alone."

In 1932 she lost the Denishawn dormitory and land by defaulting on her mortgage but she saved Denishawn House by meeting with officers of the Railroad Building and Loan Association and persuading them to let her pay only the interest on her remaining mortgage until her financial situation improved. By 1933, however, she could not meet the interest payments and her taxes were in arrears. A list of her unpaid bills totaled in excess of seventeen thousand dollars. She owed wig makers, photographers, friends, musicians, advertising agencies, her school faculty, her press clipping service, and, not least, her grocer. On the train to Greenville, South Carolina, where she had secured a stray lecture date, she wrote a poem, *I Am a Beleaguered City*. "Now they are angry," the poem concluded, "Are taking the outer city from me./I can but hasten/To my last stronghold of Silence/And wait the power of the inner law/To bring awakening and light."

The darkness deepened with word from California that her beloved mother had died. She had died peacefully, with her nurse-companion of eighteen years at her side. Ruth could not afford to attend her funeral. "Muddie dear," she reflected, "to human sense my love life with Teddy parted us, but that error can part us no longer."

As her debts mounted and the mortgage holder grew restive, Ruth discussed bankruptcy proceedings with Ted, who advised her that his tour receipts would be jeopardized and that foreclosure was preferable. In 1934 the loan company foreclosed on the Denishawn mortgage. Ruth and Ted lost over eighty thousand dollars of equity in the buildings and land which became headquarters for the American People's School. After signing the formal papers, Ruth and Ted went to the Waldorf Hotel for tea. "Thus ended a long chapter in our path of evolution," Ruth wrote in her diary. She added sadly, "I am out of vogue."

She had no place to go. With her faithful secretary, Don Begenau, she packed her belongings at Denishawn House, wept as she rediscovered old diaries and photographs. When an acquaintance offered her the use of a loft for storage, Ruth took a look and moved herself in as well. The loft was tiny, but it was free and it was hers. With hope in her heart, she christened her new home Vita Nuova.

ANGKOR-VAT

CHOREOGRAPHY: Ruth St. Denis

COSTUMES, PRODUCTION SUPERVISION: Pearl Wheeler

MUSIC: Sol Cohen

PREMIERE: August 12, 1930, Lewisohn Stadium, New York City

———◆———

SCENARIO: It is the beginning of a Khmerian day. A watchman opens the great gates of the King's palace. A milkman delivers his wares and a street sweeper uses his goatskin as a water sprinkler to dampen the earth for his broom. Girls fill their vessels with water. Preparations are underway for a feast given by the King to visiting nobles.

Dancing girls enter and perform a series of traditional poses taken from the bas-reliefs at Angkor-Vat. In the midst of their revelry, an invading army sweeps through the palace, with the Khmer King and his troops in pursuit. The attacking hordes retreat, leaving the King to observe the enactment of the legend of the Naga Queen.

The Naga Queen (St. Denis), symbol of the principle of wisdom, manifests herself as a serpent. She wears a long sarong in a snakeskin print with a six-foot, padded tail extending from its twisted hem. On her head is a towering, fan-shaped headdress with an array of seven cobra heads, ready to strike.

At the opening of her dance the Naga Queen sits with her arms extended horizontally, hands turned up in the fluted manner of the Cambodian dancer. She slowly lifts one arm from shoulder height to almost overhead, then brings that hand sharply down to her chest. With her other arm she repeats the gesture on a low diagonal, bringing her hand back sharply to touch the fingers of the other hand at chest level.

The force of her gestures suggests the male principle. The Queen's head follows each movement to its extremity, then whips back to face front.

She repeats these two gestures, but with arms softened and torso relaxed, suggesting the female principle. The sequence is concluded, as before, with a circling of the head, previously done "with the squareness of masculine movement," and now more gently, "in an attempt to convey the love element of woman versus the exploring intellectual quality of the masculine mind."

The Queen then rises on a series of chords and amplifies her seated gestures in a larger sphere, with added rhythmic footwork. She advances toward her audience, then turns her back and flings her arms upward in a prayerful attitude, then sharply brings them to the horizontal plane, symbolizing "a splitting of the heavens." She then returns to her throne.

The ballet concludes with the nightly love ritual enacted by the Naga Queen and the King of the Khmers (Lester Shafer). They see one another, rise and come together, drawn by desire. Transformed into his bride, the Queen joins the King in a harmonious dance of earthly mating. Their final pose symbolizes their symbiotic relationship, the union of the male and female principles, their bodies intertwined, their arms stretched toward the stars, "but being mortal, the King must stay on earth and become the Sovereign of his city people, while she must retreat to the realm of the Cosmic forces, there to be revitalized with wisdom and love for the succeeding night of their mystic nuptials."

———◆———

Ruth believed that *Angkor-Vat* was the finest ballet she had created since *Ishtar of the Seven Gates*. During its creation in the summer of 1930, she wrote in her diary, "I, in a fine frenzy, have found the solution of the end of my Naga dance! Sol, thundering away on the piano, trying and succeeding in getting my mood, quite wild-eyed, stopping to pat each other on the back, then he flying back to the piano and I pulling up the front of my pink practice dress to begin the dance all over again." Ted, just home from Europe, had stopped by the rehearsal hall to help her. "I dare to believe that not since *Ishtar* have I done anything as good or important."

Yet *Angkor-Vat,* for all its pleasure to its creator, represented Denishawn in decline. It was one of the few dance spectacles where a Denishawn dancer assumed the male lead opposite Ruth. Its themes suggested St. Denis' artistic preoccupation with bisexuality or androgyny, then one of the issues that preoccupied her personal life and contributed to the demise of Denishawn.

Androgyny was not a new theme for St. Denis. In *Egypta,* she said, she had dealt with "the balanced faculties of the bi-sexual or complete being, expressed in the negative and positive of day and night, in the manifold life and culture of man and woman; and in the complete cycle of life and death." Her madonna studies were an attempt to express the "feminine balance of the Godhead." She believed that all human beings contained male and female characteristics and that the artist created his works only through a resolution of the opposing elements in his nature. In 1963 she told an interviewer that "Most of us are overbalanced obviously as male and female. The artist contains within himself, eighty per cent of the time unknown to him, majority masculine or feminine. He must wait for external stimuli to make him whole." In an essay entitled "Androgyny," she wrote, "The artist has been given at birth a curse or a blessing, a genius or a degeneration. In other words he has been given a terrible responsibility which he seldom knows how to assume." This theme concerned her during most of her adult life. In her late years she lectured on the necessity for a "balanced government," with a man and a woman forming a dual American presidency. The very symbol of the Denishawn school and company, a man and a woman crouching in fetal position within the circular symbol for Yin and Yang, expressed this preoccupation, which was shared by Ted Shawn.

In *Angkor-Vat,* St. Denis attempted to work out her theory of opposites.

ELEVEN

THE SUN AND THE MOON

Ruth's most admirable quality was her honesty. She may have dissembled to those about her, but she never lied to herself. The Puritan conscience inherited from her mother led to relentless self-examination. Throughout the suspended, drab decade of the 1930s she grappled with a central conflict in her life and art, the tension between aestheticism and moralism. In personal terms, she struggled with the fear of her own sexuality. Artistically, she sought a purer expression of God in her dancing. Spiritually, she searched among the shards of a broken life and career for her truest self. As the decade began, she wrote in her diary, "I feel in some strange way that right now my soul and body are the battleground for certain powers and forces to fight out until there is peace."

Her ruined marriage was a raw wound. She probed her conscience for reasons why it had failed. She knew the obvious reasons—differences in temperament, professional rivalry, the hardships of theatrical life. "We both needed a 'wife,'" she believed, "that element that will love and protect the soaring, struggling urge for expression in beauty that is in us both." She knew that Ted had loved her and believed in her, "but I became restive when I knew he could not be two people at once. He could not fulfill his own destiny and help me to fulfill mine."

A deeper reason for the failure of her relationship with Ted, with all men, was her fundamental fear of sexual desire. "I have never even pretended to try to be a lover!" she confessed in her diary. "I have talked and longed for love all these years yet never have had the honesty, the courage to meet love squarely. How can women meet it in the fearless way that men can? unless one of two things, that they are simply animals without inhibitions of any kind or have risen to a state of such inner completeness that it becomes unimportant what they do." Ted had not known how to deal with her fears. "Teddy's love did not completely satisfy me," she wrote, "not because of any lack of physical enjoyment—as I have always thought that I was satisfied on that plane —but because of tenderness lacking, which I have so much craved. He seemed interested only in his own part of enjoyment and not in me, which is the cry of all women." She had "the most damnable fears" and at the slightest sexual suggestion became "confused, self-condemnatory, unjust, stupid." As a consequence she avoided direct relationships with men through her pose as mother-confessor. "All those boy-men that I tried to help," she wrote ruefully in 1936. "I tried, though God knows I did not call it that, to prostitute them, to buy their devotion with my love, my help, my protection. Their lack of self-confidence made them turn to me, and then when I tried to do their work for them, they naturally and inevitably hated me, all of them."

Compounding the complexity of her personal relationships were the women friends in her life. "Something in me attracts and holds them in a strange selfless devotion," she wrote. "They believe in me and serve my ideals with enthusiasm and endless patience. I in turn am egotistically unresponsive, sometimes to the point of cruelty on the merely human side, while being deeply grateful in the spiritual." She, who seemed to use the people in her life, felt used in so many of her relationships. She craved an open, honest love. It came to her in an unexpected way.

Before the demise of Denishawn, Ruth had founded a Society of Spiritual Arts. The organization began during the Follies tour as the Esoteric Group, a philosophical discussion group for her dancers. Later at Denishawn House she reorganized the group as a dancing and discussion society based on Christian Science principles. "It is not my motive to spread propaganda for Christian Science," she explained during a founding meeting, "but the very existence of our Society is based on the one Great Principle expressed throughout the writings of Mary Baker Eddy, that our concept of Life must be spiritual and not material." In connection with her society she established a small group of dancers, her "acolytes," the genesis of her Rhythmic Choir. In a typical service these girls wore neutral-colored robes and carried wrought-iron candlesticks which they placed at each corner of a large rug. They then seated themselves in a semicircle and awaited Ruth's entrance. Robed in white, she entered and took her place on a cushion in the center.

She opened the service by chanting a mantra, then began an informal talk on the relation of dance to worship. After the talk, the dancers demonstrated gestures and group designs or "Consciousness through Gesture," an application of Delsartean principles. For example, the acolytes might surround Ruth with a "circle of fear" which she broke through, or they performed "Orchestration of Emotion" exercises in which they took Ruth's central gesture and exaggerated it into group movement.

These exercises were not limited to her dancers. The congregation or audience participated in "rhythmic postures" and in the discussion of spiritual topics from the nature of God to the nature of divine art. Among the members of the society were poets, clergymen, painters, dancers, architects, and philosophers. Swami Nikhilananda occasionally came from the Ramakrishna Mission to speak about Vedanta. The famed sculptor George Grey Barnard, then in the twilight of his career, attended society meetings and participated in the rhythmic exercises. Barnard, like Ruth, sought an inner state of harmonious suspension and peace. His best-known sculpture, *Struggle of Two Natures in Man*, was an appropriate symbol for St. Denis' own struggle between the Apollonian and Dionysian sides of her nature. During one of the society meetings, Barnard told his fellow worshipers, "Nothing will ever be more perfect than this group here together, our postures, our 'being.' This is all put into painting and sculpture and we think that is the ultimate, but that is not it: it is this moment which counts. The most awful sin is to become blasé, to grow immune from the joy of the moment."

One evening in the summer of 1934 a newcomer joined their group, a Chinese poet and philosopher educated at Columbia University and in his native land, where he had served as a diplomat and director of the Chinese Government's Bureau of Economic Information. Sum Nung Au-Young had represented China at the Pan-Pacific Union in Hawaii in 1925, then emigrated to the United States where he founded the School of Chinese Philosophy and Cultural Studies in New York. Among his volumes of published poetry was *The Rolling Pearl* (1930), which drew accolades from John Dewey and Rabindranath Tagore. Edwin Markham, the popular American poet, called Au-Young "one of the greatest of modern poets." His most important work was an English translation of the bible of Taoism, the Tao Teh King.

Au-Young was twelve years younger than Ruth, handsome, elegant,

remembered by one of her friends as a "silent, smiling man." He fell in
love with Ruth and she with him. They met first to share poetry in her
tiny apartment, Vita Nuova, which she had decorated with Japanese
wall hangings, a piano, a lamp with a white jade Kuan Yin as pedestal,
Indian miniatures, Chinese paintings, and her favorite photograph of
Ted, clipped from a newspaper and inserted in a dimestore frame. This
setting became her private meeting place with Sum Nung. They called
it the "Magic Gardens." They met each Friday evening and read from
the Tao. She danced while he played the butterfly harp. For weeks she
resisted his expressions of love. In early September she asked him to
make a pilgrimage with her to Pin Oaks Farm and they took a train to
Somerville and visited the Little Place. When they returned they became lovers.

Ruth had never known sheer pleasure. Sum Nung was an artist in
love, a "sensualist who makes an occupation of love," she decided, "yet
at least he is honest." He wanted nothing from her but the pleasure of
her company. He made each tryst a work of art, with black satin sheets,
bouquets of white flowers and poems fragrant with desire. She was his
Moon and he was the Sun. In a poem for her, "Moon-Flower," he
wrote

> She is like a moon-flower
> Blossoming in its virginal beauty
> Far far above the jewelled heaven,
> Opening its fragile petals
> Only to the
> Golden sun-beam.

The intensity of their pleasure frightened Ruth. "It seemed that my
mother's reproachful eyes looked at me," she wrote, "but those artificial
strong walls of fears and evasions which had lasted so many years were
at last broken down and utterly destroyed. Now at last the final shreds
of my New England taboos and inhibitions dissolved in the beauty of
this love desire. It was the challenge to my spiritual and moral life."

Sum Nung was her tender and patient tutor. "I want to see you
grow in your consciousness a greater and more receptive soul which is
always ready to encompass the human as well as the spiritual elements," he wrote her. "Your present awareness is like the first stage of
the opening of a lotus bloom." When she grew afraid he assured her,

"Now—concerning your moods—I can say that behind them all I realize the ONE GREAT SOUL FEMININE with the jewelled crown—the real WOM-ANHOOD which is struggling for purification in that all-consuming fire of primordial love." She fascinated him. He wrote a poem about her, titled "Incomparable":

> *When I contemplate*
> *The loveliness*
> *Of peach-blossoms*
> *And the fragrance of jasmine*
> *I tenderly think*
> *Of my Beloved,*
> *Whose fragile grace*
> *Is indeed incomparable . . .*
>
> *The flowers will fade*
> *When they see her*
> *Radiant, spiritual face,*
> *As if they were ashamed*
> *Of their inconsequential existence.*

His love spurred Ruth to creativity. In 1934 she choreographed *Masque of Mary*, also called *Color Study of the Madonna*, a ritual pageant designed for presentation in a church. This was her first major production with her Rhythmic Choir, which included Anna Austin and Mary Brandt from the Denishawn days. The pageant began with the same organ prelude, "Dance of Praise," that began all services for her Society of Spiritual Arts. Next was a reading from the Gospels concerning the Immaculate Conception, then the entrance of the Madonna (St. Denis), who stood on an altar swathed in white veils while around her danced the Angels of the Heavenly Host. At the conclusion of this joyous dance, the Madonna removed her veils to stand in an Annunciation gown of deep turquoise blue. In a contemplative mood she received Gabriel with his message of creative love. The scene concluded with the dancing of "heavenly children dressed in Fra-Angelico costumes, playing on celestial instruments." The ensuing vignettes of the journey of Mary and Joseph, the birth of the Christ child, the visit of the Magi, the flight of Mary and Joseph into Egypt, and the crucifixion of Christ were depicted by choral mime and solo plastique. With each vignette the Madonna assumed symbolic veils, the red of Nativity, the purple of

Crucifixion, the gold of the Assumption. The score was by Sol Cohen, an active member of the Society of Spiritual Arts.

This new phase in St. Denis' career had several precedents. The first of her many madonnas surfaced in *Queen of Heaven,* a solo composed for the oriental tour. While she toured the Orient, Max Reinhardt brought his mystery spectacle, *The Miracle,* to the United States and commissioned a decor from Norman Bel Geddes. The Reinhardt pageant told the story of a statue of a madonna who came to life, descended into a worldly life of salacious living, then reascended to her pedestal and rightful role as the silent witness of pilgrims' prayers. There is no evidence that Ruth ever saw this play, which continued to tour the United States through 1929, but she may have discussed it with her friend Bel Geddes. A more direct influence on her madonnas was Claude Bragdon's experiments with color and the Delsarte system's scheme of symbolic colors. St. Denis may have derived the color imagery for *Masque of Mary* from Genevieve Stebbins' *Delsarte System of Expression,* which included a chapter on color and its emotional significance, and the format for *Masque of Mary* echoed Ted Shawn's pioneer work in sacred dancing.

In 1917 Shawn presented *A Church Service in Dance* for the First Interdenominational Church in San Francisco, but the performance was given in a local auditorium rather than in a church sanctuary. On his 1921 tour the same suite of dances earned him the censure of the local clergy and the Commissioner of Public Safety for the city of Shreveport, Louisiana, but he performed his sacred dances, surrounded by the city police force, and received hearty applause and a congratulatory visit from the mayor. During the same period Dr. William Guthrie sponsored rhythmic dances in his parish, St. Mark's-in-the-Bouwerie in New York City, much to the displeasure of the church hierarchy. Dancing on sacred themes or within the precincts of the church was considered controversial at best, licentious at worst, and a decade later the climate for religious dance had not improved.

Ruth's *Masque of Mary* was scheduled to debut in New York's Holyrood Episcopal Church during the Christmas season of 1934. In the parish magazine the church rector announced the performance and reminded his parishioners that the Bible taught, "Let them praise His Name in the dance," but both his congregation and his church superiors vetoed the idea and canceled the pageant. A more liberal clergyman, Dr. Daniel Russell of the Rutgers Presbyterian Church in New

York, invited St. Denis and her Rhythmic Choir to stage *Masque of Mary* in his church instead. A week after this debut the Rhythmic Choir repeated the program for more than seventeen hundred worshipers at the Riverside Church in New York. Ruth had established a new stage persona, the madonna, and a new era in her career.

Sum Nung came to the Riverside pageant but discreetly stood aside as Ted Shawn rushed back to Ruth's dressing room to congratulate her. They wept together and Ruth made Teddy promise that some day he would perform the pageant with her. Ted was in New York from time to time now. The previous year at his new home, Jacob's Pillow, a farm near Springfield, Massachusetts, he had formed his own all-male troupe of dancers. The company grew out of a semester Ted spent on the faculty of Springfield College, where he taught five hundred men who were training to be physical education directors. In the summer of 1933 he gathered his prize students and a few former dancers and began touring as Ted Shawn and his Men Dancers. For seven years they toured throughout the United States, Canada, Cuba, and England, before disbanding at the onset of World War II. They specialized in athletic, muscle-flexing dances designed to convince the American public that the art of dancing could be manly, and Shawn was widely credited with winning acceptance for male dancers.

Whenever Ted's tours brought him to New York, he visited his wife. On occasion they felt a stirring of their original feelings for each other. "It was great seeing you the other night," Ted wrote to Ruth after one visit in 1931. "Old time sparks began to fly, didn't they? There is a unique light emitted by our two carbons." But in 1934 when Ted performed at Carnegie Hall, Ruth decided not to visit him backstage after she saw his current admirer and promoter, Katherine Dreier, in the lobby. Ruth still corresponded with Ted and he occasionally sent her money. He was doing better than she, financially, with his business acumen and appetite for hard work. Ruth was hopelessly broke. When she was threatened with the loss of Vita Nuova she was unable to afford another apartment. Friends notified the city welfare department which assigned a case worker to investigate. By 1935 the welfare department subsidized Ruth's rent. Her brother helped her whenever he could and when she faced a lawsuit by a scenery transfer company, Ted converted a life insurance policy into a small annuity for her.

She worked whenever she could find a booking. In early 1935 she was a guest artist with the Pittsburgh String Orchestra in that city's

Carnegie Music Hall. She performed for society balls and gave occasional lectures. She began taking a daily dance lesson from Jack Cole, a former Denishawner and talented young choreographer. "To see me struggling with a barre is a sight," she wrote in her diary, "but it is doing me a world of good." At fifty-five, she was optimistic, eager to learn, and happy. After a visit from Sum Nung to the Magic Gardens she wrote, "I have known more sweetness and harmony in this little room than in years."

Her Rhythmic Choir was her major project. In this work Ruth felt that she harmonized her artistic and spiritual life. "Whereas before I felt and acted and lived as an 'artist' or one who feels that the outward finish of his work is vital in order to meet the artistic standards of both his own mind and the world's," she wrote, "now I feel that the techniques and standards of my artistic life must be subordinate to such realization as I have of the realm of Spiritual existence." She wanted to make dance a prayer, rather than a profession. "Dance is a living mantra," she wrote. "It is not a mere constant change of gesture and rhythm, calculated to intrigue the attention of the surface eye, but it is the very stuff and symbol of my inner creative life and the coordination of all the elements of my being."

After *Masque of Mary* she choreographed a second major pageant, *When I Meditate on Thee in the Night-Watches*, premiered at Park Avenue Presbyterian Church on February 24, 1935. After this rhythmic interpretation of the Psalms, an attorney and church elder wrote the Presbytery of New York, demanding that the Moderators' Council take action to ensure that "disgraceful scenes of this kind are not re-enacted in the pulpits." He particularly objected to Ruth's bare feet and felt the dance was "unquestionably a distinct attack upon the purity of the church." The minister of Park Avenue Presbyterian responded by defending Ruth. "In the first place," he reassured her detractor, "it was not a dance and in the second place Miss St. Denis has a real message." Ruth herself laughed at the controversy and told a reporter for the New York *Times*, "Now the fact of my putting nail polish on my toes is no different to me as a dancer than to a choir girl who puts nail polish on her finger nails. In the next five years," she predicted, "dancing in church will become so common that there will be no criticism about it from the point of novelty but it will be criticized from the point of view of the fitness of the thing they are interpreting." She enjoyed the publicity generated by the episode and her prediction proved accurate.

By the 1940s her Rhythmic Choir received only routine notice from the public and press who were quite accustomed by then to dance as worship.

Her Society of Spiritual Arts continued to meet on Thursday nights. Sum Nung often came to read from the sacred texts of Taoism. A descendant himself of Ou-yang Hsiu, the revered interpreter of the Tao Teh King of Lao Tze, Au-Young added his own special emphases to the doctrine of the Tao. He stressed the Yin and Yang principles, the complementary interrelationship of the feminine and masculine elements in life, and emphasized Lao Tze's simple methods for cultivating the physical body and "ennobling the sensuous desires and earthly pleasures." His beliefs challenged Ruth's basic sense of morality. "To the last remnants of my Protestant conscience," she wrote in her autobiography, "this relationship was the ultimate climax of my emotional sin."

She had always considered herself an aesthete, a searcher for beauty through art. Now that she had these ideal qualities in a relationship, she realized that beauty and aesthetic pleasure were not enough. Like Radha she must rise above the temptation of the five senses and reascend to her lofty but lonely throne. She tried to end her affair with Sum Nung. She resolved to leave him, then melted at the sound of his voice. She began letters of farewell, then cast them aside at the arrival of a letter or love poem from him. She felt incapable of a final act of separation.

Two of her friends urged her to make the break. One was Anne Sherman Hoyt, her newest woman friend. Anne was a plump little lady in her late fifties who wore her white hair in a bun on top. She was an aristocrat, a great-niece of the Confederate general William Tecumseh Sherman and of John Sherman, the Secretary of State in the McKinley administration. Her sister, Lady Lindsay, was married to the British ambassador to the United States. She had a tidy inheritance, and after she met Ruth she took great pleasure in being her Lady Bountiful. Ruth often visited one of Anne's three homes in Sharon, Connecticut, and she accepted money from her over the years. When Anne died in 1951 she left Ruth a legacy in her will. Ruth loved Anne but felt guilty about taking her money. She was uncomfortable when Anne sent her flowers or gifts. "There are horrible moments when I am with Anne that I feel like a 'kept woman,'" Ruth wrote in her diary. "When this mood assails me I could scream and go out and bang doors and leave everything behind!" But she also admired Anne as a "lady of the first water" who was one of the most loyal supporters of the Society of Spiritual Arts. Anne took Ruth's reputation very seriously and she cherished her image as a virginal goddess. When she learned about Ruth's affair with Sum Nung she was adamantly opposed.

Another of Ruth's new friends, a young actor and writer from California who had come to the East Coast "to connect with the theatre," became her newest "personal representative." He urged her to write her autobiography and began typing a transcript of her diaries. He moved into her apartment, then out, at Anne's insistence, and in February 1936 the three of them sailed for London. It was a trip designed to help Ruth forget Sum Nung. Just before her departure she wrote him a farewell letter, asking his compassion and assuring him that for no trivial reason "did the Moon close the gates of the magic gardens that she might enter more completely into the immortal realms." He must remember, she wrote, "the continual yearning of the moon for more tranquility and harmony in both her inner and outer life." She concluded, "The Moon left the magic gardens of time and entered the immortal garden of eternity, because of a divine necessity to attain a greater growth in the understanding of the very law which brought your imperial majesty to her needing and grateful heart." Her high-flown rhetoric did not conceal a troubled heart.

In London Ruth worked on her autobiography, saw her old friends Constance Smedley and Havelock Ellis, and stayed in a hotel operated by Rose Mazumdar, an Indian who was one of the temple priests in the first production of *Radha*. Surrounded by friends and memories of earlier visits to London, she was miserable. "My soul was in such blackness," she wrote in her autobiography, "that nothing which had previously sustained me could cast any light whatever. I had committed all the sins that, in my youth, I had sworn I would not commit." She began attending meetings of the Oxford Group, an evangelical Protestant association that took its name from a nineteenth-century effort to Catholicize the Anglican church. The current Oxford Group emphasized the religious conversion of each individual through a process of personal confession of sin, often sexual sin, and the training of the will to resist such temptation. Group members met in "Houseparty" retreats to engage in group confession and to nurture their personal relationships with God. The Oxford Group was primarily a movement for the upper classes and made its appeal to members' desire for social pres-

St. Denis in *Angkor Vat,* created for the 1930
Lewisohn Stadium concert.

Ruth, in sari, at the Taj Mahal, Agra, India, 1926.

Ruth (center) with Denishawn dancers in Jubbulpore. Left to right: Jane Sherman, Edith James, St. Denis, unknown man, Anne Douglas.

St. Denis with veena in *A Tagore Poem,* choreographed after visit to Rabindranath Tagore's university in Calcutta.

Ruth St. Denis in the *Nautch,* her most popular dance on the oriental tour.

Sum Nung Au-Young

Ruth St. Denis and her temple dancers at Denishawn House, 1933.

Ruth St. Denis as the Duchess of Marlborough in the 1944
Paramount film *Kitty*.

tige. Its publication, *The New World News*, featured names of the rich and powerful, and a historian of the movement wrote that "It was the Queen Maries, the Henry Fords, the Admiral Byrds, members of Parliament, foreign ministers and peers of the realm that were featured in the stories told at the meetings and whose names were found most often in the Group literature." As the Oxford Group evolved, it also was pacifist and anti-Communist and just before World War II the group became known as the movement for Moral Re-Armament.

Ruth became a devoted member of the Oxford Group. When she returned to the United States she affiliated with the Calvary Episcopal Church in New York, whose rector, Samuel M. Shoemaker, was the leader of the movement in America. The Rev. Dr. Shoemaker had established an Oxford Group chapter at Princeton University during his student days there, but the organization was controversial and rumors abounded that the Group fostered lurid sexual confessions. After graduation he moved to Calvary Episcopal where he was beloved for his personal approach to religion. He invited Ruth to produce her Rhythmic Choir pageants in the sanctuary of his church. During Christmas of 1937 she choreographed *Babylon*, which told the story of a woman seducing the world with pride, lust, and ambition. Ruth dedicated the work to the Oxford Group and called *Babylon* "the most dynamic of my temple dances."

As the Oxford Group became the movement for Moral Re-Armament, Ruth traveled for the organization as a speaker and participated in a "Second World Assembly" meeting that drew thirty thousand people to the Hollywood Bowl to hear the Moral Re-Armament credo of "dynamic peace for humanity." In 1939 Ruth wrote letters to celebrities, urging them to join the Oxford Group in working for world peace in a climate of impending war. She invited their participation in Moral Re-Armament Week in New York City during May of that year. Some of those on her mailing list responded with evasive letters or token contributions. Katherine Cornell begged off on the grounds that she was busy appearing in a play, but Helen Hayes' response was more forthright. "I appreciate that it is a worthy and splendid ideal," she wrote Ruth, "but unfortunately I am not wholly in sympathy with it." The Moral Re-Armament movement lost favor as pacifism became equated with treason during the war and the Oxford Group's founder, the Reverend Frank Buchman, was accused of Nazi sympathies. By then Ruth had become disenchanted with the Group. "They do fine work but they have no need for art," she wrote in her diary. "They do not understand me." In a letter to Sum Nung Au-Young she wrote that she had left the Group, then added to herself, "Was I ever meant to cooperate with any group?"

Sum Nung was back in her life. On her way to London Ruth had read his reply to her good-bye letter. "Your leaving makes me sad and depressed," he wrote, "however, true wisdom will follow you wherever you go, and my spirit will be with you always." The latter was true. "Sum Nung hovers in my echoing spaces of my being like a subtle perfume which comes and goes in its intensities," Ruth wrote. At times she longed for him; at times she was aghast at the thought of their affair. When she returned from London her new male secretary drifted on and with him, her plans for an autobiography. She refused all Sum Nung's calls, but a year later they were seeing each other again, always "for the last time." Sum Nung was ill and losing weight, and his thoughts were elsewhere, in war-torn China where, he hinted, he might return.

Ruth was at loose ends. Her Rhythmic Choir again was meeting and occasionally performing, but for little pay. She talked with Jack Cole and Anna Austin about an artistic partnership, but nothing came of it. "I have drifted away from dancing," she wrote in her diary, "I am no longer marketable." At fifty-eight she fell somewhere in the twilight zone between active performer and dancer emeritus. She auditioned for Xavier Cugat, who was organizing a variety show. It was a humiliation, "like the old Keith days" in vaudeville, "a horrible feeling of having made a fool of myself." When it seemed as if she had nowhere to go, an offer came from Dr. Paul Eddy, president of Adelphi College in Garden City, New York. Dr. Eddy and his wife had attended Ruth's "Temple Evenings" during the winter of 1936, and they were impressed with her mixture of philosophy, religion, and art. Isabel Eddy joined Ruth's Rhythmic Choir. Her husband asked Ruth to organize and direct a dance department at the university, with particular emphasis on research into the dance as an instrument of religious worship. Ruth accepted and in the fall of 1938 began an affiliation with the college that lasted into the 1960s. "To be honest I do not give much more than my name and the loan of my art objects and costumes to it," Ruth said of her new university position. "Jack and Anna and Ada and Don do the rest." Her loyal band of dancers became staff members of the department: Anna Austin, who taught oriental dance, Jack Cole and Ada

Korvin for modern dance, and Don Begenau, social dance. Ruth shared the wealth of her experience with religious dance in lectures and informal discussions, and she choreographed several rhythmic pageants for Adelphi.

Ruth's method of creating works for her religious dance choir involved parsing Christian hymns. "Get the meaning of each sentence," she told her assistants. "Sit down on the floor and somebody with a nice voice reads the hymn. Have it read with meaning and then ask the class 'what accent is on this sentence? What is the meaning you want to bring out?' When they decide on the meaning then ask 'who has some suggestions for our first meaning?' Now we are going to parse our mudras. I will take a sentence from the Psalms. 'I will lift up mine eyes to the hills.' Settle on 'I,' what does 'I' mean?" After her students selected a few gestures or mudras to express a sentence from the hymn, Ruth advised them to "get up, drop the mudras and begin to feel from the solar plexus the rhythm of the hymn. Get that well into your whole body." The next step in creating a choral dance work was the design of a floor pattern. Ruth always used floor patterns in her choreography, with attention to the symbolic qualities of geometric shapes. "The square line, the oblong, would stand for the masculine. All forms of the circle for the feminine . . . You must not restlessly keep going all the time, all over the stage. You must have a nice balance . . . you must not come to a dead end of movement." She revealed her debt to Delsarte and his observation of natural human movement. In searching for the proper gesture to illustrate a hymn of praise, she asked, "Do not children's hands, as a rule, come up when you hold up something? Some kind of instinctive movement reaching up and then there is the emotional contraction of the chest. What is wrong with that to praise God?" Her teaching method blended acting techniques, Delsartean poses, and interpretive dance. Through 1940 Ruth commuted to Adelphi, where she spent a half week, and she continued her liaison with the school after she moved to the West Coast during World War II. The university observed an annual Ruth St. Denis Day for the rest of her life.

The job at Adelphi coincided with another salutary event in her attempts to revive her career. In the summer of 1938, Ruth retired to a cabin on Long Island with a fledgling writer, Henrietta Buckmaster, who was only eighteen years old. After several false starts on her autobiography, Ruth was determined to finish it this time. She signed a contract with Harper & Brothers and over their protests insisted on Henrietta as her ghost writer. She and her mother were regular visitors to Ruth's Temple Evenings and they shared with her a belief in Christian Science. Henrietta was an impressive young woman, with one book already to her credit and a quiet sense of dignity. Though everyone else in St. Denis' entourage called her "Miss Ruth," Henrietta preferred "Ruth." They spent the summer together in a strict work regimen, deciphering Ruth's diaries, recording her memories. Henrietta screened visitors, including the various young males who were attached to Miss Ruth. By the end of the summer they had produced a document that captured Ruth's personality, her mysticism and her humor, her fantasies and her honesty. Though Ruth had a reputation to protect, she insisted on including the story of Sum Nung Au-Young, anonymously of course. Anne Hoyt objected strenuously, to no avail. The book was published in 1939 with the title *An Unfinished Life.*

The publication of her autobiography sparked a new phase in Ruth's career. With her story told, she graduated to the pantheon of senior citizens of the dance. She was considered charming rather than passé, quaint rather than merely old-fashioned. Job offers began trickling in, usually suggestions that she revive her earliest famous dances. Her Rhythmic Choir performed dates in churches and at the New York World's Fair in 1940, and in the summer of that year came an invitation to perform and teach at a dance festival at Jacob's Pillow, Ted's farm which had been leased for the summer to Mary Washington Ball, a dance educator. Miss Ball invited Ted and his Men Dancers, the ethnic dancer La Meri, the ballroom dancer Robert Knight, Dr. Elizabeth Burchenal for folk dance, and Ruth for religious dance to form the senior faculty for her first summer dance festival. Ruth performed that summer and when Ted regained control of the property and continued the festival the following year, she revived *Radha* for the first time in twenty-five years as well as her Incense and other East Indian solos. "It has restored much to my inner citadel," she wrote after that 1941 performance. "I lifted my heart to Mother just as I began 'Incense'—she must be near—smiling a little—that Ruthie has done right in going back to her own work!" The Jacob's Pillow performance confirmed the revival of her career.

At the same time Ruth met a young man destined to play a major role in prolonging her career. Walter Terry had studied dance with a student of Ted Shawn's and performed with a dance group that sent several members to Ted's Men Dancers. Ted asked Walter to join his troupe but Walter decided to continue his education and become a dance writer, which he did, joining the staff of the New York *Herald Tribune*. He became a pioneer American dance critic and soon found himself in the position of analyzing the work of both Ted and Ruth. Ted courted him assiduously and Ruth adored Walter, whom she called her "beloved Cricket." During the next two decades they collaborated on a series of programs, with Walter providing historical commentary and Ruth reviving her dances. Walter was instrumental on committees that gave Ruth awards and he also became her biographer.

Ruth found another new ally in the ethnic dancer La Meri. Born Russell Meriwether Hughes in Louisville, Kentucky, La Meri had a performing life similar to St. Denis', an early career as a movie-house dancer, a stint in a Spanish dance troupe, then years of endless touring as a solo dancer. She traveled widely and mastered native dance techniques, the *pwe* in Burma, Kathak in India, the hula in Hawaii. She wrote and published poetry and shared with Ruth a fundamental sense of humor and a shrewd intelligence. They were both strong personalities, both famous in their chosen field, and unlikely as it seemed, they became close friends. They met after one of La Meri's concerts. Ruth bounded back to her dressing room and announced that they must collaborate on a center of the oriental arts. "She was a torrent of embodied enthusiasm, as easy to avoid as a hurricane," La Meri said of Ruth. They discussed the idea of an artistic co-venture and in the spring of 1940 announced the School of Natya at 66 Fifth Avenue, where Martha Graham already had her studio. Martha was on the top floor, La Meri had the one below, and Ruth moved into the ground floor studio.

The School of Natya was a shared venture in name only. While La Meri offered classes in Indian, Japanese, Javanese, and other oriental techniques, Ruth rarely taught, and when she did, La Meri allowed her the day's "take" from the student fees. They did not share students but they did share ideas. Ruth had the notion that at long last she wanted to study authentic oriental dancing. She would summon La Meri to her studio and ask her to demonstrate some step she had noticed in her work. "I taught her the Kathak turns because she fell in love with them," La Meri said, "and she was a very quick study. But when she put them into her dance it became something else again. Technique?

She had the skill if she wanted it but emotion took over and the actual cold line of the thing was lost."

As La Meri taught Ruth various gestures and footwork, she tried in return to learn some of the secrets of St. Denis' genius. "Sometimes I would ask, 'Miss Ruth, how can you make a gesture with your hand and when you stop, the gesture just keeps on going all the way down to China?' She would look at me and say, 'You *would* ask that. My dear, I don't know!' I just wanted to nail it down practically if possible, not that I wanted to use her work, I just wanted to know it, how it could be done." The two friends collaborated on a series of fortnightly concerts called "Oriental Reunions." On one occasion at the Manhattan YMHA La Meri performed five authentic dances with Ruth following each dance with her own romantic interpretation of its style. They also worked together on a system of American vernacular and religious gesture. Ruth wanted to create a gesture language of American dance similar to the system of Hindu mudras. With La Meri as her scribe and collaborator, she filled part of a notebook with a dictionary of gestures from American sports, religion, and popular culture, until her enthusiasm and attention turned elsewhere, leaving the project unfinished.

La Meri took care of Ruth in subtle ways. Ruth was always very careless with her costumes, removing them roughly and stuffing them in her trunks. In the absence of a maid, La Meri often cleaned up Ruth's trunks and sorted her costumes. She also served as a buffer between Ruth and the landlord. On one occasion the manager of the building came to La Meri for Ruth's back rent. La Meri tactfully gave the sum to Ruth, who was ever so grateful. A few weeks later the manager returned to La Meri for Ruth's still overdue rent. She asked Ruth about it. "Darling," she chirped, "I bought some marvelous files for the photographs!" "She was completely unaware of where money should be spent. She really didn't know. She was like a child," La Meri said. "She was always skating on the edge of bankruptcy—she didn't even have enough to call it bankruptcy—but it never touched her spiritually. It was just not in her character to think about money matters." Their partnership ended when Ruth decided that she needed more space and moved uptown to a studio formerly occupied by Isadora Duncan. She continued to share concerts with La Meri and after her move to the West Coast stayed in touch with her friend. Theirs was a delightful friendship remarkably free of the manipulation that marked so many of St. Denis' relationships.

Thanks to the stimulation of the shared concerts with La Meri, Ruth was dancing again. The *Radha* revival at Jacob's Pillow generated copious publicity. In the New York *Herald Tribune* Walter Terry may have overstated the case when he described *Radha* as "one of the most demanding roles in all dance," or when he characterized St. Denis' face and body as "those of a young woman," whose movements were "undoubtedly the envy of the teen-age dancers in the audience." But he added a phrase that became the keynote of Ruth's revived career: "Ruth St. Denis remains, in my estimation, the first lady of the American dance."

The myth began. As "Miss Ruth," the "First Lady of American Dance," she prolonged her career by another twenty years. She performed the role with relish, batting her eyes with false modesty, interlacing her Irish humor with double entendres, spinning yarns of her days on the variety stage. Her publicity always stressed her amazing youthfulness, her wicked sense of humor, her trouper's sense of the-show-must-go-on. In public she became a caricature of herself and continued performing her solos well into her eighties. An important part of her new historic image was her identity as the distaff side of Denishawn. With Ted she nurtured the myth of their intact marriage, grandly celebrating their fiftieth wedding anniversary at Jacob's Pillow in August of 1964. For the occasion they performed a duet, *Siddhas of the Upper Air*. The dance consisted chiefly of a ceremonial walk up a ramp erected across the back of the stage. Ted held Ruth lightly about the waist, with both their upstage arms reaching toward the horizon. "The two of us were going up and up and up, remembering all the love of the earth but still lovers in infinite distance and infinite space, but still always up, going up," was Ted's description of the dance, but La Meri remembers Ruth saying, "Ted was scared to death. I wasn't, because I didn't think about it, but neither of us could see without our glasses."

In her role as First Lady of American Dance, Ruth presented a series of her "historic dances" at the Carnegie Chamber Music Hall in New York in December of 1941. Among the solos on her program were *Incense*, *White Jade*, *Radha* and *Cobras* and a new work, *Impressions of Chinese Theatre*, which John Martin called "long and inept." The New York *Sun* reported, however, that the concerts were well attended and warmly applauded. Ruth continued her historical series of dances at her Temple Studio on Fifty-ninth Street. The studio was always packed for the Thursday night events. Sometimes Ruth "sketched" her larger dances in solo form and she always lectured in her fascinating way, mixing utopian theories and spiritual ideas with lively anecdotes from her theatrical career. The Rhythmic Choir performed and Sum Nung Au-Young occasionally came to lecture on the Tao.

These encouraging days were marred only by the spreading world war. Years earlier Ruth had sensed that the world was on the verge of war. In her diary of July 1935, she wrote of "Russia wanting to soviet-ize the world, Japan browbeating China, Germany swaggering around again, England with her Jubilee just ended in glory, Italy grim-jawed and belligerent." As America entered the war Ruth set aside her pacifism. "My conscience is aroused," she declared in 1942. She signed on as an air warden at the Lombardy Hotel, performed in benefit con-certs for the Russian War Relief, and listened anxiously in the eve-nings to radio talk of blackouts and war. "I consider myself a war worker of the most dedicated type," she wrote in her diary, "I am work-ing to eradicate error from my own consciousness." The reality of the war for Ruth was that the young men she relied on for personal and professional assistance went to war, her bookings were curtailed, and she felt a basic need for protection. Just before Christmas of 1942 she packed her belongings and prepared to move to California where her brother and his family had agreed to take her in.

On the eve of her departure she received a last note from Sum Nung. "Dear Empress Moon," it began, "The autumn leaf has con-veyed to me such tender and loving thoughts and I profoundly appreci-ate your fleeting moments of constancy and devotion." He told her good-bye and concluded, "I know that deep in your heart your tender, loving nature will always turn to me whenever you are in communion with Nature or in the midst of Supreme Beauty. All these years, you have not changed." They had one last visit. She never saw him again.

She went to California with hope and with reservations. She had in mind a new career as a character actress and hoped to study acting and find work in motion pictures. She would live in a basement apartment in her brother's store, the Asia Bazaar, an import business he had opened in Hollywood. Japanese and oriental imports were both scarce and unpopular during the war, and Brother was struggling financially himself. His wife was not eager to see her famous sister-in-law join them. Ruth made Emily St. Denis feel that she was beneath her, a mere seamstress who had married her brother, while Ruth wrote in her own diary that Emily made her feel like a "poor relation" who needed management. Eventually the two women arrived at an accommodation, and Emily and Brother cared for Ruth during the rest of her life.

When she arrived in Los Angeles, Ruth went to work at the Douglas Aircraft factory in Santa Monica. For thirty-three dollars per week she worked the "graveyard shift" from midnight to early morning, filing requisition forms and packing boxes. Pearl Wheeler, with whom she had renewed her friendship, worked the "swing shift" in the same factory and unknown to Ruth, another famous personality from her past, the dancer Maud Allan, also worked at the plant. Each evening Ruth took a bus to the factory which was discernible in the darkness only by the huge, silver barrage balloons that hovered above it, attached by guy wires designed to ensnare approaching enemy planes. She wore Chinese blue slacks, a sweater, and a hair net and at sixty-four might have been any grandmother reporting for wartime work. She used the name "Ruth Dennis Shawn" but word got around that she was the famous Ruth St. Denis and she brought some photographs to distribute to her co-workers. Ruth loved being one of the workers. "Young people, old people, negroes, Cubans, fat people and Grandmas. All anxious to get to work and mostly talking brightly with their pals and not making a tremendous chore of the whole thing. I am fascinated at feeling this tremendous pulse of America going to work." She was "proud all over again of being an American."

Meanwhile she dreamed of founding a Temple for the Divine Dance. She wrote an essay, "A Defense Job will Build My Temple," pointing out that the usual benefit concerts that artists considered their wartime work "do not cost us the effort, the courage and pain that is for a moment comparable to what even a normal defense worker experiences." This war demanded a total commitment of energies from American artists, but Ruth added that philosophically speaking, a war of defense remained in the last analysis a war fought for "instinctive self-preservation and egocentric possessiveness. It is these very qualities that must be spiritually rooted out of us all before we shall have permanent peace. This I believe to be supremely women's work for the future of the world, and to this cause of spiritual and artistic development, as definitely opposed to all the motivations and practices of war, I dedicate my temple."

Her temple never materialized, though she tried repeatedly to establish a permanent institution. When she got her own studio in Holly-

wood she founded Theatre Intime and began Sunday evening performances with lectures and revivals of her dances. Old friends and former
Denishawn dancers surrounded her with loving support. Jack Cole,
who choreographed dances for motion pictures, taught a dance class in
her studio each week. Pearl was there and Anna Austin Crane. Visitors
came and went. One evening in her studio Anna came to her with the
news that Sum Nung Au-Young was dead. He had written Ruth of his
illness. In a last poem he had promised her

> *A world which has no nights or days—*
> *Only boundless and timeless,*
> *Where the soundless music*
> *Of Visions and Dreams*
> *Are intoned as ONE . . .*

She had written him in turn, "You must know that you were the only
human being who ever fulfilled that strange adolescent concept of love
which I had carried always in my being until I met you." Now she
wrote, "My Emperor is dethroned by a thousand furies of pain, gone
like a ship on the horizon, lost to my human eyes." Through the pages
of her diary she whispered, "You made me a woman."

BABYLON

CHOREOGRAPHY: Ruth St. Denis

COSTUMES: Adolphine Rott

MUSIC: Selections from Scriabin and Wagner

PREMIERE: Christmas 1937, Calvary Episcopal Church, New York City

———◆———

SETTING: A large Babylonian hall with a great doorway at the back. There are elevations on either side of the stage to accommodate the Kings of the Earth who wear long, fringed Babylonian costumes and tall, regal hats and black beards. Each of the ten Kings represents a sin of man unredeemed: Dishonesty, Cowardice, Pride, Lust, Ambition, Hatred, Fear, Treachery, Infidelity, Envy.

Babylon sits on a low platform at center stage. Her throne is decorated with ten heads of beasts in papier-mâché, representing the ten sins. She holds to her lips "the golden cup of abominations" and wears a "slithery and vamp-like" skirt in scarlet, purple and gold, jeweled breastplates and a tent-like veil of red and gold. She also wears arm bands, bracelets, necklaces, and jeweled fringes.

SCENARIO: Babylon sits motionless, delicate but seductive, drinking from her cup of sin. She sways slightly and assumes various postures with the cup, entreating the Kings of the Earth, representing all nations, to drink of her abominations. She ends with an imperious gesture, the cup raised over her head like a crown, summoning the nations to her feet.

She rises to dance, stepping down majestically from her throne. Proud, arrogant, commanding, she dances rhythmically and sensuously with drum and brass cymbals accentuating each beat. She circles the platform, then mounts it for the climax of her dance. The Kings of the Earth are at her feet in abject surrender. In a final dance of seduction she approaches each one in a different mood, now jealous, now possessive, now lyrical in her sweetness. The music hints at approaching doom as the nations vie for her favor, then turn upon her with their frenzy.

As the nations advance to destroy her, Babylon runs hither and thither to escape their wrath. She repels their advances, runs swiftly, then stumbles and pleads for mercy. For a moment she recovers her charm and tries to seduce the nations once again but they tear her veils and jewels from her. Trumpets howl their anger as Babylon falls back on her throne, stripped of her scarlet and purple, of her jewels and gold. The lights fade.

The lights rise dimly on a great black cross. A bell summons Babylon to Judgment. Slowly she mounts the steps of the platform and in an agony of repentance, surrenders herself with outstretched arms to the cross. The lights intensify, revealing the dark and foreboding cross to be the figure of an Archangel with outstretched arms. He wears a pleated shift, a jeweled girdle and white wig, and carries a gown for the almost-naked Babylon, a costume of flesh-colored georgette with a delicate gold design. Transformed into the Bride of Christ, Babylon dances "to the rhythms of God, glorious in her freedom, healing in her dancing, and forever victorious."

The above scenario, condensed from St. Denis' own dance notes, contains the essential elements of her religious pageants: a central female figure of great beauty and power, surrounded by framing acolytes; a Manichean struggle between Good and Evil; an androgynous figure, usually an angel, performed by a male; opulent sets and costumes and a final scene of transfiguration. *Babylon* was more dramatic and more explicit than most of her other church works. Dedicated to the Oxford Group, the dance reflected her preoccupation with sin and the Group ritual of symbolically stripping its members of lust and pride.

St. Denis' religious pageants were morality plays based on Scripture. *Babylon* took its scenario from the vision of St. John of the Apocalypse, with sections of the text read by an offstage narrator. In actual performance, the dance was adapted to the sanctuary of the Calvary Episcopal Church, with platforms added to its altar and rudimentary stage lighting installed. St. Denis' idea of a "large Babylonian hall with a great doorway at the back" remained only an idea and the lavish costumes she specified must have been modified for its 1937 premiere.

TWELVE

DANCING BEYOND TIME AND SPACE

"I HAVE LIVED so long," Ruth was fond of saying, "because in those moments when I am dancing I am beyond time and space." When she danced, all the "error" that blighted her Christian Science faith, all her money problems, the confusions and personal problems dissolved, the sense of age, vanished, and she found her truest self. She could not stop dancing. Though her body remained remarkably flexible, her troublesome knock-knees were crippled further still in an automobile accident in 1957. She frequently was overweight and her face became so wrinkled that she was forced to pull the folds of flesh severely back and fasten them under a tight band worn concealed in her headdresses. But her spirit still danced with an intensity that eradicated the ravages of age. More than one onlooker told the same story: Ruth could look one hundred years old offstage, sloppy, commonplace, and graceless. On the other side of the footlights the years fell away and she was radiant with a timeless beauty. It had something to do with the magic of makeup, the stimulation of an appreciative audience, but more to do with St. Denis' artistic gifts and her indomitable spirit.

During the last two decades of her life she continued to dance. Those who witnessed her performances remember evenings when she danced brilliantly and other occasions when she seemed a pathetic old woman who would not and could not leave the stage. She knew her own limitations. "My critics have been in this latter period of my career all too lenient," she wrote in 1950, "but they should not and they will not be asked to 'be kind' in the future. If conditions should permit my working intelligently on what I have to present—I do not mean for a moment that what I shall do at seventy-three or seventy-four will far exceed in physical dexterity what I have done in the past—that within the frame of what is possible for me to do, that it is accomplished with finish and completeness which have been sadly lacking in recent years. Allowing myself a moment of bitterness I should say, 'I have become an opportunist for money in place of an artist.'" She judged herself more harshly than her critics and audiences, who viewed the dances of her late years with warm affection and respect for the artistic sensibility that survived.

The move to the West Coast seemed to eliminate some of the tension in her relationship with Ted and they came together in April of 1945 for a joint concert, their first in fifteen years. The occasion was a gala performance at Carnegie Hall in New York, a benefit for Ted's dance festival at Jacob's Pillow. The program included La Meri and other dancers, with Walter Terry providing commentary. Ruth danced her *Brahms Waltz, Liebestraum,* and a *Nautch,* and with Ted, *Tillers of the Soil* and *Josephine and Hippolyte.* At the conclusion of their duets, Ted carried Ruth offstage. One sentimentalist in the audience, according to *Time* magazine, whispered, "Maybe they will go home together." Edwin Denby, reviewing the concert in the New York *Herald Tribune,* found that St. Denis "still has a wonderfully touching mildness and a striking clarity of movement. The tilt of the head, the turn of the wrists are in every way lovely and delicate." Denby also praised Ted's "elegant suavity of movement, and his meticulous placing of gesture." At sixty-six and fifty-three respectively, Ruth and Ted had a mellow maturity in their art that made virtuosity unnecessary.

After the Carnegie Hall concert they began serious talk of a joint tour. Ruth established the ground rules. Her own manager, Robert Sylvain, must be in charge of a joint season, she insisted, and she and Ted must decide in advance how to handle public inquiries about their relationship. "Regarding the joint publicity, I imagine the first and greatest difficulty will be to state with a certain subtlety and yet clearly what this joint appearance means," she wrote Ted. "Does it mean that we are emotionally reconciled and are refounding another Denishawn Tour? If not, why not? And just what are we doing together. We might as well face the music at the beginning, don't you think?" She suggested that they explain to the press that their joint appearances were arranged on behalf of their separate enterprises, Jacob's Pillow and her own Society of the Spiritual Arts. "Thus friends of both Ted and Miss Ruth will have the joy of seeing them together again," she wrote, "but will realize that their expanding careers, in their separate fields, is too great to permit more than a temporary appearance together. Furthermore," she added shrewdly, "Toledo or Podunk will be told that these appearances might not ever be repeated." She had learned to market herself as a historic figure.

Both Ted and Ruth needed the work. Ted had temporarily lost his Men Dancers to the war. Ruth needed the income. They both realized that they could sell themselves as a package more easily than as soloists. Ted worried about the lack of a supporting company, but Ruth wrote, "Either these local places want me as I am today, stripped of company and the usual personnel of a big tour and pared down to myself and what I can still dance—or they don't. And," she told Ted, "this applies to you equally—either they want to see you as you are (*sans* men's group) as the Artist. This is I am sure only temporary—for Praise God, when your boys come home I can wish nothing better than that you can begin again on your creative plane to continue to give America the rich contributions such as you have done in the past."

Ruth had grown to a greater appreciation of Ted, partly because of his enviable success with Jacob's Pillow, partly because her own struggles had renewed her appreciation for Ted's organizational skills. Time eased the bite of their differences, though not completely. "Certainly there has survived and even grown stronger a real love," Ted wrote her in 1945. "But as you say there are memories of old hurts and misunderstandings and seemingly when we get together on the old plane of artistic and professional partnership these same bases of misunderstanding flare into their old time strength. I find I can still be hurt by the things you do," he wrote, "but if that is the price of love, then it is cheap at the price. I would rather keep on loving and being hurt than be dead to love." They did love each other, if love be defined as years of shared experiences and memories and intimate knowledge of each other's strengths and foibles.

Over the next twenty years, Ruth and Ted performed together almost annually, at the American Museum of Natural History from 1949 through 1951, in a tour organized by Walter Terry in 1949, at Carnegie Hall in 1950. Ted served as master of ceremonies for the Carnegie Hall concert. Ruth performed several of her famous solos, including *White Jade, Incense,* her *Kashmiri Nautch, Brahms Waltz* and *Liebestraum.* When the needle stuck on the Brahms recording at the beginning of her waltz, Ruth shrugged with an eloquent gesture and began the dance again. The audience loved her for it. She also performed a work with her Rhythmic Choir, *Gregorian Chant.* A film of this dance made the same year shows Ruth in heavy draperies, turning in a shaft of light, her chorus behind her, a mass of shadowy shapes. A purple light shone from one side of the stage, a green light from the other, creating in their interplay the suggestion of a stained-glass window. To the strains of a Gregorian chant recorded in the Monastery of Solem, Ruth and her male chorus moved in simple plastique. Ruth choreographed her own madonna solo, and Jerry Green, her assistant, choreographed the group movement. Phil Baribault, the filmmaker pressed into service in the choir, said that the producers of the Carnegie Hall concert warned Ruth not to try to present a church dance on the program. "But she went ahead," he said. "She knew what she could do and she did it. It brought down the house and we had to do it again."

Ted and Ruth also performed together frequently at Jacob's Pillow, where Ted generously invited her, year after year. At the Pillow they were a legendary couple and everyone connected with the festival had a favorite story about Miss Ruth and Papa Shawn sparring at the dinner table, upstaging each other in performances. La Meri suggests that photographs from that era tell a lonelier story, with Ted often striding a few paces ahead of Ruth and both seeming to ignore the other in candid snapshots. "They were both theatre people," she said. "Miss Ruth simply didn't have any life off the stage. She wasn't breathing unless she was dancing, so to speak. Ted took it from an entirely different viewpoint, but the dance was his life too. At Jacob's Pillow he was a very reasonable man until he had to perform and then the place was turned upside down—the temperament, the problems that all of a sudden appeared were incredible! Well when you put those two people together, you couldn't have peace and harmony."

There were always fanatic devotees of Miss Ruth at the Pillow. Young dancers would gather to watch her rehearse. During the summer of 1955 in a dress rehearsal for her production of *Freedom*, Ruth made her entrance in a red gown with a blue tunic and a heavy cloak of yards of white silk jersey hanging from her shoulders. As she descended a row of steps the cape, instead of fanning behind her, twisted itself into a thick rope. Without a pause Ruth added an extra gesture and caused the cape to unfold and spread behind her like a peacock's tail. Adolphine Rott, her costumer since the 1930s, whispered, "Bless her, she has done it again!" One of the festival instructors leaned over to her pupils and said, "See Miss Ruth as often as you can while she is here. When you see her seem to grow onstage until she is much taller than she really is, don't ask me how she does it. It's her secret and it comes from within. When you see it happen, you'll know you are watching greatness."

On her trips East, Ruth saw her old students and basked in the glow of their renewed respect and praise. While touring with the Walter Terry program in 1949, she visited New York City and was invited to a party hosted by Charles Weidman in his West Sixteenth Street studio under the theatre he and Doris Humphrey had built. Martha Graham and Louis Horst were there, recently having broken their personal relationship, Ruth learned. Earlier Ruth had been to the theatre to see Martha dance. "It was a brilliant, intellectually remarkable program," Ruth thought. "I didn't enjoy it but I admired it greatly." Also at Charles's party was Doris Humphrey, looking pale and tired with the increasing burden of the arthritic condition that prematurely ended her career. John Martin, tall and sandy-haired and dignified, paused to chat with Ruth, who was quite overwhelmed with nostalgia. Even Florence O'Denishawn came to the party and each guest was presented to Miss Ruth who sat "like a mixture of Queen Victoria with a little Sheba underneath," her wide black skirt spread around her on a couch.

Back home in Los Angeles Ruth maintained a busy teaching and performing schedule. Her factory days ended in late 1943 when she accepted a job teaching oriental and religious dance at the Pasadena Playhouse. A typical class began with a group discussion, then limbering at the barre, then "period things—Louis XIV minuets or Spanish dances" devised by her assistant, Jerre Marchen. Ruth mostly talked, which had been her teaching method since the early days of Denishawn. She taught in her own school after 1946, when Brother St. Denis built her a studio and apartment of her own adjacent to his home in Hollywood. It was a handsome structure, a spacious studio with a fine wood floor and a comfortable suite upstairs. The heart of the compound was the kitchen, where Ruth and her Rhythmic Choir, which included Elyse Robert and Jerry Green, gathered on Wednesday evenings for pot-luck suppers, then cleared the table for a talk from Miss Ruth, discussion, perhaps a film or a poetry reading. Ruth lived in these pleasant surroundings for the rest of her life, hosting weekly lecture-concerts. On her sixty-eighth birthday she celebrated a Rebirthday Party at her studio and formally launched her Church of the Divine Dance, a continuation of her Society of Spiritual Arts.

Ruth had a fatal attraction to the institutions she professed to despise. In California she made repeated attempts to raise funds for a permanent institutional base. During the 1950s she dreamed of a Creative Arts Colony, patterned on the MacDowell colony, and she actually bought fifty acres of land near Hemet, California, with money inherited from Anne Hoyt and another friend. She never managed to find additional funds to implement the project. In 1962 she incorporated the Ruth St. Denis Center, with the following credo: "I believe in the Ministry of Beauty. I believe in the Divinity of the Arts. I believe that Art is the Ark of the Covenant in which all ideals of beauty and excellence are carried before the race. It is a pillar of cloud by day and of fire by night. I hereby offer my services and my God-given talents to the avowed purposes of this CENTER and pledge my allegiance to the ideals of Ruth St. Denis." Many pledged their allegiance but few pledged their funds. She left behind no institution in her own name, though the Ruth St. Denis studio still functions today as a base for a local dance company.

Ruth's acting career also never quite materialized. In 1944 she performed a small role in the ballroom scene of the Paramount film *Kitty*, a historical drama set in eighteenth-century England. She appeared in several plays over the years, including *The Madwoman of Chaillot* in the Chagrin Falls Summer Theatre in Ohio in 1954. Ruth played the title role, a demanding one for a seventy-five-year-old woman. On opening night she forgot her lines and spoke too softly and retired to her dressing room in tears. But the critic for the Cleveland *Plain Dealer*, William McDermott, forgave Ruth her lapses of memory. "What really matters," he wrote, "is personality and a command of the technical resources of acting. When Miss St. Denis comes to the stage you know that here is an extraordinary personality. Though she was not trained as an actress, she knows how to handle audiences through her long experience as a dancer." He mentioned her special skill with gesture. "Watch her hands," he wrote. "She does not overdo gestures but she uses them to her purpose with grace and harmony."

Through her work in the theatre Ruth met Harro Meller, a German refugee who came to America during the war and established a career as a villain in Hollywood films. A character actor, he was also a poet and playwright. He met Ruth in 1944 when she was a "dark, dull, gray mass of doubt and loneliness," she told a friend. "There had been no further communication *really* with Ted and of course my poor Sum Nung had long since gone to his Chinese heaven, leaving me inwardly rather a drab figure." Harro joined Ruth in a series of poetry-dance concerts in 1948 and he talked of writing her biography. He was quite in love with her and asked her to marry him. Ruth considered his proposal seriously enough to ask Ted about a divorce. He refused. "Your and my love is so established as 'Siddhas of the Upper Air' that it has survived and will survive any blows," Ted wrote her. "Our love is now such a great legend and stands as a beacon to so many people that I know neither you nor I will ever do anything to belittle it and thus hurt many people who look up to us as a rare marriage which has survived the passing of the physical tie and has emerged a greater thing than it ever was on that plane." Ruth gave up the idea of remarriage but continued her romance with Harro for more than a year and remained his friend for two more decades. They were both strong-willed, and Harro, in vain, tried to force Ruth to relinquish her dreams and schemes. "You are a peacock who desires to be an eagle. Why?" he demanded when he learned of her plans for a Creative Arts Colony. "O Ruth, Ruth, Ruth, I am horrified to think what would happen if your dream of an ART COLONY became true! There would be no more time for you for contemplation . . . you are not an organizer by any means . . . you have a dream-conception of something which in reality does not exist . . . you are far too late to begin a venture which demands decades to develop . . . are you sure, quite sure, that you really care for other artists?"

Ruth persisted with her schemes and always found supporters, mostly young men, who promised to get her into the movies or to make a film of her life or to help her establish a permanent temple. They used her for their own ambitions and came and went over the years, creating constant discord. A happy exception to the hangers-on who plagued her last years was Phillip Baribault, a former vaudevillian who had studied for the priesthood before he became part of the adagio act "Rhona and Ted." He chose the stage name "Ted" in honor of the most famous dancer of his day, Ted Shawn. Phil met Ruth in the 1940s when he was a Hollywood cameraman, and they remained close friends until her death. Phil was a perfect complement to Ruth—down-to-earth, generous, keenly interested in ideas. They became buddies and met each Thursday evening for supper and talk. Often they took long walks together, Phil scrambling to keep up with Ruth's long strides. He photographed her and made some of the finest films of her dances, always on a shoestring. "Film was not that important to her," he says.

"She didn't realize that was the way history would remember her." With borrowed equipment and sometimes only naked light bulbs, Phil filmed *White Jade, Incense, Red and Gold Saree, Tillers of the Soil,* and some of her religious dances, keenly aware that St. Denis was well past sixty and the films were, at best, poor records of her art.

Madonnas were the passion of her last years. With her Rhythmic Choir she portrayed the Virgin in *Masque of Mary, Ballet of Christmas Hymns, Healing,* and other pageants presented both in churches and in theatres. In *He Is Risen,* an excerpt from the longer ballet *Resurrection,* St. Denis portrayed Mary Magdeline, but she returned to her study of the Virgin in the *Blue Madonna of St. Mark's,* choreographed in the late 1950s. The dance began as a music visualization of Bach's *Magnificat,* developed by St. Denis with the assistance of her student and protégée, Barbara Andres. As the work unfolded it seemed to suggest four ballets or choirs around a central Madonna. Ruth's rehearsal pianist, Bob Hawkinson, suggested that she listen to a recording by a sixteenth-century composer, Giovanni Gabrielli, who was connected with St. Mark's Cathedral in Venice. Ruth liked the music and adopted it for her new work in place of the Bach. She called the dance the *Blue Madonna of St. Mark's,* a dramatic portrayal of the Virgin set in Renaissance Venice. The dance followed Mary's life from the birth of Christ to the crucifixion, from the moment she held her babe in her arms to her agony at the foot of his cross. Two angels and a Doge of Venice completed the cast. Ruth, aged eighty at the ballet's premiere, wore a blue satin robe and a halo of gold.

Whenever she was not performing, Ruth traveled as a lecturer. Her favorite topic during the 1950s and 1960s was "Balanced Government," her theory that the United States needed a dual president, both a man and a woman. Ruth had been a feminist for as long as she could remember. During World War I she told an interviewer, "A wonderful change has come over American women in the last ten years. In every aspect of life, in every relation of life, there is the truth and there is the counterfeit. Formerly women preferred the counterfeit. They liked the sugared lies of sentiment and men fed women with them. Today women want the truth only. Freedom has done it. Work has done it. The happiest women are those who realize that it is far easier as well as finer to work for themselves than to put men to work for them." Those were startling words in 1916 and forty years later her listeners were also startled when Ruth told a meeting of the Los Angeles

Breakfast Club, "Women in war are just moppers-up. They won't be doing their part until they are sitting in councils that decide whether or not to go to war." She felt that women and men have interlocking and complementary strengths and without women in positions of power, societies were dangerously imbalanced. Musing on the problems of poverty in 1965, she wrote in her diary, "All suggested remedies are a farce! They don't pretend to touch the causes of poverty—which in all places and countries are built upon the power motive (masculine) instead of the feminine Life motive!" She idolized Susan B. Anthony, Mary Baker Eddy, and Charlotte Gilman Perkins. She rejoiced when Indira Gandhi was elected prime minister of India. Yet as she looked back over her own life she wondered whether she had fulfilled herself as an artist at the expense of her womanhood. "We are caught both ways," she wrote, "we are enmeshed in the bondage of beauty or the bondage of babies. We seem to have to make an irrevocable choice. Each god we worship is a jealous god."

The last decade of her life was filled with awards which certified her role in American dance history—the Capezio Award in 1960, an award from the Dance Teachers of America in 1964, the *Harper's Bazaar* list of "100 Women of Accomplishment" in 1967, to name a few. At the age of eighty-seven, in May 1966, she performed *Incense* at Orange Coast College in California. It was her last public appearance as a dancer. She traveled on to Los Gatos, California, where she was due to present seminars on "The Dance of Life" and "The Androgyny Principle," but she suffered a bad fall and spent several weeks in bed. She recovered sufficiently to present a lecture-demonstration that winter at the University of California at Los Angeles, the institution that eventually received more than one hundred boxes of her diaries. That year she failed to attend Ruth St. Denis Day at Adelphi University, and Barbara Andres represented her, accepting Ruth's traditional roses. In the spring of 1967 Ruth fell once again and spent another period in the hospital.

Her diaries during this time were purged of the old agonies of the flesh, the worries about money and career. Instead she searched her soul in a scrawl that grew larger and larger, as if it might expand into the cosmos she hoped to conquer. With frequent references to *Science and Health,* her well-worn Bible, and Sankara's commentaries on the Vedic scriptures, she wrote in 1965, at the age of eighty-six, "The reason I dare to agree with all metaphysicians that man is now existing in *perfection* is because it is inconceivable to me that the universe could exist for one moment in imperfection. Why mankind has its illusions of imperfectability, I do not know nor have I been informed by any prophet or any teacher or thinker in a manner that satisfies my questioning." She never found a satisfactory answer for sin, for error, for imperfection, but she never stopped searching.

On July 21, 1968, she died in Hollywood after suffering a heart attack and was cremated and interred at Forest Lawn Cemetery. Her brother had a marker made for her vault. Engraved with a portrait of St. Denis in flowing robes, it bore the lines of one of her poems:

> *The Gods have meant*
> *That I should dance*
> *And in some mystic hour*
> *I shall move to unheard rhythms*
> *Of the cosmic orchestra of heaven*
> *And you will know the language*
> *Of my wordless poems*
> *And will come to me*
> *For that is why I dance.*

Incense in later years.

St. Denis as the Gold Madonna in *Color Study of the Madonna*, c. 1934.

St. Denis in *White Jade*, inspired by the Altar of Heaven in Peking.

Still dancing . . . a nautch in the 1960's.

Ruth St. Denis and Rhythmic Choir in *Gregorian Chant*

Ruth St. Denis and Phil Baribault celebrate her seventy-sixth birthday in Hollywood, 1955.

Ruth St. Denis' expressive hands.

The "Dance of Touch" from *Radha* revival, 1941.

"Siddhas of the Upper Air," married fifty years, 1964.

NOTES

Sources have been specified for direct quotations and choreographies. Readers interested in the detailed original documentation for this study may consult the doctoral dissertation of the same title, University of Texas at Austin, 1980, filed in the Perry-Casteñada Library of that institution, and on file with University Microfilms.

ABBREVIATIONS

DDD   Sherman, *The Drama of Denishawn Dance*

DS   Denishawn Scrapbooks, The Dance Collection, New York Public Library

HB   Author's interview with Henrietta Buckmaster, February 17, 1980, Boston, Massachusetts

LC   Library of Congress

LM   Author's interview with La Meri, February 18, 1980, Hyannis, Massachusetts

NA   Navy and Old Army Archives, National Archives, Washington, D.C.

NJA   Archives of the State of New Jersey, Trenton, N.J.

NJHS   New Jersey Historical Society, Newark, N.J.

NYPL   The Dance Collection, New York Public Library at Lincoln Center

PAP   Shawn, *Ruth St. Denis: Pioneer and Prophet*

PO   Patent and Trademark Office, United States Department of Commerce, Washington, D.C.

UCLA   Ruth St. Denis Collection, University Research Library, The University of California at Los Angeles

UL   St. Denis, *An Unfinished Life*

ULT   An Unfinished Life in unedited typescript, University Research Library, The University of California at Los Angeles

UM   Bentley Historical Library, University of Michigan, Ann Arbor

UT   Hoblitzelle Theatre Arts Library, Humanities Research Center, The University of Texas at Austin

ONE THE FAMILY

page 2 "The life of the play . . ." "Home Talent in 'The Old Homestead.'"

page 2 "Her posing is excellent . . ." Ibid.

page 2 Ruth Emma Hull: Census records indicate that Ruth Emma Hull's birth date was 1844, but in a sworn affidavit she declared her birth date to be Sept. 19, 1845, Widow's Pension File for Ruth E. Dennis, NA. No birth record for Ruth Emma Hull exists in Canandaigua. Other Hull family material based on United States Census records for Canandaigua, New York, 1850, New Haven, Connecticut, 1860, and Fairhaven, Connecticut, 1870; *Benham's New Haven Directory and Annual Advertiser*, vols. 1851–61; and UL.

page 3 University of Michigan Medical School: Wilfred B. Shaw, vol. 2, 789, 794; Sagendorph; "First 50 Years of MSMS (Michigan State Medical Society)–In Brief," available from Michigan State Medical Society; McGuigan, 35–38.

page 3 Ruth Emma Hull medical thesis: "Vis Medicatrix Naturae" (1872), UM.

page 3 Jackson Sanitarium in Dansville, New York: Bishop, 176–77. Dr. Jackson published *The Water Cure Journal* (Glen Haven: James C. Jackson) during the 1850s and 1860s.

page 4 The corset itself squeezed the diaphragm . . . Mary J. Safford-Blake, M.D., "Dress-Reform," in Woolson, 16–17. Other information on dress-reform in Kendall, 21–23, and Newton. General information on fashion in Carrie A. Hall.

page 5 "I am going to live to be 100 . . ." St. Denis, "The Secret of the Pharaoh's Favorite."

page 5 Quotes from Dr. Jackson: Jackson, 17–18.

page 5 Eagleswood colony: Greene, 1–19; "Raritan Bay Union's Eagleswood of the Mid-1800s Claimed Education as Its Principal Objective." Letters from Margaret Fuller and others to and from the Marcus Spring family in Raritan Bay Union and Eagleswood Military Academy Collection, NJHS.

page 5 "where industry, education and social life . . ." Greene, 6.

page 6 Tom Dennis inventions: During 1881–1907 Thomas Laban Dennis registered ten inventions with the United States Patent Office, including an electric lamp, an indicator for electric circuits, a steam engine, a phonograph, a speaking-tube and a bicycle. See Files of PO. Further detail on Tom Dennis' intellectual interests in Ruth St. Denis diary, January 1928, Box 1, UCLA.

page 6 He was born in Stourbridge . . . Birth certificate #103, *Register Book of Births 16*, District of Stourbridge, Eng. Other family information from United States Census records, Boonton, New Jersey, 1870.

page 6 Tom Dennis Civil War records: Thomas L. Dennis file, NA; *Record of Officers and Men of New Jersey in the Civil War 1861–1865*, vol. 2, 1264.

page 6 Tom Dennis-Alice Piere marriage: Marriage certificate, *Book BG*, 537, Bureau of Archives and History, NJA. Copy of divorce decree in Thomas Dennis file, NA.

page 7 Tom Dennis-Ruth Emma Hull marriage: The only record of this marriage is a sworn affidavit from an eyewitness, Jennie Spring Peet, September 30, 1919, in Widow's Pension File for Ruth E. Dennis, NA.

page 7 their daughter Ruthie was born . . . No birth certificate for Ruth St. Denis exists, but the January 20, 1879, date is verified by: affidavit in Thomas L. Dennis file, NA; marker placed by Brother St. Denis on his sister's crypt in Forest Lawn Cemetery, Los Angeles; *United States Census*, 1880, First District, Perth Amboy, New Jersey, County of Middlesex, 39; school records from the Packer Collegiate Institute, Brooklyn, New York; a birthday geeting to Ruth St. Denis from her mother, February 4, 1900, Box 29, UCLA. See Shelton, "Happy Birthday, Miss Ruth," for details of the search for St. Denis' birth date.

page 7 "born illegitimate" Interview, Phillip Baribault, April 1976, Burbank, California.

page 7 "I always have the feeling . . ." Diary, November 13, 1930, Box 6, UCLA.

page 7 "fears when I was conceived" Diary, May 24, 1935, Box 11, UCLA.

page 7 "I seem to have been born . . ." Diary, November 13, 1930, Box 6, UCLA.

pages 7–8 "bad reputation" Interview, Mrs. Carl Oberbrunner of Raritan, New Jersey, whose mother, Catherine Haring, was a playmate of Ruthie Dennis, November 1976, Somerville, New Jersey.

page 8 "Don't, the neighbors . . ." Diary, January 1928, Box 1, UCLA.

page 8 "poor me—running barefoot" Ruth Dennis letter to parents, April 12, 1900, Box 29, UCLA.

page 8 Despite the social ostracism . . . Details of St. Denis' childhood at Pin Oaks drawn from St. Denis, UL; Ted Shawn reminiscences, Sept. 8, 1971, cassette recording, NYPL; Beers, in which map of area labels family farms by name, the Dennis farm then belonging to S. C. Blackwell. School records in files of Adamsville School, Bridgewater-Raritan Regional School District, New Jersey.

pages 8–9 "Dad very angry and sullen . . ." St. Denis, ULT 29.

page 9 "Fainting and falling . . ." "Ruth St. Denis Tells of Her Dancing Life."

page 9 "deep feeling awareness . . ." Undated reminiscence by St. Denis, Box 94, UCLA.

page 9 "almost breaking my neck . . ." Sally V. Aspell letter to Ruth St. Denis, undated, Box 85, UCLA.

page 10 Mary Plunkett: Peel, vol. 2, chapters 7–10, outlines Christian Science schism and gives information on Mrs. Plunkett; also St. Denis, ULT, Box 30, UCLA.

page 10 John W. Lovell: "J. W. Lovell Dead; Former Publisher." For information on Theosophy, see Lutyens, as well as primary sources by Madame Blavatsky and her follower Annie Besant.

page 11 "seized upon my imagination" St. Denis, UL 11. Theosophical interpretation of the Cook book in Row 240–52.

page 11 "again and again that I was a bird . . ." St. Denis, UL, 1.

page 11 "To each spiritual function . . ." Stebbins, *Delsarte System*, 67. Basic tenets of Delsarte's system in Shawn, *Every Little Movement*, and in Ruyter, *Reformers and Visionaries*, 17–30.

page 12 "holding onto the old brass bedstead . . ." Ubell interview with St. Denis, 1965, phonotape 7–56, NYPL.

page 12 "remarkable talent." "Miss Davenport's Reception."

page 13 "All I remember . . ." St. Denis, UL 10. Watercress episode in Ruth Dennis letter to mother, April 15, 1891, Box 29, UCLA.

page 13 "to bridge the gap . . ." Ruth E. Dennis letter to Mrs. Nancy Miller, NYPL.

page 13 "the real birth of my art life." St. Denis, UL, 16.

page 13 "This was the day of the garden set . . ." Walter Terry interview with St. Denis, 1960, phonotape 7–57, NYPL. Information on Stebbins in Shelton, "The Influence of Genevieve Stebbins on the Early Career of Ruth St. Denis," and Ruyter, *Reformers and Visionaries*.

page 14 "statue-posing," Stebbins, "The Relation of Physical Culture to Expression."

page 14 "LIFE," Stebbins, *Dynamic*

Breathing and Harmonic Gymnastics, 3.

page 14 "There is no such thing . . ." Ibid., 61–62.

page 14 "coupled with the natural balance . . ." Ibid., 63.

page 14 Stebbins quotes: Stebbins, *The Genevieve Stebbins System of Physical Training,* 32, 70, 58–59, 85.

page 15 "chronicled the cycle . . ." "Genevieve Stebbins' Recital."

page 15 "Through Mrs. Stebbins . . ." St. Denis, UL, 16.

pages 15–16 "Egypt Through Centuries" quotes: Souvenir program, New Jersey File, UT. Also "New Dance at El Dorado," *New York Herald,* Aug. 2, 1892, 1892 scrapbook, UT.

page 16 "made me shrink . . ." St. Denis, UL, 17.

page 16 "was never demonstrative." St. Denis, ULT. Further information on Clark Miller in diary, June 8–9, 1921, Box 40, UCLA.

page 16 "Very simply mother called it . . ." St. Denis, "Prelude" essay, June 8, 1936, Box 33, UCLA.

page 16 "once witty, laughing companion . . ." St. Denis, UL 18. Other information on Lizzie Logan in Logan letter to Ruthie Dennis, November 14, 1896, Box 29, UCLA; M. E. Wall letter to Ruth St. Denis, January 14, 1920, NYPL; and *New Jersey State Census,* 1880, Somerset County, Bridgewater Township, microfilm reel T9-798, Somerset County Library, New Jersey.

page 17 "atmosphere of 'Christians.'" Ruthie Dennis letter to parents, December 5, 1893, Box 29, UCLA. Information on Moody in Findlay, McLoughlin, "Moody's Work at Northfield," and "Effective Mission Work."

page 17 "way up here at the north end of nowhere . . ." Ruthie Dennis letter to parents. Ibid.

page 18 "the most corrupt desires . . ." Moody, *Heaven,* 13.

page 18 "The very idea of Noah . . ." Moody, "The Gospel Awakening," 696.

page 18 "I just called my own . . ." St. Denis, UL, 13. Also "Ruth St. Denis Visits Somerville."

page 18 Quote from *The Old Homestead:* Cerf and Cartmell, 183.

TWO HURRYING PAST THE PICKLED CALVES

page 22 "recommended by educators . . ." Advertisement, *Werner's Magazine* (January 1898), xxiii.

page 22 Quotes concerning Worth's Museum: Program, August 29, 1891, American Playbill File, UT.

page 23 "The Only Ruth." Notice in *New York Clipper* (February 10, 1894), 786. Previous week's notice in *New York Clipper* (February 3, 1894), 769.

page 23 "hurrying by the triple-headed calves . . ." St. Denis, UL, 21.

page 23 "stood like a match . . ." Walter Terry interview with St. Denis, 1963, phonotape MGZT 7-60, NYPL.

page 23 "with a little air . . ." St. Denis, UL, 22.

page 23 "The museum is a 'museum' . . ." Mrs. Ruth Dennis letter to "Dear Boy" (Tom Dennis), undated, NYPL.

page 23 In a typical episode . . . "New York City." Social attitudes toward dancers in Ham, Cole.

page 23 "artists of the female . . ." "The New Opera Club." Cartoon accompanies article.

page 23 "grew cold with fear . . ." St. Denis, UL, 39.

page 24 "made it all very artistic . . ." Ibid., 25. The photographer was Stanford White's colleague, James Lawrence Breese.

page 24 The American attitude toward art . . . Harris, 2–25.

page 24 "Everywhere it is woman . . ." "Half Draperies at the Fair."

page 24 "the ascendant Female." Gilbert, 347.

page 24 "Pretty soon a chap . . ." "News of the Theatres," New York *Sun* (January 29, 1893), 1893 scrapbook, UT.

page 25 The Vaudeville Club: "A Club of Novel Nature"; "Vaudeville Clubrooms Opened"; "The New Opera Club."

page 25 "a thousand young men . . ." "News of the Theatres," op. cit.

page 25 "Between the cigarette smoke . . ." "The Usher."

page 26 "He was my first real contact . . ." St. Denis, UL 23.

page 26 "a subtle chill in the air" St. Denis, ULT, Box 30, UCLA.

page 26 "How could Stanford . . ." St. Denis, UL 40.

page 26 "I am a block of ice . . ." Ruthie Dennis letter to her mother, February 11, 1901, Box 29, UCLA.

page 26 "one of four Spanish . . ." These jobs mentioned in Ruth Dennis letter to "Dear Boy," op. cit.

page 26 "Ruth, premiere danseuse . . ." "Central Opera House Music Hall."

page 27 "while the breeze . . ." "Roof Garden Programmes," New York *Tribune* (July 1, 1894), 1894 scrapbook, UT.

page 27 "In nearly all cases . . ." "The Theatres in August," New York *Sun* (August 4, 1892), 1892 scrapbook, UT.

page 27 "The Only Ruth," "Notes of the Stage," New York *Times* (July 1894), 1894 scrapbook, UT.

page 27 "one of the very best . . ." "In Theatre and On Roof Last Night," New York *Herald* (July 17, 1894), 1894 scrapbook, UT. Also program, American Theatre Roof Garden, July 15–21, 1894, American Playbill File, UT.

page 27 "human beings for pigments . . ." "Improving the Ballet."

page 27 "maneuvering dancers . . ." Ibid.

page 28 Variety dancers: See "Matters of Fact"; Flitch, 81–88; Gilbert, 173; "Fell Through a Glass Trap."

page 28 Skirt dancer quotes: Flitch, 71.

page 29 "Wednesday eve I got a call . . ." Ruthie Dennis letter to "Muzzer Darling" (Mrs. Dennis), February 2, 1900, Box 30, UCLA.

page 29 "The Passing Show": Odell, vol. 15, 607–8; "On and Off the Stage," New York *Herald* (August 5, 1894), 1894 scrapbook, UT; "The Passing Show at McVicker's"; "The Passing Show."

page 29 "It is asserted . . ." "Notes of the Stage."

page 30 "Ruth LaBlanche . . ." "News of the Theatre," New York *Sun* (August 7, 1894), 1894 scrapbook, UT. See also program, Casino Theatre, August 25, 1894, American Playbill File, UT.

page 30 Pin Oaks Farm: Details of the mortgaging, parceling, buying and selling of Pin Oaks in Deed Book 1-17425, Somerset County Courthouse, New Jersey.

page 30 "I did not know . . ." St. Denis, UL, 26.

page 30 Dennis family addresses: *City Directory*, Brooklyn, N. Y., reels 19–23, New York Public Library. Information on Fort Greene area in Weld, 117–19; Habenstreit; Syrett; and Brooklyn Navy Yard files, Brooklyn Collection, Brooklyn Public Library.

page 31 "Packer's came to mean . . ." St. Denis, ULT, Box 31, UCLA. Information on Packer's in *Semi-Quarterly Reports of Scholarship*, 1896–97, Packer Collegiate Institute archives, Brooklyn; Nickerson 123–24; *Werner's Magazine* (May 1899) 300; advertisement, *Werner's Magazine* (July 1895), 542.

page 32 "mirth and music . . ." "The Ballet Girl."

page 32 "You rise say at ten thirty . . ." Ruthie Dennis letter to Tom Dennis, undated, Box 29, UCLA.

page 32 "straightened him out . . ." Ruthie Dennis letter to Ruth Dennis, October 22, 1898, Box 29, UCLA.

page 32 "for comfort and protection . . ." Letter from Ruthie Dennis to "Mama," Friday the 14th (October 14, 1898), Box 29, UCLA.

page 33 "prayed earnestly . . ." Ruthie Dennis letter to Ruth Dennis, Oct. 22, 1898, op. cit.

page 33 "So this is where we drop it . . ." Ruthie Dennis letter to Ruth Dennis, undated, Box 29, UCLA.

page 33 *A Runaway Girl:* Chapman and Sherwood, 65; *The New York Clipper Annual 1899,* 24; and "A Runaway Girl." Program, Harlem Opera House, Phroso 1900 scrapbook, UT.

page 33 Ruthie's own mother had written . . . Mr. Malone letter to Mrs. Ruth Dennis, October 24, 1894, Box 29, UCLA.

page 33 "act better than that." Ruthie Dennis letter to Mr. and Mrs. Dennis, undated, Box 29, UCLA.

page 33 Dancing lessons: "Bringing Temple Dances from the Orient to Broadway."

page 34 "I've got my bloomers on . . ." Ruthie Dennis letter to Mrs. Dennis, February 2, 1900, Box 29, UCLA.

page 34 "In this ballet d'action . . ." "Another New Gallic Farce."

page 34 "Miss Montgomery, the Mystic Girl." Ruthie Dennis letter to parents, undated, Box 29, UCLA.

page 34 "crazy on the subject . . ." Clipping from *The Green Book* (December 1912) in vol. 2 DS.

page 34 "These I devoured . . ." St. Denis, ULT, Box 30, UCLA.

page 35 "Of course I did not . . ." Ruthie Dennis letter to Mrs. Dennis, undated, Box 29, UCLA.

page 35 "If I was home . . ." Ibid.

page 35 "because your anxiety . . ." Ruthie Dennis letter to Mrs. Dennis, February 10, 1901, Box 29, UCLA.

page 35 "trying to get out of me . . ." Ruth St. Denis letter to Ted Shawn, June 1929, NYPL.

page 35 "I did all I could . . ." Diary, June 8, 1921, Box 40, UCLA.

page 35 "who are really greatly lovable . . ." Ruthie Dennis letter to "Mother Dear," February 11, 1901, Box 29, UCLA.

page 36 "You know when I have danced . . ." Ruthie Dennis letter to parents, February 22, 1900, Box 30, UCLA.

THREE FOXY QUILLER

pages 37–38 Belasco quotes: Belasco, *The Theatre Through Its Stage Door,* 6–7. Biographical information on Belasco in Timberlake, Winter, Modisett, Taubman, Gorelik, 160–66, and Belasco, "My Life's Story."

page 38 "half innocent, half-sinister . . ." St. Denis, UL, 39.

page 38 "thought in pictures . . ." Belasco, "How I Stage My Plays."

page 38 Yet his forte . . . Stevens.

page 38 Mrs. Carter had come to Belasco . . . "Training an Actress."

page 39 "ethical bluntness" . . . Timberlake, 401.

page 39 "No man will ever . . ." St. Denis, UL, 42.

pages 39–40 Ruth Dennis quotes: Ruthie Dennis letters to her parents, undated, Box 29, UCLA.

page 40 "eminently janitorious." "The Theatres: Garrick Theatre." Also " 'Zaza' May Be Suppressed."

page 40 "tho it could have been . . ." Ruthie Dennis letter to parents, April 15, 1900, Box 29, UCLA.

page 41 "With the help of Nell . . ." Ruthie Dennis letter to parents, April 23, 1900, Box 29, UCLA.

page 41 "The idea will . . ." Ibid.

page 41 "no one is here . . ." Ruth Dennis letter to parents, May 23, 1900, Box 29, UCLA.

page 41 Paris Exposition of 1900: Battersby, 10–18.

page 42 "nothing but one huge . . ." "Our European Letter."

page 42 Adams felt that the . . . Adams, 379–90.

page 42 "langorous evocation . . ." R.S. Also Battersby, 170–71 for information on Yacco.

page 43 "Father was often away . . ." St. Denis, ULT, Box 30, UCLA.

page 43 "not to be carried away . . ." Mrs. Ruth Dennis letter to Ruthie Dennis, undated, Box 29, UCLA.

page 43 *Zaza* audition: "Bringing Temple Dances from the Orient to Broadway."

page 43 "the painter in his most . . ." Moses, 123.

page 44 "a star of the first . . ." Ruthie Dennis letter to Ruth Dennis, undated, Box 29, UCLA.

page 43 *The Auctioneer:* "Plays and Players"; Mantle and Sherwood, 395; Winter, vol. 2, 12–13.

pages 44–45 *Madame DuBarry:* Ford 39–50; program, Col. Sinn's Montauk Theatre, Brooklyn, December 1, 1902, UT.

page 45 "kept woman" Ruthie Dennis letter to Ruth Dennis, February 11, 1901, Box 29, UCLA.

page 45 "an awful restlessness . . ." St. Denis, UL, 45.

page 46 "in a weary and besmudged . . ." St. Denis, ULT, Box 30, UCLA.

page 46 "Anything—anything . . ." St. Denis, UL, 43–44.

page 46 "that my destiny . . ." St. Denis, UL, 52. The original Egyptian Deities poster belongs to the Dance Collection, NYPL.

page 47 "My mother thought I . . ." Diary, May 14, 1933, Box 9, UCLA.

page 47 "There is no life . . ." Eddy, 468. Other information on Eddy in Zweig.

page 47 "What do you suppose . . ." Diary, undated, Box 14, UCLA. Letter of rejection from Anne Potter of Third Church of Christ, Scientist, to St. Denis, January 17, 1931, advised that she might reapply for membership after she had tested "for a somewhat longer period your desire and ability to rely wholly upon spiritual means for physical healing," Box 95, UCLA.

page 47 "competition is so keen . . ." Klauber.

page 48 "It was hard for her . . ." Belasco, *The Theatre Through Its Stage Door,* 8.

page 48 "which will neither tax . . ." "Woodland." See also Mantle and Sherwood, 474–75.

page 48 In this myth a deceased . . . Budge, *The Book of the Dead,* 255–59.

page 49 "Egypta, an Egyptian play . . ." Ruth Dennis, *Egypta: An Egyptian Play in One Act,* 1905, LC.

page 49 The young face . . . The photograph by H. T. Motoyoshi reproduced in Terry, *Miss Ruth,* following page 50.

page 49 Edmund Russell: Seton; Ruyter, *Reformers and Visionaries,* 24–27.

page 49 "interesting the masses . . ." Editorial notes preceding Courtenay Lemon, "Commercialism and the Drama," in the Progressive Stage Society brochure for membership, 1904, Theatre Collection, New York Public Library. Other materials on the Society in same files.

page 50 "a stage with a nobler standard," Lemon, ibid.

page 50 "Sixth Avenue darkies . . ." "A Performance of Sakuntala," *New York Dramatic Mirror* (June 24, 1905), Theatre Collection, New York Public Library. Program, Madison Square Concert Hall, 1905 scrapbook, UT.

page 50 She had in mind . . . "New Coney Dazzles its Record Multitude"; "A New Coney Island Rises from the Ashes of the Old."

page 50 "One day a dusty old volume . . ." St. Denis, "Radha" essay, Box 4, UCLA.

page 51 "If a Hindoo be asked . . ." Sir A. C. Lyall, "Brahmanism," in Lyall, 92.

page 51 "My first Indian dance . . ." St. Denis, UL, 56.

pages 51–52 Radha: Scenario for dance in Ruth Dennis, *Radha,* 1905, LC. Events leading to creation of *Radha* in PAP, vol. 1, 3–8.

page 52 "I am a Hindoo . . ." Dalliba, 184.

page 53 "fought for the bluebloods' . . ." Tully, 36.

page 53 "one of the Southern . . ." "Indians in Costume Dance for Fish Guests," undated clipping in vol. 1 DS.

page 53 "as if I were a Cherokee . . ." "Dance of Senses is Sensational," undated clipping in ibid.

page 53 Henry B. Harris: Dimmick 92–93; "Theatrical Managers Meet."

page 53 "strolled in . . ." St. Denis, UL, 64.

page 53 New York Sunday laws: "Many Police Attend the 'Sacred Concerts'"; "Sunday Night Concerts."

page 54 "Who wants de Waitah?" St. Denis, UL, 65.

page 54 "Wonderful, mysterious . . ." Advertisement accompanying "Rhoda in the Dance of the Senses."

page 54 "The entire dance . . ." Program, Proctor's Twenty-third Street Theatre, February 26, 1906, American Play File, UT.

page 54 "a virtual frost . . ." Sime, "Shows of the Week."

page 54 orientalism: Christy, 37–50; Bridges, 9–10; Chisolm, 245.

page 55 "a universal rhythm . . ." LaFollette, 572.

page 55 Exoticism: See Max Muller, Warman. Information on Fenollosa in Chisolm. Information on Coomaraswamy in Lipsey.

page 55 "Women's clubs . . ." "Truths of Buddhism Taught in Dances."

page 55 "You know you don't belong . . ." St. Denis, UL, 67. Invitation and hostess list reprinted in ibid., 67–68. Information on hostesses from Who Was Who in America.

page 56 The Incense: Documented on film in *Fifty Years of Dance* (1964), a Camera Three production, and Phillip Baribault's *Incense* (1953), NYPL.

page 57 "The Serpentine Series," Stebbins, *The Genevieve Stebbins System of Physical Training,* 131–32.

page 57 The Cobras: Documented in William Skipper film, *The First Lady of the American Dance* (1956), NYPL. Details of Hudson Theatre performance in "East Indian Dances," unidentified clipping in vol. 1 DS, and in Fenollosa.

page 58 "At last she is . . ." Fenollosa, 223.

page 58 "It's such fun . . ." Tyrell.

page 58 "Yes, Society Did . . ." Tyrell.

page 58 "At the Boom . . ." "At the Boom of the Drum Radha Kerflops."

page 58 Mrs. Jack Gardner . . . Carter, 211.

page 58 Maharaja of Baroda . . . "Reception for the Prince."

page 58 Presbyterian Building . . . "May Stop Oriental Dance"; "Dance Programme Shocks Churchmen," New York *Evening Mail* (April 12, 1906) in vol. 1 DS.

page 58 "the very forces . . ." St. Denis, UL, 79.

page 58 "I feel a force . . ." Ruthie Dennis letter to Ruth Dennis, February 11, 1901, Box 29, UCLA.

RADHA: THE MYSTIC DANCE OF THE FIVE SENSES

page 59 Radha: I have reconstructed *Radha* from the Dwight Godwin film (1941), UT; Ted Shawn's description in PAP, 28–33; the early version by Ruth Dennis, *Radha: An East Indian Idyll; A Hindoo Play in One Act Without Words* (1905), LC; and a typewritten scenario, "Radha: a Hindu Temple Dance" in uncatalogued material, Box 4, NYPL.

page 62 femme fatale: Martha Kingsbury, "The Femme Fatale and Her Sisters," in Hess and Nochlin, 183–205.

page 62 "ecstasy and joy . . ." Dennis, *Radha: An East Indian Idyll,* op. cit.

page 62 "each circle emblematic . . ." Ibid.

page 63 "representing, according to . . ." Ibid.

page 64 "borders on voluptuousness . . ." Hofmannsthal, "Her Extraordinary Immediacy," 38.

page 64 "athletic in its . . ." "The Coliseum."

page 64 "although her body . . ." Philip Hale review in Boston *Herald* quoted by St. Denis, UL, 135.

page 64 "to different persons . . ." "Ruth St. Denis in Park Theatre," Boston *Herald,* 1909 scrapbook, UT.

page 65 "And you stole . . ." Kingsbury in Hess and Nochlin, 205, op. cit.

page 65 "that which is . . ." John L. Connally, Jr., "Ingres and the Erotic Intellect," in Hess and Nochlin, 21.

FOUR THE WORLD'S ENIGMA

page 67 Automobile Club lunch: Biographical information on Kessler in Otto Friedrich's introduction to Kessler. Description of Hofmannsthal in Smedley, *Crusaders,* 144. Wedekind, Hofmannsthal, and Hauptmann in Ende. A basic source for St. Denis' European stay is Schlundt, "An Account of Ruth St. Denis in Europe."

page 68 "conscience of Germany. Laqueur, 122.

page 68 "the world's enigma . . ." Noel.

page 68 "crystalline directness . . ." Smedley, *Crusaders,* 135–36.

page 68 "I was an artist . . ." St. Denis, UL, 95.

page 68 "Words are like . . ." Thurn und Taxis, 124.

page 68 prewar Germany: Laqueur preface; Masur; Gay, 1–22.

page 69 "multiplicity and . . ." Hofmannsthal quoted in Schorske, 930.

page 69 "turned away from . . ." Janik and Toulman, 116. Information on Hofmannsthal's career and influence in Michael Hamburger's introduction to Hofmannsthal, *Poems and Verse Plays;* and Schwarz, 3–53.

page 69 "extraordinary immediacy . . ." Reprinted in English translation, Hofmannsthal, "Her Extraordinary Immediacy."

page 70 "those little, yet . . ." Hofmannsthal quoted in Nostitz, 180–81. Theory of "Praeexistenz" in Gray, 303.

page 71 "profit by the experience . . ." Chicot.

page 71 Dr. Holbrook Curtis: Dr. Curtis was an arts patron and throat specialist whose clients included important opera stars such as Enrico Caruso.

page 72 "Sir Laurence put lilies . . ." Diary, July 3, 1906, Box 40, UCLA.

page 72 "He made a habit . . ." St. Denis, UL, 78.

page 72 "a new and strange . . ." "Aldwych Theatre."

page 72 Aldwych Theatre matinee: Attendance estimated from notes in St. Denis' 1906 diary, Box 40, UCLA, and from capacity-house statistics for the Aldwych, Howard, 6.

page 72 "Monsieur X" St. Denis, UL, 80. See also diaries, July 10 and 12, 1906, Box 40, UCLA.

page 73 "She was very urgent . . ." Diary, July 3, 1906, Box 40, UCLA.

page 73 "Throw off thy bondage . . ." Noel.

page 73 "worked herself into a frenzy . . ." C.I.B.; see also Ostrovsky 68–74.

page 74 "As an American . . ." St. Denis, "The Only Radha."

page 74 "mysterious rituals . . ." "A Marigny," *L'Humanité*, August 21, 1906, 4, Douglas Hickman, trans.

page 74 An "interview" . . . Quoted in St. Denis, ULT, Box 30, UCLA.

page 74 "made such a racket . . ." Diary, September 20, 1906, Box 40, UCLA.

page 74 "The whole experience . . ." Diary, August 26–29, 1906, Box 40, UCLA.

page 74 "surely a good sign . . ." Diary, September 1906, Box 40, UCLA.

page 75 "The serpents are . . ." "A Marigny," *L'Humanité*, September 25, 1906, 4, Douglas Hickman, trans.

page 75 "Let there be no mistake . . ." "A Marigny," *L'Humanité*, September 3, 1906, 4, Douglas Hickman, trans.

page 75 "I am afraid Braffie . . ." Diary, August 13, 1906, Box 40, UCLA.

page 75 "Well the morals . . ." Diary, October 23, 1906, Box 40, UCLA.

page 75 "It goes to the limits . . ." Hofmannsthal, "Her Extraordinary Immediacy," 38.

page 76 "lifeless objects . . ." Hofmannsthal, *Aufzeichnungen*, 156, translated by Wolfdietrich Rasch in Box 95, UCLA.

page 76 "the fullest experience . . ." Kessler letter to Hofmannsthal, October 29, 1906, in *Briefwechsel*, 131, Susan Pustejovsky, trans.

page 76 when he heard that an imposter . . . Kessler letter to Hofmannsthal, November 24, 1906, in *Briefwechsel*, 137, Susan Pustejovsky, trans.

page 77 "immediately preceding the dance . . ." Kessler letter to Hofmannsthal, November 24, 1906, in *Briefwechsel*, 135–36, Susan Pustejovsky, trans.

page 77 "The basic idea . . ." Ibid., 136.

page 78 "I've fallen into another . . ." Hofmannsthal letter to Nostitz, December 12, 1906, in *Briefwechsel*, 29, Susan Pustejovsky, trans.

page 78 "If you're having soup . . ." Ted Shawn interview, September 8, 1971, reel 2, NYPL.

page 78 from Warsaw she telegraphed . . . St. Denis telegram to Braff, undated, Box 86, UCLA.

page 78 "more than the capital . . ." Johnston, 115.

page 79 "My dear child . . ." St. Denis, UL, 109.

page 79 "House full . . ." Diary, January 1907, Box 40, UCLA.

page 79 "first-class material . . ." "Ruth St. Denis," *Wiener Abendpost*, Susan Pustejovsky, trans.

page 79 "great appreciation . . ." Diary, February 1907, Box 40, UCLA.

page 79 "heavy money-making . . ." Diary, March 1907, Box 40, UCLA.

page 79 "solid and sodden . . ." Ibid.

pages 79–80 "It seems that I . . ." Diary, December 15, 1907, Box 40, UCLA.

page 80 "I'm not a machine . . ." Related in St. Denis letter to Doris Humphrey, undated, Box 3, UCLA.

page 80 "The eternal Game . . ." Recalled in diary, June 8–9, 1921, Box 40, UCLA.

page 80 "Hans without Rome . . ." Ibid.

page 80 "In a clean place . . ." *The Bhagavad-Gita*, chapter 6, verses 11–12, 49.

page 80 *The Yogi*: Described in detail in St. Denis, ULT, Box 31,

UCLA. Also filmed by William Skipper as part of *The First Lady of the American Dance* (1956), NYPL, and by Carol Lynn, *Ruth St. Denis* (1949), NYPL.

page 81 "It requires the most . . ." St. Denis quoted in "The Dances of the Orient."

page 81 "highest art . . ." "Ruth St. Denis," *Wiener Abendpost*, Susan Pustejovsky, trans.; also "Ruth St. Denis," *Berliner Tageblatt*, Susan Pustejovsky, trans.

page 81 "The most beautiful . . ." Hofmannsthal letter to Nostitz, July 7, 1908, in *Briefwechsel*, 48, Susan Pustejovsky, trans.

page 81 *The Nautch*: Details from St. Denis essay, "Indian dancing," Box 35, UCLA. Various film versions in NYPL.

page 82 "flowing, intricate movements" "Ruth St. Denis," *Berliner Tageblatt*, Susan Pustejovsky, trans.

page 82 "She is a creature . . ." Hofmannsthal letter to Kessler, February 6, 1908, in *Briefwechsel*, 175, Susan Pustejovsky, trans.

page 82 "the antithesis of that . . ." "Ruth St. Denis," *Allgemeine Zeitung*, Susan Pustejovsky, trans.

page 82 "the living image . . ." and "a living model . . ." "Fortuny's Veils," Susan Pustejovsky, trans.

page 83 "an adaptation of . . ." St. Denis, ULT, Box 30, UCLA.

page 83 "The expression of thought . . ." "Translated Dances," London *Daily Express*, Sept. 30, 1908, in vol. 1 DS.

page 83 "rapid sallies hither . . ." Flitch, 113.

page 83 "is symbolic but not . . ." Ibid., 194.

page 84 "art of movement . . ." "Theater and Music: Komische Oper," Susan Pustejovsky, trans.

page 84 "for once she threw . . ." Flitch, 193.

page 84 "a great reaction . . ." Carpenter, 240.

page 84 "whether the public will care . . ." Untitled clipping from *Lady's Pictorial*, October 8, 1908, in vol. 1 DS.

page 84 "strong element of . . ." "Scala Theatre," October 9, 1908, 3.

page 85 "THE MUMMERS ARE . . ." Smedley, *Crusaders*, 186.

page 85 "certainly one of the most . . ." "Scala Theatre," November 6, 1908, 12.

page 86 "A few persons . . ." "London Notes."

page 86 "I think never a month . . ." Hofmannsthal letter to St. Denis, July 10, 1928, Box 4, UCLA.

FIVE THE EGYPT IN YOUR SMILE

page 89 Dr. Alan Gardiner: Smedley, *Crusaders*, 137–39.

page 89 "What did Egyptian . . ." Walter Terry interview with St. Denis, 1960, phonotape 7–57, NYPL.

page 89 Amarna Letters: Aldred, 15–16, 140–42.

page 89 *False Gods*: "His Majesty's Theatre." Text of Eugene Brieux play in Tucker, 131–70. Set design in *Illustrated London News* (September 18, 1909), 385.

page 89 "the somewhat prevalent . . ." "Ruth St. Denis in Park Theatre," op. cit.

page 90 "To an Oriental . . ." "Pearls—Causes and Effects."

page 90 "pagan, not Christian . . ." Jones, 284.

page 91 "All the Orient . . ." Kingsbury, in Hess and Nochlin, 205.

page 92 "I don't know . . ." Diary, October 25, 1909, Box 40, UCLA.

page 92 Henry B. Harris: "Cohan and Harris Branch Out"; "Harris Buys the Hudson"; "Concerning Henry B. Harris."

page 92 "music in color . . ." "New Dances Here by Ruth St. Denis," New York *Times*, November 17, 1909, in vol. 1 DS.

page 92 "Monday night I . . ." Diary, December 4, 1909, Box 40, UCLA.

page 92 "one of the few times . . ." New York *Herald* (December 5, 1909) clipping in vol. 1 DS.

page 92 "one mother . . ." "Ruth St. Denis with Large Retinue in Town," clipping in vol. 2 DS.

page 93 "a consolation . . ." "The Exotic Spell of St. Denis," *Chicago Inter-Ocean*, December 19, 1909, in vol. 2 DS.

page 93 Concerned with sin: A distinction suggested by Professor Margaret Furse in her seminar on mysticism and religion, American Studies Program, The University of Texas at Austin. See also Underhill; Schlundt, "Into the Mystic with Miss Ruth."

page 93 Vivekananda adhered to . . . I have come to this understanding of Advaitan Vedanta through the writings of Sri Atmananda Guru. See also Swami Prabhavananda; Bridges, 73–79; Vivekananda, vol. 3, 497.

page 94 "the establishment of . . ." Dhar, Book Two, 950.

page 94 "The central aim . . ." Paramananda, 23.

page 94 "a number of fake . . ." St. Denis, UL, 127–28.

page 94 "The concentration of . . ." "How Ruth St. Denis Nearly Went Broke," Pittsburgh *Dispatch*, September 13, 1911, in vol. 2 DS.

page 95 "Christian Science is the . . ." St. Denis letter to Moritz Jagendorf, January 18, 1955, Box 87, UCLA.

page 95 "superficially the most . . ." "The Exotic Spell of St. Denis," op. cit.

page 95 "It would be a great . . ." Palmer telegram to St. Denis, vol. 2 DS.

page 96 The Lotus Pond: Dance reconstructed from press accounts in vol. 2 DS, and from Shawn, vol. 1 PAP, 46–47.

page 96 "She was not only . . ." St. Denis, UL, 117. Biographical information on Duncan in Duncan, Seroff.

page 97 "Each movement . . ." Duncan, "The Dance of the Future" in *The Art of the Dance*, 57.

page 97 "coordination of all . . ." Ubell interview with St. Denis, phonotape 7–29, NYPL.

page 98 "All the motions . . ." "Bringing Temple Dances from the Orient to Broadway."

page 98 "The slight sway . . ." St. Denis, ULT, Box 30, UCLA.

page 98 "the profit of rhyme . . ." Whitman, "Preface to the 1855 Edition of *Leaves of Grass*," in Whitman, 415.

page 98 "primary or fundamental . . ." Duncan, "The Dance of the Future" 12, op. cit.

page 99 "One of the bitterest . . ." St. Denis letter to Ted Shawn, May 7, 1925, NYPL.

page 99 "The 'caviar to . . .'" St. Denis letter to Ted Shawn, March 25, 1919, NYPL.

page 100 "Ruthie is a very good . . ." Quoted in Ted Shawn reminiscences, September 8, 1971, phonotape MGZTC-221, NYPL.

page 100 "I rush in . . ." "Ruth St. Denis All for Her Art" clipping from *Vanity Fair* in vol. 2 DS.

page 100 "Well, Ruthie . . ." Ted Shawn reminiscences, op. cit.

page 101 "so wonderfully lit . . ." "Miss St. Denis Dances at the Studebaker."

page 101 "thoughtful care . . ." "New Amsterdam Theatre."

page 102 "a sort of drama . . ." Parsons.

page 102 "As plays they . . ." "Dullness in Lent-End" clipping in vol. 2 DS.

page 103 "a school marm . . ." Toole, " 'Dancing? That Word Spells . . .'"

page 104 "When I turned out . . ." St. Denis, UL, 143.

page 104 "The tendency of . . ." St. Denis, "How Dancing Develops a

Beautiful Figure," syndicated article in vol. 2 DS.

page 104 "Although I don't . . ." Brother St. Denis letter to his mother, June 13, 1911, Box 29, UCLA.

page 105 Irving Lowens . . . Lowens, 266–67.

page 105 A finer distinction . . . Nye, 3–4.

page 106 "the futurists . . ." "Miss St. Denis Puzzles in New Dancing Act," New York Herald, March 12, 1913, in vol. 2 DS.

page 106 "It must be set . . ." "Local Offerings of the Week: Colonial."

page 107 "866 Rescued . . ." Headline in New York Times, April 15, 1912, 1.

page 107 "a pretty little imitation . . ." "New St. Denis Dances Provide Much Mirth," clipping in vol. 2 DS.

page 107 Bakawali dialogue: Musical score for Bakawali, bundle five, UCLA. See also clippings in vol. 2 DS, and Shawn, vol. 1 PAP, 62.

page 108 "That's where he says . . ." Ted Shawn reminiscences, op. cit.

page 108 "So she danced . . ." Hearn, "Bakawali," Stray Leaves from Strange Literature, 71.

page 109 "a well-known stage . . ."

"He Had No Eye for Art" clipping in vol. 2 DS.

page 109 "little dramas with . . ." Theatre Magazine, April 1913, clipping in Ruth St. Denis clipping file, NYPL. O-Mika details in Shawn, vol. 1 PAP, 56–60; "O-Mika: A Japanese Phantasy," essay, Box 36, UCLA.

page 109 "owing to the fact . . ." St. Denis, ULT, Box 31, UCLA.

page 110 "as bad as the . . ." St. Denis, "How Dancing Develops a Beautiful Figure," op. cit.

page 110 "showed the possibilities . . ." Ibid.

page 110 "Here was no timidity . . ." Caroline Caffin, Vaudeville, quoted in Shawn, vol. 1 PAP, 60.

page 110 "a sort of Edmund Russell . . ." "New St. Denis Dances Provide Much Mirth," op. cit.

page 110 "smacked of a cheap . . ." Keji Kishimoto, "As Seen by Japanese Eyes," Japanese Times, March 29, 1913, in vol. 2 DS.

page 110 "It may be that . . ." "Dullness in Lent-End," op. cit.

page 110 "There have been turkey . . ." "Society Dances."

page 111 "Let us cooperate . . ." Castle, 28–29.

page 112 "somewhat sicklied over . . ." "Miss St. Denis Dances at Ravinia Park" in vol. 2 DS.

EGYPTA

page 113 Egypta: I have pieced together this approximation of Egypta from Ruth Dennis' original three-scene pantomime, Egypta: An Egyptian Play in One Act, 1905, LC; Shawn, vol. 1 PAP, 48–55; St. Denis' description of dance in Walter Terry interview, phonotape 7–57 (1960), NYPL; and St. Denis speech to Society of Spiritual Arts in 1948, Yellow Folder File, Box 37, UCLA.

page 116 "Place the backs of the hands . . ." Stebbins, System of Physical Training, 35–36.

page 117 "The guests arrayed . . ." Budge, Dwellers on the Nile, 134–35.

page 117 "rather a solemn . . ." "Miss St. Denis Dances at the Studebaker."

page 119 "He was shy . . ." Diary, April 12, 1937, Box 37, UCLA. Biographical information on Shawn in Terry, *Ted Shawn*.

page 119 *Dances of the Ages:* This film included in *Denishawn Dance Film*, NYPL.

page 120 "bodily and emotional . . ." Carman, 216.

page 121 "I am a bit . . ." Shawn letter to St. Denis, ca. 1914, NYPL.

page 122 "Marriage was an inventing law . . ." St. Denis, untitled essay on marriage, February 16, 1930, Box 4, UCLA.

page 122 "For as long as I am able . . ." St. Denis letter to her mother, Box 40, UCLA.

page 122 "I sometimes feel . . ." St. Denis letter to Shawn, ca. 1914, NYPL.

page 123 "Dearest, in some hours . . ." St. Denis letter to Shawn, ca. 1914, NYPL.

page 123 "I must do my duty . . ." St. Denis telegram to Shawn, July 27, 1914, NYPL, and Shawn reply, July 22, 1914, NYPL.

page 123 "a pathetic, broken . . ." Ted Shawn reminiscences, op. cit.

page 123 "symbol of bondage." Shawn, *One Thousand and One Night Stands*, 47.

page 124 *Arabic Suite: The Arabic Suite of Dances* was later called *Ourieda, A Romance of the Desert* as an expanded dance-drama; Shawn, vol. 1 PAP, 67–68.

page 124 *The Garden of Kama:* Shawn, vol. 1 PAP, 63–64; also Mason, "Highest Art is Displayed . . ."

page 124 *The Legend of the Peacock:* DDD, 18–19.

page 125 "dark fields in himself . . ." St. Denis, UL, 160.

page 125 "It is well enough . . ." Mason, "Ruth St. Denis Best in Dance of Sea Nymph."

page 125 "There may be . . ." "Scenes of Life are Visualized by Ruth St. Denis Company," *Redlands Review*, Jan. 6, 1915, in vol. 3 DS.

page 125 "Teddy Shawn was very . . ." Los Angeles Artist Cupid to Dancing Shawns," Los Angeles *Evening Herald* clipping in vol. 2 DS.

page 125 "polite whisperings of . . ." "St. Denis-Shawn Return" in vol. 4 DS.

page 126 "I think a hundred times . . ." St. Denis, ULT, Box 14, UCLA. Though summer 1915 is often given as the date for the school's opening, various articles in the Los Angeles *Times* refer to the existence of Denishawn during that spring.

page 127 "pageant of childhood . . ." "Westward the Course of Empire."

page 127 "The Denishawn barre . . ." "Denishawn Bar" essay, Box 36, UCLA; also St. Denis, "The Education of the Dancer," *Vogue* magazine, April 1, 1917 in vol. 4 DS.

page 127 "Well, which one . . ." St. Denis, UL, 180.

page 128 "the most friendly environment . . ." Shawn in "St. Denis, Shawn, a Dialogue," phonotape MGZT 7-114, NYPL.

page 128 "We believe that to be . . ." St. Denis, "The Education of the Dancer," op. cit.

page 130 *Danse Javanese* scandal: Ted Shawn, letter to the editor in *Variety Magazine*, Feb. 18, 1916, 8 in vol. 4 DS; other clippings in vol. 4 DS.

page 130 "ran down and wheezed" San Diego *Tribune* clipping, Oct. 8, 1915, in vol. 3 DS.

page 131 "for criticism infers . . ." "Music and the Stage."

page 131 Train robbery: "Variations on Themes, Rapid and Rubato," reprint of Harry Bell letter in *Musical Courier*, June 8, 1916, in vol. 4 DS. Also clippings in vol. 4 DS.

page 131 "Miss St. Denis still . . ." Clipping in vol. 4 DS.

pages 131–32 "she sounds the first . . ." Henry C. Warnack, "Catches Mood of Great Sea," Los Angeles *Daily Times* clipping in vol. 2 DS.

page 132 "we are not restrained . . ." St. Denis, "The Education of the Dancer," op. cit.

page 132 "She added archly . . ." "Miss St. Denis Writes" in vol. 4 DS, in reply to "Dancing in Pose and Undulation," *Boston Transcript* in vol. 4 DS.

page 132 "St. Denis is a star . . ." Jack.

pages 132–33 "The psychological moment . . ." Kingsley.

page 133 "an educational example . . ." Sime, "Ruth St. Denis."

page 133 *The Spirit of the Sea:* Dance outline in Box 36, UCLA; Shawn, vol. 1 PAP 66.

page 133 "exceedingly shy and quiet . . ." St. Denis, UL, 187.

page 134 Greek Theatre pageant: Program, July 29, 1916, Berkeley Greek Theatre, author's collection; "Ruth St. Denis in Dance Pageant at University," Rochester *Post-Express* clipping in St. Denis clipping file, Reference Room, NYPL at Lincoln Center.

page 135 *Tillers of the Soil:* DDD, 25–27; Phillip Baribault film, c. 1951, NYPL.

page 136 "for God's sake . . ." Ruth E. St. Denis letter to daughter, undated, NYPL.

page 136 "I don't want charity . . ." Unidentified clipping in vol. 4 DS.

page 136 "Ever since I have been . . ." Ibid.

page 137 "step by step Divine Wisdom . . ." Diary, April 20, 1917, Box 40, UCLA.

page 137 "being changed" Ted Shawn letter to St. Denis, c. July 1918, NYPL.

page 137 "To this end, they made . . ." "Denishawn Dance Film," 1913, NYPL.

page 138 "seven-month's child . . ." St. Denis letter to Shawn, April 23, 1918, NYPL.

page 138 "You shouldn't be teaching . . ." Cohen, 33.

page 139 "I had a sick feeling . . ." St. Denis, UL, 193.

page 139 "Do not go away . . ." Diary, January 1924, Box 2, UCLA.

page 140 "bad music, bad lights . . ." St. Denis letter to Shawn, February 24, 1918, NYPL.

page 140 "Even high art . . ." St. Denis letter to Shawn, February 23, 1918, NYPL.

page 140 "four people and a . . ." St. Denis letter to Shawn, c. February 2, 1918, NYPL.

page 140 "I held on . . ." St. Denis letter to Shawn, c. February 13, 1918, NYPL.

page 141 "I am getting my peace . . ." St. Denis letter to Shawn, April 18, 1918, NYPL.

page 141 "a noble and altogether . . ." Warnack.

page 141 "the sweetness and peace . . ." St. Denis letter to Shawn, summer 1918, NYPL.

page 141 "Truly if you . . ." St. Denis letter to Shawn, undated, NYPL.

page 142 *The Spirit of Democracy:* Described in program, B. F. Keith's Washington, D.C., Theatre, January 6–12, 1919, in *Keith's Book*, UT Coll.

page 142 "I want to touch . . ." St. Denis letter to Shawn, April 1, 1919, NYPL.

page 142 "lead me on . . ." St. Denis letter to Shawn, March 25, 1919, NYPL.

page 142 "Just as people are sick . . ." Diary, December 19, 1919, Box 40, UCLA.

page 142 "I saw what happened to my mother . . ." Diary, December 20, 1919, Box 40, UCLA.

page 143 "Little Tedruth . . ." Diary, November 12, 1919, Box 40, UCLA.

THE SPIRIT OF THE SEA

page 144 *The Spirit of the Sea* (group): DDD, 87–90; St. Denis' choreographic notes, "The Spirit of the Sea: Plot," Box 36, UCLA.

page 146 Havelock Ellis . . . Quoted by Ted Shawn, *Every Little Movement,* 66.

SEVEN MUSIC MADE VISIBLE

page 147 "an eye dancer . . ." Walter Terry interview, 1960, phonotape 7–57, NYPL.

page 147 "You might show . . ." St. Denis letter to Shawn, June 20, 1929, NYPL.

page 148 Dalcroze system: Jaques-Dalcroze, Findlay.

page 149 "the art of expressing . . ." Jaques-Dalcroze, "How to Revive Dancing" in *Rhythm, Music, and Education,* 176.

page 149 "she stopped when . . ." St. Denis, UL, 215.

page 149 "she rarely walks . . ." Jaques-Dalcroze, 183.

page 149 "the scientific translation . . ." St. Denis, "Music Visualization."

page 150 *Second Arabesque:* DDD, 38–40. This dance revived by Klarna Pinska for the Joyce Trisler Danscompany, November 1976, New York City. Choreographic notes in Box 36, UCLA. I have reconstructed this dance by comparing St. Denis' dance notes with the piano score, with the assistance of pianist James Coote.

page 151 "A joyous, lyric dance . . ." "St. Denis Typed Copies of Essays" file, Box 39, UCLA.

page 151 "This would not have been true . . ." Bell letter to June H. Rhodes, January 23, 1900, NYPL.

page 152 "a departure from . . ." "St. Denis Dancers Enter a New Field."

page 152 "art so extremely new . . ." "East Indian Dances."

page 152 "opened a new world." "Artistry of Ruth St. Denis Dancers."

page 152 *Kuan Yin:* Choreographic notes in Box 36, UCLA. Also DDD, 45–46. With revisions, this was probably the same dance as *Kwannon* (1929), St. Denis' study of a Japanese goddess to the same Satie score.

page 153 "where there is an emotional . . ." St. Denis, "Music Visualization" essay in program, November 12, 1920, Trinity Auditorium, Los Angeles, box 1, file 4, Arthur Todd Collection, University Research Library, University of California at Los Angeles.

page 153 "seemed to be about . . ." DDD, 57.

page 153 "In all visualization . . ." St. Denis, "Music Visualization" in program, op. cit.

page 153 "massed in one corner . . ." Alice R. Gillette letter to St. Denis, August 30, 1959, Box 93, UCLA.

page 153 *Scarf Dance:* Also known as *Valse Caprice;* DDD, 49–50.

page 153 *Soaring:* Choreographic notes, Box 36, UCLA; also DDD, 53–56.

page 154 "When I go alone . . ." From script for *East Indian Suite from Tagore,* Box 36, UCLA.

page 154 "Ted now has his own . . ." Diary, March 17, 1920, Box 40, UCLA.

page 155 "What you want . . ." St. Denis letter to Shawn, undated, c. 1921, NYPL.

page 155 "sense of pride . . ." St. Denis letter to Shawn, undated, c. 1915, NYPL.

page 155 "I do not expect you . . ." Ibid.

page 155 "a perfectly tremendous . . ." St. Denis letter to Shawn, August 1920, NYPL.

page 156 "hesitated to risk . . ." Smedley, *Crusaders,* 236.

page 156 "Drama proceeds from . . ." Smedley, *Greenleaf Theatre Elements,* 76.

page 156 "She is gifted with . . ." "Miriam at Greek Theatre," *Christian Science Monitor,* August 12, 1919, in Louis Horst Scrapbooks, vol. 2, NYPL.

page 156 "In countless places . . ." Quoted in vol. 1 PAP, 85.

page 157 "when the foundations . . ." Shawn letter to St. Denis, August 28, 1920, NYPL.

page 157 "the first native American . . ." Kendall, 167. Also "Toltec Pageant at the Pantages" and DDD, 59–63.

page 157 "Ted Shawn is immense . . ." Lewellyn Totman, "Ted Shawn Wins in Dance Concert at New Garrick," Duluth *News Tribune,* September 24, 1921, in Horst Scrapbooks, vol. 2, NYPL.

page 157 "very sweet friendship" Shawn letter to St. Denis, November 7, 1921, NYPL.

page 158 Ted developed a close . . . Shawn letter to St. Denis, February 5, 1920, mentions his affair with "Bobby" and praises St. Denis for her "remarkable breadth of mind," NYPL.

page 158 "She is hen-brained . . ." Shawn letter to St. Denis, March 21, 1922, NYPL.

page 158 "It is the opportunity . . ." Shawn letter to St. Denis, December 17, 1921, NYPL.

page 158 "This day I am unmarried . . ." Diary, December 1921, Box 40, UCLA.

page 158 "We are building . . ." Shawn letter to St. Denis, July 11, 1922, NYPL.

page 158 "This is your first big . . ." St. Denis letter to Shawn, c. May 1921, NYPL.

page 159 "Who in the whole world . . ." Shawn letter to St. Denis, May 30, 1921, NYPL.

page 159 "Ruth St. Denis, High Priestess . . ." Program in Louis Horst Scrapbooks, vol. 2, NYPL.

page 159 "otherwise I appear . . ." St. Denis, ULT, Box 45, UCLA.

pages 159–60 "our three little stars," St. Denis letter to Shawn, March 22, 1922, NYPL.

page 160 "Betty May, Martha . . ." Shawn letter to St. Denis, March 22, 1922, NYPL.

page 160 "It's so much more dignified . . ." Shawn letter to St. Denis, undated, c. 1922, NYPL.

page 160 "We are offering this . . ." St. Denis letter to Shawn, March 22, 1922, NYPL.

page 161 "Run diagonally to right . . ." *Brahms Waltz No. 15* choreographic notes, Box 36, UCLA. This dance and *Liebestraum* in DDD, 71–74.

page 161 "and this inspiration . . ." Horst. *Liebestraum* notes in diary, December 14, 1935; film version made at Jacob's Pillow, c. 1950, NYPL. Both *Liebestraum* and *Brahms Waltz* were reconstructed by Klarna Pinska for the Joyce Trisler Danscompany in 1976, with dramatic values accentuated.

page 162 "To be sure, I had . . ." St. Denis, UL, 224.

page 162 "Miss St. Denis' dancing . . ." Ruth St. Denis, London *Times.*

page 163 "Your old slogan . . ." Shawn letter to St. Denis, January 19, 1922, NYPL.

page 163 "I have severed . . ." Shawn letter to St. Denis, January 16, 1922, NYPL.

EIGHT THE DENISHAWN EMPIRE

page 166 *The Crapshooter:* DDD, 112–13.

page 166 *Betty's Music Box:* DDD, 78–79.

page 166 *Cuadro Flamenco:* DDD, 97–101. Portions included in film, *Death of Adonis, Cuadro Flamenco, Hoop Dance, Scarf Dance* (1924), NYPL.

page 166 *Juba Dance:* Kendall, 174.

page 166 *Maria-Mari:* DDD, 74–76.

page 166 *Danse Americaine:* DDD, 84–85.

page 166 *Revolutionary Étude:* DDD, 64–66.

page 166 *The Vision of the Aissoua:* DDD, 119–22.

page 167 *Dance of the Black and Gold Sari:* Film versions include the Marcus Blechman–William Skipper "First Lady of the American Dance" (1956), Phillip Baribault *Red and Gold Saree* (1950), and in *Ruth St. Denis* (1950), all in NYPL. See also DDD, 81–84.

page 167 "*Rond de jambe* . . ." Choreographic notes for *Black and Gold Sari*, Box 36, UCLA.

page 168 "Always in Miss St. Denis' work . . ." "Ruth St. Denis in Dances of the East."

page 168 "Why will America . . ." "Miss Duncan Dances; 3,000 Cheer Speech."

page 168 "She had all the mystery . . ." Graham.

page 168 "Isadora relieved women . . ." Walter Terry interview, January 26, 1963, phonotape MGZT 7-60, NYPL.

page 169 "You dance with a duchess . . ." Shawn reminiscences, September 8, 1971, NYPL.

page 169 The same dancer sensed . . . Jane Sherman Lehac letter to the author, August 24, 1977.

page 169 "She did not always . . ." Anna Austin Crane letter to the author, March 28, 1980.

page 169 "Why don't you give up . . ." Jane Sherman Lehac letter to the author, op. cit.

page 170 "She acted all the time . . ." Author's interview with Clifford Vaughan, May 2, 1976, El Monte, California.

page 170 "Paul has the true . . ." Shawn letter to St. Denis, August 29, 1922, NYPL. See also Lentz, a clipping kindly brought to my attention by Arthur R. Mathis, Jr.

page 171 "I have no education . . ." Poem included in Wheeler letter to St. Denis, undated, NYPL.

page 171 "The reason I turn . . ." St. Denis letter to Shawn, August 11, 1926, NYPL.

page 172 "I dare not . . ." Shawn letter to St. Denis, February 4, 1922, NYPL.

page 172 "rather too intimately . . ." "Denishawn Dancers Return to Chicago and Win Applause."

page 173 "He's the best material . . ." Shawn lettter to St. Denis, c. May 1924, NYPL. The student was Howle Moore, who may have been the same as Howle Fisher, another Denishawn dancer.

page 174 "done with a saggy dip . . ." St. Denis, "Indian Dancing" essay in *Writings on Dance* notebook, Box 35, UCLA. This *Nautch* also in DDD, 35–38 and Appendix G.

page 174 "even, quick, quiet . . ." St. Denis' choreographic notes for *Nautch* in Box 36, UCLA.

page 175 *Cuadro Flamenco:* DDD, 97–101; "Denishawn Dancers in Diverse Program." Excerpt from dance in film *Death of Adonis* . . . , NYPL, op. cit.

page 175 "Chinese? You've got . . ." Walter Terry interview with St. Denis, 1960, op. cit.

page 175 *Ishtar of the Seven Gates:* Typed description in Box 36, UCLA; program notes, Manhattan Opera House, box 1, file 4, Arthur Todd Collection, UCLA; DDD, 102–6.

page 175 "It is a marvel . . ." "Denishawn Dancers' Program Nets $1,000 . . ." St. Paul *Pioneer Press*, March 8, 1924, in Horst Scrapbooks, vol. 2, NYPL.

page 176 "though she sometimes stoops . . ." "Ruth St. Denis and Denishawn Dancers Score Again at

State," Uniontown *Herald,* March 14, 1925, in ibid.

page 176 The Feather of the Dawn: DDD, 90–94.

page 177 "Not so Miss Ruth . . ." Cohen, 40.

page 178 "conceptual clarity to . . ." "Ouspensky's Universe."

page 178 "The phenomenal world . . ." Ouspensky, 145.

pages 178–79 "In art it is necessary . . ." Ibid.

page 179 "the line, the curve . . ." St. Denis, "God Geometrizes" essay in *Temple Records* notebook (1929–32), Box 37, UCLA.

page 180 "color-music . . ." Bragdon, 116.

page 180 "The children were engrossed . . ." St. Denis, "Creative Era of the Religious Dance" essay, Box 33, UCLA.

page 181 "I am a vegetable . . ." St. Denis letter to Shawn, c. 1924, NYPL.

page 181 "your own being convinced . . ." Shawn letter to St. Denis, June 29, 1924, NYPL.

page 181 "God help me . . ." Diary, September 27, 1924, Box 2, UCLA.

page 181 "Artistically speaking . . ." St. Denis letter to Shawn, July 9, 1924, NYPL.

page 182 "I see men and women . . ." St. Denis, "The Dance as Life Experience" 1.

page 182 "The spectacle of a singer . . ." Ibid. 3.

page 182 "external freedom . . ." St. Denis letter to Shawn, c. 1924, NYPL.

page 182 "With a month's study . . ." Quoted in Mrs. Ruth E. St. Denis letter to Ruth St. Denis, May 10, 1920, NYPL.

page 183 "Run right and catch . . ." Choreographic notes for *Schubert Waltzes,* Box 36, UCLA.

page 183 "rode the music." Author's interview with Clifford Vaughan, op. cit. Film version in *Waltzes and Straussiana* (1925), NYPL.

page 183 "*Seated on the box* . . ." Choreographic notes, *The Balinese,* Box 36, UCLA.

page 184 "Here is the eloquent . . ." "Denishawns Surpass All Past Efforts," Houston *Chronicle,* January 13, 1924, in Horst Scrapbooks, vol. 2, NYPL.

page 184 "It cut across . . ." Earl and Shirley Ubell interview, op. cit.

page 184 "Every creative artist . . ." Margerie Lyon, "Denis-Shawn Dialogue: Ruth St. Denis and Ted Shawn on Tour, Season 1927–28," tour letter, Box 2, UCLA.

page 184 "I have been looking . . ." St. Denis, UL, 258.

NINE THE ORIENT AND BEYOND

page 187 "full of the knowledge . . ." Diary, August 12, 1925, Box 2, UCLA.

page 187 "left the camp . . ." St. Denis, UL, 259.

page 188 "They weren't great . . ." Author's interview with Clifford Vaughan, op. cit.

page 188 "June insists on . . ." Brother St. Denis diary, September 5, 1925, Box 30, UCLA.

page 189 "We later surmised . . ." Ibid., August 19, 1925. A basic source on the Orient tour is Sherman, *Soaring.*

page 189 "an hour and a half . . ." St. Denis, "American Movies in Japan" essay, Box 2, UCLA.

page 190 A Legend of Pelée: DDD, 124–25; program, Ziegfeld Follies 1927–28, Box 1, Arthur Todd Collection, UCLA. Also see Lovell.

page 191 "We have never been . . ." *Hochi Shimbun,* September 7, 1925, in collected reviews in translation, NYPL.

page 191 "amazed at my ignorance . . ." Isamu Susno, "Western Classic Dancing: A Tribute to Denishawn Dancers," *Japan Times*, September 13, 1925, NYPL.

page 191 "Two women have entered . . ." Diary, September 13, 1925, quoted in St. Denis, UL, 268.

page 192 "She takes up the piece . . ." Diary, March 10, 1926, Box 40, UCLA.

page 192 "I have the financial morals . . ." Diary, May 25, 1926, Box 40, UCLA.

page 193 "The annual 'war' . . ." Diary, undated, Box 2, UCLA.

page 193 "Strange dead period . . ." Diary, October 19, 1925, Box 40, UCLA.

page 193 "so weird" Brother St. Denis diary, November 9, 1925, Box 40, UCLA.

page 193 "for an instant of time . . ." Diary, November 1925, Box 2, UCLA. See S. H. Hansford, "Altar of Heaven" in Wheeler, 215–20.

page 194 "To worship the four . . ." Diary, June 1926, Box 2, UCLA.

page 194 "The part of Java . . ." Brother St. Denis diary, August 5–7, 1926, Box 40, UCLA.

page 194 "Ted, Brother . . ." Sherman, *Soaring*, 134.

pages 194–95 "She should only have known . . ." Ibid., 45.

page 195 "It is nervy . . ." Ibid., 158.

page 195 "My experiencer is working . . ." Diary, October 19, 1925, Box 40, UCLA.

page 195 "We work like dogs . . ." Diary, November 1925, Box 2, UCLA.

page 196 "one of the only sixteen . . ." Advance press kit, Judson Tour, NYPL.

page 196 "It's hard to realize . . ." Diary, December 25, 1925, Box 40, UCLA.

page 196 "We came to the Orient . . ." Brother St. Denis diary, December 27, 1925, Box 40, UCLA.

pages 196–97 "Last night in bed . . ." Diary, January 17, 1926, Box 2, UCLA.

page 197 "Ted is easily . . ." Diary, c. January 26, 1926, Box 40, UCLA.

page 197 "because she has wanted to break . . ." Doris Humphrey letter to her mother, undated, #3-C261.1, Doris Humphrey Collection, NYPL.

page 198 "for some reason deep down . . ." St. Denis, UL, 288.

page 198 "I am beginning to see . . ." Quoted in St. Denis, ULT, Box 31, UCLA.

page 199 La Meri, the American . . . LM.

page 199 "having a richness and purity . . ." Shawn, *Gods Who Dance*, 92.

page 199 "She opened the door . . ." Marian Horosko interview with Nala Najan, c. 1963, phonotape MGZT 5–70, NYPL.

page 199 Rukmini Devi, a major . . . Author's interview with Rukmini Devi, January 1977, Madras, India.

page 199 Two female impersonators . . . Brother St. Denis' film of these dances in *India Dances* film, NYPL.

page 200 "India, old, dying . . ." Diary, March 1, 1926, Box 40, UCLA.

page 200 "the heart of spiritual India . . ." St. Denis, UL, 288.

page 200 "It is before us . . ." Diary, March 16, 1926, Box 40, UCLA.

page 201 "Pearly, who has always . . ." Ibid.

page 201 "hotly defending the influence . . ." St. Denis, UL, 292.

page 202 "Visions of emeralds . . ." St. Denis, UL, 293.

page 202 "the orbits of a mentality . . ." St. Denis, UL, 294.

page 203 "We are grateful that . . ." Diary, undated, Box 40, UCLA.

page 203 "the older ones like Doris . . ." Ibid.

page 203 "Start upstage center . . ." *Burmese Dance* notes in Box 36, UCLA; see also DDD, 142–45.

page 204 "Clouds hanging over harbor . . ." Diary, undated, Box 40, UCLA.

page 204 "There is nobody out front . . ." Diary, August 26, 1926, Box 40, UCLA.

page 205 "Their dance is the admiration . . ." Untitled review in *Hochi Shimbun,* September 7, 1925, in collected reviews in translation from the Orient tour, NYPL.

page 205 "a feeling of cool white . . ." "White Jade" essay, Box 34, UCLA.

page 206 "It has all been very interesting . . ." Diary, November 8, 1926, Box 40, UCLA.

page 206 "I went on a long journey . . ." Diary, June 6, 1926, Box 40, UCLA.

page 206 "When I am dancing . . ." Diary, undated, Box 2, UCLA.

White Jade

page 207 *White Jade:* Setting described in "White Jade" essay, Box 34, UCLA. Score in bundle 5, UCLA. Film versions include Phillip Baribault, *White Jade* (1948), Marcus Blechman's *First Lady of American Dance* (1956), and Carol Lynn's *Ruth St. Denis* (1949–50). See also DDD, 155–57.

page 208 "In the opening scene . . ." Diary, December 14, 1935, Box 37, UCLA.

page 209 "The light falling on white . . ." Duncan, "The Dance of the Future" in *The Art of the Dance,* 56–57.

page 209 "I am Kuan Yin . . ." St. Denis, "White Jade," Box 32, UCLA.

ten I Am a Beleaguered City

page 211 "Twelve years married . . ." Diary, August 14, 1926, Box 40, UCLA.

page 211 "Like the Orient contract . . ." Diary, August 9, 1925, Box 2, UCLA.

page 212 *In the Bunnia Bazaar:* DDD, 157–61.

page 212 *General Wu Says Farewell To His Wife:* DDD, 145–48.

page 212 *A Javanese Court Dancer:* DDD, 134–37. Film version in *Moments from Famous Dances* (1932–33), NYPL. See also diary, December 14, 1935, Box 37, UCLA.

page 213 *The Cosmic Dance of Siva:* DDD, 131–34.

page 213 "exceptional richness and beauty . . ." "Denishawns in Pantomime."

page 213 "Where was I . . ." Quoted in St. Denis diary, October 22, 1929, Box 4, UCLA.

page 213 Even in his old age . . . LM.

page 214 "Miss Ruth could laugh . . ." Author's interview with Clifford Vaughan, op. cit.

page 214 "The whole institution . . ." Diary, c. November 1927, Box 2, UCLA.

page 214 "Miss Ruth has no plans . . ." Doris Humphrey letter to her mother, c. May 1927, C 265.13, Doris Humphrey Collection, NYPL.

page 215 "muchly namesake." Estelle Dennis letter to author, March 20, 1980.

page 215 "This kind of life . . ." Diary, December 1, 1927, Box 2, UCLA.

page 215 "I am lazy! . . ." Diary, undated, Box 2, UCLA.

page 216 "a Strokish person . . ." Diary, January 1928, Box 2, UCLA.

page 216 "It was casting pearls . . ." Diary, c. November 1927, Box 2, UCLA.

page 216 "Must I endure . . ." Diary, c. November 5, 1927, Box 2, UCLA.

page 217 "My concept of institution . . ." Margerie Lyon, ed. "Ruth St. Denis and Ted Shawn on Tour, Season 1927–28," newsletter, Box 2, UCLA.

page 218 "I can't stand . . ." Episode recounted in diary, October 26, 1927, Box 2, UCLA.

page 219 "I am so glad . . ." St. Denis letter to Fred Beckman, November 28, 1927, NYPL.

page 219 "It is a terrible test . . ." Diary, December 1, 1927, Box 2, UCLA.

page 219 "My, but it looks . . ." Entire visit described in diary, December 27, 1927, Box 2, UCLA, and in St. Denis, UL, 311.

page 220 "Doris feeling her freedom . . ." Diary, February 14, 1928, Box 2, UCLA.

page 220 "only after a half hour . . ." Diary, undated, Box 2, UCLA.

page 220 "Well, this is a gala . . ." Diary, January 15, 1928, Box 2, UCLA.

page 220 "My intuitions tell me . . ." Diary, February 1, 1929, Box 2, UCLA.

page 220 "Ted is so earnest . . ." Diary, February 22, 1928, Box 2, UCLA.

page 220 "But there are limits . . ." Diary, February 1928, Box 2, UCLA.

page 220 "One day—as all things . . ." Fred Beckman letter to St. Denis, undated, NYPL.

page 220 "There is a great mystery . . ." Ibid.

page 221 "What was it in him . . ." Diary, undated, Box 2, UCLA.

page 221 Ruth was vaguely anti-Semitic . . . In her diary of January 1, 1935, she wrote, "I must rise above the fear and resentment of business-Jewish control . . . ," Box 11, UCLA.

page 221 Her only mention of anti-Semitism . . . Diary, May 10, 1933, Box 9, UCLA.

page 222 "This was the first time . . ." Cohen, 62.

page 222 "Well, our first Directors' meeting . . ." Diary, June 19, 1928, Box 3, UCLA.

page 222 "I have given many 'shows' . . ." St. Denis letter to Humphrey, June 1928, Box 3, UCLA.

page 222 "directed my life . . ." Humphrey letter to St. Denis, undated, NYPL.

page 223 "Don't let either of us . . ." St. Denis letter to Humphrey, July 2, 1928, NYPL.

page 223 "All art is autobiographical . . ." Diary, August 6–7, 1926, Box 40, UCLA.

page 223 "We are overwhelmed and yet . . ." St. Denis poem, "The Lamp," Box 45, UCLA, published in abbreviated form in St. Denis, Lotus Light, 25. Choreographic notes for The Lamp in Box 35, UCLA.

page 224 "leans much more strongly . . ." J.M.

page 224 "has become weak and artificial . . ." Ibid.

pages 224–25 "quite understanding notice" Diary, August 1928, Box 3, UCLA.

page 225 "To discover that the body . . ." St. Denis, untitled essay, July 7, 1935, Box 10, UCLA.

page 225 By 1933 she wrote . . . Reprinted in Cohen, 125.

page 225 "a magnificent example of . . ." Diary, August 11, 1937, Box 14, UCLA.

page 226 "Dear John . . ." St. Denis letter to Martin, November 15, 1955, NYPL.

page 226 "pupils can be accommodated . . ." Advertisement in The Dance Magazine, September 1928, 3, in Box 135, UCLA.

page 226 "in rather a Byzantine fashion . . ." General interview and remarks by Klarna Pinska before Congress on Research for Dance conference, Philadelphia, November 1976.

page 226 "Pearly is trying to get . . ." St. Denis letter to Shawn, undated, NYPL.

page 227 "She is stifled . . ." Diary, May 10, 1933, Box 9, UCLA.

page 227 He opposed the idea . . . Shawn letter to St. Denis, June 14, 1930, NYPL.

page 227 "What do I hope to gain? . . ." Diary, July 3, 1930, Box 5, UCLA.

page 228 "An action of this kind . . ." Shawn letter to St. Denis, November 23, 1947, Box 91, UCLA.

page 228 "a prose poem of movement." Program, The Forrest Theatre, New York, December 27–31, 1929, Box 1, Arthur Todd Collection, UCLA.

page 228 "as though looking over . . ." Choreographic notes for "Tagore Poem," Box 36, UCLA.

page 229 "They scarcely do credit . . ." "Denishawns Appear in American Classics."

page 229 "I saw us entering . . ." St. Denis letter to Shawn, undated, NYPL.

page 230 "If Teddy does not take . . ." Diary, September 30, 1929, Box 4, UCLA.

page 231 "Now that between you two . . ." St. Denis, *Lotus Light,* 38. Title of the poem was "A God to Worship."

page 231 "As a poet, Ruth St. Denis . . ." Benét.

page 231 "The whole institution is falling . . ." Diary, May 10, 1933, Box 9, UCLA.

page 231 "sadly inept and amateurish . . ." Martin, "Oriental Dancing by Ruth St. Denis."

page 231 "My recital, personally . . ." Diary, May 10, 1933, op. cit.

page 232 "Now they are angry . . ." St. Denis, "I Am a Beleaguered City," *Love Poems* notebook, Box 32, UCLA.

page 232 "Muddie dear . . ." Diary, May 2, 1932, Box 9, UCLA.

page 232 "Thus ended a long chapter . . ." Diary, May 4, 1934, Box 10, UCLA.

page 232 "I am out of vogue." Diary, Jan. 27, 1934, Box 9, UCLA.

ANGKOR-VAT

page 233 *Angkor-Vat:* Dance reconstructed from "Notes on Khmer's Ballet," Box 35, UCLA; "Angkor-Vat" notes, Box 36, UCLA; *Angkor-Vat* memo, Oct. 28, 1965, Box 86, UCLA; program, August 12–14, 1930, Lewisohn Stadium, New York City, Box 1, File 3, Arthur Todd Collection, UCLA.

page 234 "I, in a fine frenzy . . ." Diary, July 17, 1930, Box 5, UCLA.

page 235 "the balanced faculties . . ." St. Denis, ULT, Box 31, UCLA.

page 235 "feminine balance of the Godhead." St. Denis, "A Color Study of the Madonna: An Essay," October 2, 1958, Box 87, UCLA.

page 235 "Most of us are overbalanced . . ." Terry interview with St. Denis, op. cit.

page 235 "The artist has been given . . ." St. Denis, "Androgyny," *Music Notes* notebook, Box 35, UCLA.

page 235 "balanced government" Diary, August 20, 1965, Bundle 3, UCLA. Clipping from San Francisco *Sun Examiner and Chronicle,* May 1, 1966, in Box 130, UCLA.

ELEVEN   THE SUN AND THE MOON

page 237 "I feel in some strange way . . ." Diary, February 16, 1929, Box 2, UCLA.

page 237 "We both needed a 'wife' . . ." Diary, December 13, 1929, Box 4, UCLA.

page 237 "but I became restive . . ." St. Denis, ULT, Box 45, UCLA.

page 237 "I have never even pretended . . ." Diary, undated, c. February 1926, Box 2, UCLA.

page 238 "Teddy's love did not . . ." Diary, February 16, 1929, Box 2, UCLA.

page 238 "the most damnable . . ." St. Denis letter to Shawn, July 1, 1929, NYPL.

page 238 "All those boy-men . . ." Diary, undated, c. July 1936, Box 14, UCLA.

page 238 "Something in me attracts . . ." Diary, June 9, 1933, Box 9, UCLA.

page 238 "It is not my motive . . ." St. Denis, quoted in minutes from February 4, 1932, meeting of Society of Spiritual Arts, *Temple Records 1929–32* notebook, Box 37, UCLA.

page 239 "Nothing will ever be more . . ." Barnard, quoted in minutes from November 5, 1931, meeting of Esoteric Class at Denishawn House, in ibid.

page 239 "one of the greatest of modern . . ." Markham quoted on jacket of Lao Tze. See also "China Seeks Capital for Movie Theatres," and Au-Young for biographical information.

page 240 "silent, smiling man . . ." HB.

page 240 "sensualist who makes an occupation . . ." Diary, April 7, 1935, Box 11, UCLA.

page 240 "She is like a moon-flower . . ." Au-Young, "Moon-Flower," Box 10, UCLA.

page 240 "It seemed that my mother's . . ." St. Denis, "Rebirth" essay, Box 34, UCLA.

page 240 "I want to see you grow . . ." Au-Young letter to St. Denis, January 24, 1935, Box 94, UCLA.

page 241 "Now—concerning your moods . . ." Ibid.

page 241 "When I contemplate . . ." Au-Young, "Incomparable," Box 10, UCLA.

page 241 "heavenly children dressed in . . ." St. Denis, "Masque of Mary" essay, Box 45, UCLA. See also notes in *Dance Dramas* notebook, Box 35, UCLA; narrative in *Temple Records 1929–32* notebook, Box 37, UCLA; and "An Interpretation of the Masque of Mary," *Literature IV* notebook, Box 34, UCLA.

page 242 "Let them praise His Name . . ." See "St. Denis: Dr. Fosdick Says Yes . . ."

page 243 "It was great seeing you . . ." Shawn letter to St. Denis, c. September 1931, NYPL.

page 244 "To see me struggling . . ." Diary, August 9, 1934, Box 10, UCLA.

page 244 "I have known more sweetness . . ." Diary, August 27, 1934, Box 10, UCLA.

page 244 "Whereas before I felt . . ." Diary, June 28, 1934, Box 9, UCLA.

page 244 "Dance is a living mantra . . ." Ibid.

page 244 "disgraceful scenes . . ." James E. Bennet, quoted in McDowell.

page 244 "In the first place . . ." Rev. Edmund Melville, quoted in ibid.

page 244 "Now the fact of my putting . . ." St. Denis, quoted in ibid.

page 245 "ennobling the sensuous . . ." Au-Young, preface to Lao Tze.

page 245 "To the last remnants of . . ." St. Denis, UL, 369.

page 245 "There are horrible moments . . ." Diary, April 10, 1935, Box 11, UCLA.

page 246 "lady of the first water," Mimeographed letter from St. Denis to friends, summer 1940, Box 97, UCLA.

page 246 "to connect with the theatre," St. Denis, UL, 371. Also diary, September 20, 1935, Box 11, UCLA.

page 246 "did the Moon close . . ." St. Denis letter to Au-Young, January 22, 1936, Box 13, UCLA.

page 246 "My soul was in such blackness . . ." St. Denis, UL, 376.

page 247 "It was the Queen Maries . . ." Clark, 84.

page 247 "the most dynamic of my . . ." St. Denis, "Scribblings," Box 17, UCLA.

page 247 "dynamic peace for humanity." Diary, August 4, 1939, Box 16, UCLA. Also see "Moral Re-Armament," Box 16, UCLA.

page 247 Katherine Cornell begged off . . . Cornell letter to St. Denis, Box 86, UCLA.

page 247 "I appreciate that it is . . ." Hayes letter to St. Denis, April 20, 1939, Box 86, UCLA.

pages 246–47 "They do fine work . . ." Diary, September 17, 1937, Box 14, UCLA.

page 248 In a letter to Sum Nung . . . St. Denis letter to Au-Young, October 1937, Box 14, UCLA.

page 248 "Was I ever meant to co-operate . . ." Diary, February 17, 1937, Box 14, UCLA.

page 248 "Your leaving makes me sad . . ." Au-Young letter to St. Denis, January 31, 1936, Box 12, UCLA.

page 248 "Sum Nung hovers in my . . ." Diary, March 17, 1937, Box 13, UCLA.

page 248 "I have drifted away . . ." Diary, July 10, 1937, Box 13, UCLA.

page 248 "like the old Keith days . . ." Diary, August 18, 1942, Box 17, UCLA.

page 248 "To be honest . . ." Diary, January 10, 1939, Box 16, UCLA.

page 249 "Get the meaning of each . . ." St. Denis, "Wisdom Comes Dancing" essay, July 1957, p. 2, in Box 131, UCLA.

page 250 "It has restored much . . ." Diary, July 12, 1941, Box 17, UCLA.

page 251 "She was a torrent . . ." LM.

page 251 "I taught her the Kathak . . ." Ibid.

page 252 "Sometimes I would ask . . ." Ibid.

page 252 "Darling, I bought some . . ." Ibid.

page 253 "one of the most demanding . . ." Terry, "The Dance."

page 253 "The two of us were going . . ." Shawn, narrative for film *Fifty Years of Dance*, NYPL. See also Hughes.

page 253 "Ted was scared . . ." LM.

page 253 "long and inept." Martin, "The Dance: Ruth St. Denis Program." More favorable notice in "Dance Series Begun by Ruth St. Denis."

page 254 "Russia wanting to sovietize . . ." Diary, July 31, 1935, Box 11, UCLA.

page 254 "My conscience is aroused." Diary, October 2, 1942, Box 17, UCLA.

page 254 "I consider myself a war worker . . ." Diary, July 5, 1942, Box 17, UCLA.

page 254 "Dear Empress Moon . . ." Au-Young letter to St. Denis, October 3, 1942, Box 17, UCLA.

page 255 "poor relation" Diary, undated, Box 17, UCLA.

page 255 unknown to Ruth, another famous . . . McDermott.

page 255 "Young people, old people . . ." Diary, February 2, 1943, Box 18, UCLA.

page 255 "do not cost us . . ." St. Denis, "A Defense Job Will Build My Temple," February 4, 1943, Box 29, UCLA.

page 255 "instinctive self-preservation . . ." Ibid.

page 256 "A world which has no nights . . ." Au-Young, untitled poem inscribed "To Empress Moon from the Sun," December 28, 1936, Box 42, UCLA. For details of Au-Young's death see cert. 12458, Bureau of Records, Dept. of Health, Borough of Manhattan, N.Y.

page 256 "You must know . . ." St. Denis letter to Au-Young, August 19, 1937, Box 14, UCLA.

page 256 "My emperor is dethroned . . ." Diary, May 28, 1943, Box 18, UCLA.

BABYLON

page 257 *Babylon:* Reconstructed from choreographic notes, "Babylon," Boxes 17 and 35, UCLA.

page 258 "to the rhythms of God . . ." Choreographic notes, Box 35, UCLA.

TWELVE DANCING BEYOND TIME AND SPACE

page 261 "I have lived so long . . ." St. Denis quoted in LM.

page 261 "My critics have been . . ." St. Denis, "The Confessions of St. Denis" essay, Box 39, UCLA.

page 262 "Maybe they will go home . . ." "High Priestess Returns."

page 262 "still has a wonderfully . . ." Denby.

page 262 "Regarding the joint publicity . . ." St. Denis letter to Shawn, June 28, 1945, Box 19, UCLA.

page 263 "Either these local . . ." Ibid.

page 263 "Certainly there has survived . . ." Shawn letter to St. Denis, October 3, 1945, Box 85, UCLA.

page 263 When the needle stuck . . . Author's interview with Phillip Baribault, July 13, 1975, Burbank, California.

page 264 "But she went ahead . . ." Ibid. *Gregorian Chant* filmed by Baribault, NYPL.

page 264 "Miss Ruth simply didn't have . . ." LM.

page 264 "Bless her, she has . . ." Episode described in William Thomas letter to St. Denis, summer 1955, Box 42, UCLA.

page 265 "It was a brilliant . . ." Diary, March 28, 1946, Box 20, UCLA.

page 265 "like a mixture of Queen Victoria . . ." St. Denis, group letter, October 4, 1949, Box 23, UCLA.

page 265 "period things . . ." Diary, October 1943, Box 18, UCLA.

page 266 "I believe in the Ministry . . ." Ruth St. Denis credo on membership card, Box 141, UCLA.

page 266 "What really matters . . ." McDermott.

page 266 "dark, dull, gray mass . . ." St. Denis letter to Henrietta (Buckmaster?), July 25, 1947, Box 21, UCLA.

page 267 "Your and my love . . ." Shawn letter to St. Denis, November 23, 1947, Box 91, UCLA.

page 267 "You are a peacock . . ." Meller letter to St. Denis, October 12, 1959, Box 92, UCLA.

page 267 "Film was not that important . . ." Author's interview with Phillip Baribault, op. cit.

page 268 *He Is Risen:* Dance described in Stella Worden, "A Day at Miss Ruth's Studio," Box 90, UCLA. Film version by Phillip Baribault, NYPL.

page 268 *Blue Madonna of St. Mark's:* Dance reconstructed from St. Denis, "Current Biography" notes, Box 126, UCLA; Smith; costume details in St. Denis letter to Alfred Stury, September 2, 1964, Box 94, UCLA.

page 268 "A wonderful change . . ." Greeley-Smith.

page 269 "Women in war are just . . ." "Ruth St. Denis Says Women Should Decide . . ."

page 269 "All suggested remedies . . ." Diary, August 29, 1965,
Bundle 3, UCLA.

page 269 "We are caught both
ways . . ." St. Denis, ULT, Box 32,
UCLA.

page 269 "The reason I dare . . ."
Diary, November 9, 1965, Bundle 1,
UCLA.

page 270 "The Gods have
meant . . ." St. Denis, "Calling" in
Lotus Light, 1.

SOURCES

MAJOR COLLECTIONS OF RUTH ST. DENIS
PAPERS AND DANCE MEMORABILIA
(Code letters for these collections are given in parentheses.)

1. RUTH ST. DENIS COLLECTION, DEPARTMENT OF SPECIAL COLLECTIONS, RESEARCH LIBRARY, UNIVERSITY OF CALIFORNIA, LOS ANGELES (UCLA). This collection includes two hundred bound volumes of Ruth St. Denis' handwritten journals, dating from 1900 through 1968. Within those journals are St. Denis' outlines and notes for many choreographies, including *Ishtar of the Seven Gates*, the *Cadman Nautch*, *Soaring*, *O-Mika*, and others. The collection also contains sheet music for St. Denis' dances, at least five hundred books from her personal library, sound tapes of accompaniment for her dances, programs, letters, photographs, costumes, and properties.

2. RUTH ST. DENIS COLLECTION AND THE DENISHAWN COLLECTION, DANCE COLLECTION, LIBRARY AND MUSEUM OF THE PERFORMING ARTS, THE NEW YORK PUBLIC LIBRARY AT LINCOLN CENTER, NEW YORK CITY (NYPL). This archive contains an extensive collection of photographs and a voluminous personal correspondence between Ruth St. Denis and Ted Shawn. Also included are the Denishawn scrapbooks, programs and itineraries, books, articles, audio materials including tape recorded interviews with St. Denis, and the most complete archive of St. Denis dances on film.

3. HOBLITZELLE THEATRE ARTS LIBRARY, HUMANITIES RESEARCH CENTER, UNIVERSITY OF TEXAS AT AUSTIN (UT). Within this rich archive of dance and theatre materials are photographs and programs related to Ruth St. Denis, as well as scrapbooks which document the American variety theatre at the turn of the century.

4. LIBRARY OF CONGRESS. Ruth St. Denis' first two choreographies were registered as "plays without words" in the Library of Congress. See Ruth Dennis, *Egypta: An Egyptian Play in One Act* (1905), and *Radha: An East Indian Idyll; a Hindoo Play in One Act Without Words*.

5. NEW JERSEY STATE LIBRARY. Important documents relating to Ruth St. Denis' early life are contained in the archives of the State of New Jersey, including marriage records, census records, and historical documents.

6. New Jersey Historical Society, Newark, New Jersey. The Raritan Bay Union and Eagleswood Military Academy Collection, 1849–73, contains documents pertinent to the early years of Ruth St. Denis' parents' marriage.

7. The Somerville Free Public Library, Somerville, New Jersey. Scrapbooks and newspaper clippings pertinent to Ruth St. Denis' childhood are housed in this library's New Jersey Room.

OTHER UNPUBLISHED SOURCES

1. Properties Documents related to Pin Oaks Farm are found in "Lease and Agreements Docket," County Courthouse, Somerset County, Somerville, New Jersey.

2. Military Information on Thomas Laban Dennis' military service and his marriage to Ruth Emma Hull is included in Widow's Pension File for Ruth E. Dennis and Thomas Laban Dennis File, Navy and Old Army Branch, Military Archives Division, National Archives, Washington, D.C.

3. Inventions Records of Thomas Laban Dennis' patent applications are obtainable from Files of Patent and Trademark Office, United States Department of Commerce, Washington, D.C. Individual inventions described in *Annual Report of the Commissioner of Patents,* issued by the Patent Office.

4. Education Documents related to Ruth Dennis' education at the Packer Collegiate Institute are contained in the institute archives, Brooklyn, New York. See *1896–1897 Semi Quarterly Reports of Scholarship* in that archive. Ruth Emma Hull's medical thesis, "Vis Medicatrix Naturae" (1872), is located in Bentley Historical Library, Michigan Historical Collections, The University of Michigan, Ann Arbor, Michigan.

INTERVIEWS

Author's interview with Phillip Baribault, July 13, 1975, Burbank, California.

Author's interview with Henrietta Buckmaster, February 17, 1980, Boston, Massachusetts.

Author's interview with Rosemary Glenn, April 20, 1976, Burbank, California.

Author's interview with La Meri, February 18, 1980, Hyannis, Massachusetts.

Author's interview with Clifford Vaughan, May 2, 1976, El Monte, California.

SECONDARY SOURCES

Among the most basic secondary sources are Christena L. Schlundt's *The Professional Appearances of Ruth St. Denis and Ted Shawn;* St. Denis' autobiography, *An Unfinished Life;* Ted Shawn's *Ruth St. Denis: Pioneer and Prophet,* and Jane Sherman's *The Drama of Denishawn Dance.*

BOOKS

Adams, Henry. *The Education of Henry Adams,* 1918. Reprint. Boston: Houghton Mifflin Company, 1961.

Aldred, Cyril. *Akhenaten, Pharaoh of Egypt—A New Study.* London: Thames and Hudson, 1968.

Allan, Maud. *My Life and Dancing.* London: Everett and Company, 1908.

Amaya, Mario. *Art Nouveau.* London: Studio Vista, 1966.

Armitage, Merle. *Dance Memoranda,* ed. Edwin Corle. New York: Duell, Sloan & Pearce, 1947.

Atmananda Guru, Sri. *Atma Darshan.* Austin: Advaita Publishers, 1972.

———. *Atma Nirvriti.* Austin: Advaita Publishers, 1972.

———. *Atmananda Tattwa Samhita.* Austin: Advaita Publishers, 1973.

Au-Young, Sum Nung. *The Industrialization of China.* Honolulu: Institute of Pacific Relations, 1925.

———. *Some Aspects of China's Resources.* Honolulu: Institute of Pacific Relations, 1928.

Baldwin, Charles C. *Stanford White.* New York: Dodd, Mead & Company, 1931.

Battersby, Martin. *The World of Art Nouveau.* New York: Funk & Wagnalls, 1968.

Beasley, Norman. *Mary Baker Eddy.* New York: Duell, Sloan & Pearce, 1963.

Beebe, Lucius. *The Big Spenders.* New York: Doubleday & Company, 1966.

Beers, F. W. *Atlas of Somerset County, New Jersey.* New York: Beers, Comstock, and Cline, 1873.

Belasco, David. *The Theatre Through Its Stage Door.* New York: Harper & Brothers, 1919.

Benham, John H., ed. *Benham's New Haven Directory and Annual Advertiser.* New Haven: John H. Benham, 1861.

The Bhagavad-Gita, trans. Ann Stanford. New York: Herder and Herder, 1970.

Bishop, Emily. *Americanized Delsarte Culture.* Meadville, Pennsylvania: Flood and Vincent, The Chautauqua Century Press, 1892.

Bloom, Eric, ed. *Grove's Dictionary of Musicians.* New York: St. Martin's Press, 1954.

Bowers, Faubion. *The Dance in India.* New York: Columbia University Press, 1953.

Bragdon, Claude. *More Lives Than One.* New York: Alfred A. Knopf, 1938.

Breasted, James Henry. *A History of Egypt.* New York: Charles Scribner's Sons, 1905.

Bridges, Hal. *American Mysticism: From William James to Zen.* New York: Harper & Row, 1970.

Brockett, Oscar G. *History of the Theatre*, 1968. Rev. New York: Allyn & Bacon, 1974.

Budge, E. A. Wallis. *The Book of the Dead*, 1895. Reprint. New York: Dover Publications, Inc., 1967.

———. *Dwellers on the Nile*, 1885. Rev. London: The Religious Tract Society, 1926.

———. *The Gods of the Egyptians or Studies in Mythology*, 2 vols. London: Methuen & Co., 1904.

Caffin, Caroline. *Vaudeville*. New York: Mitchell Kennerley, 1914.

Carman, Bliss. *The Making of Personality*. Boston: L. C. Page and Company, 1908.

Carpenter, Edward. *My Days and Dreams: Being Autobiographical Notes*. London: George Allen & Unwin, 1916.

Carter, Huntly. *The Theatre of Max Reinhardt*, 1914. Reprint. New York: Benjamin Blom, 1964.

Carter, Morris. *Isabella Stewart Gardner and Fenway Court*. Boston: Houghton Mifflin Company, 1940.

Castle, Mr. and Mrs. Vernon. *Modern Dancing*. New York: Harper & Brothers, 1914.

Cerf, Bennett, and Cartmell, Van H., eds. *S.R.O.: The Most Successful Plays in the History of the American Stage*. Garden City, New York: Doubleday, Doran and Company, 1945.

Chapman, John, and Sherwood, Garrison P., eds. *The Best Plays of 1894–99*. New York: Dodd, Mead & Company, 1955.

Chisholm, Lawrence. *Fenollosa: The Far East and American Culture*. New Haven: Yale University Press, 1963.

Christy, Arthur E., ed. *The Asian Legacy and American Life*. New York: The John Day Company, 1942.

Clark, Walter Houston. *The Oxford Group: Its History and Significance*. New York: Bookman Associates, 1951.

Cohen, Selma Jeanne. *Doris Humphrey: An Artist First*. Middletown, Connecticut: Wesleyan University Press, 1972.

Cole, Arthur C. *The Puritan and Fair Terpsichore*, 1942. Reprint. Brooklyn: Dance Horizons, n.d.

Comini, Alessandra. *Egon Schiele's Portraits*. Berkeley: University of California Press, 1974.

Cook, Mabel Collins. *The Idyll of the White Lotus*, 1884. Reprint. London: Theosophical Publishing Society, 1896.

Coomaraswamy, Ananda, trans. *The Mirror of Gesture: Being the Abhinaya Darpana of Nandikesvara*. New Delhi: Munshiram Manoharlal, 1970.

———, and Noble, Margaret E. *Myths of the Hindus and Buddhists*, 1913. Reprint. New York: Dover Publications, 1978.

Cross, Whitney R. *The Burned-Over District*, 1950. Reprint. New York: Harper & Row, 1965.

Curry, S. S. *Foundations of Expression*. Boston: The Expression Co., 1920.

————. *Classic Selections From the Best Authors Adapted to the Study of Vocal Expression.* Boston: School of Expression, 1888.

Dalliba, Gerda. *An Earth Poem and Other Poems.* New York: G. P. Putnam's Sons, 1908.

Daly, Joseph Francis. *The Life of Augustin Daly.* New York: The Macmillan Company, 1917.

Delaumosne, Abbe. *Delsarte System of Oratory,* 1882. Rev. New York: Edgar S. Werner, 1893.

DeMiglio, John E. *Vaudeville U.S.A.* Bowling Green, Ohio: Bowling Green University Popular Press, 1973.

Devi, Ragini. *Dances of India.* Calcutta: Susil Gupta Private Ltd., 1928.

Dewey, John. *Democracy and Education,* 1916. Reprint. New York: The Macmillan Company, 1932.

Dhar, Sailendra Nath. *A Comprehensive Biography of Swami Vivekananda,* 3 vols. Madras: Vivekananda Prakashan Kendra, 1975–76.

Dimmick, Ruth Crosby. *Our Theatres To-Day and Yesterday.* New York: The H. K. Fly Company Publishers, 1913.

Doubleday, H. A., and de Walden, Lord Howard, eds. *The Complete Peerage.* London: The St. Catherine Press, 1932.

Drummond, Henry. *Drummond's Addresses.* Chicago: Donohue, Henneberry and Co., n.d.

Duncan, Isadora. *The Art of the Dance,* 1928. Reprint. New York: Theatre Arts Books, 1969.

————. *My Life.* New York: Boni and Liveright, 1927.

Eddy, Mary Baker. *Science and Health with Key to the Scriptures,* 1875. Rev. Boston: Joseph Armstrong, 1907.

Ellis, Havelock. *The Dance of Life.* Boston: Houghton Mifflin Company, 1923.

Emerson, Charles Wesley. *Physical Culture.* Boston: Emerson College Publishing Department, 1916.

Emerson, Ralph Waldo. *Selections from Ralph Waldo Emerson,* ed. Stephen Whicher. Boston: Houghton Mifflin Company, 1960.

Findlay, Elsa. *Rhythm and Movement: Application of Dalcroze Eurhythmics.* Evanston, Illinois: Summy-Birchard Company, 1971.

Findlay, James F., Jr. *Dwight L. Moody: American Evangelist, 1837–1899.* Chicago: University of Chicago Press, 1969.

Flitch, J. E. Crawford. *Modern Dancing and Dancers.* Philadelphia: J. B. Lippincott Company, 1912.

Ford, James Lauren. *Mrs. Leslie Carter in David Belasco's DuBarry.* New York: Frederick A. Stokes Company, 1902.

Frohman, Daniel. *Daniel Frohman Presents.* New York: C. Kendall and Willoughby Sharp, 1935.

Fuller, Loie. *Fifteen Years of a Dancer's Life.* Boston: Small, Maynard & Company, 1913.

Gay, Peter. *Weimar Culture: The Outsider as Insider,* 1968. Reprint. New York: Harper Torchbooks, 1970.

General Catalogue, The University of Michigan, 1837–1890. Ann Arbor, Michigan: Published by the University, 1891.

Georgen, Eleanor. *The Delsarte System of Physical Culture.* New York: The Butterick Publishing Company, 1893.

Gilbert, Douglas. *American Vaudeville: Its Life and Times.* New York: Whittlesey House, McGraw-Hill Book Company, 1940.

Giles, Herbert A., et. al., eds. *Great Religions of the World.* New York: The North American Review Publishing Co., 1901.

Gorelik, Mordecai. *New Theatres for Old.* New York: Samuel French, 1940.

Gray, Ronald D. *The German Tradition in Literature.* Cambridge: University Press, 1965.

Guernsey, Otis L., Jr., ed. *Guernsey Directory of the American Theatre, 1894–1971.* New York: Dodd, Mead & Company, 1971.

Habenstreit, Barbara. *Fort Greene, U.S.A.* New York: The Bobbs-Merrill Company, 1974.

Hall, Carrie A. *From Hoopskirts to Nudity: A Review of the Foibles of Fashion, 1866–1936.* Caldwell, Idaho: The Claxton Printers, Ltd., 1938.

Hall, G. Stanley. *Educational Problems,* 2 vols. New York: D. Appleton and Company, 1911.

Ham, Mordecai. *The Modern Dance: A Historical and Analytical Treatment of the Subject.* San Antonio: San Antonio Printing Company, 1916.

Harris, Neil. *The Artist in American Society: The Formative Years, 1790–1860,* 1966. Reprint. New York: Clarion Books, 1970.

Hearn, Lafcadio. *Shadowings.* Boston: Little, Brown & Company, 1900.

———. *Stray Leaves from Strange Literature.* Boston: James R. Osgood and Company, 1884.

Hendricks, Gordon. *The Kinetoscope: America's First Commercially Successful Motion Picture Exhibitor.* New York: Arno Press, 1972.

Hess, Thomas B., and Nochlin, Linda, eds. *Woman as Sex Object: Studies in Erotic Art.* New York: Newsweek Books, 1972.

Hofmannsthal, Hugo von. *Aufzeichnungen.* Gesammelte Werke in Einzelausgaben, 1959.

———. *Hofmannsthal: Selected Essays,* ed. Mary E. Gilbert. Oxford: Basil Blackwell, 1955.

———. *Poems and Verse Plays,* ed. Michael Hamburger. New York: Pantheon Books, 1961.

———, and Kessler, Harry Graf. *Briefwechsel, 1898–1929,* ed. Hilde Burger. Frankfurt am Main: Insel Verlag, 1968.

———, and Nostitz, Helene von. *Briefwechsel.* Frankfurt am Main: S. Fischer Verlag, 1965.

Howard, Diana. *London Theatres and Music Halls, 1850–1950.* London: The Library Association, 1970.

Inness, George, Jr. *The Life, Art and Letters of George Inness.* New York: The Century Company, 1917.

Isherwood, Christopher, ed. *Vedanta for the Western World,* 1960. Reprint. New York: The Viking Press, 1973.

Jackson, James Caleb. *Dancing: Its Evils and its Benefits.* Dansville, N.Y.: F. Wilson Hurd & Co., 1868.

Janik, Allan, and Toulman, Stephen. *Wittgenstein's Vienna.* London: Weidenfeld and Nicolson, 1973.

Jaques-Dalcroze, Émile. *Rhythm, Music and Education.* London: Chatto & Windus, 1921.

Johnston, William M. *The Austrian Mind: An Intellectual and Social History.* Berkeley: University of California Press, 1972.

Jones, Howard Mumford. *The Age of Energy: Varieties of American Experience, 1865–1915.* New York: The Viking Press, 1970.

Jullian, Philippe. *The Orientalists: European Painters of Eastern Scenes.* Oxford: Phaidon Press, 1977.

———. *The Triumph of Art Nouveau.* London: Phaidon Press, 1974.

Kalidasa. *Sakuntala,* tr. Laurence Binyon. London: Macmillan and Co., 1920.

Kendall, Elizabeth. *Where She Danced.* New York: Alfred A. Knopf, 1979.

Kessler, Count Harry. *The Diaries of a Cosmopolitan, 1918–1937.* London: Weidenfeld and Nicolson, 1971.

Koch, Robert. *Louis Tiffany: Rebel in Glass.* New York: Crown Publishers, 1964.

La Meri. *Dance Out the Answer: An Autobiography.* New York: Marcel Dekker, 1977.

Lao Tze. *Tao Teh King,* tr. Sum Nung Au-Young. New York: March and Greenwood, 1938.

Laqueur, Walter. *Weimar: A Cultural History, 1918–1933,* 1974. Reprint. New York: Capricorn Books, 1976.

Laurie, Joe, Jr. *Vaudeville: From the Honky Tonks to the Palace.* New York: Henry Holt and Company, 1953.

Le Favre, Carrica. *Physical Culture Founded on Delsartean Principles.* New York: Fowler & Wells, 1892.

Leavitt, M. B. *Fifty Years in Theatrical Management, 1859–1909.* New York: Broadway Publishing Co., 1912.

Lipsey, Roger. *Coomaraswamy: His Life and Work.* Princeton, N.J.: Princeton University Press, 1977.

Loti, Pierre. *India.* London: Laurie, 1913.

Lovell, John. *Martinique, St. Vincent, Guadalupe, St. Lucia, Dominica, Barbados and the Danish West Indies.* Brooklyn: Library Publishing Co., 1902.

Lowell, Marion, ed. *Harmonic Gymnastics and Pantomimic Expression.* Boston: Marion Lowell, 1895.

Lowens, Irving. *Music and Musicians in Early America.* New York: W. W. Norton & Company, 1964.

Lutyens, Mary. *Krishnamurti: The Years of Awakening.* New York: Farrar, Straus & Giroux, 1975.

Macdonald, Allan H. *Richard Hovey: Man and Craftsman*. Durham, N.C.: Duke University Press, 1957.

MacKaye, Percy. *Epoch*, 2 vols. New York: Boni & Liveright, 1927.

The Macmillan Encyclopedia of Music and Musicians, ed. Albert E. Weir. New York: The Macmillan Company, 1938.

Malone, Dumas, ed. *The Dictionary of American Biography*. New York: Charles Scribner's Sons, 1943.

Mantle, Burns, and Sherwood, Garrison P., eds. *Best Plays of 1899–1909*. New York: Dodd, Mead & Company, 1947.

Masur, Gerhard. *Imperial Berlin*. New York: Basic Books, 1970.

Max Muller, Friedrich, ed. *Sacred Books of the East,* 50 vols. Oxford: Oxford University Press, 1875.

McCausland, Elizabeth. *George Inness, An American Landscape Painter*. New York: American Artists Group, 1946.

McCullough, Ed. *Good Old Coney Island*. New York: Charles Scribner's Sons, 1957.

McDonagh, Don. *Martha Graham*. New York: Popular Library, 1973.

McGuigan, Dorothy Gies. *A Dangerous Experiment: 100 Years of Women at the University of Michigan*. Ann Arbor: Center for Continuing Education for Women, 1970.

McLean, Albert F., Jr. *American Vaudeville as Ritual*. Lexington: University of Kentucky Press, 1965.

McLoughlin, William G., Jr. *Modern Revivalism: Charles Grandison Finney to Billy Graham*. New York: The Ronald Press Company, 1959.

Menen, Aubrey. *The Mystics*. New York: The Dial Press, 1974.

Modisett, Noah Franklin. *A Historical Study of the Stage Directing Theory and Practice of David Belasco*. Ph.D. dissertation, the University of Southern California, 1963.

Moody, Dwight L. *"The Gospel Awakening," Comprising the Sermons and Addresses, Prayer-Meeting Talks and Bible Readings of the Great Revival Meetings Conducted by Moody and Sankey*, ed. L. T. Remlap. Chicago: J. Fairbanks and Co., 1879.

———. *Heaven; Where It Is; Its Inhabitants, and How to Get There*. Chicago: F. H. Revell, 1880.

Moore, Lillian. *Artists of the Dance*. New York: Thomas Y. Crowell Company, 1938.

Morgan, Anna. *An Hour with Delsarte: A Study of Expression*, 1889. Reprint. Boston: Lee and Shepard Publishers, 1895.

Moses, Montrose J. *The American Dramatist*. Boston: Little, Brown & Company, 1911.

The New York Clipper Annual. New York: The Frank Queen Publishing Co., 1899–1900.

Newton, Stella Mary. *Health, Art and Reason: Dress Reformers of the 19th Century*. London: John Murray, 1974.

Nickerson, Marjorie. *A Long Way Forward: The First Hundred Years of the Packer Collegiate Institute.* Brooklyn: The Packer Collegiate Institute, 1945.

Northrop, Henry Davenport. *New Popular Speaker and Writer.* Publisher unknown, 1900.

Nostitz, Helene von. *Aus Dem Alten Europe: Menschen und Stadte,* 1924. Rev. Weisbaden: Insel Verlag, 1950.

Nye, Russel. *The Unembarrassed Muse: Popular Arts in America.* New York: The Dial Press, 1970.

Odell, George C. D. *Annals of the New York Stage,* vols. 13–15. New York: Columbia University Press, 1942, 1945, 1949.

Oliver, George B. *Changing Pattern of Spectacle on the New York Stage, 1850–1890.* Ph.D. dissertation, Pennsylvania State University, 1956.

Ostrovsky, Erika. *Eye of Dawn: The Rise and Fall of Mata Hari.* New York: Macmillan Publishing Co., 1978.

Ouspensky, P. D. *Tertium Organum: A Key to the Enigmas of the World,* tr. Nicholas Bessaraboff and Claude Bragdon, 1922. Rev. New York: Vintage Books, 1970.

Palmer, Winthrop. *Theatrical Dancing in America: The Development of the Ballet from 1900.* South Brunswick, New Jersey: A. S. Barnes, 1978.

Paramananda, Swami. *Emerson and Vedanta.* Boston: The Vedanta Centre, 1918.

Peel, Robert. *Mary Baker Eddy,* 3 vols. New York: Holt, Rinehart & Winston, 1966, 1971, 1977.

Perugini, Mark Edward. *A Pageant of the Dance and Ballet.* London: Jarrolds, Publishers, 1935.

Powell, Lyman P. *Mary Baker Eddy: A Life Size Portrait.* New York: The Macmillan Company, 1930.

Prabhavananda, Swami. *The Spiritual Heritage of India.* Garden City, New York: Doubleday & Company, 1963.

Record of Officers and Men of New Jersey in the Civil War, 1861–1865, 2 vols. Trenton: John L. Murphy, Steam Book and Job Printer, 1876.

Rosen, Marjorie. *Popcorn Venus.* New York: Avon Books, 1973.

Row, T. Subba. *A Collection of Esoteric Writings.* Bombay: The Tatva-Vivechaka Press, 1910.

Ruhl, Arthur. *Second Nights.* New York: Charles Scribner's Sons, 1914.

Ruyter, Nancy Chalfa. *Reformers and Visionaries: The Americanization of the Art of Dance.* New York: Dance Horizons, 1979.

Sagendorph, Kent. *Michigan: The Story of the University.* New York: E. P. Dutton & Company, 1948.

St. Denis, Ruth. *Lotus Light.* Cambridge, Massachusetts: The Riverside Press, 1932.

———. *An Unfinished Life.* New York: Harper & Brothers, 1939.

Schlundt, Christena L. *The Professional Appearances of Ruth St. Denis and Ted Shawn: A Chronology and Index of Dances 1906–1932.* New York: The New York Public Library, 1962.

———. "The Role of Ruth St. Denis in the History of American Dance,

1906–1922." Unpublished Ph.D. dissertation, University of California at Claremont, 1958.

Schopenhauer, Arthur. *Samtliche Werke*, ed. Eduard Grisebach, 6 vols. Leipzig: Druck und Verlag von Philipp Reclam jun., 1921–24.

Selz, Peter, and Constantine, Mildred, eds. *Art Nouveau: Art and Design at the Turn of the Century*. New York: The Museum of Modern Art, 1959.

Seroff, Victor. *The Real Isadora*. New York: The Dial Press, 1971.

Shaw, Frances A. *The Art of Oratory System of Delsarte*. Albany: Edgar S. Werner, 1882.

Shaw, Wilfred B., ed. *The University of Michigan: An Encyclopedic Survey*. Ann Arbor: University of Michigan Press, 1951.

Shawn, Ted. *Every Little Movement: A Book About François Delsarte*. Pittsfield, Massachusetts: Eagle Printing and Binding Company, 1954.

———. *Gods Who Dance*. New York: E. P. Dutton & Company, 1929.

———. *Ruth St. Denis: Pioneer and Prophet*, 2 vols. San Francisco: John Henry Nash, 1920.

———, and Poole, Gray. *One Thousand and One Night Stands*. Garden City, New York: Doubleday & Company, 1960.

Sherman, Jane. *The Drama of Denishawn Dance*. Middletown, Connecticut: Wesleyan University Press, 1979.

———. *Soaring: The Diary and Letters of a Denishawn Dancer in the Far East, 1925–26*. Middletown, Connecticut: Wesleyan University Press, 1976.

Smedley, Constance. *Crusaders: The Reminiscences of Constance Smedley*. London: Duckworth, 1929.

———. *Greenleaf Theatre Elements*. London: Duckworth, 1923.

Sobel, Bernard. *A Pictorial History of Vaudeville*. New York: Bonanza Books, 1961.

Spitzer, Marian. *The Palace*. New York: Atheneum, 1969.

Stebbins, Genevieve. *Delsarte System of Expression*, 1885. Rev. New York: Edgar S. Werner Publishing & Supply Co., 1902.

———. *Dynamic Breathing and Harmonic Gymnastics*. New York: Edgar S. Werner, 1893.

———. *The Genevieve Stebbins System of Physical Training*, 1898. Rev. New York: Edgar S. Werner, 1913.

———. *Society Gymnastics and Voice-Culture*. New York: Edgar S. Werner, 1888.

Swedenborg, Emmanuel. *Heaven and Hell*, 1778. Reprint. New York: Pillar Books, 1976.

Symonds, John. *Madame Blavatsky: Medium and Magician*. Longacre, London: Odhams Press, 1959.

Syrett, Harold Coffin. *The City of Brooklyn, 1865–1898: A Political History*. New York: Columbia University Press, 1944.

Taubman, Howard. *The Making of the American Theatre*. New York: Coward-McCann, 1965.

Terry, Walter. *Miss Ruth: The "More Living Life" of Ruth St. Denis.* New York: Dodd, Mead & Company, 1969.

————. *Ted Shawn: Father of American Dance.* New York: The Dial Press, 1976.

Thompson, Denman. *Denman Thompson's The Old Homestead.* New York: Street & Smith, 1889.

Thoreau, Henry David. *Walden: or, Life in the Woods,* 2 vols., 1854. Reprint. Boston: Houghton Mifflin Company, 1897.

Thurn und Taxis, Princess Marie. *Memoirs of a Princess,* tr. Nora Wydenbruck. London: The Hogarth Press, 1959.

Timberlake, Craig. *The Bishop of Broadway: The Life and Work of David Belasco.* New York: Library Publishers, 1954.

Tucker, S. Marion, ed. *Modern Continental Plays.* New York: Harper & Brothers, 1929.

Tully, Andrew. *Era of Elegance.* New York: Funk & Wagnalls Company, 1947.

Underhill, Evelyn. *Mixed Pasture: Twelve Essays and Addresses,* 1933. Reprint. Freeport, New York: Books for Libraries Press, 1968.

————. *Mysticism: A Study in the Nature and Development of Man's Spiritual Consciousness.* New York: E. P. Dutton & Company, 1912.

Veblen, Thorstein. *The Theory of the Leisure Class: An Economic Study of Institutions,* 1899. Reprint. New York: Vanguard Press, 1932.

Vivekananda, Swami. *The Complete Works of Swami Vivekananda,* 3 vols. Calcutta: Advaita Ashrama, 1973.

Warman, Edward B. *Hindu Philosophy in a Nutshell.* Chicago: A. C. McClurg and Company, 1910.

Weld, Ralph Foster. *Brooklyn Is America.* New York: Columbia University Press, 1950.

Wheeler, Mortimer, ed. *Splendours of the East.* London: The Hamlyn Publishing Group, Ltd., 1970.

Whitman, Walt. *Complete Poetry and Selected Prose,* ed. James E. Miller, Jr. Boston: The Riverside Press, 1959.

Wilkinson, J. Gardiner. *A Popular Account of the Ancient Egyptians,* 2 vols. London: John Murray, 1854.

Willson, A. Leslie. *A Mythical Image: The Ideal of India in German Romanticism.* Durham: Duke University Press, 1964.

Winter, William. *The Life of David Belasco,* 2 vols. New York: Moffat Yard and Company, 1918.

Woolson, Abba Goold, ed. *Dress Reform: A Series of Lectures Delivered in Boston, on Dress as It Affects the Health of Women,* 1874. Reprint. New York: Arno Press, 1974.

Zweig, Stefan. *Mental Healers: Franz Anton Mesmer, Mary Baker Eddy, Sigmund Freud,* tr. Eden and Cedar Paul. Garden City, New York: Garden City Publishing Company, 1931.

ARTICLES

"A Marigny," *L'Humanité*, August 21, 1906, p. 4.

"A Marigny," *L'Humanité*, September 1, 1906, p. 4.

"A Marigny," *L'Humanité*, September 3, 1906, p. 4.

"A Marigny," *L'Humanité*, September 25, 1906, p. 4.

"A Marigny," *L'Humanité*, October 2, 1906, p. 2.

"Aldwych Theatre," London *Times*, July 6, 1906, p. 10.

"Altar Inspires St. Denis; Awed in Havens Home," San Francisco *Examiner*, April 8, 1911, p. 3.

"Amusements: Niblo's Garden," New York *Times*, October 5, 1880, p. 4.

"Ancient Egyptian Rites Seen in Dance," New York *Times*, December 13, 1910, p. 13.

Arlen, Walter. "Program of Dances Offered," Los Angeles *Times*, November 17, 1958, section 4, p. 8.

"Artistry of Ruth St. Denis Dancers," Atlanta *Constitution*, December 14, 1920, p. 4.

Arvey, Verna. "A Contrast—Two American Dancers," *The American Dancer*, July 1931, p. 11.

"At the Boom of Drum Radha Kerflops," New York *Telegraph*, March 23, 1906.

"Aurilla Colcord Poté," *Werner's Magazine*, December 1896, p. 1185.

B.C. "Snakes and Ale," New York *Times*, November 15, 1932, p. 24.

B.G. "Music: Polyhymnia Makes Its Debut," New York *Times*, April 13, 1931, p. 16.

"The Ballet Girl," New York *Times*, December 22, 1897, p. 6.

"A Bare-Legged Dancer," New York *Globe and Commercial Advertiser*, March 30, 1906.

Barzel, Ann. "European Dance Teachers in the United States," *Dance Index*, April–June 1944.

Belasco, David. "How I Stage My Plays," *The Theatre*, December 1902, p. 32.

———. "Money Rules the Stages, World's Worst Trust," Chicago *Tribune*, January 12, 1908, p. 27.

———. "My Life's Story," *Hearst's Magazine*, March 1914–December 1915.

Benét, William Rose. "Round About Parnassus," *The Saturday Review of Literature*, November 12, 1932, p. 241.

"Bringing Temple Dances from the Orient to Broadway," New York *Times*, March 25, 1906, section 4, p. 2.

C.I.B. "Sacred Dances of Brahmanism," New York *Daily Tribune*, June 25, 1905, section 5, p. 4.

"Capezio Dance Award Won By Ruth St. Denis," New York *Times*, December 15, 1960, p. 58.

Cassidy, Claudia. "Miss Ruth Dances and the Calendar is Not a Little Confounded," Chicago *Tribune*, May 21, 1951, section 2, p. 1.

"Central Opera House Music Hall," *New York Clipper,* May 26, 1894, p. 182.

Chicot. "Radha," *Variety,* February 17, 1906, p. 6.

"China Seeks Capital for Movie Theatres," New York *Times,* January 20, 1926, p. 30.

"Cities in which Ruth St. Denis and Ted Shawn have played during the last three years . . . ," *The Denishawn Magazine,* summer 1925, inside back cover.

"A Club of Novel Nature," New York *Daily Tribune,* January 8, 1893, p. 22.

"Cohan and Harris Branch Out," New York *Times,* June 15, 1908, p. 7.

Cohen, Barbara Naomi. "The Franchising of Denishawn," *Dance Data,* no. 4.

Colbron, Grace Isabel. "Dancing and Pantomime," *Cosmopolitan,* August 1904, pp. 387–93.

"The Coliseum," London *Times,* April 20, 1909, p. 10.

Collins, Charles. "The Exotic Spell of St. Denis," *Chicago Inter-Ocean,* December 19, 1909.

"Concerning Henry B. Harris," New York *Times,* April 21, 1912, section 7, p. 8.

"Concert Replaces Dancing," New York *Times,* August 23, 1928, p. 25.

"The Current Plays," *The Theatre,* December 1905, p. 293.

"Dance Series Begun by Ruth St. Denis," New York *Sun,* December 5, 1941.

"Dancer's Home is Destroyed," Los Angeles *Times,* November 10, 1919, section 1, p. 7.

"Dancers to Aid Chinese Relief," New York *Times,* May 20, 1942, p. 22.

"Dancers to Don Tunics Again Today," New York *Times,* April 11, 1923, p. 16.

"Dances Assist Alumnae," New York *Times,* May 27, 1935, p. 14.

"The Dances of the Orient: Ruth St. Denis Back with New Acquirements," New York *Sun,* November 14, 1909.

"Dancing Praised by Dr. G. Stanley Hall," New York *Times,* March 24, 1904, p. 1.

"The Delsarte Matinee," New York *Times,* February 13, 1889, p. 4.

"The Delsarte Matinee," New York *Times,* March 26, 1890, p. 4.

Denby, Edwin. "Legendary Stars," New York *Herald Tribune,* April 18, 1945.

"Denishawn Dancers Delight a Throng," New York *Times,* August 7, 1929, p. 29.

"Denishawn Dancers Give Varied Program," New York *Times,* August 21, 1928, p. 27.

"Denishawn Dancers in Diverse Program," New York *Times,* April 5, 1924, p. 18.

"Denishawn Dancers Return to Chicago and Win Applause," Chicago *Tribune,* April 3, 1923, p. 21.

"Denishawns Appear in American Classics," New York *Times,* December 23, 1929, p. 18.

"Denishawns Delight Second Audience," New York *Times*, December 28, 1929, p. 10.

"Denishawns Draw Throng," New York *Times*, August 27, 1931, p. 22.

"Denishawns in Pantomime," New York *Times*, April 5, 1927, p. 30.

"Dr. Ruth E. St. Denis, Dancer's Mother, Dead," Los Angeles *Times*, April 29, 1932, section 1, p. 13.

"East Indian Dances," Los Angeles *Times*, February 9, 1921, section 3, p. 4.

"Effective Mission Work: The Northfield Training School," New York *Daily Tribune*, April 4, 1892, p. 3.

Ende, Amelia von. "Giants of the German Drama," *Theatre Magazine*, July 1912, pp. 5–8, xi.

"Entertained by Miss Stebbins," New York *Times*, November 26, 1892, p. 9.

"Expert Classes Dancing as 'Rhythmic Hugging,'" New York *Times*, January 9, 1935, p. 24.

F.J.S. "A Defence of the Male Dancer," *New York Dramatic Mirror*, May 13, 1916, p. 9.

"Features of a Delsarte Matinee," New York *Tribune*, March 21, 1888, p. 4.

"Fell Through a Glass Trap," *New York Dramatic Mirror*, December 14, 1895, p. 13.

Fenollosa, Mary McNeil. "The East Indian Dances of Miss Ruth St. Denis," *The Golden Age*, April 1906, pp. 219–23.

"Fortuny's Veils," *Berliner Tageblatt*, November 25, 1907, p. 3.

"Genevieve Stebbins' Recital," *Werner's Magazine*, May 1895, p. 388.

Graham, Martha. "Ruth St. Denis—1878–1968," New York *Times*, August 4, 1968, p. 30.

Greeley-Smith, Nixola. "Vanity Turns Woman Into Peacock But the Chosen Symbol is a Man," Minneapolis *Journal*, February 7, 1916.

Greene, Maud Honeyman. "Raritan Bay Union, Eagleswood, New Jersey," *Proceedings of the New Jersey Historical Society*, January 1950.

"Half Draperies at the Fair," *Music and Drama*, March 18, 1893, p. 4.

Hall, G. Stanley. "Some Relations Between Physical and Mental Training," *Werner's Magazine*, October 1895, pp. 724–28.

"Harmony in the Vaudeville," New York *Times*, September 12, 1893, p. 9.

"Harris Buys the Hudson," New York *Times*, April 2, 1908, p. 7.

Hastings, Baird. "The Denishawn Era: 1914–1931," *Dance Index*, June 1942, pp. 88–99.

"Henry B. Harris," New York *Tribune*, April 21, 1912, p. 4.

"Henry B. Harris' Plans," *New York Clipper*, August 26, 1911, p. 2.

"High Priestess Returns," *Time* magazine, April 30, 1945, p. 68.

"His Majesty's Theatre," London *Times*, September 15, 1909, pp. 10–11.

Hofmannsthal, Hugo von. "Die Unvergleichliche Tanzerin," *Die Zeit*, November 25, 1906. Reprinted as "Her Extraordinary Immediacy," *Dance Magazine*, September 1968, pp. 37–38.

"Home Talent in 'The Old Homestead,'" *Somerset Unionist Gazette*, March 2, 1893, p. 5.

Horst, Louis. "The Musician Comments," *The Denishawn Magazine*, Summer 1925, p. 7.

Hughes, Allen. "Ruth St. Denis and Ted Shawn: After Fifty Years, Dance Goes On," New York *Times*, August 12, 1964, section 2, p. 40.

"Improving the Ballet," *Werner's Magazine*, May 1897, pp. 435–36.

J.M. "The Dance: Fine Programs at the Stadium," New York *Times*, August 26, 1928, section 7, p. 7.

"J. W. Lovell Dead; Former Publisher," New York *Times*, April 22, 1932, p. 17.

Jack. "Ruth St. Denis," *New York Clipper*, February 5, 1916, p. 13.

Kingsley, Walter J. "Ruth St. Denis Turns Away Thousands at Palace Theater," *New York Dramatic Mirror*, February 12, 1916.

Klauber, Adolph. "The Understudy—a Factor in Modern Theatricals," New York *Times*, May 15, 1904, section 3, p. 2.

Kobbe, Gustav. "Augustin Daly and His Life-Work," *Cosmopolitan*, August 1899, pp. 405–18.

LaFollette, Fola. "Dancing of To-Day," *The Bookman* (January 1913), pp. 570–73.

Lentz, Gloria. "Medford Man Danced with the Best of Them," *Burlington County Times*, January 29, 1978, magazine section, p. 9.

"The Light of Asia," New York *Times*, October 10, 1928, p. 32.

"Local Offerings of the Week: Colonial," *New York Clipper*, November 11, 1911, p. 7.

"London Notes," *Variety*, May 8, 1909, p. 11.

Macdonald, Nesta. "Isadora Reexamined: Lesser Known Aspects of the Great Dancer's Life," *Dance Magazine*, July–December 1977.

"Many Actors and Actresses Sail," New York *Daily Tribune*, April 5, 1900, section 1, p. 6.

"Many Police Attend the 'Sacred Concerts,'" New York *Times*, January 29, 1906, p. 2.

Martin, John. "The Dance: Aiding Folk Culture," New York *Times*, April 16, 1933, section 9, p. 6.

———. "The Dance: Award," New York *Times*, January 1, 1961, section 2, p. 8.

———. "The Dance: A Document," New York *Times*, September 24, 1939, section 9, p. 8.

———. "The Dance: Far and Near," New York *Times*, June 5, 1938, section 9, p. 8.

———. "The Dance: A Greek Re-Creation," New York *Times*, May 29, 1932, section 8, p. 12.

———. "The Dance: Hanya Holm," New York *Times*, January 2, 1938, section 10, p. 8.

———. "The Dance: Influence of Ruth St. Denis," New York *Times*, April 23, 1933, section 10, p. 6.

———. "The Dance: Miscellany; Ruth St. Denis and La Meri Join Forces—

Tours at Home and Abroad," New York *Times,* May 26, 1940, section 9, p. 8.

———. "The Dance: Miscellany; Ruth St. Denis Center in Former Duncan Studio," New York *Times,* October 19, 1941, section 9, p. 2.

———. "The Dance: New England," New York *Times,* August 15, 1937, section 10, p. 8.

———. "The Dance: Notes and Programs," New York *Times,* May 26, 1946, section 2, p. 4.

———. "The Dance: A Periodical," New York *Times,* November 30, 1941, section 9, p. 2.

———. "The Dance: 'Radha' Again," New York *Times,* July 20, 1941, section 9, p. 8.

———. "The Dance: Ruth St. Denis, the American Dancer, Will Tour Europe in Search of New Inspiration," New York *Times,* January 8, 1928, section 8, p. 6.

———. "The Dance: Ruth St. Denis Program," New York *Times,* December 6, 1941, p. 15.

———. "The Dance: Season's End," New York *Times,* May 12, 1940, section 9, p. 8.

———. "The Dance: Summertime," New York *Times,* July 6, 1941, section 9, p. 8.

———. "Denishawn Dancers Seen at Stadium," New York *Times,* August 25, 1931, p. 17.

———. "Oriental Dancing by Ruth St. Denis," New York *Times,* April 30, 1933, section 2, p. 3.

———. " 'Radha' is Danced by Ruth St. Denis," New York *Times,* December 5, 1941, p. 28.

———. "Revival of 'Radha' by Ruth St. Denis," New York *Times,* July 12, 1941, p. 16.

———. "Ruth St. Denis Turns the Calendar Back," New York *Times,* April 24, 1933, p. 12.

Mason, Redfern. "Highest Art is Displayed by Danseuse," San Francisco *Examiner,* February 22, 1915, p. 10.

———. "Ruth St. Denis Best in Dance of Sea Nymph," San Francisco *Examiner,* October 13, 1915, p. 8.

"Matters of Fact," *New York Dramatic Mirror,* December 14, 1895, p. 17.

"May Stop Oriental Dance," New York *Tribune,* April 13, 1906, p. 11.

McDermott, Lacy. "Maud Allan: The Public Record," *Dance Chronicle,* vol. 2, no. 2, 1978, pp. 85–105.

McDermott, William F. "Ruth St. Denis Stars at Chagrin Falls in 'Madwoman of Chaillot,'" Cleveland *Plain Dealer,* June 17, 1954.

McDowell, Rachel K. "Dance by Ruth St. Denis in Church Stirs up a Presbyterian Row," New York *Times,* February 28, 1935, p. 21.

"Miss Davenport's Reception," *The Unionist Gazette,* May 11, 1893, p. 5.

"Miss Duncan Dances; 3000 Cheer Speech," New York *Times,* October 8, 1922, p. 30.

"Miss St. Denis Dances at the Studebaker," Chicago *Tribune*, February 20, 1911, p. 10.

"Miss St. Denis Drops Her Lecturer," San Francisco *Examiner*, April 6, 1911, p. 9.

"Moody's Work at Northfield," New York *Times*, August 12, 1895, p. 2.

"Mrs. Frederic Beckman," New York *Times*, January 23, 1947, p. 23.

"Mrs. Genevieve Stebbins' Matinee," New York *Tribune*, January 26, 1894, p. 7.

"Mrs. Thomas L. Dennis," New York *Times*, April 29, 1932, p. 12.

"Music and the Stage," Los Angeles *Times*, April 25, 1911, section 2, p. 5.

"Narcissus and Other Scenes," *The Director*, October–November 1898, reprinted in *The Director*, Brooklyn: Dance Horizons, n.d., p. 272.

"New Amsterdam Theatre," New York *Daily Tribune*, December 13, 1910, p. 7.

"New Barrie Play a Delicate Whimsey," New York *Times*, December 26, 1916, p. 9.

"New Coney Dazzles its Record Multitude," New York *Times*, May 15, 1904, p. 3.

"A New Coney Island Rises from the Ashes of the Old," New York *Times*, May 8, 1904, section 3, p. 5.

"The New Opera Club," *Music and Drama*, March 18, 1893, p. 6.

"New York City," *New York Clipper*, December 14, 1895, p. 647.

Noel, Margaret. "To Ruth St. Denis, Dancing," *Theatre Magazine*, July 1906, p. 193.

"Notes of the Stage," New York *Times*, July 29, 1894, p. 19.

"Now We May Hear Music of the Hindus," San Francisco *Examiner*, April 2, 1911, p. 4.

"1,340 Perish as Titanic Sinks," New York *Tribune*, April 16, 1912, p. 1.

"Our European Letter," *New York Clipper*, July 14, 1900, p. 430.

"Our London Letter," *New York Clipper*, August 18, 1906, p. 686.

"Ouspensky's Universe," New York *Times Book Review*, October 25, 1931, p. 16.

Parsons, C. L. "Ruth St. Denis: An American Terpsichore," *New York Dramatic Mirror*, February 22, 1911, p. 7.

"The Passing Show," New York *Times*, May 10, 1894, section 8, p. 5.

"The Passing Show at McVicker's," Chicago *Tribune*, September 30, 1894, p. 38.

"Pearls—Causes and Effects," *Vanity Fair*, November 1913, p. 67.

"Personal Culture," *Werner's Magazine*, December 1895, p. 990.

"Plays and Players," *The Theatre*, November 1901, p. 4.

"Prof. Megahey's Legerdemain," *Somerset Unionist Gazette*, November 6, 1890, p. 5.

"Programs of the Week," New York *Times*, August 23, 1931, section 8, p. 6.

"The Progressive Stage Society," *The Theatre*, January 1905, p. xiii.

R.S. "The Exposition Theatres," New York *Times*, September 16, 1900, p. 18.

"Rain Stops Dancing at Stadium Concert," New York *Times*, August 29, 1931, p. 16.

"Ramakrishna—Vivekananda Centre," *The Message of the East*, June 1933, pp. 189–90.

"Raritan Bay Union's Eagleswood of the Mid-1800s Claimed Education as Its Principal Objective," Perth Amboy *Evening News*, September 28, 1963, p. 6.

"Ravinia's Frantic Efforts to Get a Dancer," Chicago *Sunday Tribune*, July 6, 1913, section 2, p. 2.

"Reception for the Prince," New York *Times*, May 21, 1906, p. 18.

"The Rehabilitation of Terpsichore," *Current Literature*, July 1908, pp. 86–91.

"Reveals Mysteries of Hindoo Dances: Ruth St. Denis Gives a Striking and Artistic Portrayal at the Hudson Theatre," New York *Globe*, March 23, 1906.

Roberts, Mary Fanton. "The Art of Motion Belongs to Every Human Being: An Appreciation of the Modern Dance-Drama," *The Touchstone*, May 1919, pp. 99–110.

"Rodha (sic) in the Dance of the Senses," New York *Times*, February 4, 1906, section 3, p. 3.

"A Runaway Girl," New York *Times*, August 28, 1898, section 2, p. 14.

"Ruth St. Denis," *Allgemeine Zeitung*, March 18, 1908, p. 3.

"Ruth St. Denis," *Berliner Tageblatt*, May 2, 1908, p. 2.

"Ruth St. Denis," London *Times*, May 16, 1922, p. 6.

"Ruth St. Denis," *Wiener Abendpost*, January 3, 1907, p. 5.

"Ruth St. Denis at the Hudson Theatre," New York *Globe*, November 18, 1909.

"Ruth St. Denis in Dances of the East," New York *Times*, October 11, 1922, p. 22.

"Ruth St. Denis in Park Theatre," Boston *Herald*, December 28, 1909.

"Ruth St. Denis in White Plains," New York *Times*, September 26, 1931, p. 25.

"Ruth St. Denis Says Women Should Decide Whether Men Go to War," Los Angeles *Examiner*, April 8, 1954, p. 1.

"Ruth St. Denis Tells of Her Dancing Life," *New York Review*, December 5, 1909, p. 5.

"Ruth St. Denis Visits Somerville To Gather Facts for Autobiography," *Somerville Courier-News*, May 26, 1938.

Ruyter, Nancy Chalfa. "American Delsartism: Precursor of an American Dance Art," *Educational Theatre Journal*, December 1973, pp. 421–35.

St. Denis, Ruth. "The Dance as Life Experience," *The Denishawn Magazine*, vol. 1, no. 1, p. 1.

——. "Does the Tango Need a Defender? If So Here She Is," Chicago *Sunday Tribune*, June 15, 1913, section 2, p. 1.

——. "The Independent Art of the Dance," *Theatre Arts*, June 1924, pp. 367–72.

——. "Music Visualization," *The Denishawn Magazine*, vol. 1, no. 3, Spring 1925, p. 1.

——. "The Only Radha" in "Letters to the Editor from 'Herald' Readers," New York *Herald* (Paris edition), August 20, 1906, p. 8.

——. "Ruth St. Denis' Ideas for the Dance Theatre," *Christian Science Monitor*, October 23, 1917.

——. "The Secret of the Pharaoh's Favorite," Atlanta *Journal*, February 26, 1911.

——. "Visualizing a Symphony—An Experiment in Musical Education," *Musical Courier*, December 26, 1931, p. 42.

"St. Denis Dancers Enter a New Field," Los Angeles *Times*, December 19, 1919, section 11, p. 7.

"St. Denis: Dr. Fosdick Says Yes; Bishop Manning Doubtful," *Newsweek*, January 12, 1935, p. 22.

"Says Dance Aids Culture," New York *Times*, February 10, 1932, p. 20.

"Scala Theatre," London *Times*, October 9, 1908, p. 3.

"Scala Theatre," London *Times*, November 6, 1908, p. 12.

Schlundt, Christena L. "An Account of Ruth St. Denis in Europe, 1906–1909," *American Association for Health, Physical Education, Recreation Research Quarterly*, March 1960, pp. 82–91.

——. "Into the Mystic with Miss Ruth," *Dance Perspectives*, no. 46, Summer 1971.

Schorske, Carl E. "Politics and Psyche in fin de siècle Vienna: Schnitzler and Hofmannsthal," *The American Historical Review*, October 1960.

Schwarz, Egon. "Hugo von Hofmannsthal as a Critic," in *On Four Modern Humanists*, ed. Arthur R. Evans. Princeton: Princeton University Press, 1978, pp. 3–53.

Seton, Harold. "All Sorts of Hamlets," *Theatre Magazine*, July 1919, p. 56.

Shelton, Suzanne. "Happy Birthday, Miss Ruth," *Dance Magazine*, January 1979, p. 25.

——. "The Influence of Genevieve Stebbins on the Early Career of Ruth St. Denis," *Dance Research Annual*, vol. 9, 1978, pp. 33–49.

——. "Ruth St. Denis," *New York Dance*, November 1976.

——. "Ruth St. Denis: Dance Popularizer with 'High Art' Pretensions," in *American Popular Entertainment: Program and Papers of the Conference on the History of American Popular Entertainment*, Myron Matlaw, ed. Westport, Connecticut: Greenwood Press, 1979, pp. 259–70.

Sherlock, Charles R. "Where Vaudeville Holds the Boards," *Cosmopolitan*, February 1902, pp. 411–20.

Sime. "Ruth St. Denis," *Variety*, February 4, 1916, p. 17.

——. "Shows of the Week," *Variety*, February 24, 1906, p. 8.

Smith, Wayne C. "Jacob's Pillow Annual Dance Season Opens," Springfield *Union*, July 1, 1959.

"Society Dances," New York *Tribune*, April 12, 1912, p. 1.

"Somerset Hall Gave Audience Vaudeville Acts," Somerset *Messenger-Gazette*, October 23, 1969, p. 5A.

Stebbins, Genevieve. "The Relation of Physical Culture to Expression," *Werner's Magazine*, September 1897, p. 98.

Stevens, Ashton. "An American Bernhardt in a Record Production," San Francisco *Examiner*, June 14, 1904, p. 5.

"Stockings and Garters Seem Censors' Idea of Real Art," *The Arkansas Democrat*, January 18, 1921, p. 6.

"Sunday Night Concerts," *Variety*, January 27, 1906, p. 2.

"Swami Paramananda," New York *Times*, June 22, 1940, p. 15.

"Tagore in Recital," New York *Times*, December 15, 1930, p. 5.

"The Temple Restored," New York *Daily Tribune*, November 26, 1893, p. 19.

Terry, Walter. "The Dance," New York *Herald Tribune*, July 12, 1941.

———. "The Legacy of Isadora Duncan and Ruth St. Denis," *Dance Perspectives*, no. 5, Winter 1960.

"Theater and Music: Komische Oper," *Neue Preussiche Zeitung*, November 3, 1906, p. 5.

"The Theatres: Garrick Theatre," London *Times*, April 17, 1900, p. 3.

"Theatres," New York *Times*, December 19, 1897, p. 9.

"Theatrical Managers Meet," New York *Daily Tribune* (January 12, 1906), p. 7.

"Titanic Sinks Four Hours After Hitting Iceberg; 866 Rescued by Carpathia, Probably 1250 Perish; Ismay Safe, Mrs. Astor Maybe, Noted Names Missing," New York *Times*, April 15, 1912, p. 1.

"To Open a School for Latest Talent," New York *Times*, October 4, 1908, section 2, p. 9.

"Toltec Pageant at the Pantages," Los Angeles *Daily Times*, October 6, 1920, section 3, p. 4.

Toole, J. Lawrence. " 'Dancing? That Word Spells the Tragedy of My Life,' Sighs Ruth St. Denis," San Francisco *Examiner*, April 9, 1911, arts section, p. 3.

———. "Dazzle of Color Aids Ruth St. Denis: Gorgeous Stage Pictures Clothe Dances," San Francisco *Examiner*, April 4, 1911, p. 5.

"Training an Actress," *Werner's Magazine*, February 1896, p. 161.

"Truths of Buddhism Taught in Dances: A New Jersey Girl's Interpretation of Hindu Mysteries," New York *Sun*, February 4, 1906, p. 2.

Tyrell, Henry. "Yes, Society Did Gasp When 'Radha' in Incense-Laden Air 'Threw Off the Bondage of the Earthly Senses,'" New York *World*, March 25, 1906.

"The Usher," *New York Dramatic Mirror*, January 21, 1893, p. 2.

Van Vechten, Carl. "Salomé: The Most Sensational Opera of the Age," *Broadway Magazine*, January 1907, pp. 380–91.

"Vaudeville Clubrooms Opened," New York *Daily Tribune,* November 28, 1893, p. 7.

Wagnalls, Mabel. "Stories of the Operas," *Werner's Magazine,* January 1895, pp. 39–44.

Warnack, Henry Christeon. "Drama," Los Angeles *Times,* July 1, 1918, section 2, p. 8.

"Westward the Course of Empire," Los Angeles *Times,* June 4, 1915, section 2, p. 1.

Wilbor, Elsie M. "New York School of Expression," *Werner's Magazine,* October 1895, pp. 782–84.

" 'Zaza' May be Suppressed," New York *Daily Tribune,* April 21, 1900, p. 2.

INDEX